TAKEOVER

ALSO BY MOIRA JOHNSTON

The Last Nine Minutes: The Story of Flight 781

Ranch: Portrait of a Surviving Dream

TAKEOVER

THE NEW WALL STREET WARRIORS: THE MEN, THE MONEY, THE IMPACT

Moira Johnston

A BELVEDERE BOOK
ARBOR HOUSE • NEW YORK

Manufactured in the United States of America

10 9 8 7 6 5 4 3 2 1

Library of Congress Cataloging in Publication Data

Johnston, Moira, 1934-
Takeover: the new Wall Street warriors.

"A Belvedere book."
1. Consolidation and merger of corporations—United
States. 2. Tender offers (Securities)—United States.
I. Title.
HD2746.5.J64   1986   338.8'3'0973   86-10818
ISBN: 0-87795-784-3

ACKNOWLEDGMENTS

I was introduced to the subject of corporate takeovers at twenty thousand feet, sharing a Mesa jet with T. Boone Pickens as he launched his bid for Phillips Petroleum. It was a rare and privileged introduction, for which I wish to thank Boone, Bea Pickens, and the people at Mesa Petroleum. Through subsequent visits to Amarillo over the winter of 1984–85, I learned extraordinary lessons about maintaining resilience, graciousness, and good humor under pressure.

From that beginning, I have explored the subject from many perspectives and through innumerable sources, the most important being the dozens of people who appear in this book. This is not a piece of psychohistory. Every word, thought, and feeling is drawn from face-to-face, in-depth interviews with the principals, as well as from rigorous research into the paper blizzard of documentation that has accompanied the take-over phenomenon. If the characters are more personalized than in most "business" books, it is because the best men and women in the takeover game, while caught up in the consuming urgency of their own deals, gave to the project with a rare commitment of time, energy, and candor. It is their book, and I thank them.

A number of people devoted hours to giving me superb stories and insights, which, because of the book's structure, scarcely appear. Ronnie and Sam Heyman taking on "the club" to win GAF. William Haselton putting me in the CEO's seat during successive waves of attack on St. Regis. Andrew Sigler and James Keogh presenting the views of the Business Roundtable. NASD's Jack Guion explaining the dynamic evolution of America's stock exchanges and markets. The many people involved in Ted Turner's bid for CBS. The analysts who shared their wisdom and research. And more. I hope their generous effort is reflected in a broadened grasp of the subject and in the rounded view I have tried to present.

How can I properly thank the professional support system that has inspired and sustained me? John Dodds, my editor at Belvedere Books/Arbor House, brought ever-expanding enthusiasm for the project and the seasoned judgment of one of the very best in the business. Raised in a corporate environment, Arbor House publisher Eden Collinsworth was an uncommonly sensitive and knowledgeable participant in the genesis and development of *Takeover*. I am blessed to have as my agent Michael Carlisle of the William Morris Agency, a friend and comrade whose astuteness and creativity helped me negotiate fields of scorched earth and poison pills to achieve the book he believed I could and should write. I wish to pay special tribute to my daily partner on the project, Sheilagh Simpson, an editor and writer who poured formidable editorial, research, and organizational skills and boundless energy into a complex project. Without her contribution, I could not have completed the book.

I would like to thank a few dear friends: Curt and Joan Hurley, whose home was my Park Avenue hotel throughout the summer of 1985; Diane Perry for research assistance; and Flemming Fischer, loyal friend to the Johnston family and to the project. My wonderful children, Christie and Don, helped me keep balance and humor—again!

TAKEOVER ALERT

This list includes only the major players featured in this book. They have been selectively chosen to give a balanced view of the people, processes, and issues of the takeover wars. Many other firms and individuals were involved in the corporate control struggles listed below.

Key to the Lineup:

LBO   LEVERAGED BUYOUT
PF   PROXY FIGHT
TO   TENDER OFFER
NM   NEGOTIATED MERGER

CROWN ZELLERBACH CORPORATION

TARGET:
CROWN ZELLERBACH CORPORATION   TO & PF
    MANAGEMENT: William T. Creson, CEO
    BOARD MEMBER: Warren Hellman
    OUTSIDE COUNSEL: Wachtell, Lipton, Rosen & Katz, Martin Lipton
    INVESTMENT ADVISER: Salomon Brothers Inc
    PR FIRM: Kekst and Company, Inc., Gershon Kekst
    PROXY SOLICITOR: D. F. King & Co., Inc., John Kelly

BIDDER AND DISSIDENT SHAREHOLDER:
SIR JAMES GOLDSMITH
    INSIDE STAFF: Roland Franklin
    OUTSIDE COUNSEL: Skadden, Arps, Slate, Meagher & Flom, Joseph Flom, Blaine Fogg
    INVESTMENT ADVISERS: Rothschild, Inc., Robert Pirie; Drexel Burnham Lambert Incorporated

TRANS WORLD AIRLINES, INC. (TWA)

TARGET:

TWA　　　　　　　　　　　　　　　　　　　　　　　　TO

　　MANAGEMENT: C. E. Meyer, vice-president and CEO, Richard
　　　Pearson
　　BOARD MEMBERS: Robert McNamara, Peter Ueberroth
　　OUTSIDE COUNSEL: Skadden, Arps, Slate, Meagher & Flom, James
　　　Freund
　　INVESTMENT ADVISER: Salomon Brothers, Ira Harris, Michael
　　　Zimmerman
　　PR FIRM: Kekst and Company, Inc.
　　PROXY SOLICITOR: D. F. King & Co., Inc.

BIDDERS:

I. TEXAS AIR
　　MANAGEMENT: Frank Lorenzo, CEO
　　OUTSIDE COUNSEL: Wachtell, Lipton, Rosen & Katz, Richard Kat-
　　　cher
　　INVESTMENT ADVISER: Drexel Burnham Lambert Incorporated,
　　　Leon Black

II. ICAHN & CO., INC.
　　INSIDE STAFF: Alfred D. Kingsley
　　INSIDE COUNSEL: Gary K. Duberstein
　　OUTSIDE COUNSEL: Weil, Gotshal & Manges, Stephen Jacobs
　　INVESTMENT ADVISER: Drexel Burnham Lambert Incorporated,
　　　Leon Black

UNION: AIR LINE PILOTS ASSOCIATION (ALPA)
　　Captain Harry R. Hoglander, chairman, Master Executive
　　　Counsel
　　OUTSIDE COUNSEL: Cohen, Weiss & Simon, Bruce Simon
　　INVESTMENT ADVISER: Lazard Frères & Co., Eugene Keilin

UNOCAL CORPORATION

TARGET:

UNOCAL CORPORATION　　　　　　　　　　　　　TO & PF

　　MANAGEMENT: Fred L. Hartley, chairman and CEO, Claude
　　　Brinegar, senior vice president and director
　　INSIDE COUNSEL: Sam Snyder
　　OUTSIDE COUNSEL: Gibson, Dunn & Crutcher (Los Angeles),
　　　Andrew E. Bogen; Morris, Nichols, Arsht & Tunnell

(Wilmington), A. Gilchrist Sparks; Wilmer, Cutler & Pickering (Washington), Juanita A. Crowley; Susman, Godfrey & McGowan (Houston), Randall Wilson

INVESTMENT ADVISERS: Dillon, Read & Co., Inc., Nicholas Brady, Franklin Hobbs; Goldman, Sachs & Co., Stephen Friedman, Peter Sachs

COUNSEL: Sullivan & Cromwell, Ricardo Mestres, Jr.

PROXY SOLICITOR: D. F. King & Co., Inc., Arthur F. Long, Dan Burch, John Kelly

PR FIRM: Hill & Knowlton, Richard Cheney

BIDDER:
MESA PARTNERS II

T. Boone Pickens, Jr.

MANAGEMENT: Mesa Petroleum Corp., David Batchelder, Sidney Tassin

OUTSIDE COUNSEL: Baker & Botts (Houston), Robert Stillwell; Skadden, Arps, Slate, Meagher & Flom, Joseph Flom; Richards, Layton & Finger (Wilmington), Charles Richards

INVESTMENT ADVISER: Drexel Burnham Lambert Incorporated, Fred Joseph, John Sorte, Michael Milken

PR FIRM: Kekst and Company, Inc.

PROXY SOLICITORS: The Carter Organization, Inc.

GETTY OIL

TARGET:
GETTY OIL COMPANY   NM

MANAGEMENT: John McKinley, CEO

INVESTMENT ADVISER: Goldman, Sachs & Co., Geoffrey Boisi

SHAREHOLDERS: The Sarah Getty Trust, Gordon Getty; The Getty Museum

COUNSEL: Wachtell, Lipton, Rosen & Katz, Martin Lipton

BOARD MEMBER: Laurence Tisch

BIDDERS:
I. PENNZOIL

MANAGEMENT: J. Hugh Liedtke, CEO

II. TEXACO

INVESTMENT ADVISER: First Boston Corporation, Joseph Perella, Bruce Wasserstein

COUNSEL: Skadden, Arps, Slate, Meagher & Flom, Morris Kramer

REVLON, INC.

TARGET:
REVLON, INC.   TO & LBO
OUTSIDE COUNSEL: Wachtell, Lipton, Rosen & Katz, Martin Lipton
INVESTMENT ADVISER: Lazard Frères & Co., Felix Rohatyn

BIDDER:
PANTRY PRIDE INC.
MANAGEMENT: Ronald O. Perelman
OUTSIDE COUNSEL: Skadden, Arps, Slate, Meagher & Flom, Stuart
   Shapiro, Donald Drapkin
INVESTMENT ADVISER: Drexel Burnham Lambert Incorporated
PR FIRM: Kekst and Company, Inc.
PROXY SOLICITOR: D. F. King & Co. Inc.

LBO BIDDER:
FORSTMANN LITTLE & CO.
INVESTMENT ADVISER: Goldman, Sachs & Co.

THE OUTSIDE PLAYERS:

RISK ARBITRAGE:
Bear, Stearns & Co.
   Alan Greenberg, CEO, Robert Steinberg, Nancy Havens-Hasty,
      Calvert D. Crary
Ivan F. Boesky Corporation
   Ivan F. Boesky

RESEARCH ANALYSTS:
Kurt Wulff, vice president, Donaldson, Lufkin & Jenrette Securities
Corporation

BANKS:
Security Pacific Corp.
   Russell Freeman, senior legal counsel

CORPORATE EXECUTIVES:
Atlantic Richfield Co. (ARCO)
   Robert O. Anderson, chairman

LITIGATION:
Moran v. *Household International Inc.*
   PLAINTIFF: John A. Moran

COUNSEL FOR PLAINTIFF: Skadden, Arps, Slate, Meagher & Flom, Irving Shapiro, Stuart Shapiro
DEFENDANT: Household International, Inc.
MANAGEMENT: Donald Clark, CEO
BOARD OF DIRECTORS: John Whitehead, John A. Moran
COUNSEL FOR DEFENSE: Wachtell, Lipton, Rosen & Katz, Martin Lipton; Richards, Layton & Finger (Wilmington), Charles Richards
INVESTMENT ADVISER: Goldman, Sachs & Co.

REGULATORY AGENCY:
Securities Exchange Commission (SEC)
Gregg A. Jarrell, chief economist

SHAREHOLDERS:
Council of Institutional Investors
Jesse M. Unruh, treasurer of California
Manufacturers Hanover Investment Corporation
Victor J. Melone, president

THIRD MARKET AND STOCK EXCHANGES:
Jefferies & Company, Inc.
Boyd Jefferies, CEO

Adapted from *Corporate Control Alert,* a newsletter published by the *American Lawyer.*

TAKEOVER

INTRODUCTION

IT is the American dream: for a kid from the Bronx or a boy from rural Wisconsin to sit at the very center of the turbulent takeover wars that are transforming Wall Street and corporate America, and make millions by the age of thirty-five. To be a warrior in the struggles for corporate control that, month after month, create more action in the economy, more controversy and headlines than any other business event of the 1980s. To negotiate and shuffle the assets and power of the largest corporations in the Fortune 500. To ride the dizzy escalation in scale from $20 million mergers to Gulf, Getty, and Revlon, where numbers less than $1 billion have little meaning and where not even Exxon is invulnerable to attack. To unseat the financial establishment. And get the gratification of war without risking a drop of blood.

In the heat of a deal, it is easy to believe you are at the white-hot heart of the universe. A target company may be in Los Angeles or Bartlesville, Oklahoma; the initiators of a raid—Sir James Goldsmith, T. Boone Pickens—may be in Paris or Amarillo. Computer-age telecommunications may disperse the action across the country. But the nerve center is always in New York City, within a few square blocks of Wall and Broad streets, and of Park and Fiftieth Street on the Upper East Side.

Why are they drawn to these battles—the lawyers and investment bankers, the proxy fighters and arbitragers, the entrepreneurs, money managers, and financial analysts who constitute the smartest and most aggressive elite Wall Street has ever seen? The challenge of the chess game partly. The thrill of

1

battle. Greed, of course. Like professional mercenaries, most are for hire by either side. They fight their campaigns in an arena rampant with white knights, poison pills, springing warrants, and hostile front-end loaded bust-up tender offers. And they are in it to win.

On the surface, money may seem to be the Holy Grail that propels them from battle to battle. It is certainly the most visible report card. But there is something more than greed that drives this new warrior. A few have come from pampered suburbs and social privilege. But at the highest echelons, they are more often from the Virginia coalfields, the streets of Far Rockaway or Newark, the shops, farms, and factories of post-immigrant America where the hard, bright light of opportunity still shines with a diamond brilliance that has been largely dulled by affluence since the days of the frontier. Rediscovering the founding principles of hard work, risk, and the rewards of enterprise, they have grasped life and forged it into something bigger than it was. Some burn out young, but at least it is with the heady knowledge that they have tasted life and changed their world.

They are not, of course, all heroes. It is a revolution. And revolutionaries tend to go to excess. Some are back-knifing buccaneers, amoral as Machiavelli. Some are "deal junkies" who start to sweat if they go more than two days between battles, and whose vision is no loftier than that day's stock price. But these new Wall Street warriors have touched a lost chord in America. Individualists in the traditional American mold, they are demonstrating that the code of gray caution lived by post–World War II corporate man falls pitifully short of a full-blown experience of life. Perhaps they come closer to the true Renaissance man—a man of commerce, ambition, and swaggering individualism—than the more popular image of velvet-robed humanist. At a time of low productivity, the decline of what had seemed our most stable industries, and a crisis of competition in the international marketplace, it is time for a sensitive probe into the hostile and controversial world this new financial breed inhabits. Useful answers for America may be found there.

The new Wall Street warriors did not invent takeovers. Thrust by the accidents of history and timing to the heart of a remarkable convergence of events, they ride the crest of the fourth wave of mergers and acquisitions in this century. What *is* new is the size, the hostility, and the destructive implications for corporations, as well as the introduction of the individual entrepreneur into the game. These struggles for corporate control are fought with such intensity, such urgency, that there is little time to think about their redeeming social value. But some do. For the takeover campaigns of the 1980s are driven by forces far larger than any one skirmish or raider. They thrust into head-to-head conflict fundamental principles and issues that touch the lives and prosperity of us all. They are issues that have inspired wars before: free markets versus regulation, federal versus state power, corporate democracy, the role and sanctity of that powerful institution the corporation, and the strength of our financial and, indeed, of our American free enterprise system. They are the clash of two conflicting elements in our national character: the capitalist, who has marched to the beat of Adam Smith's free trade theories since the nation's founding; and the humanist, marching to nonmaterialist values, who tries to buffer the poor from the law of the jungle with benevolent social programs. Critics and champions lock horns in debate over the long-range impact of takeovers on companies, their people and communities, and, beyond them, on the economy and even national security.

The war is still too young to assess. While the jury is out, the current takeover wave will almost certainly continue to roll, its shape and strategies adjusting to the changing regulatory, political, and economic climate. Guns loaded with the most advanced "device of the day," warriors will fashion ever new forms of tender offers, proxy contests, leveraged buyouts, and financing techniques. For the new Wall Street warrior is a master of creative resilience, and a new idea lasts about thirty minutes.

There were signs that the current wave might have crested during the fierce struggle in the spring of 1985 between Fred

Hartley and T. Boone Pickens for control of Unocal. The fury of the hostile wars in Big Oil seemed spent. First Boston's Joe Perella predicted a return to more peaceful negotiated mergers. As the shock of Crown Zellerbach falling to Sir James Goldsmith reverberated through San Francisco, Crown's defense lawyer, Marty Lipton, said, "It's called into question the desirability of hostile takeovers." And the stock market's stunning rise in the first months of 1986 was a deterrent, narrowing the spread where takeovers' profits lie.

Yet as 1986 began, takeover activity had reached unprecedented intensity. Day after day, the most active stocks on the New York Stock Exchange were rumored or actual takeover targets; nearly 5 percent of the stock market's 31.6 percent rise to new highs was credited to takeover activity. By 1985, takeovers had become a growth industry with transactions reaching a value of nearly $200 billion, up from $122 billion the previous year, and a mere $10 billion in 1975. They involved an estimated three thousand mergers, takeovers, buyouts, and divestitures, with thirty-five of the announced deals valued at more than $1 billion. More than $20 billion profits had poured into the pockets of the shareholders of America's public companies, and sufficient billions into federal coffers as taxes to help reduce the national debt, as Boone Pickens loved to claim. Generating the excitement of a gold strike, takeovers were attacting even the most conservative financial institutions and investors.

By 1985, the wave had spread from oil, where it began, to industries that had been considered immune—airlines, television networks, banks. It struck institutions that had seemed sacrosanct—Revlon, CBS, TWA. There were multibillion-dollar leveraged buyouts of Beatrice and Macy's. Philip Morris gobbled up General Foods; Nabisco consumed R. J. Reynolds. There was an epidemic of voluntary "restructuring," as hundreds of corporations tried to avoid attack with radical corporate surgery—a phenomenon triggered by the threat of takeover. Lower interest rates, a supportive regulatory environment, and eager investors with apparently bottomless pockets created a climate ever more favorable to takeovers. In

November, Ivan Boesky, "king of the arbitragers," told a
packed hall of entrepreneurial minded business students at the
University of California's Berkeley campus, "We're going to see
the biggest movement of mergers and acquisitions America has
ever seen. If last year was $120 billion, the stage is set for more,
and more, and more." And Perella's crystal ball revealed that,
"Five years from now, there will be more pools of private
capital, more entrepreneurs like Carl Icahn running large
established companies, and new upstarts to replace them." The
sheer critical mass of drive and creative power on Wall Street
would transcend the cyclical nature of mergers and acquisitions, he believed. "If it isn't one kind of a deal, it will be
another. And it will be a global market for profit, with the
predominant flow of foreign takeover capital into the U.S.
because it is viewed as a secure part of the world and is just such
a big, big market—the United States is 35 percent of the world's
GNP."

◆   ◆   ◆

ON the surface, the causes of the takeover wars were glaringly
obvious. The "Eureka!" event was the discovery of the undervalued asset. In the early 1970s, financial analysts and smart
corporate executives and financiers had begun to identify
dozens of companies in which the stock price languished far
below the appraised value of the underlying assets. Bargains!
With inflation having raised the cost of building plants and
finding oil, it was suddenly cheaper to buy than to build. It was
quickly discovered that, once bought, a company's discrete
assets—its divisions—were worth far more sold off individually
than as part of the whole. Asset spin-offs were just one of many
restructuring techniques invented to liberate those inherent
values, run the stock price up, and get instant gratification for
the shareholder in the form of huge profits.

The oil industry's undervalued assets, its oil reserves, sat
shiny and seductive as nuggets in a creek. Smart entrepreneurs
like oilman T. Boone Pickens saw that the vehicles for liberation
of those values were at hand. There had been a revolution in
the shareowning of America's public companies. The individual shareholder who had bought shares and tucked them away

in portfolios for long-term gains had given way to institutional investors managing billions of pension fund dollars, and required, by law, to achieve high performance every quarter. His job depended on quick profits. If an entrepreneur made a tender offer—an offer to buy a controlling number of shares at a price far higher than the trading price of the stock—institutions would leap to tender their shares and grab the profit, and the entrepreneur could acquire commanding blocks of stock.

As excitement surrounded the stock and it started to move up, another breed of investor entered the game, adding a vital component. They were risk arbitragers who bought stock the moment a bid was announced and kept on buying (usually from institutions, who preferred to take their profits and play it safe), driving the price up farther in the hope that a still higher bid for the stock would appear. In the institutional investor and arbitrager, the raider had found his allies.

One more element was needed to launch the multibillion-dollar megadeals that are the hallmark of today's wave of takeovers. Capital. The vast reservoirs of capital only the largest corporations commanded. How could an individual entrepreneur buy the millions of shares tendered to him in a takeover fight—the shares that must be bought to gain control? That, too, was at hand in the enterprising minds of investment bankers at Drexel Burnham Lambert, who had already taken the low-rated, high-yield bonds that had earned the name "junk" as the downgraded bonds of troubled companies and adapted them to raising capital for growth, often high tech, companies. In 1984 they had turned junk bonds to borrowing money to finance tender offers and other forms of buyouts. Out there, waiting to play, was an emerging source of capital, a source dubbed by First Boston's Perella the "private pools of predatory capital" that were ready to initiate raids, or back them. The Texas Bass family and the Canadian Belzbergs are archetypes. Paying commitment fees to investors simply for keeping their money on "standby" during the struggle for control, as well as very high interest, Drexel Burnham's "junk bonds" attracted larger sums of money than had ever been available through normal banking and investment channels. By giving the individual "little guy" a chance to play, junk bonds democratized the capitalist system.

With the collaboration of entrepreneur, institutional investor, arbitrager, and pools of capital, the basic elements were in place. T. Boone Pickens could sit in the Texas Panhandle and challenge the largest corporations. Even Exxon, the world's largest industrial company, was not immune. "It would take about $35 million to start an Exxon deal," Pickens joked in a speech. "They think they're so big, they're safe."

A remarkable new financial network was ready to intercept the slow-rolling forces of change and accelerate the process.

◆　◆　◆

THE forces that underlie the more obvious causes may be too large to be perceived by the men who lead the revolution. "They're financial operators who can't see the long-term implications of their course of action," says Irving Shapiro, former chief executive officer (CEO) of Du Pont and now a lawyer with the premier takeover firm, Skadden Arps—a man with a rare view of both sides. Those who do raise their eyes and look around see that they play against a backdrop as big as the transition from the rusting industrial age to the technology-intensive information age. The stage for the first act was no less than the contraction of the Age of Oil, and the wrenching effort of American industry to regain its competitive edge in the world's markets.

A changing attitude toward American business was in the air. "Since the Great Depression, industry had been the enemy, something that ought to be criticized and restrained," says Shapiro. "As far back as the TNEC congressional hearings in the early 1940s, industry was the whipping boy." Regulation, antitrust, taxes, the Supreme Court—all had conspired to treat business like a beast to be kept caged. "But there's been a sea change," Shapiro exults.

In the late seventies, a free market spirit began to take hold, a spirit fanned by the Reagan administration. Perhaps disillusion with the utopian dreams of the late sixties had forced recognition that a vibrant economic system was still the best underpinning for the good life and a strong nation. Enforcement of antitrust laws that had kept business from getting too big and protected corporations from unwelcome mergers were relaxed. Deregulation threw protected industries—telecommunications, banking, airlines, trucking, and securities—into open competition. As patterns of over forty years were reversed, business began to have a free rein. Entrepreneurs, suppressed in monolithic corporations and eclipsed by the sixties' rejection of materialist goals, had first flexed their muscles in Silicon Valley. Now they were on the loose on Wall Street.

Change swept the financial community. Deregulation—symbolized by "May Day," May 1, 1975, when fixed commissions on stock transactions ended—threw Wall Street, too, into the open competitive marketplace. It undermined the old reliance on golf club relationships and put establishment "white shoe" investment banking and law firms at a disadvantage to hustling young firms using sophisticated research and aggressive marketing techniques. The all-purpose investment banker who served his corporate client over decades was fading before the specialist; the clubby bonds between corporate boards and their Wall Street advisers were crumbling before a deal-by-deal spirit. Wall Street came to be viewed as an industry, like any other. And firms that didn't adapt died or were gobbled up in the wave of consolidation that engulfed the Street.

As the word *brilliant* replaced *well connected*, a new breed was making the fortunes. They were the specialists who dominated the major corporate control struggles. A club of, at most, one hundred men.

By the early eighties, this new breed of entrepreneur was becoming a role model for a new greening of America—a greening based on the dye of dollar bills. The University of California's Berkeley campus, home of the free speech movement, saw enrollments plateauing in all departments except the business school, which boomed. T. Boone Pickens, first and most famous of the corporate raiders, was accorded folk hero status as he spoke to standing-room-only crowds on campuses from Stanford to Columbia. Ivan Boesky, the risk arbitrager whose speculation in the outcome of takeovers has earned him an estimated $150 million fortune, reaffirmed to a student audience at Berkeley that greed was okay, as they cheered a very different hero than those of the sixties.

The powerful men who form the infrastructure for this remarkable era in our economic history fill the pages of this book, breathing life into the deals and unfathomable numbers. Most are specialists in both modes, attack and defense. The men on the insiders' short lists. It is not a definitive list, nor a definitive history. But the men and the deals have been selectively chosen as models, and metaphor, for the larger group. There are investment bankers: First Boston's Joe Perella and Bruce Wasserstein; Goldman Sachs's Steve Friedman and Peter Sachs; Morgan Stanley's Bob Greenhill and Joe Fogg; Drexel Burnham's Fred Joseph, John Sorte, Jim Balog, Chris Anderson, and Michael Milken, whose junk bonds unilaterally extended Wall Street to Beverly Hills. There are Lazard Frères' Felix Rohatyn and Eugene Keilin, Salomon Brothers' Ira Harris, Jay Higgins, and Michael Zimmerman, Dillon Read's Nick Brady and Fritz Hobbs. There are two towering law firms: Skadden Arps, with the legendary Joe Flom leading his front line of Fin Fogg, Morris Kramer, Jim Freund, and father and son Irving and Stuart Shapiro; and Wachtell Lipton with its star, Marty Lipton, creator of the poison pill, and one of his protégés, Dick Katcher. There is Weil, Gotshal with Stephen Jacobs lawyering for Carl Icahn.

There are the risk arbitragers: Ivan Boesky; and "Ace" Greenberg's "arbs" at Bear, Stearns, led by Bob Steinberg. Block trader Boyd Jefferies in Los Angeles, star of the burgeoning "third market," the man who, alone in the United States, kept the market open when hurricane Diana closed down the nation's stock markets last fall. Public relations specialists Gershon Kekst, and Hill and Knowlton's Dick Cheney are here. And veteran proxy fighter Arthur Long. There are the institutional money men who are emerging as a determinant force in takeovers, men like Vic Melone of Manufacturers Hanover Trust and California's treasurer, Jesse Unruh, who gave voice to the growing shareholder activism in the Council of Institutional Investors. There are the leveraged buyout specialists, Forstmann Little, fast-rising rivals of Kohlberg,

Kravis, Roberts & Co. There is financial analyst-turned-activist Kurt Wulff, who scans the oil industry for investment bankers Donaldson, Lufkin & Jenrette and counsels T. Boone Pickens.

There are the corporate CEOs, trying to stem the tide, dealing with destiny with varying degrees of rage and responsiveness. Phillips's Bill Douce, ARCO's Robert Anderson, TWA's Dick Pearson, Crown Zellerbach's Bill Creson, and Unocal's Fred Hartley, an oilman who held the ramparts with unparalleled grit. Finding themselves on the firing line as never before in American corporate history, there are the boards of directors—TWA's Robert McNamara and Peter Ueberroth, Crown Zellerbach's Warren Hellman. Household International's John Moran and John Whitehead.

And there is a pilot, TWA's Captain Harry Hoglander, who proves that an employee can play a pivotal role in the outcome of takeover and in the fate of his company.

There are the scholars and economists who stand like a Greek chorus behind the protagonists, raising their voices in support or condemnation of the takeover wars. Scholars from the University of Chicago's School of Economics promote the laissez faire, free market spirit of the Reagan administration, a spirit expressed in that testament to takeover, the 1985 Economic Report of the President. Their theories dominate the Securities and Exchange Commission (SEC), the body that regulates takeovers. There is chief economist of the SEC Gregg Jarrell, a young Chicago alumnus for whom raiders are "inventors" and valuable instruments of corporate reform, and the movement's highest profile scholar-champion, visiting Harvard professor Michael Jensen, whose writings in the *Harvard Business Review* have become the takeover manifesto: "The takeover market . . . provides a unique, powerful, and impersonal mechanism to accomplish the major restructuring and redeployment of assets continually required by changes in technology and consumer preferences." Yes, there would be pain, Jensen admits. "But innovations that increase standards of living in the long run initially produce changes that reduce the welfare of some individuals, at least in the short run. The development of efficient truck and air transport harmed the railroads and their workers; the rise of television hurt the radio industry. New and more efficient production, distribution, or organizational technology often imposes similar short-term costs."

A bold and influential body of opposition speaks out against the abuses of takeover. They are the voices of economist Peter Drucker, lawyer Marty Lipton, investment banker Felix Rohatyn, and CEO Andrew Sigler who speaks for the Business Roundtable, a powerful lobbying consortium of two hundred of the United States' largest corporations. With speeches, essays in the *Wall Street Journal,* and congressional hearings as his forum, Rohatyn attacks the high level of debt created by junk bonds and argues that the hostile takeover process "completely fails to take into account the fact that a large corporation is an entity with responsibilities to employees, customers, and communities, which cannot always be torn apart like an erector set." Public concerns over takeovers' potential damage underlay the rounds of congressional hearings that went on through 1985. With Rep. Timothy Wirth's House Energy and Commerce Committee and New York Senator Alphonse D'Amato's Securities Subcommittee as principal forums for debate, the hearings left more than fifty pieces of proposed legislation in their wake. In Washington to hear his chairman defend junk bonds and takeovers against Missouri Senator Thomas Eagleton's flaying of TWA suitor Carl Icahn as "a 24-karat pirate motivated by one instinct—greed," Drexel Burnham's Jim Balog made the wry comment, "You can talk about the beneficial effects of takeovers in macro-economic terms. But on the Hill, there are no senators from Macro. There are senators from states."

The voices, pro and con, speak a new language, a lurid vocabulary so rife with terms of "predation, crime, and warfare" that its "lexical violence" alone may be evidence of need for reform of hostile takeovers. So said a report of the U.S. Senate Committee on Banking, Housing and Urban Affairs. Some fluency in the language eases entry into a hostile and complex world. First, a *hostile takeover* is a merger resisted by the acquired company, and can be launched in several forms. It can be a *tender offer,* a public offer to buy some or all of the stock of a corporation within a specified time period. A *two-tier tender offer* is an offer to pay an attractive price (often cash), for a controlling share of a company's stock, the *front end,* and then to acquire the rest, the *back end,* usually at a lower price and with securities rather than cash. Designed to stampede shareholders into tendering for the higher price, the *two-tier front-end-loaded tender offer* is now considered a crude and coercive first-generation takeover technique. It was vital to *bootstrapping* bidders with limited capital who could only make bids for control by *leveraging,* or borrowing, the money to make their bids, the process that created the great lumps of new corporate debt that so worry takeovers' critics. The two-tier offer is losing popularity to all-cash offers, and to such techniques as *leveraged buyouts,* or LBOs, in which a group of investors, often the corporation's management, buy out the publicly owned stock, taking a company private, and using the company's own assets as collateral to borrow the money. The billions in capital needed to buy stock is often borrowed by issuing *junk bonds,* securities that pay a high rate of interest to investors because they are unsecured by specific assets and are rated below investment grade by Standard & Poor's. Control of a company can be gained, too, by *open market purchases,* in which a raider buys a controlling interest (at least 51 percent) of a stock directly in the stock market, or by *proxy fights,* in which control can be won by getting enough proxy votes from shareholders to gain seats on the board of directors—far less expensive than a tender offer.

The takeover glossary is rich with words to describe defensive techniques. Hostile bids may be foiled by a *white knight,* a third party invited in to acquire the target company and "save" it from the hostile bidder. One of the earliest ways of getting rid of a raider was with *greenmail,* which bought back a raider's block of stock at a *premium,* or higher price than the going market price, discriminating against other shareholders. A whole host of devices has been adopted by boards of threatened companies to thwart hostile bids: the voting power of the raider's stock can be *diluted* by issuing stock with *special voting rights,* which defies the basic principles of corporate democracy by giving perhaps ten votes per share, and placing it in hands friendly to the corporation. And most contentious of all defensive devices, boards can adopt a *poison pill*, which poisons the value of the bidder's investment when he is forced, by certain triggering events, to swallow it. Properly called the Share Purchase Rights Plan, it was invented by lawyer Martin Lipton in his 1982 defense of El Paso Natural Gas, and typically takes the form of a special issue of stock that converts, when a hostile bidder completes a takeover, into the rights holders' right to buy two shares of the acquired company's stock for the price of one, raising the cost of acquisition to forbidding levels. The value of a raider's investment can also be diluted by identifying a company's prime *crown jewel* assets and giving a preferred suitor a *lockup*, or option to buy or control them, reducing the company's value to the hostile bidder.

Survival has forced corporate boards to new levels of inventiveness. They have adopted *staggered boards*, which elect only a portion of the board each year, preventing an acquiring company from replacing an entire incumbent board all at once. And they adopt *supermajority provisions*, which require a supermajority shareholder vote of 70 or 80 percent to approve critical decisions such as mergers.

Command of the new language is a passport into one of the most spirited national debates of the century and the provocative questions it asks:

Are corporations sacred entities with their own right to life? Vancouver financier Edgar Kaiser, heir to Henry Kaiser's industrial empire, says, "I can't believe my grandfather intended every company he founded to live forever." Yet under attack, TWA and CBS claimed status as national treasures. Are they? And how deep is our emotional dependency on the continuity and stability of institutions—corporation, church, or presidency?

What are the limits to a corporation's rights to protect itself? Who is to define them? As corporations ignore principles of corporate democracy and exclude large shareholders from profitable stock offers, state and federal courts struggle with the issue.

The emerging shareholder. Does he have more rights than a corporation's other constituencies, its employees and customers, for example? What *are* the proper roles, the proper relationships, for shareholders, management, and boards of directors? The boardroom has become the laboratory for the search for new balances of power that reflect the shareholder's stake in the company.

And debt, the concern above all others. As oil prices plunged in early 1986, there was anxiety over whether the debt taken on by Phillips, Unocal, and Chevron in takeover battles made them less resilient in a volatile oil market. Are junk bonds, as Rohatyn has speculated, part of a great bubble of debt that could burst under the pressure of economic downturns?

And finally, the $11 billion question forced by the historic November 1985 court award against Texaco in the wake of its takeover of Getty Oil: does a handshake constitute a contract? A citizen's jury in Houston thought so. Was the jury's decision a call for reevaluation of Wall Street's codes and ethical standards?

◆ ◆ ◆

HERE, then, is a road map through the takeover wars. Focus is on the campaigns of 1985, a year that saw the climax battle of the great oil mergers, a quantum leap in the pace of activity, and the strong emergence of the next phase of the corporate revolution—the voluntary restructuring that engulfed corporate America by the end of 1985. It is a story of power, money, and, above all, people, as seen through the eyes of the close-knit club that runs the deals. Focus will be on three of the major corporate struggles of 1985: Unocal, Crown Zellerbach, and TWA. They were initiated by the heaviest-hitting and most interesting of the entrepreneurs—T. Boone Pickens, Sir James Goldsmith, and Carl Icahn. But other deals echo throughout the story—Texaco-Getty, CBS, Revlon, Household, Union Carbide. For takeovers can best be understood as a synthesis of deals, each unique but tightly interwoven into the larger fabric and incestuous network of men.

The fight for Unocal puts Boone Pickens's credibility on the line against takeovers' most determined opponent, CEO Fred Hartley. A clash of archetypes, its generals are two oilmen who fight for opposing destinies, for oil and for industrial America. Unfolding into the full-blown panoply of war with a cast of hundreds, Unocal introduces the basic issues, players, and processes—the pieces that make up the complex mosaic of takeover.

The Crown Zellerbach struggle, in which elegant British-French financier Sir James Goldsmith sweeps over Marty Lipton's feared poison pill defense and marches to control of the San Francisco–based forest products company, reveals takeovers as a growing international phenomenon attracting foreign raiders and investors, and erupting in Canada, Britain, Japan, and Australia. Sharing center stage with the charismatic Goldsmith is the poison pill, symbol of the clever defense and attack devices that consume extravagant amounts of lawyers', bankers', courts', and corporations' time, energy, and money, and that test the most basic issues.

These two battles prepare the ground for Carl Icahn's takeover of TWA, which, more than any other, shows the human side of takeover and its impact on the employee. A textbook view of deregulation's impact on an industry, TWA tests one of the uncertainties of takeover: can a raider, once in control, manage better than the entrenched management he displaced? It will be one of the important questions of the late 1980s.

Love them or hate them, Icahn, Pickens, Flom, Lipton, Boesky, and the rest stand at the edge of a fundamental transformation of our industrial system. The corporation—still, by consensus, the best vehicle for productivity in a capitalist society—and the culture that runs it will never be the same again. We will not know until the dust settles toward the end of the decade whether the long-term costs in social disruption and disabling debt have been too high. Or whether the preeminence of quick profits as a national goal—indeed, a national god!—will satisfy, for long, the other sides of the American spirit. Viewing the battlefield at the end of 1985, Irving Shapiro observed, "The net effect has been to force every company to look at its productivity. Industrial America is in healthier shape in 1986 than in 1976. It doesn't mean there isn't pain with the health. Large change always comes with some pain and bloodletting. And this is a large change."

CHAPTER 1

‍

On July 25, 1985, in Bedford Hills, a stately suburb an hour north of New York City, two dozen corporate chief executives stepped from air-conditioned cars and limos and ambled across acres of green lawn. Here, in the civilized languor of management consultant John Diebold's estate, Cassiobury, they would suspend the hostilities and join a seminar on the struggles for corporate control that, this summer of 1985, preoccupied the minds of American businessmen. Gathered here by Diebold and *Chief Executive* magazine, the group included veterans. Harris Ashton, CEO of General Host, had survived four takeover attempts. David Moxley, managing partner of the big accounting firm Touche Ross, was quickly surrounded by CEOs hungry to know about Touche Ross's Hot Line to Wall Street, where target corporations or raiders could call, night or day, for information on the tax implications of takeover. "You didn't used to have to get tax advice over the weekend," he said with a laugh.

In this controlled environment, they would confront the enemy—notorious raider Carl C. Icahn. The man trying to take over TWA. There had been nothing new in the *Wall Street Journal* that morning. Back in June, Frank Lorenzo's Texas Air Corporation had come in as a white knight, TWA's friendly savior, and would probably buy Icahn out for some enormous profit. But Icahn apparently still held over 30 percent of TWA's stock. What if he *did* get control of TWA? Was he *fit* to run an airline? Would he bust it up? They'd ask him.

But first amenities. Like figures in an impressionist painting, the men chatted in the dappled shade of linden trees, sipping white wine, gleaning pearls of insight from two of Wall Street's elite warriors, here to join Icahn as stars of the seminar. One of the panelists, Joseph R. Perella, his neat-clipped black beard topping a lean six-foot-four frame, was the investment banker who had put the First Boston Corporation at the epicenter of mergers and acquisitions. Raised in an Italian family in Newark, his Harvard Business School degree had been his passport across the Hudson River and out of a tedious accounting job to multimillionaire status as co-head of the most aggressive financial team on Wall Street. His team epitomized the revolution in Wall Street from gentlemen bankers who despised hostile transactions and waited for clients to call to an aggressive, "Why aren't we in the deal?" marketing stance. First Boston's team had helped the Du Pont company to a $7.8 billion takeover of Conoco Oil, Perella's first megadeal. Over an intense three day period he and his partner Bruce Wasserstein had helped Texaco negotiate its $10 billion-plus takeover of Getty Oil, the second largest merger in history. Pennzoil, enraged that Getty had been snatched away from what Pennzoil had believed was an agreement to buy, was challenging the Texaco transaction at this moment in a jury trial that was just getting under way in Houston. But no one took it seriously in the light of precedent and tradition. Pennzoil's agreement had never been signed. And they all knew a deal was not done until it was signed. Or as the saying went in the takeover fraternity, "The opera's not over till the fat lady sings." For Perella, Texaco had been a triumph he'd celebrated with champagne at the Four Seasons. But most weekends he weeded his vegetable garden at his

house in Westhampton, a precious outlet for an Italian love of
the soil.

Perella's fellow panelist, lawyer Stuart L. Shapiro, could also
take Diebold's guests to the heart of the takeover wars. His
resonant voice, mellow Renaissance style, and fierce will to win
helped make him one of the most successful litigators in
Skadden, Arps, Slate, Meagher & Flom, the law firm most
famous for taking the attack side of takeover battles such as T.
Boone Pickens's. Perella's father, a PhD in economics who
worked as an accountant for Lionel Corp., had given Perella a
taste of the business world. But Shapiro had been raised with a
privileged view of corporate power. Stuart was the son of
Irving Shapiro, former CEO of Du Pont and one of the
founders of the Business Roundable—a bastion of the prevailing corporate culture. There was delicious irony in the fact that
Stuart's father, now a partner in Skadden Arps, too, had just
returned to the courtroom for the first time in thirty-five years
to argue a landmark case against a corporation, Household
International, the case Stuart had tried and lost at a lower court
level.

With the decision of the Delaware Supreme Court still pending, the case would be a bellwether of how far companies could
go to defend and entrench themselves from takeover. The case
tested a clever legal device called a poison pill, designed to
deter a raider by making a company lethal to swallow. Termed
"the atomic bomb of takeover defense arsenals," it would be,
corporations hoped, a weapon to help end the wars. The
Delaware ruling could have enormous impact on the CEOs at
the Diebold seminar. For if Household won, it would give
management another weapon in wars that were increasingly
hard to win. If the Shapiros won, it would fan the flames of war.

But it was nearly lunchtime. Where was Carl Icahn? Then,
stepping out of a silver Mercedes and guiding his white-haired
mother by the elbow across the lawn, Icahn slipped amiably
into the midst of men whose corporations, at that moment,
might be his targets. This was Icahn? This lanky, affable guy in
tan slacks and sports coat who looked more like a country club

golfer? This was the predator stalking TWA? And he had
brought his sweet mother along, smiling and dressed in blue
blouse and skirt. Carl had urged her to come. She'd be returning to Florida in a few days; it would be a nice lunch and a
chance to see her son in action. Icahn couldn't be all bad.

Over a lunch of chilled borscht and chicken breasts with
mustard caper sauce, good talk resonated from paneled walls
that had graced the Elizabethan home of the Earl of Essex,
inspiring Diebold's wry introduction to the seminar: "The first
hostile tender offer was probably made by Essex in the Rye
House Plot, when he made a partial tender offer for the crown
of England." But the event that hovered over the seminar was
the lobbying going on in New York Governor Cuomo's office
that day for and against an antitakeover bill that sat on his desk,
to be signed or vetoed within thirty days. It was a bill that could
undercut Ted Turner's current bid for CBS, bring hostile
takeovers of New York–based companies to a crashing halt, and
virtually wipe out the use of junk bonds, the controversial
financing that was vital to the takeover wars. It had triggered
Diebold's theme: "Do the states or the United States need
additional legislation or regulation?"

"If they pass legislation, you won't have takeovers anymore,
and the U.S. will become a second-rate power," Icahn asserted,
audaciously proposing takeovers as the answer to America's
failure to compete in international trade, the nation's hair shirt
of the eighties. The steel industry had fallen into its sink of
inefficiency, Icahn claimed, "because there weren't guys like me
around." The CEOs bristled. Shapiro, the poised litigator,
softened Icahn's claim. "There's no groundswell of concern to
justify legislation at this time, and nobody's smart enough to
write a law that works," he said with a droll smile. We do have
the Williams Act, the governing law for takeovers, Perella
reminded, designed in 1968 to create a level playing field for
both targets and raiders—the most basic right of any schoolboy.
Icahn had closed his eyes during some of the introductory
comments, but the phrase "level playing field" was a battle alert.
"I don't think it's such a level playing field, unless you go
through with a tank," he said. "There are some kamikaze

boards out there that will do *anything*—blow up the company—to keep me out. They'll sue you, they'll dilute you—"

"Who's ever diluted you, Carl?" Perella challenged. "There's a lynch mob out there if they try it." Icahn snapped back, "Disney tried it! Carter Hawley Hale—*they* diluted! What about Dan River?" He could have gone on. He had just fought dilution in the Baxter takeover that Perella's team had masterminded, and at that moment Texas Air was trying to dilute the value of his investment in TWA, trying to drive him away. An impatient CEO charged, "You're not interested in the health of a company, Carl, and in your glib and charming way you let the press think it's the real world, but you haven't *lived* in the real world of the CEO." At that, Icahn loosed a unilateral indictment of the American management class: "I've been on boards. And I say that management is the reason we have problems. It's the anti-Darwinian theory—the survival of the *un*fittest. The guy who's CEO, he's a nice guy, head of the fraternity, good at surviving. He's worked twenty years to get his fiefdom. It would be *crazy* for him to make the guy coming up who's smarter than him number two. You don't see the *best* men!"

Perella deftly diverted to the basic issue for CEOs. How could they defend themselves from Carl Icahn? They were all watching the *Wall Street Journal* for an announcement that the European raider, Sir James Goldsmith, had taken control of Crown Zellerbach Corporation. Embroidered into its defensive package by the Crown board was a poison pill triggered when Goldsmith acquired 20 percent of the stock, an event that would make it intolerably expensive for him to acquire 100 percent of the company. But ignoring it, Goldsmith had been able to buy 51 percent and gain control without suffering the impact of the pill. It was the very same pill being tested in the Household case. Unilaterally adopted by Crown's and Household's boards of directors without shareholder approval, the pill multiplied the target company's purchase price two or three times in a hostile acquisition and simply made it too expensive to merge. They hoped. But there was the specter of Goldsmith's easy victory. Were these ingenious devices dreamed up by lawyers illusionary Maginot Lines that gave you a false sense of security? "Poison pills, bylaw amendments, proxy contests, white knights," Perella said, shrugging. "The only real defense is to have 51 percent of your stock in friendly hands."

"The only real defense," Carl said, reducing the discussion to the gospel of the takeover wars, "is to have your stock price up. I think the stock market is a real good report card. If a company's run well, its stock price should reflect it. But if there's a big spread between your appraised value and your stock price, you better get that price up or someone else will do it for you." Taking swipes at flies that were using his balding forehead as a landing strip, Perella added chapter and verse: "Yes, you can refocus assets, unbundle, look at repurchase of shares . . ." In other words, restructure, the buzzword that encompassed the radical surgery and lopping off of assets done to gain efficiencies, bring your stock price up, and save yourself from takeover. Corporate America was caught up in a frenzy of restructuring.

But no matter what efficiencies might be gained by hacking off the fat and the unproductive assets, it was a painful process. The CEOs listened with nervous interest to Stuart Shapiro's reasoned doubts about the justice of the pill he and his father had twice attacked in court. Leaning back, arms stretched over the sofa, Shapiro studied his cigar smoke as it curled upward: "Poison pills raise fundamental issues of shareholder democracy. If shareholders don't have the right to approve something that can destroy a company's options under attack, is the system working?" The room took on a chill as Perella made Stuart's speculation academic: "When Goldsmith went over 20 percent, Crown Zellerbach walked into the Valley of Death." In practice, the pill had failed to stop the raider.

♦   ♦   ♦

On that same morning, July 25, 1985, Sir James was returning to Paris on the Concorde. One of Europe's richest, most elegant and elusive entrepreneurs, Jimmy Goldsmith bestrode like a colossus not only England, Europe, and the tax-shelter paradises of the Caribbean, but now the United States as well. Europe's second largest grocer, as he wryly called himself, king of a conglomerate empire assembled with Alexandrian speed and appetite in the sixties, owner of a string of magazines and newspapers, including France's most influential newsmagazine, *L'Express,* he had pursued capitalism against the socialist wave with dazzling success and—as a British tabloid noted—with golden balls. But born of a British Jewish father and French Catholic mother, raised in the family's French hotels and long domiciled in England, he was increasingly a spiritual and political alien in France and England. In the seventies, he had watched the stream of Arab oil money divert from London to American investments, and Wall Street eclipse the City of London as the nexus of international finance. In 1981, he had watched the nationalization of French industry that had forced him to sell his bank, Banque Occidentale.

His roots and family were still in England and France. But America was where the excitement was. And where entrepreneurial capitalism still flourished. He was now dismembering his European empire with the vigor with which he had created it, and was refocusing his acquisitive lust and vast capital resources on corporate America. He now lived one-fourth of the year in New York, and had joined Pickens and Icahn in the takeover wars. All three had daring, tenacity, and steel-trap strategic minds. But Goldsmith brought a grasp of the global scene that products of Far Rockaway and the Texas Panhandle could never match.

On arrival at JFK Airport by Concorde the previous morning, Sir James was whisked by limousine to a brick town house on East Eightieth Street marked only by a discreet number, buzzer, and locks. Inside, moving past marble busts of two powerful Florentines, Cardinal Soderini and his brother, for whom Machiavelli had worked as secretary of the influential governing committee Dieci di Balia, he crossed a three-story atrium carved from the bowels of the staid old Victorian town house, bypassed the polished oval desk and stiff brocade of the boardroom to his left, and climbed a splendid curved stairway to the drawing room where Goldsmith's team waited, watched by a haughty bust of a Medici. There, in a setting of pale gold walls and sofas, Oriental rugs, a library of burnished leather-bound French classics and Churchill's histories, and lofty windows dressed in thick red brocade, Goldsmith and his team refined the terms of surrender that would be negotiated with Crown Zellerbach that afternoon.

For eight months, Goldsmith had pursued his corporate prey, buying shares through a global network of shell companies and partnerships that stretched from Liechtenstein to the Cayman Islands. He had acquired a controlling share of the company's stock, 51 percent, and had come to preside over the transfer of Crown Zellerbach into his hands. Lawyers and investment bankers had been negotiating the agreement all week, the climax to a long and bitter battle. Today, the two principals, Goldsmith and Zellerbach's CEO, William T. Creson, would sign the armistice that would end the war. He would fly back to Paris chairman of the board of Crown.

Creson and Goldsmith met at noon at the offices of Wachtell, Lipton, Rosen & Katz, the firm founded by Martin Lipton, the lawyer who had created the poison pill. Goldsmith, a commanding presence in an exquisitely tailored Italian suit over his six-foot-three frame, exuded a political, personal, and economic philosophy that was alien to the American corporate system. At fifty-two, he was everything the organization man was not. At twenty-one, he had convinced Bolivian tin heiress Isabel Patino to elope with him, a continental sensation that had left him devastated when Isabel died of a brain hemorrhage in late pregnancy just months later. With a disarming cleft in the chin, his broad, handsome face remained, more than thirty years later, as smooth, polished, and implacable as his marble busts. He was still dashing, but now Croesus-rich. He kept his beautiful women—wives, ex-wives, and lovers—and scattered troops of progeny in households in London, Paris, and on Eightieth Street without a flicker of moral guilt. He stayed close to his French family and former wife Ginette, while maintaining his current wife, the former Lady Annabel Birley, and their children in Ormeley Lodge, a stately Georgian mansion on Richmond Park in London. He had secretly married Lady Annabel, a statuesque, square-jawed blonde, in Paris in 1978 after a scandalous transcontinental liaison with her when she was still married to Mark Birley, one of Goldsmith's Eton contemporaries and owner of the smart nightclub Annabel's. In New York, his companion for several years has been a young French reporter with *Paris-Match*, Laura Boulay de la Meurthe, who lived openly with him at his apartment in the Carlyle Hotel, and in the town house on Eightieth Street which is now his operating base in New York.

He so transcended the level of fears and priorities that consumed most corporate boards that he had chosen to attend a critical Crown board meeting by satellite hookup from his yacht off the coast of Turkey, where he was cruising with friends. With a knighthood from the Queen in his pocket, he had delighted in puncturing ballooning speculation over what corporate white knight might rescue Crown Zellerbach from his evil grasp with the comment, "Well, I'm white. And I'm a knight."

Yet America was where a sophisticated financial animal now needed to be. "Since an early age," he says, "I had rejected the prevailing cultures of England and France, which seemed to me the cultures of decay." He made his fortune in the sixties by exploiting the undervalued assets that he saw as symptoms of this decay. "English companies had rotted, and when a company rots, its stock price usually does not reflect its fundamental value." Goldsmith was finally frustrated by decades of conflict with the system, and by the "gentrification" of the middle class that stripped it of the lusty mercantile spirit that had built the British Empire. In a sensational criminal libel case, he sued the gossipy magazine *Private Eye* for stories tying him, by implication, to a suicide, a murder, and the disappearance of several of his acquaintances. Although he had won an apology from *Private Eye*, the British press had excoriated him and made his name synonymous with scandal. Here in the United States, free from the socialism and "corporate statism" he despised, there was still room for the full play of an entrepreneur of Renaissance vision and dimensions. Like a hunting falcon cruising for opportunity, he had scanned the continents and oceans and dived at the speed of light at the glittering piles of profits sitting in the balance sheets of America's corporations. In 1973, Sir James had come company shopping on Wall Street. He had bought the Grand Union supermarket chain, then gone hunting for timber. Trees. An asset no one but he seemed to see as the jewels they would be in five or ten years as use of the world's forests outstripped reforestation. This ability to see value where others cannot is the gift of the great raider.

Leaning back, long legs stretched out, his face the cool enigma he had perfected in his teens doing high-stakes gambling in the casinos of Europe, Sir James Goldsmith entered the final, formal negotiations. Wachtell Lipton's lawyers had already drafted terms of the agreement. Lawyers on both sides had sweated over them and drawn up an agenda for the meeting. Both Goldsmith and Creson were backed by formidable teams. The two legendary lawyers Marty Lipton and Joseph Flom had been head to head on the transaction, as they had been on deals for the past twenty years, Lipton on Zellerbach's team, Flom on Goldsmith's. There were Blaine V. ("Fin") Fogg, a lawyer on Flom's front line, investment bankers Chris Anderson of Drexel Burnham Lambert Incorporated for junk bonds, and Rothschild's Bob Pirie, a former Skadden Arps lawyer who headed up Goldsmith's financial strategy. There were Roland Franklin, head of Goldsmith's North American operations, CEO Bill Creson and George James from Crown, outside Crown director Warren Hellman, and pairs of back-up lawyers from both Wachtell and Skadden Arps.

Creson held his dignity. But for him it was a terrible moment. He had himself been swept to power by a coup d'état that, four years earlier, had thrown out weak management that had allowed the 115-year-old San Francisco company to slide into decline. With aggressive slashing and management reforms, he had been turning it around. The market hadn't perceived the changes yet, but it was happening. He needed a little more time. "In two more years, it would have worked. It would have been too expensive then for Jimmy to buy," takeover public relations specialist Gershon Kekst said as he saw events overtake Creson's plans.

Bringing grace to the painful task, Goldsmith moved politely through the agenda of items Crown Zellerbach might argue but must ultimately accept. Goldsmith felt no rush of emotion. This was simply business. He'd been through it a hundred times. When he'd made his first points, the eyes of the inside teams turned toward Creson. The lead-off response came not from Creson though, but from Warren Hellman, grandson of the founder of Wells Fargo Bank, and now a San Francisco investment banker with Jewish establishment credentials to match those of old James D. Zellerbach, grandson of the founder, who died in 1963. An attractive, lean ultramarathoner who had raced to the presidency of Lehman Brothers in New York at twenty-nine, he spoke Goldsmith's language much more comfortably than did Creson. It was as if, intuitively, a voice more like that of the founding entrepreneur, not a professional manager's, needed to be heard at the gallows.

The principals left the meeting in the late afternoon, with the fine-tuning in the hands of the team that had lived and breathed the deal since December 1984. At 9:00 P.M., Creson and Goldsmith signed the agreement. With a signature, Crown Zellerbach ceased to exist as an independent company. The headline next morning in the *Wall Street Journal* would read "GOLDSMITH WINS FIGHT FOR CROWN ZELLERBACH CORP," while Sir James caught the Concorde back to Paris.

◆ ◆ ◆

CROWN Zellerbach might have lost its war, but Unocal would carry the scars and burdens of its victory for years. July 25 was the day the nation's twelfth-largest oil company would perform one of the bold acts of restructuring forced on it as the price of independence after a wrenching battle with T. Boone Pickens. Today—or tomorrow, if the climate seemed more welcoming—it would release into the market the first few units of its master limited partnership. Unocal had spun off some of its oil reserves into a partnership, which would send profits from Unocal's oil production directly out to shareholders. Franklin W. ("Fritz") Hobbs of Dillon, Read & Co. Inc., one of Unocal's two investment bankers through the ordeal, called this "an attempt . . . to demonstrate to the world some of the inherent values inside Union Oil."

Unocal needed Lester Winterfeld's vote of confidence. Just

retired as senior oil analyst at Manufacturers Hanover Trust, Winterfeld came in as a consultant now only one or two days a week. He had come in early from the country this morning, and he shook his head with concern as he called up Unocal quotations on the terminal in his windowless office in the shadow of Rockefeller Center. Unocal's balance sheet was now heavy with over $3 billion in new debt taken on to buy back a chunk of its own stock, a move to help defeat Pickens and make itself less attractive to other bidders. The company had lost its sex appeal in the stock market the moment Pickens abandoned his bid to seize control. Unocal's board had hurled Pickens's bid for $54 a share back in his face as "grossly inadequate." "Now it has an 80 percent debt ratio and its stock is selling for $29," said Winterfeld. "I think Fred Hartley lost."

What had thrust this unassuming man to the cutting edge of the takeover wars? Winterfeld's job is to evaluate oil companies. He takes their pulse and makes the recommendations that guide the investment decisions of portfolio managers who, at Manufacturers Hanover, control $22 billion of pension fund money, which must be kept actively invested in the market. It was those buy or sell orders that moved Unocal's stock price up or down. For these so-called institutional investors now controlled an estimated 70 percent of the stock on the New York Stock Exchange, and held the success or failure of a hostile bid in their hands. Winterfeld had an extra dimension of power: he sat on the proxy committee that voted the shares "Manny Hanny" had under its control in proxy contests, where fights for seats on the board of directors often decided the outcome of struggles for corporate control. The proxy was an increasingly popular weapon of war.

Among the most wooed men in the financial world, Winterfeld and his fellow analysts, a day earlier, had gone to the Plaza Hotel for a meeting and glittering reception staged by ARCO, the big Los Angeles oil company that had just taken on billions of new debt to restructure itself in order to avoid takeover. ARCO's CEO, Robert Anderson, already impressive as the largest individual landowner in the United States, and something of a hero since his voluntary actions, had flown in with his senior executives to reassure the oil analysts about the changes, sugarcoating some bad news about low quarterly earnings with an upbeat slide show, cocktails, and hors d'oeuvres. Winterfeld was not easily dazzled. "When I saw Anderson up in his gorgeous boardroom with its art collection in Los Angeles I thought, 'This boardroom is worth as much as your whole *stock* is worth.' He didn't look to me like a man who was going to lean down and create a more efficient company." But he was doing it now. As was Unocal. Union Limited Partners would start trading at $23 a share. Would Winterfeld, and the market, smile on it?

◆　◆　◆

TEN blocks away, TWA Captain Harry R. Hoglander plunged into the honking, snarling gridlock of traffic girdling the Pan Am Building, headed for the pilots' union office, which had become his command post since this battle for the airline began. He was a warrior by default, caught in a war he had not initiated, but could not escape. What did he know about takeovers? Or Carl Icahn? But here he and Icahn were, yelling profanities at each other in broad New York accents in labor negotiations that would decide the fate of the airline.

What Hoglander had quickly learned was that once "in play," something would happen. The airline would be sold, busted up, or taken private. And the world he had known as an airline pilot would be changed forever. He had found himself leading not only TWA's thirty-three hundred pilots but the thirty-four thousand pilots of the Air Line Pilots Association into a strange new world of takeover and deregulation in which the pilot was just another asset. It was the end of the era, launched by Lindbergh, when flight held such glamor and cockpits such concentrations of the "right stuff" that the mantle of folk hero had shifted from cowboy to the pilot. The end of status honored in salaries that soared to $150,000-plus for 747 captains. Just weeks before, the terrorist hijacking of TWA's Flight 847 from Athens had shown the stuff pilots were made of; TWA's crew had maintained its cool and courage throughout the hostage crisis. Theirs had been a horrifying but clear-cut war. Harry's was an intangible war—one he was convinced threatened the performance the guys on Flight 847 had shown. The system was at risk: the structure of training, performance checks, discipline, seniority, pay scales, working conditions, and, above all, pride and loyalty—that had given TWA ten years without a crash.

Harry's war wasn't, ultimately, with takeovers. It was with change—the change that was transforming the aviation industry since deregulation in 1978. He knew his pilots must compromise or become dinosaurs in the drive for routes and passengers. Their salaries could not compete with the $30,000 that Continental pilots had averaged ever since Frank Lorenzo took them over and broke the union. And yet how could balance sheets show the uncertainties about jobs and money that all TWA employees and their families faced? How safe would the airline be if the structure was dismantled, sacrificed to cost cutting?

And now TWA, his company, wanted Frank Lorenzo of Texas Air to buy the airline. The Darth Vader of deregulation, as far as the pilots were concerned. He broke the unions and stripped the job of dignity, Harry believed. The company had committed to him without even talking to the unions. Harry had read about it in the *New York Times,* for chrissake. Drexel Burnham was raising junk bonds for Lorenzo right now to buy the airline. Drexel could pull miracles out of a hat. They'd raised $3 billion for Boone Pickens in less than a week on Unocal.

Harry was risking it all. His job. Twenty years of seniority. The chance to fly. If Lorenzo got the airline, Harry knew he'd be the first to go. "They have ways to get rid of you. They'll fail you on a check ride. Lorenzo takes no prisoners," he muttered, scanning intuitively to avoid midairs with taxicabs as he maneuvered through the traffic, hot in his rumpled seersucker suit with the pants a little too short. Ruggedly handsome but half shaven, he looked harassed. A stack of phone messages would be waiting.

They were juggling about a dozen balls in the air, trying to find alternatives to Lorenzo as the envelope of time narrowed from days to hours. There was Icahn, calling night and day, at two or three in the morning, then again at five, trying to wear them down, threatening to sell his stock to Lorenzo if the unions didn't come around and make concessions. There were Mr. X's guys, flying in today to crunch numbers with Chase Manhattan and Citicorp to see if he could get the financing together for a higher bid than Lorenzo or Icahn. There was a rush of hope last week when Frank Borman of Eastern had wanted to come in, then disillusionment when that hope faded. They were still flirting with half a dozen other options, trying to stall Icahn because they feared he might bust up the airline. But the fucking unions couldn't get together! His pilots, the machinists, the flight attendants—they all had their own petty agendas. Instead of a united front, they were negotiating behind one another's backs.

As he started taking the calls, he flashed on the weekend coming up. To relieve the tension, he'd fly to Saint Louis and fly with the National Guard. He'd take up the little T-33 jet trainer and do some aerobatics. "Flying, every day is a sunshine day for me because I always see the sun," he mused. "When you're coming out of a murky, lousy, stinking day and you go through the clouds on top . . ."

The phone rang. A voice who would only identify himself as someone from one of the printers who specialize in proxy and tender offer materials said, "Lorenzo's got his financing. I just saw them printing up the proxy stuff to go out to shareholders."

Harry said the words pilots say when they first discover they have a serious emergency and throw everything they have into saving the airplane: "Oh, shit."

CHAPTER 2

JULY 25, 1985, had been taking shape at least a year earlier in secret acts, and in events buried in board meetings and on the inside pages of the *Wall Street Journal*.

The summer of 1984 was a summer of building defenses, as the wave of hostile takeovers engulfed first the oil industry and then spread out to other industries. It was lawyer Marty Lipton's summer. He was doing aggressive marketing of the poison pill. He had invented it, as he had invented an arsenal of sophisticated defense devices that could be embedded in a corporation's bylaws or adopted by boards of directors to deter takeover raids, exploding under the feet of raiders who marched too far into the territory with stock purchases and hostile tender offers. His progress from corporate board meeting to board meeting that summer reminded one of a pre-Reformation cardinal touring the provinces with his bejeweled crown and retinue, selling indulgences that would absolve sin and assure safe passage into heaven.

And best to buy defenses early, before attack. If your stock began mysterious fluctuations in the market, it was Wachtell

Lipton you called, and Marty Lipton you wanted to see. In a legal career that had spanned the modern history of mergers and acquisitions, he had, at fifty-three, become the second most famous takeover lawyer in the nation. Joseph Flom, of Skadden Arps, was number one, a small man who cast a shadow Lipton's portly frame could never quite escape.

Lipton had seen his first hostile deal in 1952, when he graduated from the University of Pennsylvania's Wharton School to become a bag carrier for corporate attorney Lincoln ("Pud") Morris of Selig and Morris. It was a three-year defense of Fairbanks Morse against Penn Texas and archetypal corporate raider Leopold G. Gilverstein. Wharton School had been intended as a step toward investment banking, the ambition his father, a factory manager, had had for him since Lipton's Jersey City childhood. But with Penn Texas, and glamorous clients like Mike Todd and Elizabeth Taylor sweeping through the office, he was hooked on law. Flom was already there, ahead of him.

Lipton first saw Flom in action when the two faced each other in a proxy fight in the late fifties, even before Lipton had started his own firm, Wachtell, Lipton, Rosen & Katz, in 1965 with several old Wharton classmates. "Joe already had a reputation twenty-five years ago," says Lipton of the man who would become his arch rival for supremacy of the field. "There were only two or three proxy fights a year then—they were rare, and a deal of $10 million was very big." But in 1965, Lipton did "the deal of the year." It was under $100 million—Illinois Central Industries. But it was very important to the firm. On that deal he met Ira Harris, a young man just starting a meteoric rise at Salomon Brothers Inc, the investment bankers. They would become a team, with Harris hiring Lipton as Salomon's lawyer and the two working so closely together on so many deals that, a lawyer colleague cracked in 1985, "Lipton's really just a senior partner of Salomon."

Flom's star was rising. "By 1970, Joe was the country's leading expert," says Lipton, who, in 1973, recognized his rival in the *Michigan Law Review:* "One member of the New York bar has become so renowned for his specialized defenses against takeovers that the first question on Wall Street is 'which side has him?' " The old and prestigious investment bankers Morgan Stanley & Co. Incorporated and their corporate finance chief, Robert F. Greenhill, had been watching Flom and decided he was the man to hire for takeover matters. "By 1974," says Lipton, "Flom and Greenhill were leading the pack. They absolutely dominated it. The rest of Wall Street was getting restive. They didn't know how to compete." The same year, Lipton's opportunity came. With Wall Street watching, he helped financier Laurence A. Tisch, still a Lipton client, and his corporate vehicle, Loews Corporation, challenge the CNA Insurance Company in Chicago. "It was considered impossible to take over an insurance company, but we did. It was the high-profile deal of the year." Wall Street had found a way to fight Flom and Morgan Stanley: "Get Lipton!"

The famous Regency breakfasts started then. "Flom and I," says Lipton, "would meet at the Regency Hotel two or three mornings a week and conference through breakfast. They went on for years." Other takeover lawyers started coming there, too, hoping to lip-read. "It got too crowded. We've stopped them now." But the Regency breakfasts helped give birth to a myth that still wreathes the two in an aura of power: the belief that, no matter who the other players are, every major takeover deal is ultimately orchestrated by Flom and Lipton in secret meetings. The Regency breakfasts became a provocative crumb that fed the news-hungry press and competitors, extending the myth. "But it just isn't *true*," Lipton says, not entirely convincingly. "They *don't* get together and work out everything. Absolutely not," agrees proxy fighter Arthur Long, who started in the game with Flom and Lipton in the sixties. "Take the poison pill. Would Flom support Marty putting in poison pills when he's going to have to fight them in court?"

Lipton's personal legend built through the New York City financial crisis in 1975 to 1977, when he joined banker Felix Rohatyn on the pro-bono committee that saved New York from bankruptcy. The man who moves like a gray eminence through the takeover wars, Rohatyn had been born in Vienna, a member of a prosperous Polish-Jewish family. Escaping Europe via Casablanca and Rio de Janeiro to New York in 1942, he had joined the New York office of the very private French investment banking house Lazard Frères & Co. after graduating from Middlebury College in 1949. Smart, French-speaking, and a refugee who had escaped the Nazis at the same time, he became the protégé of the late André Meyer, the man described by *Fortune* as "the most important banker in the Western world" and by his biographer, Cary Reich, as a man "who spun a web of wealth and influence over two continents." Confidant to presidents, Jackie Onassis, and the industrial giants of the world, Meyer saw Rohatyn as his heir. But Rohatyn turned down the chance to take over the reins of Lazard from Meyer. Like Meyer, he had a very practical notion of wealth that had come from stuffing the family's few remaining gold coins in toothpaste tubes as they escaped Biarritz. Like Lipton, he loved the hands-on thrill and challenge of masterminding deals that influenced the fate of corporations and the shape of economic events. "New York City was in crisis," says Lipton. "I was on it full time in the fall of '75." Savoring memories of the ultimate power trip when he and Rohatyn simultaneously manipulated a city's and a corporation's destiny, he adds, "At the same time, Felix and I were fighting each other in Colt's bid for Garlock. We solved it in the hall during a recess at City Hall."

By the late seventies, the battles were getting intense. Until then, corporations had still been in the growth mode of the sixties, the age of conglomeratization, when you acquired companies to expand or diversify. "The bust-up game was beginning. I began to question hostile takeovers and develop a philosophy," says Lipton. As they became a national phenomenon, Lipton, with his academic credentials as adjunct professor at New York University School of Law, became one of the most vocal opponents of hostile takeovers. Rohatyn was outspoken, too, but saw abuses and benefits in both attack and defense in takeovers, and continued to represent both sides as investment banker. But Lipton had chosen his side; he worked it with a crusader's passion.

While Flom was advising T. Boone Pickens on his earliest

hostile bids and at the same time defending great corporations, Lipton became the guru of defense. Intense eyes magnified to the point of bulging by thick horn-rimmed glasses, Lipton brought a powerful intellect to bear on defending corporate America. He seemed a genius at devising new defenses to slow or defeat attacks, defenses a board of directors could vote in without shareholder approval. They needed only to evoke the Business Judgment Rule, an honor system adopted by most states, which gives management and boards of directors broad freedom and authority to act in the interests of their company without shareholder approval. The Rule operates on the assumption that management is responsible and knows best. Under threat of takeover, it could become a defensive shield.

Counseling threatened corporations, Lipton began to recommend a variety of "shark repellents." There were staggered boards, where only two or three board members came up for election each year, making it impossible for dissidents to throw out an entire board. There were special voting rights—stock held by friendly hands that had not one, but perhaps ten, votes per share in a proxy fight, an explosively controversial violation of the notion of one share, one vote, which had been as basic to corporate as to political democracy. There were scorched earth and PacMan defenses, white and gray knights, porcupine provisions, and sandbag tactics. The special language of takeovers proliferated as fast as the weapons Lipton created, as he saw "junk-bond bust-up takeovers replacing the two-tier bootstrap bust-up takeover." Poison pills came in a variety of forms.

As companies became increasingly scared, the invention of devices became an iconoclastic specialty that gave Lipton the aura of high priest. His firm was paid $4, $5, and up to $10 million fees for the big transactions as the number of hostile bids and mergers increased exponentially in both size and amount. By 1984, there was a record of twenty-five hundred merger-and-acquisition transactions involving $122 billion.

◆   ◆   ◆

"THE first use of the poison pill was when I got a call to defend El Paso Natural Gas against Burlington & Northern Railroad in '82," Lipton recalls. "I was in the middle of the fight for General

American Oil. Flom was helping Pickens, and I got the last plane out of Dallas for New York. El Paso was in crisis. There was an offer for half of El Paso's stock. They had no defenses." The idea came to him: "Why can't we create a special class of stock?" Attached to that stock would be rights that would be activated when a raider acquired 20 percent of the stock. When swallowed by the raider, the poison went to work. It gave shareholders the right to buy additional shares to dilute the raider's holdings, and, more ingenious, the right, if their company was acquired, to buy stock in the newly merged company at a bargain price. Two for one, in effect. It could increase the cost of acquiring the company by billions. It would simply knock out the bootstrapping raider who didn't have a big war chest of money, or burden him with multimillions or billions of dollars in debt if he was able to borrow the money. Lipton named it the Share Purchase Rights Plan. But it was quickly christened the "poison pill" by the *Wall Street Journal.* The El Paso board adopted it, but that conflict settled before the pill could be used.

♦ ♦ ♦

"OOPS, My Company Is on the Block" was the title of the *Fortune* magazine article in July 1984 that scared Donald C. Clark to death and put his preparations for war into high gear. The CEO of Household International, a large financial services corporation in Prospect Heights, Illinois, summoned Lipton to a special board meeting on August 14, 1984. He summoned Goldman, Sachs & Co., his investment bankers, too. The front line of defense. In May, Goldman had produced a report that declared Household "vulnerable." Since then, the Murchisons, wealthy Texans, had surfaced with a letter of interest in acquisition. And now the threat lay within as well as without. One of his own directors, John Moran, Household's largest shareholder, was planning, Clark feared, to acquire the company. Clark and Moran had met in New York to talk about it. Moran had not made a hostile bid, though. He had said he wouldn't. But . . .

On the surface, it was an elephant worrying about a flea. Moran's private investment company in New York, Dyson-

Kissner-Moran, was a mere 1 percent the size of Household. It had a dozen employees. Household's stock was worth $1.7 billion. But with the emergence of junk-bond financing, which allowed you to borrow almost any sum, fleas were waging war.

But surely Moran was a gentleman. A twinkling-eyed Irishman who could carry off a paisley silk foulard and gray bowler with a business suit, he was suave, soft-spoken, gracious. And he had a streak of daring that belied his traditional investment banking background. He belonged to Cresta, the "crazy bobsled club in Saint Moritz," as a friend describes it, was a horseman and pilot, and loved white-water rafting and scuba-diving on the Great Barrier Reef. Cold-blooded cunning did not seem his style.

Dyson-Kissner-Moran (DKM) had never made a hostile bid, although it had made many friendly negotiated acquisitions. It was watching Household, however. At $25 a share, Household's stock was well below "book," or estimated net, value, and DKM had bought a half million shares in the spring. It was a steal at the price, they thought. But studying the "black book," their very private list of investments and candidates for investment, DKM's acquisition analysts began to see it as more than that. Household was a true conglomerate with discrete, separate divisions—Household Finance, National Car Rental, a furniture and grocery store, a merchandising division. It would be easy to break up and sell off some of the divisions to generate cash and buy the company. It and another company on whose board Moran sat, American Natural Resources, looked like excellent candidates for a leveraged buyout, or LBO, a technique that allows the group who wants to acquire the company to use that company's own assets and cash flow to fund the purchase and pay back their debt. LBOs were being used more and more as a means for management to buy the company they work for and take it private. Fast becoming the trendiest technique in takeovers, LBOs would be taking Macy's, Levi Strauss, and Beatrice private before the end of 1985.

As they brainstormed, Moran and his partners moved Household up to a priority position in the book, and Moran met with Clark and Household's chief financial officer to discuss an LBO. Moran had agreed in his meetings that he would not make an unfriendly offer for the company. He was a gentleman. There was no specific threat to Household on August 13 as Moran flew to its board meeting in Prospect Heights.

Takeover preparedness, however, would be the issue of the board meeting on August 14; Marty Lipton would be its star. Lipton had prepared a thick notebook, which was mailed by Household to all the directors just a week before the meeting. It was normal to give the directors time over the weekend to review the agenda. But to Moran this seemed rushed for issues of such magnitude. The evening before the meeting, the directors were invited to an informal dinner in the corporate dining room. But before that, all the directors except Moran had been invited to a meeting where the pill was discussed. To an increasingly nervous Clark, Moran had become a Judas in their midst.

Next day, the directors met for an all-day meeting, not unlike meetings being held in boardrooms across the nation. Lipton, with the equivalent of Churchillian exhortations to "fight them on the beaches," presented the proposals. First was a commitment to independence, a resolve that "the investment of the shareholders and the long-term interests of the corporation as a whole will best be served if the corporation continues as an independent company." He recommended bylaw changes that would make it more difficult for a raider to use the proxy mechanism to get his message before the annual meeting, where boards could be thrown out. And then Lipton presented the poison pill.

Setting up a climate of threat was Goldman Sachs's presentation by Gordon McMahon, complete with a slide show that depicted, as an attorney described it, "the rape and pillage of the boardroom by takeover." It was, as described in court testimony, Goldman's "standard anti-takeover speech." Lipton's notebook had made it clear that the Share Purchase Rights Plan, the poison pill, was not the perfect defense. Activated when a raider went over 20 percent, it gave anyone who held it the right to buy the target's stock for half price when and if the company was 100 percent acquired and merged. "The plan would not prevent takeovers. It would have no effect on a raider who is willing to acquire control and not obtain 100 percent ownership until after the rights have expired," according to Lipton. But if the plan did not deter a takeover, it would "virtually assure that any takeover attempt would be for cash and for all the shares of the company's common stock." It would, he believed, prevent junk-bond takeovers that bought stock by issuing low-grade unsecured bonds, or front-end-loaded two-tier tender offers that left some of the shareholders out.

Two-tier tender offers were becoming one of the negative catchphrases of the takeovers wars. As opposed to an offer to buy all of a company's stock at one price, they were an offer to buy part of the stock first at a premium price per share for cash or high-rated securities—loading the "first tier" or "front end" with tempting profit. But for the rest—the "second tier" or "back end"—a lower price was generally offered, to be paid in much less attractive securities. Two-tier offers allowed individual raiders such as Pickens to make bids for control of huge companies without having to come up with cash for all the shares. But there was a short deadline for tendering shares to the first tier, and with the back end often hardly more than a vague promise, shareholders generally rushed to offer their shares to the first tier rather than risk getting left out in the less profitable back end. It gave professional and institutional investors a great advantage, for they monitored the tender offer materials minute by minute and could act quickly. An individual shareholder might throw away the mail and never even know about the first-tier offer. As the takeover wars warmed up in the fall of 1984, the front-end-loaded two-tier offer was under attack as coercive.

The Share Purchase Rights Plan would not only put an end to the two-tier offers cash-short raiders had relied on, Lipton claimed, it would add $6 billion to a raider's cost of taking over Household.

The threat was there. With Drexel Burnham having just

proved in the Gulf deal that it was able to raise junk-bond financing in huge amounts for any bootstrapper, an unprecedented weapon was at hand for the lone-wolf raider. What corporation was immune? Drexel had financed the raids of Pickens against General American and Gulf, of Steinberg against Walt Disney, Lipton reminded, and most alarming, Leucadia's current bustup bid for Avco, a financial services company like Household. Clark blanched. Household had just been called and offered parts of Avco by the raiding company. It could just as easily be dismembered parts of Household being offered. Clark urged that the plan be adopted. Now.

Moran was appalled. He hadn't been told they were going to vote on the rights this morning. The board was being whipped into a state of threat, he felt, and railroaded into approving a defensive plan he was sure the directors did not fully understand. It was so confusing that Lipton himself had claimed that part of its deterrent force was that "the plan creates rather complicated situations that may be difficult for a potential raider to evaluate." If raiders, with their armies of expert lawyers and bankers, could not understand it, what chance had directors, in one hour's discussion? Shareholders hadn't even been asked. Once adopted, the rights would be carved in stone, part of the corporate bylaws. And the triggering of the pill, Moran feared, could backfire on Household. Like a grenade with the pin in, the rights could be kept deactivated until the moment a raider bought 20 percent of the stock. But once activated, they were unredeemable. And as Moran understood its implications, they could deter not only the raider but anybody else, a friendly white knight perhaps, from gaining control. Management and boards might not like it, but the fact was that takeovers did have the effect of moving the target stock price up. And as arbitrager Ivan F. Boesky loved to remind, "That's why people buy stock. To have it go up. If there's any other reason, I've never heard of it." The poison pill, Moran feared, could immutably reduce these profitable options for the shareholders.

And *would* it deter a raider? Lipton himself had made it clear

that it was not a catchall preventive for takeover. It appeared
that a raider might still gain control by buying stock in the open
market, unaffected by the pill unless he tried to merge. Moran
spoke up against voting precipitously. So did John C. Whitehead, senior partner of Goldman Sachs and one of the outside
directors on Household's board. Whitehead's voice was one of
the most respected on Wall Street; about to retire, he would
become deputy secretary of state in Reagan's cabinet. He
warned that adopting the defensive pill would only highlight
Household as a vulnerable target, and attract raiders. But the
board voted fourteen to two to adopt the pill, joining Crown
Zellerbach in what would become a groundswell of such adoptions. Colgate-Palmolive. Owens-Illinois. Lipton was on a roll.

Moran had to leave the meeting right after lunch. As Household's Kingair flew him to a finance committee meeting of the
board of directors of American Natural Resources in Detroit,
he viewed the morning and became increasingly disturbed.
The pill was wrong, and probably illegal, he believed. And what
was its real motive? There was no overt threat, even though
Moran had been treated like the enemy. "The directors voted
for the plan for the sole and primary purpose of entrenching
themselves in office. A lot of boards don't want anybody to
shake up their little country club. This is one of them."

Within three days of Household's adoption of the pill, John
Moran called Joe Flom. On August 17, Moran sued Household
in the Delaware courts, where Household was incorporated,
and Household became a name on a court docket. Lipton later
told Flom in one of their tête-à-têtes, that if he had known
Moran was going to sue, he wouldn't have proceeded with the
pill. But it was too late. Flom's first team of litigators, Stuart L.
Shapiro and three colleagues, would try the case for Moran in
September and lose at the chancery court level. It would be
tried again on appeal by the Delaware Supreme Court in the
spring, and would hover over the takeovers wars, undecided,
for most of 1985. As the issues it raised—the two-tier tender
offer, the use and abuse of the Business Judgment Rule in
takeovers, and the limits of a corporation's right to take action

to prevent takeovers and limit options without the approval of shareholders—swelled into national concerns, Moran's suit against Household would grow, even before that final decision, to landmark status. *John A. Moran, et al v. Household International, Inc., et al* would influence the shape of the takeover wars well beyond 1985.

CHAPTER 3

In San Francisco, Crown Zellerbach had adopted the pill on July 18, a month before Household. In one of the great ironies of the takeover wars, that act may have triggered the very thing Crown dreaded most. As Fin Fogg, Goldsmith's lawyer in the subsequent struggle for control, relates it, "Roland Franklin, who runs all Goldsmith's deals, told me why Goldsmith started buying shares in Crown: when the company put in its poison pill, they made a statement to the effect that 'this will keep someone like Goldsmith away.' The day Goldsmith read that, he started buying Crown Zellerbach shares." For all Goldsmith's poise and brio, he had his sensitive spots. In this hostile arena, how you were perceived was everything. He had endured a battering from the British press over his criminal libel suit against *Private Eye*, was seeing some of that spill over into American media, and intended to resist a negative image taking hold in the United States.

It would be several months before Goldsmith would surface as a large shareholder of Crown Zellerbach. For, in the late summer of 1984, the heavy-hitting raiders were cruising, keeping Wall Street and corporate America nervous.

◆   ◆   ◆

IN September, Carl Icahn had secretly bought his first shares of TWA, still under the 5 percent mark, when he would have to declare it to the Securities Exchange Commission, which monitors and regulates takeover events. Icahn did not yet have nearly the celebrity of T. Boone Pickens. While Pickens rode the crest of the megadeals that began in the oil industry, Icahn's ambitious eye had roamed over a number of industries, looking for opportunity. So far, he had been known primarily for investing in a company, scaring it to death, and selling back to the company or to a friendly white knight at a higher price than other shareholders received in what was becoming notorious as greenmail.

He had so far made far less money than Pickens on his deals; Pickens's Mesa Petroleum and his partners had made over $400 million pretax on Gulf Oil alone. The streets of Far Rockaway had flavored Icahn's speech with a broad New Yorkese that made Pickens, with his droll Texas style, seem a disarming exotic. "The neighborhood was black, Irish, Jewish, and those streets were *mean,*" Icahn asserts. Yet the accidents of birth and upbringing had produced a man who was, by late 1984, becoming one of the most daring players of the takeover wars. Icahn did not learn risk taking from his mother. "Maybe it was a reaction," he muses. "She was a teacher from Brooklyn, afraid to venture out in the world. Always saying, 'Don't do this. Don't do that.' My father was a lawyer, but he never made any money. I was always driven to excel." A keen mind that made him the first from Far Rockaway High to get into Princeton drew him to philosophy and medicine before he discovered law and commerce. While Pickens studied petroleum engineering at Oklahoma State, Icahn's philosophical heroes were the twentieth-century empiricists: "very rational, very analytical . . . the same kind of thinking as chess."

James Freund, a Skadden, Arps lawyer whose firm had opposed Icahn in his battle earlier that year to take control of

ACF, a manufacturer of railroad cars, had seen hints of Icahn's larger strategies. "Icahn had always been known as a green-mailer, but every time I'd say to his lawyer, 'Let's take Carl out,' he'd say, 'You watch, Carl's in for the long haul.'" Icahn had indeed taken control of ACF, defeating a variant of the poison pill in court, and instead of busting it up, he had set about to manage the company. It was a $469 million deal—nearly half a billion dollars. But the size of deals was escalating so fast that deals of this magnitude were invisible in the press compared to Chevron's $13.3 billion acquisition of Gulf, or Texaco's takeover of Getty for $10.3 billion, the two largest so far. Wall Street hadn't yet made enough profit from Carl Icahn's bids to give him the attention Boone Pickens was getting. But Icahn had his plan. "In takeovers, the metaphor is war," he said. From the study of history, he had learned—and now applied—the cardinal principle of winning, not just waging, a war: "The secret is reserves. You must have reserves stretched way out ahead. You have to *know* that you could buy the company and not be stretched." He had been moving more slowly than Pickens toward the big game, but when he struck, his reserves would be there. As 1985 unfolded, reserves—the ability to fight on many fronts and hang in—would be a critical factor for both men in two of the most dramatic battles of the year.

◆　◆　◆

As summer moved into fall of 1984, stocks of possible target companies were fluctuating nervously. "Pickens on the Prowl?" the *Wall Street Journal* asked, as the Street and the press tried to guess what his next target would be. Mobil? Sun? Phillips?

Pickens had come off the Gulf deal a hero on Wall Street. Mayor Ed Koch had stopped short of a ticker tape parade to present him with a crystal apple at a gala dinner given by the traders and arbitragers of the Regency to honor him for the windfall his deals had brought to a needy city. In March, Chevron had taken over Gulf Oil in the largest merger in history, a $13.3 billion transaction. Pickens had triggered the whole thing, initiating a sensational proxy fight with Gulf in Delaware, where Gulf was incorporated. He had not set out to take over Gulf, but seeing opportunity in Gulf stock that was trading at around $38 per share, had urged Gulf to spin off some of its oil reserves into a royalty trust, as Mesa had done, a device he believed would get profits flowing directly to shareholders and move Gulf's stock price up. He had urged restructuring and had converted to a proxy bid for the company when Gulf had rejected the royalty trust.

As he made his move in Gulf, Pickens was coming off his bid to conquer Cities Service, an oil company twenty-three times the size of his Mesa Petroleum. He had built the oil and gas exploration and production company from $2,500 capital in 1956 to assets of, by early 1985, $4 billion, which made him a large "independent," but small among the majors. Cities Service had been a cliff-hanger: Mesa had barely escaped being gobbled up by a counterbid from Cities Service; Gulf had come and then gone with shocking suddenness as Cities Service's white knight; and finally, Armand Hammer's Occidental Petroleum in Los Angeles had bought the entire company at a premium price of $53 per share, up from $35 when Pickens began. As Mesa Petroleum pocketed $31.5 million pretax profit, Pickens's legend was launched. Moving on to the even larger Gulf, Pickens had narrowly lost the proxy struggle. But at a special Gulf shareholders meeting in Pittsburgh on December 2, 1983, he had taken the floor to speak on behalf of not only Gulf's, but America's 42 million shareholders, and scored great gains in national news exposure. America has always been attracted to bonanzas and self-made men. But Pickens was something more. Here was a distant relative of Daniel Boone standing up to a glowering array of corporate power with the same guts Daniel Boone had shown facing Indians and grizzlies on the frontier. He had stood and reasserted a fact that had been forgotten by the corporate bureaucracies of post World War II—that shareholders, not management, own America's public companies. In the forgotten shareholder Pickens had identified his theme and his constituency.

He had subsequently sold his Gulf shares to Chevron for $80 per share, and Gulf shareholders rode his coattails to more profits than they had ever dreamed of making from the stock. The stock had soared more than 40 points since Pickens made his move on the stock. Pickens went forward from Gulf with a firm grip on the role of champion of the American share-holder. His bids had made $446 million profits for Mesa. His first three big deals—Cities Service, General American Oil and Gulf—poured, as he loved to claim, $9 billion into the hands of shareholders, with $2 billion of that going to the federal treasury in taxes. He had proved that a little guy could chal-lenge the giants and make things happen. He was not yet a household word, but was being watched and followed with increasing fascination by the financial community and press. With blood lust, his growing army of fans wanted him to go for bigger and bigger targets. So far, he had not yet succeeded in taking one over. Would he win the next?

◆   ◆   ◆

IN Los Angeles, Fred L. Hartley, CEO of Unocal Corp., the toughest and feistiest CEO in Big Oil, was mad as hell. Twice during the summer, Unocal stock had gone crazy in the market on unfounded rumors. The first, in July, was a rumor that Standard Oil of Indiana was going to take Unocal over and pay it $52 a share. In twenty-four hours, the stock went up $10 per share. The New York Stock Exchange called Hartley. Hartley knew it *could* have been a viable rumor. "Standard of Indiana doesn't operate on the West Coast. Watching everyone get bigger and them staying the same size—well, it was a good rumor. But it was an absolute lie!" He believed it was planted by an arbitrager who would buy stock in advance, get the lie out, get the stock pushed up, and then sell at a profit. It was creating false information for greed, for gain. The stock market halted trading in Unocal stock, and the price subsided to normal levels, only to explode again. The rumor: Mr. Hartley's plane was seen in Chicago, home of Amoco; he was in negotiation. This time he called the stock exchange: "I'm right here in Los Angeles. Why in hell don't you do something about it? You've got a bunch of crooks operating in that place of yours. Bring in the FBI or something! You've got a racket going on."

At the end of the third week in November, the "stock watch" desk at the Broad Street offices of New York proxy specialists D. F. King & Co. Inc. was tracking unusual activity in Unocal stock, one of its clients. King's chairman, Artie Long, one of the most colorful pioneers of the current takeover wars, reported the movement to corporate secretary Robert Hedley. On November 1, D. F. King was put on retainer, its "stock watch" now officially on duty.

"Fred, you're under accumulation," Dillon Read's chairman, Nicholas Brady, had called and told Fred Hartley as his people picked up the same unexplained action in Unocal stock. An investment banker for Unocal for over thirty years, Dillon Read was always watching. "It's a fingertip thing," said Fritz Hobbs, Dillon, Read's chief mergers-and-acquisitions man, trying to explain the intelligence network on Wall Street. "It's like the British intelligence in World War II—a bunch of people on Wall Street whose antennae are out everywhere. If you've been in the business long enough, you're hooked into that world. You know the key players, the lawyers, the proxy solicitation firms. You're hooked into it through your own arbitrage operation and stock watch people. Clues come off the floor of the stock exchange from changes in the trading patterns. It's ill defined. There are no printed facts. But you can read the tea leaves with incredible accuracy. By November, December, we knew." But they couldn't be sure it was Pickens.

"We had a strong suspicion Pickens was behind it," says Peter Sachs, oil mergers specialist at Goldman Sachs, the investment bankers who run neck and neck with First Boston for aggressive leadership in the giant mergers. "We'd never worked with Unocal. But we'd been talking to them and told them that Unocal was on Pickens's 'due list,' " says Sachs. In October, the trading desk and risk arbs started picking up the kind of intriguing pattern only noticed by those who are "deep in the flows" of the takeover environment. Houston investment adviser Fayez Sarofim had been placing big orders through Goldman Sachs for both Phillips and Unocal stock, buying the two on alternate days. A discreet handful at Goldman Sachs had guessed Pickens's secret: since October 21, he had been buying both. But Peter Sachs was puzzled. The art of raiding requires that you buy your initial block of stock in absolute secrecy, so that you don't start an epidemic of buying that will drive the stock up. You follow strategies of Byzantine complexity and deviousness to conceal your move on a company. Pickens was perceived as a cool, smart strategist who played his cards very close to the chest. "So I can't imagine why he'd use Fayez when Fayez does so much business with us." Had he glimpsed a crack in Pickens's image of strategic perfection, he wondered?

◆   ◆   ◆

IN Amarillo on December 4, the TV weather station was alerting Oklahoma and the Panhandle that the first storm of the winter was moving in, and the pale yellow sky had turned to a dull snow-laden gray. From Bhopal, India, first word of the horror of mass death from toxic gas was coming in snatches on the news. A deadly leak from a Union Carbide chemical plant. Ghastly images of limp, sari-wrapped bodies piled in the streets. The news was instantaneously integrated and transmuted by the market into a loss of 15 points in Union Carbide stock as it skidded from $48 down to $33.

That day in New York, oil analyst Kurt Wulff had just mailed his pre-Christmas newsletter wishing "Happy Holideals" to his investor clients. Satisfied that the restructuring and takeover movement he had promoted since the early seventies was rolling well in the oil industry, he continued to nag at the few holdouts to change and recommended Phillips Petroleum as a prime target, as he had since 1981.

On December 4, Unocal's Fred Hartley was in Spain shooting quail with two of his fellow Big Oil CEOs, John McKinley of Texaco and William Douce of Phillips. Late that night, Douce took a call from his corporate headquarters in Bartlesville. It was the call Hartley had feared would be for him. More news had just come across the Dow Jones tape. At 3:36 P.M., Pickens had announced that he owned 5.7 percent of Phillips's stock and was making a bid for at least 10 percent more, "a step in obtaining control of Phillips." The enemy had shown his face. Pickens was making a tender offer. In his book *Tender Offer,* a former CEO, Dorman Commons, who saw the San Francisco–based company he commanded, Natomas, wrenched from his hands within a week of an uninvited tender offer, describes an unfriendly tender offer as "an offer to purchase shares of a corporation, using cash or securities as payment . . . made directly to shareholders, bypassing management." There is nothing less tender in the commercial transactions between men.

Douce called an executive meeting in Bartlesville for the next day. In New York, Wachtell Lipton and Morgan Stanley men grabbed their briefcases and rushed to the airport, brandishing defensive strategies and poison pills. Morgan Stanley had devised the "scorched earth" tactics that had helped Carter Hawley Hale Stores and Walt Disney Productions stay independent. Douce flew home to defend the nation's tenth-largest oil company, and to urge shareholders to hold firm to their stock until the company had had time to formulate a response. Hartley breathed a little easier, unaware that he was still being secretly stalked.

◆   ◆   ◆

IN Chicago two days later, a slight, gray-suited businessman with sandy, slick-brushed hair, a hang-dog sag to his eyes, and a slight pout to his lower lip slipped with loose-muscled grace through the bustling Christmas crowd in the old Marshall Field store. To most, Marshall Field is one of the most elegant of the traditional department stores. To the takeover community, it was the target, in 1982, of attacks by Carter Hawley Hale and Carl Icahn that led to its merger with Louisville-based Batus. This noon, it was Boone Pickens's stage. His hostile bid for Phillips two days earlier was the sensation of Wall Street and the business news. As he moved now through Texas and Oklahoma and on Wall Street, he was beginning to see raised fists and hear the exhortation, "Go get 'em, Boone!" But his fame had still scarcely gone beyond the business pages. Few of the shoppers knew that they were brushing by the most celebrated, vilified, and certainly most controversial business figure of the early 1980s. Moving through packed aisles booby-trapped with pretty girls aggressively spraying perfume, he, his bodyguard, and cadre of aides pressed toward a standing-room-only crowd of financial analysts overspilling the luncheon tables and lining the walls of a huge dining hall upstairs. Past men and women in full-length minks, through alleys of cheeses and gourmet hot dogs, ribbons, lights, and Christmas trees, past tables of friends and families laughing and gossiping through gala pre-Christmas lunch in the Dickensian warmth of the paneled Wedgewood Room, he walked into the white blaze of television lights.

At fifty-six, still fit as a college athlete, Pickens ambled to a dais hung with festive wreaths and the satin seal of the Investment Analysts Society of Chicago, and rolled into an amiable joke: "If I'd planned my schedule better, I could have done my Christmas shopping on the way. I might not get a lot of shopping done this year." The laughs had that edge of intensity that comes from the excitement of privileged contact with Boone Pickens at the launch of a new campaign. Billions would change hands before the deal was done. At Pickens's bid of $60 a share, Phillips was worth $9.3 billion. With a whopping 47 percent of Phillips stock in institutional hands, some of those billions should flow to the pension funds, banks, trusts, and investment consultants these analysts worked for. At the McDonald Securities breakfast that morning, where Pickens spoke to powerful managers of portfolios such as the Sears $1 billion-plus pension fund, memories of the glittering piles of profits from Pickens's previous deals had glowed warmly, setting the theme of the introduction by his host: "When I got home last night, my son had got a call from the *New York Times* and asked me, 'Who is Mr. Pickens?' I said, 'Well, son, in Wall Street, at this season of the year, he's called Santa Claus.' "

Sugarplums danced in their heads. Phillips stock had already moved up nearly 10 points since Pickens had filed his tender offer two days ago, soaring from $45 to as high as $56 yesterday in frantic trading. It was up from $35 in October, when Pickens started buying. Most of these investors had bought the stock months or years ago. They could tender their shares to Pickens for $60, his offering price, and make a beautiful profit. Or, if it played through like Gulf, a white knight would come in and outbid Pickens for the company and pay them an even higher price. In this morning's *Journal*, oil analyst Kurt Wulff had predicted that a major oil company would come in with a

$65 offer. The appraised "breakup" value of its assets was even higher—an estimated $80 a share. For a stock that had been trading around $40, there was a lot of money to be made in that spread. It could be a great Christmas.

But what if . . . ? In every takeover deal, playing with "what ifs" is an obsessive sport. What if no white knight came forward? With so many mergers in the past two years, there were fewer oil companies left to come to Phillips's rescue. And what if, instead of being bought by a white knight, Phillips bought some other oil company to dilute the value of its stock? Or if Phillips PacManned, and gobbled Mesa in self-defense? It would be great for Mesa shareholders. But for Phillips? And what if oil prices continued to slide, reducing the value of Phillips's oil reserves, and Pickens got scared that his bid was too high and sold back to Phillips?

What if he greenmailed? It was most raiders' modus operandi. If he sold his shares back to Phillips for a higher price than the market value, it could leave shareholders stuck with a stock that would plunge overnight. No, no, Pickens wouldn't greenmail. He had railed against it. There had been a reassuring quote from Pickens just yesterday that "the partnership will not sell any Phillips shares owned by it back to Phillips except on an equal basis wtih all other shareholders." He was the shareholders' champion. Equality for all shareholders was the most basic tenet of his crusade. If he took greenmail, he'd lose his credibility and be dead for the next deal.

And he clearly wanted, really wanted, to win control of the company. To prove he could run one of the giants. "Me and my wife, Bea, would move to Bartlesville," he told the crowd, the country boy drawl broadening. "Ah'm from Holdenville, a little town just south of Oklahoma, and ma wife's from Natoma . . ." His first job as a petroleum engineer had been with Phillips. He had lived in Bartlesville. "I gave them four good years." And ultimately, there was more money in it for him if he got control of the company. Boone would never sell back.

Pickens exited Marshall Field trailing a *New York Times* reporter, who tried to take notes as they jostled through the crowd. "Why Phillips?" It was the first question everyone asked.

Pickens would answer it beguilingly on TV in New York: "It was one we could get our arms around." The *New York Times* handed off to an *L.A. Times* man, who rode with Pickens in the limousine to Mesa's Falcon jet, waiting at O'Hare Airport to take Pickens to New York. "Nothing much has happened since we made our bid, except for the stock going up," he mused. But the one certainty in every takeover deal was that, once set "in play," something would happen.

◆   ◆   ◆

SIX days later, on December 12, Sir James Goldsmith surfaced as a buyer of both Crown Zellerbach and Colgate-Palmolive stock. In the required filing with the SEC and Federal Trade Commission, he revealed that he might buy up to 25 percent of both companies. As regulatory agencies extracted financial intimacies from him, he marveled that the term *elusive* could still attach to him. "The day you invest in a public company in America, you've got to accept the fact that everything is public. Anyone can go through the SEC's files and see every detail of my financial position *revealed,*" he said, laughing.

But his motives were elusive. Where Pickens seemed to be following a straight track, going after oil companies for takeover but settling for profit if that didn't work out, Goldsmith confused Wall Street by moving on three tracks. His five-year corporate war with the monster French oil company Elf-Acquitaine, still moving through French courts, was an act of principle. It was ideologically driven, as was his acquisition of *L'Express* magazine, which gave him a voice of influence in the French press for his conservative political and economic views. In 1983, when he'd acquired the forest products company Diamond International, inventor of the safety match, he had summarily busted up the company, selling off all the assets except the forests, earning himself the title "asset stripper." And yet he'd clearly bought the Grand Union supermarket chain in 1973 for growth. As he transformed the chain to respond to the food revolution in America—hiring designer Milton Glazer and new management from the retail clothing field, and training fishmongers, bakers, and butchers to bring a European marketing flavor to the chain—he claimed, "This is the absolute *opposite* of asset stripping."

His abortive run at another forest products company, St. Regis, earlier in the year had revealed one clear pattern: "I do believe in forests. I do believe in forest lands. Everybody says they're a disaster. But they're still making profits. And forest lands will one day be as valuable as they were." He didn't give a damn about the divisions that made toilet tissue and coated paper. Viewing forests with a global eye, he saw them in the context of dwindling global supply, shifting consumer needs, and swings in the export market. The United States, he noted, was one of a shrinking number of exporters of wood. "I may prove disastrously wrong," he admitted. But he was buying timber.

The news of his Crown Zellerbach and Colgate-Palmolive acquisitions triggered a flurry of action in both stocks. It set up concern in San Francisco, a city that had seen, in San Francisco–based Chevron's acquisition of Gulf, the liquidation of a huge corporation and its impact on the city of Pittsburgh. Vacationing at the Mexican resort of Careyes on the coast between Manzanillo and Puerto Vallarta that Christmas, San Francisco's chief administrative officer, Roger Boas, played tennis on Sir James's private court at his villa in a wooded compound high above the intense blue of the Sea of Cortez, while Goldsmith watched. Over a drink afterward, Boas gently probed Goldsmith's interest in Crown Zellerbach. He developed the dialogue over the next few days as they partied with "the same network of expatriates," as Boas describes it, "a snazzy set of French, Belgians, and Italians." At one party, Goldsmith got very jumpy when a photographer tried to take his picture with Boas, and joked, "You wouldn't want your picture taken with me and have it shown back in San Francisco." Boas did not know of the innocent photograph of Goldsmith's third wife, Annabel, and a casual friend, Lord Lucan, in the Sunday *Times,* which had launched the libel case that had so damaged Goldsmith's image in England.

"Why are you doing this?" Boas asked Goldsmith. "The assets seem to be of little value right now."

"I think the forests are a great asset for the long term," Goldsmith replied. "The problem is staying power. I *have* staying power."

Of the man who might well become one of the major corporate figures in his city, Boas says, "He had enormous presence, but little pretense. His ego was subordinated to the people and events around him; it was in control."

Playing tennis in San Francisco's Presidio Park one morning after his return, Boas ran into a Crown Zellerbach director, Warren Hellman.

"I met a guy who wants Crown's timberlands," Boas said.

"Is he for real?" Hellman asked.

"He's so real he's going to buy those timberlands," Boas warned him.

But Goldsmith's intentions were lost in larger events. The storm that had hit the Panhandle on December 4 had gathered up into a fury of national consequence in Bartlesville, Oklahoma.

◆ ◆ ◆

THE church was filled with hushed anxiety as the minister spoke: "Our board of directors is in a distant city, needing your prayers to know what to do." The prayers of Bartlesville reached out to the Helmsley Palace in New York, where Douce and his key executives, lawyers, and investment bankers were bunkered, strategizing round the clock. Their prayers reached out on the evening network news, touching a chord across the nation. Bartlesville had risen with a unity and determination scarcely seen in America since World War II. One of the few surviving company towns, Bartlesville lived or died by Phillips Petroleum. The largest corporation in the state of Oklahoma, Phillips employed eight thousand of the town's forty thousand people and was the economic lifeblood of the city. Pickens's bid had triggered all the fear and emotion of America's threatened industrial regions. The "rust belt." Steel and automobiles. Unions. Farmers. It raised the worrisome issues of low productivity, trade deficits, and the threat of Japan. But mostly it raised the fear of job loss. The fear of Phillips closing down, of having to migrate to new towns, of Bartlesville becoming a ghost town. Gulf had vanished from Pittsburgh. Right here in Oklahoma, in Tulsa, Cities Service had been dismantled and stripped when Occidental took over; 22,500 employees had been reduced to 4,000. They hadn't forgotten; Pickens had started that, too.

It didn't matter how often Pickens said he would not move or close the company, how often he evoked his own and his wife's deep Oklahoma roots, or his commitment to move to Bartlesville. He could not be heard above the uproar. As television crews poured into town to cover the growing story, Bartlesville became the symbol of an intuitive human resistance to change, an emotion that is the takeovers wars' most powerful opponent.

It erupted first in raging anger. "It's the most ruthless, vicious, dastardly stealing in U.S. history," a resident proclaimed to the clapping and cheers of a town rally. Fanned by Phillips, the emotion was quickly organized and focused. The Chamber of Commerce staged town meetings. "Boone-Busters" T-shirts and "I Love Phillips" buttons appeared. Students wrote postcards to the president. There was a Boone-Busters float in the Christmas parade.

And Bartlesville turned to prayer. "In our Lord we put our faith," the minister said.

If rejection by his native state hurt, the unflappable Pickens never let it show. "I doubt that I could be elected mayor of Bartlesville," he joked in one of his dozens of television interviews. But he and his team were in New York, and under increasing pressure. Hovering over the deal was the specter of declining oil prices. OPEC had met in an emergency meeting in Geneva the previous week. The oil cartel's control of world oil prices was threatening to collapse; OPEC member Nigeria, as well as Norway, Britain, Canada, and Mexico, had dropped their crude oil prices, in defiance of the $29-a-barrel benchmark price OPEC was trying to hold. All Pickens's sophisticated calculations could fall into disarray if prices fell too far. He could end up paying $60 per share for Phillips, a price based on Phillips's oil reserves being worth a certain price per barrel, and find himself owning reserves worth much less as the price of oil deteriorated. Lower prices would reduce income and cash flow needed to pay down the new debt. One of the riskiest aspects of oil mergers, it had cast a cloud over the wisdom of the $13 billion-plus price Chevron had paid for Gulf. There was a threshold price per barrel below which any debt-burdened oil company would be plunged into bankruptcy. At $60, by his team's calculations, he could maintain his "comfort factor" down to $20 a barrel, but no lower. Drexel and Mesa consulted with the dean of international oil analysts, Charles Maxwell of Cyrus J. Lawrence Inc. They talked to much-published energy consultant Daniel Yergin, of Cambridge Energy Associates in Boston. They studied evaluations of the company by J. S. Herold, Connecticut-based oil analysts whose evaluations were considered among the most authoritative in the industry. But Pickens relied on his own analysis as much as anybody's.

And other factors were converging. Bartlesville's emotional resistance had touched an entire nation. Phillips had hired private detective Jules Kroll to dig up dirt on Pickens, an act Pickens responded to by suing in Amarillo for an injunction against "a campaign of harassment" of friends, family, and former employees. There were charges that Pickens was guilty of insider trading, of giving tips on his takeover targets to his friends at the Amarillo Country Club, and the SEC was launching a formal investigation. There was Phillips's continuing legal pressure to stop Pickens on the grounds that his standstill agreement with a previous target, General American Oil, which prohibited him from attacking it for fifteen years, extended also to Phillips, the new owners of General American. It was pending in the Delaware courts.

On December 20, a Delaware court rejected Phillips's attempt to hold Pickens to the standstill agreement. It was a win for Pickens, removing formal obstacles to takeover. It made settlement suddenly more urgent for Douce than for Pickens. Phillips made the traditional call that initiates settlement negotiations, and two days before Christmas a settlement was signed. Boone had sold back. Phillips would buy Pickens's shares for $53 per share and pay his $25 million expenses; in return, Pickens would support a recapitalization and stock buyback plan designed to pay better returns to the shareholders and buoy the stock price—a complicated package Phillips claimed would be worth $53 per share to the shareholder, like Pickens's. Pickens's profit would be $75 million pretax after expenses, his second-highest profit from a takeover bid.

Next day, Phillips stock plunged nearly 10 points, closing at just over $45 on the New York Stock Exchange. Within two hours of the opening bell, Phillips had lost $1.54 billion in value, nearly 20 percent of its total capitalization.

In Bartlesville, the churches devoted sixty-six seconds of their Christmas Eve services to silent prayer.

◆ ◆ ◆

"BOONE sold back."

Ivan Boesky, king of the arbitragers, thought the phone connection from New York to Barbados must be bad. "He sold back?" he said.

From his New York office came confirmation of the impossible: "Yeah, Boone sold back."

Boesky had an estimated $40 million invested in Phillips. He and his fellow risk arbitragers had information networks second only to the CIA. Every scrap of information, every nuance of rumor, was a clue to what might happen, and when to buy and sell so they didn't get caught by a falling market. Boesky had lawyers poised in every courtroom, at every congressional hearing that could possibly affect the outcome of a takeover transaction. For arbitragers make their money in the few weeks or months between the time a takeover deal is announced until it culminates one way or the other. It seldom exceeds three months. Buying into a target stock only after a takeover bid is announced, arbitragers make their profit in the spread between the starting price of the stock and the much higher price when the deal is consummated. They dart in and out of the market like bees at a hive, sifting news and rerolling their strategies every half minute. They only make big money if something happens—a takeover or restructuring. If a deal died and the stock dived, their stock could lose millions in value in minutes. If they smell a deal falling through, they sell their stock at the speed of light. Information and timing are everything.

Arbs maneuver where angels and even the most aggressive

institutional investors fear to tread. Professional investors love to have them there, for arbs give them liquidity—a place to sell their stock and turn their investment into cash if the risks grow greater than a cautious investor can carry without sedation. Risk arbitrage is not a profession for the faint of heart. Loyalty or long-range views of a company do not exist. "It may seem callous. But I am indifferent to who succeeds or fails as long I make a profit," Boesky has said. Carl Icahn loves to joke, "I've told my wife, if I need surgery, get me the heart of an arb. It's never been used."

On vacation, Boesky hadn't been reading for a few weeks, but he knew Boone's pattern. He'd made money on it before. And he had been fine-tuning the art of risk arbitrage for twenty years. He'd learned from mistakes. The Cities Service debacle was still raw. He lost an estimated $18 to $24 million in "the biggest bath arbs have ever taken" when Gulf walked away from its bid for Cities Service. But 70 percent of the deals he invested in worked out. Now this. He paused and tried to digest it, then said to New York, "That's the only thing Boone wouldn't do. He would do everything else, but he would never sell back. He *sold back?*"

"Yeah, he sold back."

"It's Christmas. I was looking forward to a feast," said Boesky. Within the hour, he was on a plane to New York, as the value of his investment plunged.

◆   ◆   ◆

THE *New York Times* reported an analyst's comment: "The arbs have been hurt. They'll be very cautious about backing him in his next deal." But controversy and criticism only seemed to strengthen the Pickens mystique as it gathered momentum in early 1985. The nation was witnessing the making of a folk hero. He seemed to fill a psychic need for a nation disenchanted by the failed dreams of the sixties and searching for affirmation of the old can-do capitalistic values. A need for someone to say, as he did to a packed house at the UCLA School of Business, "You want to make money. And you want to make it honestly." His entrepreneurial spirit played well on campus. Thirty-three-year-old San Francisco advertising executive Gregg Sherwood summed it up: "Boone Pickens makes you bite the bullet and face how you really feel about founding principles like the free enterprise system." His fame may have been a product, in part, of the image making of public relations specialists Gershon Kekst and Pickens's own rigorous exploitation of the media. But there was also a mythic element that probably sprang from his origins. He was the embodiment of frontier values, the little guy who makes it from the rough and gritty rangelands and oil patch of Oklahoma and the Texas Panhandle. He faced attack the way pioneers had faced mountains. Confronting the storm of criticism that that followed his sellback to Philips, he charged into a speech in Los Angeles by demanding, off the top, "If anybody here thinks I greenmailed Phillips, put your hand up." As hands shot up all over the room, he quietly told of the greenmail he had four times been offered and refused, then asked again for a show of hands. As only one hand went up, he let his case rest with masterly effect. Even Pickens's name was the stuff of legends. An unabashed fan as she greeted him on the *CBS Morning News,* Diane Sawyer compared him to J. R. Ewing and almost gushed, "We've turned you into a mythical giant," even though the most fire she struck from the mild-mannered Texas gentleman was the admission that, for fun, he does "handball, family for Thanksgiving, and hunt." But Pickens's consistency and low-key style, in contrast to his spectacular deals, only made him more disarming, and in subsequent interviews with Sawyer, he had clearly become a network pet. Even as Boesky was licking his wounds, *Time* magazine was preparing a cover story on T. Boone Pickens.

CHAPTER 4

◆◆◆

FEBRUARY 14, 1985. It was one of the most memorable Valentine's Days since the 1929 Chicago massacre.

In Amarillo, Pickens's staff readied the announcement they would release to the wire service at the close of the market that Pickens had acquired 7.9 percent of Unocal's stock. Unocal's Valentine's surprise. But it was not a declaration of war. Pickens's investment group, Mesa Partners, was acquiring Unocal stock, they said, "for investment purposes only." The same day, he filed his 13D with the SEC, the document that must be filed within ten days of acquiring 5 percent of a company. That single sheet of paper was the event that transformed the months of rumors into a call to arms. Yet Unocal had begun as a passive move. Pickens had made no bid for the company. He had simply become a Unocal shareholder. Fred Hartley was not flattered. As the press called Hartley in Los Angeles for comment, he mustered enough humor to congratulate Pickens for his good taste in stock. But he did not invite his new shareholder to tea.

In New York on Valentine's Day, one of the last scenes of the Bartlesville drama was being played through. At the offices of the New York City Comptroller Harrison J. Goldin in lower Manhattan, California State Treasurer Jesse M. Unruh and his new baby, the Council of Institutional Investors, were behind closed doors quizzing Boone Pickens about his sellback of stock to Phillips. Smelling of greenmail to Unruh, that act had helped trigger this meeting of the council, a consortium of money managers who, between them, control $100 billion in pension fund money, millions of it invested in Phillips Petroleum. Their proxy votes could swing or kill the recapitalization plan that had emerged as part of the settlement agreement with Pickens. That plan, being challenged by Carl Icahn as unfair to shareholders, would go to a shareholder vote in Bartlesville next week, on February 22. It was shaping up as the largest contested proxy fight in history. And it would be the first big opportunity for the council, and for its founder, Jesse Unruh, to intrude themselves into the takeover arena. National television cameras would be rolling at Bartlesville.

In the halls outside the meeting room, a group of women from Bartlesville were turning the council meeting into a church social, handing out heart-shaped "I Love Phillips" cookies in an eleventh-hour attempt to swing votes for the company plan.

Fending off cookies, a parade of principals in the Phillips deal filed in to be grilled—Pickens, Phillips's CEO Bill Douce, Carl Icahn, arbitrager Ivan Boesky, oil analyst Kurt Wulff. The sessions were closed. But television crews scavenged for shots of the stars and grabbed them for press conferences afterward. It was great theater. The cookies. The moms of Bartlesville. Pickens.

Pickens had become a secondary player in the Phillips deal, obligated by his settlement agreement to support the company's recapitalization plan. It was now Carl Icahn who was carrying the attack forward, soliciting votes and shares for his proxy fight to defeat the recapitalization plan and for his tender offer to buy the entire company. It was Icahn and Douce who had most to gain or lose from support of the council. Icahn's tender offer had been filed just the day before this meeting. With nearly half of Phillips stock held by institutional investors, the special meeting on February 22 had become a battle for institutional votes.

But the real story was the revolution this meeting represented: the rise of the institutional investor to a crucial role in the takeover wars. The proxy votes and blocks of stock they control are the prize both CEOs and raiders fight for; they can determine the outcome of these struggles. The nation's "fiduciaries"—the men and women who invest America's pension fund dollars—have been thrust to the front lines. A hostile tender offer is, essentially, an invitation to shareholders to tender, or sell, their shares to a raider as a means of gaining control. Without the support of institutional investors, who control most of those shares, hostile struggles for power cannot be won or successfully resisted.

That Unruh and his colleagues could command appearances from this group speaks for the power of the investment portfolios they controlled. For the institutional money managers inside and outside the council who manage America's pension funds control what is already the largest concentration of money in the world—a $1.5 trillion lump, which, in five years, is expected to reach $3 trillion. Making himself the voice of an economic force of such enormous impact may be the most brilliant strategy of Unruh's long political career.

That Unruh should be here at all, ringmastering a command performance of the takeover stars, is a testament to survival instincts that have always put him where the power is. He is a gruff, muscular tank of a man whose short-clipped moustache is out of character with his bulldozer drive to reform whatever institution he touches and transform it into a seat of power. A sharecropper's son born into a Mennonite family in Newton, Kansas, raised in Texas, he has always shown uncanny skill at sensing the routes to power. In the sixties, the route lay in human rights, social activism, and Democratic politics. It lay in close alliances with the Kennedys and a power base in the nation-state of California. As Speaker of the House, he consolidated state power in the Speaker's chair, and gave that job, and a lackluster assembly, the stature and effectiveness appropriate to California's emerging role in post–World War II America. The state had emerged as a vibrant social laboratory whose GNP ranked it as the seventh-largest nation in the world. "I passed civil rights legislation so forward-looking that it's still on the books and has never been surpassed," he says proudly. He was at Bobby Kennedy's side in Los Angeles when Kennedy was shot and was the first to grab the assassin Sirhan and hold him for custody.

For a few years, he seemed to wander in the desert. He ran against, and lost to, Ronald Reagan for governor. He was eclipsed by fellow Democrat Jerry Brown during Brown's years as governor. He despised Brown and his neo-hippie friends and his appointments so much that, even several years after Brown left the governorship, he barbs him in speeches with one-liners that still get a laugh. Elected treasurer in 1974, Unruh might have been swallowed into the bureaucracy of Sacramento and vanished. But one of the shrewdest politicians ever produced in California, he set about to make the plain office adjacent to the splendidly refurbished capitol that had eluded him the launching pad for a new drive for power. Disenchantment with the failed ideals of the sixties and seventies had spawned a return to material values.

With his election as treasurer, Unruh was on track again. Following his own maxim—"Money is the mother's milk of politics"—he took firm hold of California's purse strings and put himself on thirty powerful finance boards. Most important, he got himself appointed to the boards of two state pension funds, the California Public Employees Retirement System (PERS) and the California State Teachers Retirement System (STRS), which together total $37 billion—two of the largest in the United States. He has made his office an extension of Wall Street. Wall Street competes not only for California's pension funds in stock market investments, but for the $8 billion of underwriting business he brings each year when he goes to New York to raise the state's capital requirements. With the council, he had the vehicle to lever his financial clout into national visibility and influence that surpasses anything he knew during his days as Speaker of the House.

He created the Council of Institutional Investors in 1984 as

spearhead of a new activism among the institutional investors—
the traditionally gray and prudent men who are stewards of
our retirement dollars. Although Unruh has final fiduciary
responsibility, he does not personally make day-to-day investment decisions. He hires portfolio managers to do that for
him—members of the fraternity of money managers at banks,
insurance companies, investment management companies, and
corporations who run the nation's pension fund billions
through their fingers. A passive voice in the marketplace in the
past, they had bought stocks for the long haul, supported
management with their proxy votes, or, as a feeble protest,
simply sold their stock if they were unhappy with management.
"Now we've started voting with our heads and not our feet,"
says Unruh. It was a foiled takeover of Texaco in 1983 that
shook him into action. "I was outraged that Texaco was paying
the Bass brothers greenmail," he says of the genesis of the
council. California's funds had large Texaco holdings, and they
lost $15 million in value when the stock dropped after the
payoff to the Bass brothers. Unruh hadn't known what was
going on. He'd had no control over events that could strike the
value of the state's pension funds. Now, as a unified group,
perhaps they could halt these disasters. They could exchange
information; they could call management and raiders to accountability; and they could open a dialogue, as they were
doing here in New York on Valentine's Day.

The council was the driving wedge of a larger revolution—
the awakening of the nation's 42 million shareholders, who had
forgotten that they, not management, control America's publicly owned companies. Proxy votes and annual meetings had
become mere formalities, an hour every year when management paid lip service to corporate democracy and to their role
as hired steward of the shareholder's investment. There were
often some troublesome gadflies at the meetings, but the individual shareholder seldom raised his voice. With the growth of
pension funds, the individual's stake in the market had been
displaced by great funds that moved into the market from GM,
Sears, and General Foods; from counties, states, teachers' and
truckers' unions; from IRAs and physicians' retirement plans.

Those dollars joined the more traditional institutional money in insurance companies, banks, S&Ls, and trust funds until, by 1985, roughly half of the nation's stock was held in institutional hands. According to SEC chairman John Shad, "Institutions account for an estimated 70 percent of daily volume on the New York Stock Exchange, and about 45 percent of total public stock ownership." The power of these vast funds gives anyone with even a dollar in a pension fund a stake in the takeover wars.

Most of the founding members of the Council of Institutional Investors controlled public pension funds; most, like Unruh and his co-chairman, Jay Goldin, were elected officials. Although the council's doors were open to the entire institutional community, to corporate as well as public pension fund managers, it was the public sector—the pension funds of the nation's counties, cities, and states—that played the more powerful role in the takeover wars. For unlike corporate funds, they were not taxed on transactions and could buy and sell with almost the speed and flexibility of arbitragers, moving in and out of the market, their purchases of a fast-moving stock helping to run the price of a target's stock up in a takeover bid. In a hostile tender offer, they held huge blocks of stock that they could tender to a raider, and give him success. And they wielded another power. Corporations usually gave the voting rights for their pension fund stock portfolios to the money managers they hired to handle those funds. Public funds like California's, however, generally gave the investment decisions to money managers but kept control of the voting rights. The votes they cast were often the determining votes in proxy contests.

With exponentially expanding power has come pressure and the potential for abuse.

Pension fund money has become a force for influencing social and political policy. It intrudes into management and boardroom decisions. Union pension funds have become a bargaining tool with management. They are becoming a political weapon, used to influence such policies as apartheid. Unruh strongly resisted that use, as divestment of stocks doing busi-

ness in South Africa became a hot political issue in California
and across the land. "I don't want to play God," he said, as he
watched his friend Jay Goldin use New York City's $15 billion
pension fund to strike a blow against apartheid, selling off
investments in corporations that did not divest themselves of
their South African interests. Victor J. Melone, chief investment officer for Manufacturers Hanover Investment Corporation's $22 billion pension fund portfolio in New York, sees the
decision to divest as often in conflict with the sound investment
decisions fiduciaries are obligated, by law, to make. They are
bound by the "prudent man" rule, which requires that investment decisions be based on getting the highest possible performance of the stock. "The U.S. does stand for something in
the world—human rights," Melone says from Manny Hanny's
headquarters adjacent to Rockefeller Center. "But do you take
upon yourself the exclusion of 170 of Standard & Poor's 500
companies in your portfolio?" The institutional investor often
found himself in personal conflict. No matter what his feelings
about the injustice of apartheid, politically driven investment
decisions were not necessarily the best and most responsible for
the performance of his portfolio.

Performance! That was where the real pressure lay. Institutional investors work under increasing pressure to have the
stocks in their portfolios perform well, with that performance
no longer measured by the year, but by the quarter, day, and
hour.

That pressure has been fanned by the Department of Labor,
which regulates pension funds. Regulatory power of all corporate and, increasingly, public, pension funds is concentrated in
the Department of Labor's pension fund act, ERISA (Employee Retirement Income Securities Act). ERISA's potential
power is only hinted at today. But by the year 2000, it could
control half the equity in the United States. Unruh's counsel
Tom Aceituno only half jokingly speculates, "It is not beyond
the realm of fantasy that, by 1990, the nation's economy could
be controlled by some mid-level functionary in the Department
of Labor!" Supporting the Reagan administration's pro-
takeover policy, then-head of ERISA Robert Monks urged
fiduciaries to take takeover profits. "Gulf was sitting around

$40, went to $80, and Bob Monks was saying that you, as a fiduciary, must participate in the short-term gains," says Vic Melone at Manufacturers Hanover. "Is it good for the pension fund in the short term? Yes. But I'm concerned about a time horizon that never goes beyond the quarter. I see near-permanent damage to the health of the acquiring companies. Monk's not indictable for what he's said. But it has an impact."

This pressure to perform in the short term is compounded by a system of ceaseless evaluation and public exposure of a fiduciary's performance. "Pension consultants hire and fire portfolio managers and monitor performance," says Melone. "Performance is measured against the performance of Standard & Poor's index, and those ratings are published quarterly. It shouldn't be hard to outperform Standard & Poor's—it's a ho-hum index. But for the past two years, as a group they have not, and they're under the gun." Hostile takeovers, with their fast runups of stock and premium prices paid for a target's stock, have been the beleaguered fiduciary's best friend.

This short-term outlook is alien to everything fiduciaries are trained to do. Conservative men accustomed to looking for long-term value in corporations, they have been forced to become high rollers. "The wave of the future is that institutions are going to own corporate America, and how do you force the institutional investor to exercise a broad-based, rather than a narrow, provincial judgment?" asks former Du Pont CEO Irving S. Shapiro, now a lawyer in Skadden Arps's Wilmington office since retirement from Du Pont. "We're dealing with a transformation. The stock that used to be held by families is held by institutions that have no loyalty at all to the corporation. Boone Pickens, Icahn—the institutional investor doesn't care if he's a raider or not; if he can make a dollar from the transaction he's going to be for it. He can justify whatever he does on fiduciary duty, and what he wants to do most times is show good earnings this quarter."

Richard Dixon, Los Angeles County's treasurer and guardian of its $5 billion pension fund, sums up the growing concern: "This focus on the short term—on the quarter, instead of the year or the decade—is reaching an obscene climax."

◆   ◆   ◆

KURT Wulff's appearance before the Council of Institutional Investors wasn't a media event, like Pickens's. Looking like an elongated John Kennedy, a thatch of thick brown hair across his forehead and a look of boyish eagerness that belied his banker's suit, Kurt Wulff was neither raider nor CEO. But to the men here he was a star, one of the top two or three oil analysts on Wall Street. Votes from this group and their colleagues across the country had won him the academy award for financial analysts—First Team rank in the annual rankings by *Institutional Investor* magazine—an honor worth highest prestige and bonuses to analysts who win, and many millions in business to their firms. Produced for the investment banking firm of Donaldson, Lufkin & Jenrette Securities Corporation (DLJ), "Kurt's work" had become required reading for the large institutional investors looking for good advice on where to invest in the oil industry and how to boost their performance with profits on takeover plays.

One of a new breed on Wall Street, the activist-analyst, Wulff has brought derring-do and crusading zeal to a profession that has suffered, like the institutional investor, under the image of passive number cruncher. His job is to study the oil industry and make recommendations of stocks to buy. But he has gone beyond that to become a passionate advocate of change in the industry. His analyses of the oil industry and recommendations of what to buy and sell have become an uncannily accurate road map for the takeover wars. His outspoken arguments for getting value up and out to the shareholders through restructuring has made him a kind of prophet to a movement that has spread from its genesis in oil to any industry in which unexploited values can be found. To the oil industry, Kurt's work is often treachery, an invitation to attack. A self-fulfilling prophecy of doom for any luckless company that finds itself on Wulff's list.

Of all the new Wall Street warriors, Wulff has had as intimate a view as any of the birth in the oil industry of today's hostile wave.

Three days a week, Kurt hunkers down in the cellar office in his home in suburban Short Hills in New Jersey, working at three computers, producing the newsletters that have made him a figure of influence in the takeover wars. Naming names on his "most vulnerable to restructuring or takeover" list, he has seen DLJ lose corporate finance business as a result of his outspokenness. "It's the price you pay to hold on to your objectivity," he says philosophically. "The nature of the thing is that Morgan Stanley has had all the oil company contacts locked up from years gone by anyway. But what we say plays well with the institutional investor," he says with a buoyant confidence that stops just short of arrogance. His institutional clients thank him for good ideas by placing stock orders through DLJ's trading desk, paying profitable commissions. In the crassest terms, that is his job. To get business for the stock trading side of DLJ.

On a more subtle level, the symbiotic relationship between aggressive oil analyst, institutional investors, and raiders (or "initiators," as Wulff prefers to call them) like T. Boone Pickens is what gave birth to takeovers in the oil industry.

Wulff was here before the council today because, as usual, he was in the thick of it. Carl Icahn had hired him as adviser in his fight against Phillips's recapitalization. "My material on Phillips was the rationale for Carl Icahn to solicit votes against the management," Wulff said with undisguised pleasure. His analysis of Phillips's recapitalization package—his assessment that it was worth a mere $42 per share to the shareholder, $11 less than Pickens received in his settlement—was the underpinning for the tender offer and proxy contest Icahn was waging simultaneously with a tender offer for $55 a share for assets Wulff's analysis showed to be worth $75 a share or better. "I had taken a public position in a column in the *New York Times* that the deal management was proposing wasn't very favorable. I didn't mind them placing 30 percent of the stock in employees' hands, but they were also proposing that for any important vote, there had to be a supermajority vote of 70 to 75 percent of the stock voted for it, and with 30 percent of the stock in friendly hands, it would be impossible for a dissident ever to get a supermajority."

The contact with Icahn had been made socially, at a party in

New York. Senator Jacob Javits's niece, who worked for DLJ, had met Icahn at a party, urged him to read Wulff's research, and Icahn had called. Icahn had hired Wulff because he needed credible support for his attack on Phillips's recapitalization from, as Icahn said in the tender offer filed just the day before this council meeting, "one of the foremost oil analysts in the country." But prestige gave Wulff no immunity from attack.

Taking up arms against a corporation could lose his firm corporate business again. DLJ would get $1.4 million from Icahn for its work on the Phillips deal; advising on the corporate side, Phillips's investment bankers, Morgan Stanley and First Boston, would get ten times that. But as a man with a mission, this was a fight Wulff wouldn't miss. "In the early seventies, I was closely identified as a Phillips booster, and kept recommending it through '76, '77." He felt sentiment for a picture in his den of his lanky body draped over a Texas longhorn in the old Frank Phillips home in Bartlesville. The relationship had begun to cool after '82. "That year, I began recommending Phillips for some restructuring potential, but I wouldn't say it was an invitation to raiders. I went to an analysts' meeting in Bartlesville, sat beside Bill Douce, the chairman, at dinner, and explained my restructuring ideas. He referred to 'my work' in his speech." But Wulff's frankness had compromised the closeness. By the time of publication of his pre-Christmas letter for 1984, dismayed that Phillips had not done any substantial restructuring on its own, Wulff proposed a takeover price for both Phillips and Unocal of $60 per share. "I doubt that Phillips or Unocal would hire me as an adviser right now," he said with a chuckle.

His outspokenness had thrust him into the war rooms, to consult with generals. As Gordon Getty struggled with what to do with Getty Oil in January 1983, Wulff flew to San Francisco to explain his ideas in the music room of the Getty mansion overlooking the bay. "A nice enough house for a millionaire, perhaps, but for a *billionaire*?" quips the irreverent Wulff. He has advised Boone Pickens since 1971, stayed with him and his wife, Bea, in their sprawling town house in Amarillo, with its indoor tennis court, and delights that "Pickens had done an enormous amount to implement the same ideas I support." He has met with the CEOs of most of the Seven Sisters of the oil industry.

But like the ancient messenger killed for bearing bad news, Wulff has been ceaselessly attacked since entering the investment industry in 1971. He has been subpoenaed, verbally abused, and his firm blackballed for his ideas. A few months before his appearance before Unruh's council, he had been deposed by lawyers from five legal firms on his meeting with Gordon Getty, testifying under oath for ten hours that his analysis of the restructuring potential at Getty did not include inside information from Gordon Getty. Years earlier, one of his fellow analysts was roughed up out of anger at Wulff for writing negative things about a natural gas company. Marathon Oil halted questions and closed down an analysts' meeting in Finley, Ohio, when Wulff asked pointed questions. "Gulf actually had their investment bankers publish a critique of me and my research and circulated it amongst investors—an unprecedented act. It was so blatantly negative that it was great advertising for us," he says.

"As I got strong reactions—and then turned out to be *right*— I got more confident in my analysis." He had just testified on Phillips, having been subjected to aggressive interrogation "in which the lawyer was trying to tear down my research, trying to get me to admit that if we changed one assumption, then the whole conclusion would change." They could discredit anything—Wulff's taste in ties, wines, or wife. But his assumptions! "There is always a moment when I get my feelings up and give a *very* firm response. I came back saying, 'There isn't anyone else in the world you could get to give you better assumptions.' " As he replayed the exchange for his wife, Louise, she laughed. "A lawyer is no match for my husband when it comes to talking about oil and gas analysis."

He had lacked that confidence when Louise started prodding him toward taking advantage of his own hidden talents. Nor did he have any idea of the dimensions of the revolution he would help unleash when he started working in San Francisco for Chevron as a chemical engineer in the summer of 1962.

Oil hadn't even attracted him. "I was trained at the University of Wisconsin, and most of the opportunities in Wisconsin were in the paper industry, not oil." But George Keller, now chairman of Chevron, had recruited him, and he had come to California at a time when "Jesse Unruh was the kingpin in state politics . . . We were building a hydrocracker in Oakland, part of the boom in refinery building. The industry was growing, oil prices were strong, and the engineer was king. Management were all engineers." OPEC had just been formed but was still an infant, trying to organize itself into an effective cartel to control the world's oil prices. But even then, as he and Louise walked to work together from The Lodge, the singles residence on Sutter Street where they both lived, he was sensing vulnerabilities in the industry that would inspire his basic theories: first, that small companies are more efficient than large. "Management is more accountable to investors in small companies." Why shouldn't big companies be broken up into several smaller companies, he wondered. Mildly frustrated that his own talents might never surface in the huge bureaucracy of Chevron, he applied the theory first to himself. "Chevron has got to have many people like me buried in the organization—it's just too big," he speculated to Louise. Unleashing his talents would become a priority for Louise. By the time they married a few months later, she had already quit her job at E. F. Hutton, rented an apartment, and laid the challenge before him: "You never work at night. Don't you have any goals? Is there some-thing wrong with you?" She laid an application for Harvard Business School before him. "I wanted to stay in San Francisco. But after spending a week on the application form, I didn't have the energy to apply to Stanford." He laughs at Louise's purposeful interest in his career: "She may have pushed a little. But it was the direction I probably would have gone anyway."

After Harvard, he might have stayed with the consulting firm Arthur D. Little had Louise not been convinced that he was not "fully appreciated." She retrieved from a wastepaper basket a questionnaire from an executive search specialist that led to his job at Donaldson, Lufkin & Jenrette. "I wanted to be an oil industry analyst. It seemed the best way to make money, use my chemical engineering, and explore some of these ideas I

had about management." Rebuffed in earlier attempts to enter
Wall Street because he had no analyst experience, he joined
DLJ just as the young firm was beginning to rebuild the in-
depth research for the institutional investor they had pioneered ten years earlier during the blossoming of small "bou-
tique" research houses in Wall Street, then lost when the
market collapsed during the late sixties. It was the beginning of
a professionalism and computer-aided, high-tech rigor in research that would replace the more informal methods of the
past, based mostly on balance sheets and information gleaned
from someone on the board.

Within the year, he had enraged his first company, a small
pipeline company, Coastal States, by sending its chairman a
prepublication draft of his bleak predictions for the company's
Texas gas contracts, with recommendations that his clients sell,
rather than buy, Coastal stock. "I thought he'd be glad to see it.
The chairman of Coastal, Oscar Wyatt, came running to the
president of DLJ, called lawyers, and threatened that, if my
predictions were true, he would have to cancel our private
placement of $100 million of debt and call off his merger with
Colorado Interstate. I was sufficiently intimidated that I didn't
publish all at once, but dribbled it out gradually. A month later,
in an unusually cold winter, there were gas shortages in Texas
that made my projections for four years out materialize immediately. A few months later, the SEC suspended trading in
Coastal stock for six months."

And Wulff was beginning to talk about the discovery that
would become the basis of the wave of hostile takeovers just
gathering steam in 1972—the undervalued asset.

At that time, he still had no real sense of the scale and scope
of the historic stage onto which he had stumbled. Or that the
aberrations he was detecting in the oil industry were symptoms
of something far larger. They were the creaks and groans of an
aging industry, the most powerful industry the world has ever
known. "For thirty or forty years we'll still have some big plays
in oil," says Wulff. But oil companies were not replacing their
reserves. The United States, and eventually the world, was
running out of oil. As Boone Pickens loved reminding audi-

ences, "Gulf had not replaced its reserves for twelve years. Now you have to say that's a trend." Since Gulf's fall to Chevron, the Seven Sisters were Six. It was an industry in liquidation.

Wulff had begun to detect the symptoms while he was still at Arthur D. Little, analyzing small oil exploration companies. As he ran his numbers through his computer, and, at home, his slide rule, he discovered that the companies' stocks were selling too low. They weren't reflecting the appraised value of their most basic asset—the oil reserves in the ground. It was so obvious. The value of assets might be hard to measure in an airline, where you had intangible assets like airline routes and goodwill as well as hardware. They were hard to evaluate in the huge integrated oil companies that involved themselves in every aspect of the industry, from drilling and production to refining and selling the oil at retail gas stations. But allowing for fluctuations in the price of oil, the value of a pool of black stuff in the ground could be calculated. Once in production, its future volume was predictable; a price could be assumed, and a value easily calculated. And the value of oil reserves was not complicated by labor or equipment obsolescence, in contrast, say, to airlines. Wulff began to ask, "If the reserves are worth $30 a share, why is the company's stock selling at $10?"

Others were beginning to ask the same questions. Why, asked international oil consultant Daniel Yergin of Cambridge Energy Associates in a *New York Times* editorial, should Wall Street think Gulf is worth $38 a share, when Standard of California is willing to pay $80 a share? He explained the difference in terms of "time horizons." Said Yergin: "Wall Street is, at the most, looking ahead only a couple of years, and what it sees is a substantial energy surplus. Higher prices, conservation, recession, technological advance—all have worked together to call forth energy supplies considerably in excess of what the market now requires. So the reserves of Gulf and the other oil companies are hardly worth a premium—especially with talk of further falls in oil prices. Yet take a longer perspective, say 10 to 15 years, and the surplus may well have eroded, putting pressure once again on supplies. Those companies that are positioning themselves for the 1990s are willing to pay a premium for United States oil reserves."

In Wulff's view, "Wall Street puts a low value on Gulf and integrated oil companies because it fears that the cash flows from the properties will not be diverted to the shareholders but will be dissipated in poor investments."

Though the reasons why may be debated, identification of the undervalued asset was the event that would trigger the takeover wars and drive the stock market to record highs in 1985—a discovery so basic and exploitable that, like any great invention whose time has come, it was discovered simultaneously by a small core of like-minded men, such as T. Boone Pickens. Pickens was the enterprising founder and CEO of a small but ambitious independent exploration and production company in the Texas Panhandle, Mesa Petroleum. He had started Mesa's predecessor, Petroleum Exploration Inc., on a $2,500 shoestring in 1956 and had expanded aggressively by buying oil properties, exploring and drilling for oil and gas, forming Mesa Petroleum in 1964. He was a "wildcatter," one of the risk-taking breed of independents that does speculative drilling for oil—and finds more of it than the integrated giants of Big Oil.

Undervalued assets existed in many industries. But they had special urgency in the oil industry. If the values weren't liberated soon and released to shareholders, they might never be realized. For if the industry was in slow but irreversible liquidation, stock values would only decline as the oil reserves that backed them were depleted over time.

Wulff was not predicting doomsday. "I just had a strong feeling that if the properties of a company are worth more, that value has to come out some way." How could they be released? He built his confidence first on small exploration companies, playing with a concept that, by 1985, would become a household word: *restructuring.* It was a catchall word for a variety of financial and organizational changes that are perceived by the shareholders as making the company more efficient in the future, and therefore its stock worth more today. A company could sell off some of its assets; it could divert excess cash from unprofitable diversifications and use it to buy back a chunk of its own stock, concentrating the asset values in fewer shares; it could put its oil reserves into trusts and partnerships, which sent oil income pouring out directly to shareholders. Inviting boundless entrepreneurial creativity, restructuring would correct the three deadly sins of corporate America: diversification, overcapitalization, and integration. Wulff would emblazon the three words on his banner. He traveled to companies, talked to CEOs, lobbied in Washington, brought an annual meeting to a halt by making unwelcome suggestions, and urged with dogged consistency in his writings that corporations restructure voluntarily. If they didn't, it might be done for them, he cautioned. By takeover.

Boone Pickens had noticed the possibilities even before Wulff joined DLJ. Seeing the undervalued asset as a way to buy more oil reserves cheaply for his fast-growing company, he made a hostile bid in 1969 for Hugoton Production; he took it over, adding to Mesa's reserves a large stake in the superbly productive Hugoton gas field in southwest Kansas, the largest producing gas field in the United States. Here was a man with similar ideas, ready to implement Wulff's ideas and to add creative wrinkles that would extend Wulff's thinking. It was inevitable that Wulff and Pickens would meet and share ideas. By phone and personal meetings in New York, Amarillo, and at analysts' meetings and seminars around the country, Wulff and Pickens forged the professional relationship that would mature into the multibillion-dollar deals of the early eighties. As they watched the restructuring of exploration companies come to pass through a rash of takeovers, both Pickens's and Wulff's confidence grew. "By the late seventies, I thought, Why couldn't there be takeovers of small, integrated companies? I applied what I'd learned, and in 1981, I recommended Marathon Oil for its restructuring potential." The reign of terror had begun in the oil patch.

That letter—Wulff's August 3, 1981, monthly analysis—is chillingly prophetic. In hindsight, it was a raider's road map. It was titled "Restructuring." There was, he said, "investor disenchantment with integrated companies," an ill for which "the cures are simple." Integration could be reversed by "spinning off refining/marketing. Overcapitalization can be corrected by increasing debt and reducing equity with stock repurchase and/or spin-offs of unrelated businesses or even oil and gas reserves in a royalty trust. Restructuring can be on a voluntary basis, as in Shell or Sun, or involuntary as in the case of Conoco."

His letter was a compelling argument for the end of the era of integration. It was something most had never questioned. Mobil and Gulf had, for decades, drilled, refined, and sold oil and gas from stations that were as familiar a part of the American landscape as billboards and telephone poles.

Wulff was asking a much subtler question. Should an entity, simply because it is large, rich, and familiar, be immune from the roiling process of change that affects all organisms and social institutions? "There may have been a day many years ago when control of refining/marketing was important to oil producers. . . . If there were a surplus of U.S. crude oil production, there might be benefits to controlling market outlets. But so long as the U.S. imports oil, by definition there is not a surplus of domestic production. Thus, the business arguments are weak at best." And then he launched his plea for smaller companies: "The stock market argument against integration appears to be very powerful. . . . And managements who insist on the irrational and incompatible combination of refining/ marketing with exploration and production are doing their stockholders a disservice by making it impossible to realize a stock price more in line with underlying value. Ultimately, the simple benefits of the spin-off are that an exploration/production company will sell for more in the stock market than an integrated company. The stock market," he emphasized, "is voting for smallness."

He was making an argument for the unthinkable—the breakup of the monolithic oil company.

As long as it was small exploration companies being gobbled up, the industry could ignore the fundamental change going on in the nature of mergers and acquisitions. But when he named Marathon as a target, it began to hit home. Wulff was recommending voluntary change. But the reality was that these would not be friendly acquisitions of a company for growth, as in the past. Although unintended, the consequence of Wulff's work was swift and violent liquidation. The death of great corporations.

Marathon, Conoco, and Cities Service, among the smallest of

the integrateds, were at the top of his list. All three had stocks selling for far less than the values placed on their assets by analysts like himself. Marathon proceeded to fall to U.S. Steel, then Conoco to Du Pont, both in 1981, and Cities Service to Occidental. In 1982 they became the first $3 billion-plus mega-deals that showed that size was no object to takeover. Their undervalued assets were the lure. All three fell to other large corporations eager to buy assets cheaply.

But with the Cities Service takeover, a sensational new element had been added: T. Boone Pickens, challenging giants twenty times his size. "In '82, we saw a new way to make money," Pickens said of the Cities Service deal, in which Cities Service almost swallowed Mesa in the process of being bid for by Gulf, before finally being "saved" by Occidental. Until then, it hadn't been thought that individual investors—what First Boston's Joe Perella calls "the private pools of predatory capital"—could ever be large enough to try to buy a giant. The invention of junk-bond financing for takeovers by Drexel Burnham permitted individuals to borrow sums no bank had ever loaned before. The lone-wolf raider taking on a giant added an element of human drama to takeovers that was not there when one big corporation took over another. As the stakes climbed to the billions, and personalities became part of the equation, the nation as a whole began to take an interest.

Next in size on Wulff's recommended list were Phillips, Gulf, and Unocal. In 1984, Gulf fell to Chevron—another Pickens-initiated deal—and Getty to Texaco. Phillips had stayed independent, but was certainly restructuring. Wulff was writing headlines for his research letters like "Goodbye Cities Service," "Goodbye Gulf" and "The Phillips Phizzle." DLJ hadn't earned a cent from the Getty deal, but it had been a landmark event in the maturing of Wulff's theories. In 1983, the then-richest man in America, Gordon Getty, found himself steward of the Getty Trust. Getty's secretary had called on Getty's behalf and asked to see Kurt's work. "I knew that once he had read it, any sensible person would want to implement some of those ideas, so I called him and arranged to meet. I spent all weekend on my computer preparing my proposal, and in January 1983, I flew to San Francisco to meet with him. I had some thoughts on a royalty trust," the concept Wulff credits Pickens with having added to his restructuring repertoire. "We'd already had Conoco, Marathon, and Cities Service. But the idea of selling the whole company, of liquidating, was still so much of a shock that I didn't even propose that as a realistic alternative. We talked about what Getty might be worth *if* it was liquidated. But I didn't suggest that he do that," says Wulff. "But there is nothing sacred about remaining intact."

Gordon Getty did not buy Wulff's, or DLJ's, services. But late in 1983, Getty Oil was swept up in a takeover. In a week of fierce competitive strategizing, Texaco snapped it up for $10.6 billion, the largest deal up to that time. Its undervalued stock sold to Texaco for $128 per share. Getty, too, had been restructured.

Wulff's latest letter, of February 1, 1985, titled "The Last Holdout," had focused on Unocal, and now, on the very day that he was meeting with the Council of Institutional Investors, Valentine's Day, Pickens had announced his acquisition of Unocal stock. "Suddenly we are talking about the largest companies in the world! We aren't working on Exxon yet, but Mobil certainly," said Wulff, his confidence soaring with vindication of his ideas. As he churned out his newsletters, he was daring to ask his clients, "Why should $80 value in property in *Mobil* sell for only $30 on the stock market?"

◆ ◆ ◆

THE tension at the council meeting was palpable. This room held forces that could swing the vote for Icahn or Phillips. At this moment, all over Wall Street and uptown, the lawyers, investment bankers, proxy fighters, and the principals themselves were hounding the big institutional investors with calls, hustling hard to win proxy votes. Bartlesville was praying again for deliverance. For the special shareholder meeting in Bartlesville that would determine whether Phillips's restructuring would be by its own, or Icahn's, hand was just a week away. As Wulff listened to Pickens address the council, he was struck by the ironies. Here he was opposing Pickens, Wulff's spiritual ally through the whole wild history of the restructuring crusade.

And there was Boone supporting the company he had tried to
take over, fighting Wulff and Icahn. Pitted, too, against his old
associates at Drexel Burnham, who were raising junk bonds for
Icahn. Only Pickens's fast wit and unflappable amiableness
could let him turn *this* into a triumph. "You could tell it was
awkward for him. But, still, he made the best impression on the
group," Wulff marveled. "I don't know how he did it. While
saying he supported the recapitalization, he let them know that
he really didn't."

Wulff was disappointed that he couldn't hear Phillips's CEO,
Bill Douce. "Douce wouldn't let me in the room to hear his
presentation to the council. I was *forbidden* to be there. My old
friend Bill!" said Wulff, his optimism over the vote on February
22 rising with the violence of Douce's reaction. Still measuring
the effectiveness of his ideas by the vehemence of the response
from management, he wondered if Unocal's Fred Hartley out
in Los Angeles would respond to his February 1 "Last Holdout"
newsletter. He'd really whacked Hartley with that one, attacking him for persisting with "the folly of integration," for
"spending half a billion dollars on a shale-oil plant which still
does not work more than a year after its intended start-up . . .
instead of repurchasing 7 percent of its stock." And by embarrassing Fred Hartley with a status report on the oil industry:
"The 18 largest companies from four years ago are 12 companies today. Of those 12, four have bought other companies
through megadeals, and seven are repurchasing their own
stock. One company has so far escaped from being the object of
any take-over or voluntary change in financial structure. . . .
Unocal is the last holdout." Pickens's acquisition of Unocal stock
had not yet been announced as he sat with the council. As they
played through the final act of the Phillips deal, the first shot of
an even more violent war was about to be fired. Wulff knew
that, if attacked, Hartley would put up a fight for Unocal that
would make Bartlesville seem like a ladies' bridge game.

◆   ◆   ◆

FEBRUARY 22. Bartlesville schoolchildren massed across the
street from the auditorium waving red heart-shaped balloons
and "I Love Phillips" signs, as hundreds of employees, execu-

tives, battling teams of lawyers and investment bankers, and
press representatives from all over the nation filled the auditorium and several closed-circuit locations set up throughout the
building. The Phillips presence was everywhere, almost every
surface of the building imprinted, carved, or hung with the
"Phillips 66" logo. Shiny red hearts were pinned to the breasts
of hundreds of business suits and secretaries' dresses. Up in the
bleachers, several dozen television cameras were poised to roll.

A pudgy young man with his gray suit coat and tie a little
askew took his seat toward the back of the auditorium. Alfred
D. Kingsley, Icahn's intimate business associate since even
before Kingsley had graduated from New York University's law
school, carried a proxy card pledging Icahn's 60 million votes
against Phillips's recapitalization plan. He had a telecopy machine set up at the Holiday Inn outside Bartlesville, and proxy
solicitors were running votes over to Kingsley even as the
meeting began. Kingsley was almost certain they had won.
Compressed into less than two weeks, the proxy blitz he, Wulff,
and Icahn had waged was the most intense campaign he and
Icahn had fought in their twenty years together. Of all the
campaigns—Bayswater, Tappan, Hammermill, ACF—this was
the one that would put Icahn in the very top tier of raiders, or
"corporate entrepreneurs" or "initiators," as they were vari-
ously called. Icahn had started buying Phillips stock when
Pickens's deal collapsed. With his close-knit investment group,
he had proposed a leveraged buyout of the entire company,
with its $13 billion worth of assets. Drexel Burnham had said
the magic words: that they were "highly confident" they could
raise the financing, a role for which they would receive between
$10 to $15 million in fees. "At first, I didn't know what those
words meant," said Kingsley, "but Joe Fogg at Morgan Stanley
just scoffed when I showed him the first Drexel letter that only
said 'confident,' and told me that only the words 'highly confident' meant they could really raise the money." Apparently it
was some kind of inside code that Drexel Burnham really could
get commitments for the needed billions. He didn't know that
the words that would soon be awaited like the Second Coming
by Wall Street whenever Drexel Burnham was out raising

financing for a new deal were being born here, in Phillips.

It was a war of letters. In the frantic few weeks since Icahn had started buying stock, letters between Icahn and Phillips had flown like diplomatic missives between warring Renaissance princes. It was Icahn's way. To buy a substantial chunk of stock, then write a letter to the company or board inviting corporate action that would raise the stock's value. He didn't just blast them with a tender offer. There was a certain gallantry to it, like a glove thrown down as a challenge for a duel. But behind the velvet glove was the will to buy 100 percent of the company if it came to that. What he was trying to do was force Phillips to make their restructuring more profitable for shareholders, of which he was the largest. Kingsley had helped Icahn orchestrate the barrage of letters from Kingsley's "library," the small office on the twenty-seventh floor of 1270 Avenue of the Americas, where he sat behind a disheveled mountain of paper that overflows his desk and rings the room in stacks of briefs, books, and files.

The sparring had been fast, and full of brinkmanship. Just three weeks before the meeting, Phillips had announced adoption of a poison pill, joining Crown Zellerbach and Household. It had been designed by Marty Lipton to activate when a raider owned 30 percent of the stock. Armed with Kurt Wulff's analysis that the company's recapitalization offer to shareholders was worth far less than the price Pickens had been paid and was therefore unfair to shareholders, Icahn launched a proxy fight, the tender offer, and demands to withdraw the poison pill. Lawsuits were filed by both sides. And Phillips wrote back with a classic corporate plea, calling on Icahn's basic decency not to "attempt to force the bustup and liquidation of Phillips, and the resultant hardship to the thousands of employees who would be thrown out of work, all for the purpose of you making a few dollars more per share profit on the stock you bought during the past few weeks."

The plea did not sway Icahn. "I think it's terrible," Carl said. "They turn down Boone's first offer of $60, buy him off with $53, and give the shareholders $43. I came in, bought stock, and called up First Boston and Morgan Stanley and said, 'Hey,

look, why don't you put some more points on there?' All they
had to do was call me back and say, 'Okay, we're going to put
another 3 or 4 points on the table.' " One of his team heard
Icahn say, 'Lipton wouldn't let them call me back, and I don't
think they realized it. Never! If Phillips stays independent,
Lipton will say, 'I've saved you from the two most notorious,
horrible raiders in the world, Pickens and Icahn.' I say, 'You
will have cost Phillips a *billion dollars extra!*' "

It would finally all come down to the institutional vote.
Kingsley and Icahn had been making calls until the minute the
Bartlesville meeting began. Kurt Wulff had been making calls.
This would be the largest, most nationally visible test of
whether the fiduciaries were going to stand up to management.
The key for Icahn was Capital Guardian. Its portfolio held 6
million shares of Phillips stock—a huge chunk of Phillips
pension funds. "These decisions," said Kingsley, "are easiest for
public pension funds, like Unruh. They don't have anyone to
answer to. They control their votes, and just decide how they
want to do it. But," he said, "a money manager managing funds
for a large corporation like Phillips has a very tough time
voting against management. They may have control of buying
and selling the securities. But they may or may not have voting
power. They may have standing instructions to vote with management, regardless of what they, as money managers, feel."

It would take a stiff back for Capital Guardian to vote against
Phillips. For Al knew that "whoever has the power to say, 'You
can run $50 million of our money,' is also empowered to tell
them, 'If there's a controversial vote, vote in favor of management.' " If you didn't, you could lose the account. If Capital
Guardian voted against Phillips, it would be a watershed for the
institutional investor. And Icahn would win.

As the meeting convened, Douce made his plea for support
of the recapitalization. And Al Kingsley looked around as
questions from the floor began. He could see one of Pickens's
key financial people, Sidney Tassin, toward the front to the
right. He had flown in by Mesa jet to cast Pickens's proxy
representing 8.9 million votes for Phillips—the largest block of
votes Douce would receive. The Phillips team was milling

around up front to the left, staying close to Douce and key
executives, whispering and consulting. There was Marty Lipton himself, thick glasses, balding curly hair, and the soft,
somewhat corpulent body of an academic. But in an expen-
sively cut dark blue suit, moving with confidence and economy
of motion, Lipton oozed power. Morgan Stanley's Joseph F.
Fogg darted like an alert little bird, eyes intense behind his
glasses, his brow furrowed. Fogg and Pickens had worked
together on General American, but were crossing swords now,
as Fogg testified against Pickens on the standstill issue in an
affidavit for an Oklahoma court. There was A. Gilchrist Sparks
of Morris, Nichols, Arsht & Tunnell, Phillips's Delaware counsel. And First Boston's Bruce Wasserstein, a mergers-and-
acquisitions legend in his mid-thirties. Joe Flom, who had
advised Pickens in his previous battles, had to sit this one out
because of a conflict of interest, and he hated it.

In this partisan crowd, Pickens and Icahn were the enemies.
The emotion that had unified Bartlesville before Christmas
swept the hall, as old and young employees took the floor. Lee
Hill Boyer, retired after thirty-five years, the last four based in
Norway, gathered his courage and addressed Bill Douce: "My
forty-five hundred shares represent over half of my net worth,
and I've been very worried about them since December 4. I
have no love for Mr. Pickens and I don't care if management
loses its jobs. I was *very* disappointed that management paid
Mr. Pickens $53 and $25 million expenses without going to the
board." He glared at Douce, and took a breath. "But I'm going
to vote for it. It's the personal equation. I fear for the people
who live in Bartlesville, and for the retired people who stay on
here for the rest of their lives." He sat down to heavy applause.
A shareholder, John Petticoe, took the mike and snapped at Al
Kingsley, "Why did Icahn get *into* this company? Why didn't he
stay *out* of this company?"

A handsome young man in a clerical collar rose to calm the
waters, and the hall went still. "There came into Egypt a
pharaoh who did not know Joseph. That's what Bartlesville is
afraid of—a pharaoh who does not know Joseph. We are afraid
that ownership will change to people who do not care." He

paused, and his voice seemed about to break as he went on in an intense whisper: "Without care, there is no community. There is no civilization."

Kingsley had to speak. He gave his shirt a bit of tuck-in and took the mike. "I'm Alfred D. Kingsley. I represent the Icahn group. We love Bartlesville, Phillips, all the people. We don't want to bust up Phillips. What *we're* against is the recap." He got a weak trickle of applause. But it didn't really matter. It was all over for the recap plan. The first person to take the floor as questions began had been Jesse Unruh's counsel, Thomas Aceituno, who had flown in from Sacramento. His casual sports coat and schoolteacherly moustache disguised the power of the proxy card he had just cast. Speaking for the 124,000 shares held by the California State Teachers Retirement System and, beyond that, for the voting power of California's $38 billion in pension funds and Unruh's new council, he said, "We are long-term investors. We have owned Phillips stock for many years—we're in it for the long haul. And there are certain aspects of the recap plan we don't approve . . . the staggered board, the poison pill—if it's not a poison pill then a difficult vitamin to swallow." Douce stayed poised, his hands gripping the edges of the podium. "We're opposed to greenmail, and we think the payment to T. Boone Pickens *was* greenmail. We are voting in opposition to the recapitalization."

Kingsley ran numbers through his head. He knew, as very few here yet knew, that, at the eleventh hour, Capital Guardian had given Icahn its vote. California was icing on the cake. The recap was dead. "This is the coming of age for the institutional investor," Kingsley crowed. An aide heard Icahn explode when he heard the news, "I can't believe that guy Lipton. He just cost Phillips shareholders $2 *billion.* Marty Lipton is the raider's best friend!" Lipton's firm, Wachtell Lipton, would make a reported $10 million in fees.

Phillips was forced to change its recap to pay all shareholders a package equal in value to what Pickens received. "It was worth $52, $53," says Kingsley, "we tendered and got all the pieces. We made a profit of $30 million." But there was no permanent relief from uncertainty for Bartlesville. Carrying more than $5 billion new debt to pay the costs of war and the final recapitalization, Phillips would remain fearful of every step OPEC took that might weaken oil prices, and of persisting takeover rumors. Douce had said at the meeting, "We have been vulnerable for years. We will continue to be vulnerable." By the end of 1985, Phillips was named the fifth-least-admired corporation in the United States by *Fortune* magazine.

CHAPTER 5

SAM A. Snyder had planned to leave for Bangkok on February 15 for an arbitration. In his thirty-year-long climb to the position of Unocal's assistant general counsel, he had negotiated all over the world—the Middle East, Africa, Southeast Asia, wherever Union's global oil network reached. Those stamps in his passport were a measure of the distance he'd traveled from the coalfields of West Virginia, where his dad had died young and Sam had won scholarships to law school at Southern Methodist University in Dallas. He was due for a promotion just two months from now, to general counsel of Union Oil of California, just renamed Unocal. Not quite one of the Seven Sisters, but the nation's ninth-largest oil company. Suddenly, he wondered if there would be a company left by then. "About one in the afternoon on February 14, the piece of paper was delivered to us. Pickens had filed his 13D. I knew I wouldn't be going anywhere anytime soon." That night, he drove home to Pasadena and started work at "Mac," his Macintosh computer, calling up the tentative battle plan he had been developing over the past year.

Sam Snyder had dealt with disaster before in his three decades as a lawyer with Unocal. In January 1969, an oil spill from a Union-operated drilling rig in the Santa Barbara Channel had coated the shore with twenty thousand barrels of oil and imprinted on the world's consciousness shocking images of oil-soaked seabirds dead on the beaches. The event that helped trigger the environmental movement, it left Fred Hartley with an image of brutish insensitivity he has never shed. Snyder still shuddered at thoughts of the day Hartley's statement on the spill came out misquoted in the *Wall Street Journal* as, "I'm amazed at the publicity for the loss of a few birds." His actual quote, "I am always tremendously impressed at the publicity that death of birds receives versus the loss of people in our country in this day and age," had been lost in the uproar. In 1976, there was the explosion of Union's tanker, *Sansinena*, in Los Angeles Harbor, an unexplained horror that killed eight people, destroyed the ship, and damaged docks and buildings.

And Unocal had faced struggles for control before. Union Oil had, in fact, been created by the merger of three wildcatting little oil companies in 1890. In 1905, the vulnerable young oil company based north of Los Angeles in Santa Paula had feared loss of control and tried to quiet rumors that Standard Oil had bought out Union with words that are very familiar today: "We positively assert that neither the Standard Oil nor any of its allied companies is either directly or indirectly interested in your company. And neither is your company . . . interested directly or indirectly in the Standard." Shareholder support had been galvanized, finally, by the drilling of "Old Maud," the world's greatest gusher at the time, spewing a million barrels of oil in its first hundred days.

The company had survived a rash of ambitious efforts to seize control just before and during World War I, days of litigation, proxy contests, and fights between the founding and controlling Stewart family, boards of directors, outside financiers, and aggressive competitors. There had been bids by a British group headed by Earl Gray, former governor-general of Canada. There had been a disruptive internal struggle with Union's own treasurer, John Garrigues, who, before he was fired, tried to grasp Union as a vehicle for his imperial ambitions to acquire control of the lumber and oil industries, the financial interests, and, finally, the politics of the entire Pacific Coast. There had been power struggles over attempts to make Union the nucleus of an international oil colossus whose financing would come from a Wall Street consortium led by financier Bernard Baruch.

But the most instructive to Sam Snyder as he searched the past was the 1960 raid by none other than Phillips Petroleum. It had started precisely like Pickens's purchase of Unocal shares. In fact, the June 1, 1960, letter sent to Union shareholders was uncanny. Just change the word *Phillips* to *Pickens* and Snyder could have written it himself the day after Valentine's: "Several days ago we received word that Phillips Petroleum Company had reported to the SEC in Washington that it had purchased and now owned in excess of one million common shares of Union Oil, or slightly over 12 percent of the total outstanding. This is the first knowledge that your board of directors or management had of Phillips's acquisition of stock, as the shares had been purchased in other names and in such a manner as not to disclose the identity of the real owner. More recently, Phillips advised your management that it had purchased these shares solely as an investment, because of its confidence in their intrinsic value, and had no purpose or intention to seek any merger or consolidation." That raid had come to an end three years later, when Phillips sold its shares to entrepreneur Daniel K. Ludwig. Ludwig finally sold back to Union Oil in 1965, an act that would force Hartley on the defensive at the company's upcoming annual meeting, twenty years later, when a journalist attacked it as greenmail—a word not invented in 1965.

Union Oil had, itself, merged with Pure Oil in 1965, erasing the name "Pure Oil" from the industry but creating the ninth-largest oil company in the United States—a titan whose $1.7 billion assets of global oil and gas reserves, supertankers, pipelines, refineries, chemicals, and seventeen thousand service stations in thirty-seven states could withstand any attempts to wrest control, it was believed. There had been a flurry of opposition to that merger, involving several of today's big financial and corporate players—Lazard Frères, Allied Chemical Company, Lehman Brothers, and H. L. Hunt.

But there was a critical difference in it, and in all the struggles of the past. They had been, essentially, the flexing of muscles by asset-hungry oil companies wanting to expand and grow, part of the process of building the multinationals of Big Oil, which would become the single most powerful economic and political force in the world. The Pure Oil merger did not cast a pall over Chicago, its home, but was celebrated by both companies at Union's diamond anniversary lunch and board meeting in the quaint old wooden building in Santa Paula where Union Oil had been founded in 1890. Almost twenty years to the day before Pickens started accumulating Unocal shares, the feisty Hartley had made what may be his most charming statement, saying on that festive event that Union aspired to be "not another Goliath in the oil industry, but a bigger David." Like Pure and Phillips, most of those earlier struggles could be contained, negotiated, or rejected by the board. If you *were* bought, it wasn't for dismemberment.

Snyder had been there through Phillips, Pure Oil, Santa Barbara, the *Sansinena* explosion. But he had also known industrial hostility from childhood. With both his father and grandfather on the management side in the West Virginia coalfields, he'd had to fight his way through the Depression against militant members of the United Mine Workers. But today's swift and devastating financial assaults on a company couldn't be dealt with by plugging an oil seep or punching back. It was a game you couldn't practice. But you could try to prepare. Snyder had been doing that since long before the Valentine's Day surprise that Pickens had acquired 7.9 percent of Unocal stock "for investment purposes only." "From that moment, the mood was, 'We're under siege,'" says Snyder. It was time to activate the defense team and put into practice some of his preparations for a moment he had known would come. He had healthy respect for Boone Pickens. "I'd been eyeball to eyeball with him years ago in Amarillo, when I first started out with Union Oil. He was a good oilman. And he was smart."

"It was quite obvious as early as three years ago that Unocal could be a target," says Snyder. "You could read prognostications of the pundits on the Street, the analysts, and see that others they had referred to had gone into play." The stock had started the year at around $35, within a few points of its high in 1980, while analysts were saying the stock was worth about $78. What an invitation! But who would it be? Another oil company? He ran through the list. "Well, Mobil's a possible aggressor. Who might have a use for our assets? Standard of Indiana? Probably the nicest fit for a cash-rich company would be Standard of Ohio. But one assumed they were gentlemen," Snyder had mused. No, it would probably be a raider. The Bass brothers? The Canadians, the Belzbergs? Pickens? "Intelligence is the prime resource in any war. We began to marshal information. We had to know the players better than they knew us," says Snyder. He and his staff gathered and searched briefs, SEC filings, and testimony. They scanned clips, litigation, state statutes. Patterns began to emerge. "These people had their ritualistic dance, always with the same players, and with an almost predictable outcome." The surprise element is what he would be looking for.

He'd been watching Phillips closely, trying to learn from other takeovers. One of Phillips's counsel had told Snyder, "Phillips's management lost control to their lawyers and bankers when they left Bartlesville and moved their headquarters to New York and the Helmsley Palace." The decision had already been made by Valentine's Day that, if attack came, control would remain in the Unocal headquarters in downtown Los Angeles, on the corner of West Fifth and Boundry at a major interchange of freeways that Snyder called "panic junction." Hartley would hold the reins. Claude Brinegar, senior vice-president and director, would play five-star general to Hartley's field marshal. Sam Snyder would consider himself Hartley's sergeant major.

The morning after Valentine's Day, Snyder sent copies of

Pickens's 13D filing with the SEC to the lawyers he had standing by. He did not call Marty Lipton for a poison pill. "We had
decided we would not go to the firms usually seen in these
plays." They would try to break the patterns and throw Pickens
off stride. They would go, instead, to Houston and Los
Angeles. Copies of the 13D went to Andrew Bogen of 414-
lawyer Gibson, Dunn & Crutcher in Los Angeles for securities
work, and, for anti-trust, to Randy Wilson with Susman, Godfrey & McGowan, "a 19-lawyer Yuppie firm in Houston that
was *way* out of character for us and for takeovers."

But New York, Washington, D.C., and Delaware could not be
ignored. There was experience there that would be needed. In
Delaware, where the nation's most sympathetic corporate climate has attracted half the Fortune 500 companies to incorpo-
rate and made corporate law a growth industry, he called
Gilchrist Sparks of the Morris, Nichols, Arsht & Tunnell law
firm. Morris, Nichols would handle the Delaware litigation that
inevitably erupted in these struggles. They had represented
Gulf against Pickens. Sparks was just finishing up with Phillips;
he'd been in Bartlesville on the company's side that week for
the big recap meeting so would have fresh insights into Pickens
and his team. In Washington, D.C., Snyder called Dick Cass,
Lou Cohen and Ted Levine of Wilmer, Cutler & Pickering.
They would steer Unocal through the regulatory arena—SEC,
FTC, Federal Reserve. But working with Andy Bogen in Los
Angeles, Wilmer, Cutler would also work on general strategy as
they had for other West Coast firms caught up in control
struggles. Carter Hawley Hale. Kaiser Steel. Steinberg's bid for
Walt Disney Productions. Wilmer, Cutler would be part of the
inside team in Los Angeles.

◆   ◆   ◆

ON February 19, Pickens quietly increased his holdings to 8.5
percent. Irwin L. Jacobs, the Minneapolis raider known as "Irv
the Liquidator," announced that he had acquired a "substantial
stake" in Unocal. Within days, Pickens would move his stake up
again to 9.5 percent.

On February 25, the Unocal board made several changes in

its bylaws, fortifying the shark repellents that had been put in place two years earlier. Then, it had adopted a staggered board that elected only one-third of the board each year, making it impossible for a raider to gain control of the board all at once. At the same time, it had added the requirement of a supermajority vote of 80 percent of the shareholders, if not approved by three-fourths of the board for any bylaw changes proposed by a dissident trying to merge with the company. Now, it extended the notice period required for nominations of directors or the introduction of any new motion to thirty days before a shareholder meeting. Previously, you could propose a slate up to twenty-four hours before a meeting. It would give Pickens very little time to wage an effective proxy fight before the upcoming annual meeting on April 29. As the nation's business press reported from the front, Unocal was digging its trenches deeper.

◆　◆　◆

UNOCAL went to New York for investment bankers. Nicholas F. Brady at Dillon Read got a call. With its thirty-year relationship with Unocal—an increasingly rare thing in Wall Street—Dillon Read was almost family. Less expected was the call to Goldman, Sachs, a dominant force in takeover defense. Goldman's marketing efforts over the past year were paying off. Goldman's Los Angeles man, Peter Barker, had kept in regular contact with Philip Blamey, Unocal's chief financial officer. He had set up several dinner meetings with Hartley and Goldman's senior partners, Stephen Friedman and John Whitehead. Friedman is on everyone's short list of most important players in mergers and acquisitions, and Whitehead's distinguished career in corporate finance was about to be climaxed by his appointment as deputy secretary of state in the Reagan cabinet.

First contacts had been made. The day after the February 25 board meeting Snyder, Hartley, Brinegar, Blamey, and Neil Shmalle, then director of economics and planning, flew to New York to meet with Goldman's Friedman and Peter Sachs, the firm's specialist in oil industry takeovers. "Fred Hartley views the financial community as vermin. But they asked us to work for them as we walked in the door," said a delighted Sachs.

Hartley also hated the words *investment banker*. They would be advisers.

"As soon as we were hired, Steve and I started our lists of 'what ifs.' We drew up on a piece of paper—forget the order—what are all the things Boone Pickens could do? It was our job to identify alternatives. Not make decisions," says Sachs. "We may give fairly strong advice, but pulling the trigger can't be delegated." That philosophy suited Sam Snyder and Fred Hartley just fine. "Once Steve and I had started our 'what ifs,' our other job was to get up to speed on the operation of each division of the company. We put together a team to fly to Los Angeles to dig in and find out."

◆ ◆ ◆

NEW York was also the home of two specialties that get fewer headlines than most other players, but may be responsible for more of them. Proxy solicitation and public relations are deeply woven into both attack and defense in the takeover process. Snyder called Hill and Knowlton, Inc.'s Richard Cheney to do public relations. Cheney had worked for Pickens on the Gulf deal, but had been replaced by Gershon Kekst, Cheney's arch-rival, on Phillips. "I've got more business from being fired by Pickens," Cheney said gamely as Kekst gained momentum in the field. "Unocal knows I know the enemy." Kekst would work with Pickens on Unocal as well, helping orchestrate the public perception that was vital to the way a campaign unfolded. TV, newspapers, magazines, the way ads and letters to sharehold-ers, management, and politicians were phrased—all could whip up enthusiasm among arbs and institutional investors, inflame a Bartlesville, or win sympathy in Congress or the SEC. It was critical to get the message across to key journalists, TV pro-grams, and publications. The *Wall Street Journal*. Louis Rukey-ser's "Wall Street Week." Dan Dorfman. "Adam Smith's Money Line." "The Today Show." "The McNeil/Lehrer Newshour." *Fortune* and *Time*. Cable News Network (CNN). The *Journal's* Tim Metz. Robert Cole at the *New York Times*.

◆ ◆ ◆

"TELL me! How many shares does the *New York Times* own?" roared proxy solicitor Arthur F. Long, pricked with annoyance that some of the public relations firms were trying to cut in on the takeover proxy contest business he and many on Wall Street believe he single-handedly developed into a sophisticated craft that encompasses "stock watch" services, strategy for annual meetings, investor and press relations, and the drafting and timing of the letters to shareholders that are vital to the strategy of a deal. Perhaps the most flamboyant, fight-scarred veteran of all the Wall Street warriors, Long is the man behind the sedate name, D. F. King & Co., Inc., printed at the bottom of the big proxy ads that appear almost daily in the *Wall Street Journal,* the ads that announce the day's breaking struggle for shareholders' votes. The action he had seen as a navy coxswain on landing craft at Okinawa and football player at Columbia had helped prepare him for the front lines of the takeover wars.

Long is a bear of a man whose bellowing and profane style disguises high skills and a code of honor and fierce loyalty that only rarely coexist with the competitive spirit of today's Wall Street. His presence all but overwhelms D. F. King's conservative offices, which he continues to keep at 60 Broad Street, resisting the lemminglike charge uptown that is making Wall Street more an idea than a place. "Those assholes are never in the *room,*" he went on, flailing at the flacks and nouveaux proxy men who hadn't been there. When Artie said *room,* he meant war rooms and boiler rooms, the rooms in the lawyers' and bankers' offices and in the fancy hotels, where only the insiders who were privy to the highest level of strategy planning could go. The room that was light-years away from the bedroom in the Mennonite farmhouse where he, a boy from Brooklyn, had spent his summers—the room where corn grew right up to the window. Now, a very different room was where you had to be. You lived with a phone in your hand. When the stock watch desk was at its most active in February and March, he'd say, "How could you run up $37,000 in phone calls in two months?"

Proxies are the voting rights that attach to almost every share of publicly held stock in America's corporations. Those votes, either mailed in or delivered personally to annual or special shareholders' meetings, are what elect the board of directors,

approve bylaw and charter amendments, and accept or reject
any issue brought before shareholders. When a hostile proxy
contest comes up, the war is waged by ads in the financial press
and by a thick and endless stream of proxy statements and
letters mailed to the shareholders. The King staff writes and,
when cleared, works with printers to lay out and—most important—to time the mailing of the truckloads of proxy statements,
letters, and ads, the amendments, addendums, and supple-
ments that pour out ceaselessly during a hostile contest. For
each major proxy contest, there are generally four to seven
mailings and three to five prominent ads. "The attention span
of the shareholders gets shorter and shorter; your mailings
have to get shorter and shorter," says Long. They have employees who, at times, sleep at the printers in lower Manhattan who
thrive on the takeover wars. The trend pleases Long deeply.
"They're coming back my way. A proxy fight is the cheapest
way to gain control of a company. You don't have to buy 50
percent of the stock. You just need votes."

Like his office, the larger part of Long's busines is sedate. To
his dozens of corporate clients, he is the man kept on retainer
to conduct routine proxy solicitations for annual meetings. "We
do four hundred proxy solicitations a year. It's 60 percent of
our business," says Long. But the real Artie Long is the man a
company calls, night or day, when they're about to fight or
defend a war, often bypassing their usual proxy firm. Long
keeps a stock watch desk at his offices, where every fluctuation
of clients' stock is monitored like heartbeats; his proxy fighters
roam the country, mobile listening posts for any scrap of
information that can equip them to fight effectively. Proxy
contests often decide who wins or loses a takeover war. And yet
Long didn't get the big fees he saw the lawyers and investment
bankers get. It rankled. "We're the lowest paid in the crowd," he
complained. But money wasn't everything.

"I was the first person hired on Unocal. Why? Because I
know the enemy," he said in a loud, conspiratorial stage whisper over lunch at one of his Wall Street hangouts, Michael Two.
A white telephone rang steadily, turning the table into his
command post over a three-hour lunch of soft-shell crabs and

Napa Valley chardonnay. A client, Long Island Lighting (LILCO), kept calling, its approval of a nuclear power plant stymied by controversy over evacuation schemes. Artie was helping phrase the company's stance to the press and to the shareholders. A major food company, a household word, called, wanting to meet with him the next day. "They've got the cash for a big deal." But King would be cut out of that one by a conflict of interest. The target turned out to be one of their 110 retainer clients. To sit here was to glimpse the earliest signs of events that would not reach the papers for days, months—or never! Long was in the throes of the big recap contest for Phillips, and of *two* proxy fights for National Intergroup against successive attacks by Leucadia, winning both for his client. Unocal was a client the stock watch desk was monitoring closely. He felt the old adrenaline rush when the call came. Pickens had 7.9 percent of the stock, a passive investment so far. But he knew Boone.

Arthur Long did know the enemy. He knew Flom, who would be back advising Pickens on this one, after sitting Phillips out. Long had worked for both Morgan Stanley and Pickens, who were opposed in the Phillips deal. He had worked for Pickens on Hugoton, Southland Oil, Cities Service, and General American Oil. He'd worked against him on Gulf, Phillips, and, now, Unocal. D. F. King was hired February 18, and the next day, Long was on the plane for Los Angeles for a meeting with Claude Brinegar at the Unocal headquarters scheduled for February 20.

Long would be bringing to the party experience and insight of a veteran of the modern history of mergers and acquisitions. His war stories bristle with bias, pride, and outrage. And the fiercest kind of loyalty to his long time associations. But he was there at creation. The men who would become stars of the takeover wars are not legends to Long. They are the friends he met for breakfast at the Regency. Their names evoke the history of the takeover wars. Flom, Lipton, Arthur Fleischer, Arthur Liman, the lawyers. Rohatyn, Perella, Brady, Bob Greenhill, Marty Siegel, Steve Waters, Ron Friedman, Frank and Paul Manheim of Lehman Brothers, the investment bankers. "Ivan Boesky was an arbitrager at Edwards & Hanley in the sixties, before there was risk arbitrage in the takeover game. My son worked for him summers when he was in college." And Joe Flom? He and Long had bought their first horse together in 1965—"a cheap little nag, but we won three races in four starts at Belmont and Aqueduct," he recalls. They'd wakened a printer on a weekend in Youngstown, Ohio, in 1962 to get proxy material printed and mailed, with Flom protesting, "You're crazy, I've got to clear material with the SEC!" "You want your mailings to be the first, most, and last—the last vote is the one that counts," Long reminds him. He had hollered at Flom, "You'd *better* clear Monday because you're going to *mail* on Monday." Representing General Fireproofing against Alphonse Landa, they had done it and won.

It had been a wild frontier. "Until 1968, you had the Securities Act of 1934, but there were no rules, no Williams Act, nothing. It was a shooting gallery. Every Saturday, I'd get a call from some company saying, 'I'm going to get hit in the ass,' and if I wasn't on the opposition, they'd hire me to defend. Every Monday, you were playing in another city. It was Gallagher and Sheen!" Using his own cryptic language laced with undecipherable X's, Y's, and M's, he evoked that primordial time when "it was rape and pillage. And, in my opinion, many of those fine Tiffany lawyers and bankers—old-line firms like Shearman & Sterling; Cravath, Swaine & Moore; Sullivan & Cromwell; your Morgan Stanley and First Boston, the X—they didn't want to participate in hostile takeovers. So three little firms said, 'We'll get into it.' " Skadden Arps; Wachtell Lipton; Fried, Frank; and Paul, Weiss, Rifkind. "I'd joined this tiny proxy solicitation firm, D. F. King, and done my first hostile deals in 1960, 1961. I stumbled and fell, but I learned a lot. And I had a good teacher. My father worked for and was an associate of one of the early tycoons—Thomas Fortune Ryan. A week before my father died in the early fifties, he told me, 'Son, what you'll see in the next twenty years is companies becoming more aggressive in acquiring other companies.' "

It was his father's death in 1954 that launched Artie Long's friendship with Joe Flom. "Skadden, Arps & Slate, which was three lawyers who'd started their own firm out of Dewey, Ballantine, was executing my father's will. There was a hustling guy there named Joe Flom. He was the first associate in the firm in 1948, a partner in 1954. Six years later, when I went into this business, we'd have dinner together. I'd fought a couple of fights, and Joe was interested. We started having dinner together three nights a week—at Manny Wolf's or the Assembly. We were *kids!* When I'd get a call from a company who needed a lawyer, and not always, but often, I'd recommend Flom."

For Long, the current hostile cycle "started to bust loose in 1960, when the flamboyant entrepreneur Jimmy Ling hired him to assist in "price, terms, and conditions" on what Long claims is the era's first tender offer, a bid for the Chance Vought Corporation—a major manufacturer for the military, whose Corsair fighters nobody wanted in 1961—a company with a low stock price and a strong balance sheet. The deal spawned some of the best war stories, like the night Ling, who had been refused a meeting with Chance Vought's CEO, Fred Detwieler, found out where he planned to dine, then marched in and presented Detwieler with his offer. "It must have ruined his dinner," says Long. But it was healthy for Vought stock. Transformed into Ling-Temco-Vought (now LTV Corp.) its common stock moved from $2 to $150 in just five years, from 1960 to 1965. "Ling was one of a kind. One of the most imaginative and creative businessmen I ever met. What flair!" Long reminisces, "Everything to Jimmy was a military project, especially when he was looking at another acquisition. His accomplishments seem all the more amazing to me considering what I've heard about his humble early years in Texas, an enlisted man in World War II, and without the benefit of much formal education." Long saw in Jimmy the same kind of thinking about undervalued assets that drives the hostile bids today. "The first thing Jimmy looked for was value. But in a different way. He'd say, 'Here's an undervalued company. I could leverage the whole thing, and the company could buy itself.' Jimmy Ling did the first leveraged buyout twenty-five years ago."

Long's view of Ling's earliest deals is as good a guidebook for financing and strategies of today's leveraged buyouts as could be found. Here, twenty-five years ago, Jimmy Ling recognized that the parts of a company, its discrete assets and divisions, were often worth more than the whole—one of the basic principles of today's restructuring. His spinning off of assets at a price high enough to raise the value on the rest of the assets pioneered the principles that would be used in the eighties. It is a kind of creative thinking about assets—the ability to look at assets as dynamic entities to be manipulated and massaged into endlessly varied vehicles for maximized profit—that connects Ling with later entrepreneurs like Pickens and Icahn. "Jimmy's acquisition of Wilson in 1967 was, in my opinion, the first form of a leveraged buyout. Ling borrowed foreign money when he didn't get financing here to purchase 100 percent of Wilson and Company. Wilson was composed of three separate companies, three divisions known as 'meatballs, golf balls, and goof balls'—meat packing, sporting goods, and pharmaceuticals. Jimmy subsequently sold off to the public roughly 20 percent of Wilson. And the market price of the part he sold off reflected a higher market price than he originally paid for 100 percent of Wilson. That was the first true LBO," Long claims.

It was still a time when most acquisitions were for growth, not bust-up. Bigger was still deemed better. And as inflation rose, it was cheaper to buy than to build. Many see the start of the hostile takeover era as 1972. But Long credits the day in 1964 when J. Hugh Liedtke, founder and still chairman of Pennzoil, called him as "the start, with LTV Corp., of the hostile wars as we know it today." "Liedtke said he was preparing to make a tender offer for a gas company, and would I be available to help with price, terms, and conditions." That night, Long flew to Houston to meet with Pennzoil executives and was told the target—United Gas. Liedtke took a gentler route twenty years later in negotiating a merger in late 1983 with Getty Oil. But his fighting spirit would prove unimpaired as he sued Texaco for stealing his sweetheart, Getty Oil, days later. As the Unocal deal began, his lawsuit had not yet gone to trial, but was scheduled for July in Houston. With that lawsuit, Long's old client would make an impact on Wall Street and takeovers that surpassed anything Long had seen him do.

That beginning, according to Artie Long, was five years before he got a call from Boone Pickens, who was about to launch his first hostile bid for another gas company, Hugoton Production. "In '68, I got a call from Mesa Petroleum, I think it was Boone, saying, 'I'd like to discuss an exchange offer for a company considerably larger than ourselves, Hugoton Production, selling at half the price–earnings multiple that Mesa's selling for.' Christ, Hugoton was ten times the size of Mesa in assets. It was daring!" A successful exchange offer of Mesa securities for Hugoton stock—it was the acquisition whose reserves in the Hugoton gas field in Kansas would be a quantum leap in size and stature for Mesa Petroleum. It was the deal that made oil analysts begin to take notice of Pickens and his growing little company. "Boone was smart. He knew what to do, he just needed a little help on how to do it. I shake a bit when I think of those days. Boone was working with New York Securities, a small investment firm. My first meeting with Boone and his friend Wales Madden was in their offices." Long had been matchmaker for Flom and Pickens, the team that would terrorize the oil industry. "We're sitting in Oscar's in the Waldorf, the little restaurant downstairs—Boone, Wales, my partner John Cornwell, and me. And Boone asks me for my thoughts on legal counsel, and I recommend Joe Flom. I called Joe on the phone right then to see if he was interested in representing Mesa. He was."

He and the early few were on to something so good that the rest of the crowd began to try to get some of the action. Now what had been a tiny closed club is a fiercely competitive industry. "The bankers and lawyers who used to recommend Skadden, Arps and Lipton wouldn't recommend them anymore! Now I say, 'In '68, you guys with the white buck shoes told me you'd never get into the business. Now where do you make most of your money? You're all competing like hell!' They wrote me up in the *Times* in '60, and I said, 'You're going to see a billion-dollar tender offer.' Now I've been involved in

ten $8 billion deals." He has seen proxy firms such as The
Carter Organization capitalize on the takeover wars, and grow
to run neck and neck with D. F. King in numbers of big deals
they were involved in. "But I've done more, I've won more,"
Long says with a grin.

On March 5, Long flew to Washington to meet with Unocal
officials and Goldman's Steve Friedman to discuss Pickens's
Valentine's Day filing and Unocal's annual meeting, coming up
April 29.

◆　◆　◆

IT would be good to be in the war rooms with Nick Brady
again, Long thought. Nicholas Brady was one of Long's oldest
friends on Wall Street. They'd done the Purolator deal to-
gether in the sixties when Tung Sol Electric was acquired by
Purolator. Brady's father, James Cox Brady, was chairman of
Purolator at the time. Like Flom, Nick owned "parts of several
horses" with Long, racing them in the New York Wheel—
Belmont, Aqueduct, and Saratoga. Nick had got him into the
Jockey Club, the prestigious association that registers all Thor-
oughbreds in the United States and Canada and maintains the
American stud book. They would both be going to the Jockey
Club's Roundtable Conference in Saratoga in August. "I'm the
poorest man in the club," Long hooted as his name joined Du
Pont and Mellon on the membership list. "I just got his name a
little higher on the list. He was a good man, and they were too
stuffy to see that," says Brady modestly.

It was important to Nick Brady to be in the war room. Dillon
Read was one of the white-shoe firms trying to make a transition to the competitive takeover arena. Brady was a little
sensitive to a recent story in the *New York Times* that had
described his involvement in Unocal as a reentry into the
mainstream of investment banking. "We've been here all along.
Old Mr. Clarence Dillon was doing big acquisition deals in the
twenties." But they didn't do as many. They didn't have a big
mergers-and-acquisitions team blitzing the market. Fritz Hobbs
of Dillon Read admired First Boston's Joe Perella and Bruce
Wasserstein for "taking a mergers-and-acquisitions department
that was small potatoes, going out and marketing the living hell

out of it, and making it the most aggressive in the business," whereas Morgan Stanley, he felt, "just sat there waiting for the phone to ring. The phone just isn't going to ring any longer because there are too many people already calling your client." He was describing the new Wall Street. The complacent old-line WASP firms had seen the business vanish, while aggressive firms with creative ideas and nothing to lose were inheriting the earth. The last few holdouts of the personalized merchant banking tradition like Dillon Read and Lazard Frères had been branded boutiques, "a perjorative term meaning 'You're not in the game,' " said Hobbs, defensively. "But Felix at Lazard is in the same game Perella's in. And so are we. We may do fewer deals, but we're in the game."

Nick Brady epitomizes the style that prevailed through the fifties and sixties. He is tall and elegant, with a lean, patrician face and a gracious manner that lets him serve wax paper-wrapped roast beef sandwiches at his boardroom table as if it were a champagne hunt breakfast. The Oriental rugs, hunting prints, polished Chippendale-style chairs, and fresh bouquets of flowers in the lobby—traditional banker's trappings—exude a quiet quality and taste. He has family wealth, powerful social connections, the right schools behind him. Vice-President George Bush and Secretary of State George Schultz are good friends. He's a member of the Bohemian Grove near San Francisco, the forested camp along the Russian River where, each summer, corporate jets fly in the nation's corporate and political power structure. He has shared his camp, Mandalay, with Henry Kissinger and Gerald Ford. He belongs to the Jockey Club, owns and races horses. And he was in the Senate briefly in 1982, appointed to finish the term of Harrison Williams when Williams was indicted and jailed over the Abscam scandal. Brady had swiftly returned to the action on Wall Street. "I couldn't believe it took them sixteen years to get a bill on something as important as nuclear waste." Brady, for all his genteel establishment style, was not about to be left behind in a game he'd played as early as any of them.

But in Unocal, Dillon Read would have to share the investment banking role with Goldman, Sachs, the company that

Long remembered in 1960, when he came to Wall Street as
"zero. Goldman, Sachs was just a little Gus Levy X. Now they
are second to none." Every move, every shred of financial
analysis and strategic thinking Dillon Read did, would be
measured against Goldman, Sachs's superstrategists. "Was I
happy about it?" said Hobbs. "No. My pride was hurt. I'd been
on the account, done Unocal's last debt offering. The problem
with being small is that these companies feel they have to have
the clout of a big firm. It hurt a little that they didn't think we
could do it by ourselves. . . . But," he added, "I knew Goldman
Sachs as guys we could work with as our partners, and that is
rare. I also knew this would be a showdown. We had a very
strong client with the support of his board and his people, and
an opponent who is just as strong and clever with an unbeliev-
able track record. All the elements were there for a classic
confrontation. We were happy to be part of it.

"To be honest, I was excited and I was scared," Hobbs said,
smiling. "Do I lack confidence? No. But there's no way to go
into these things overconfident when someone is as strong as
Boone, an old friend's in trouble, and there's so much at stake."
Poised at the starting line with the best in the world, hyperven-
tilating with good healthy fear, was where Hobbs had been
before. He had rowed at two Olympics—as stroke of the heavy
eights Harvard crew at Mexico City in 1968 and, with his
brother, on the national crew in Munich in 1972. He bristled
with the competitive intensity that put you on the A team in the
takeover wars. Yet his background came close to the fading
white-shoe tradition. Franklin W. Hobbs IV had been raised in
an upper-middle-class, suburban New England family in Con-
cord, Massachusetts, the oldest of four children, all of them
high achievers. "My father always said, 'Don't count on any
money, because if I have any money I'm going to spend it. But
you can have any education you want.' He never pushed me,
but he felt very strongly that if you did something, you did
your best." He had motivational techniques. "My wife laughs at
me when I say how cute our kids are. She says, 'You could have
been cute, too, but in all your pictures you had a crew cut.' I
had a crew cut because my father cut our hair, and the deal was

that if we didn't get certain grades we got a crew cut. I always had a crew cut."

Thus motivated, Fritz—blond, handsome, and full of high purpose—achieved Harvard for undergraduate and business school. He neither smoked nor drank. "I was going to save the world. In the late sixties, there was still a strong sense of purpose and social service, and the way to be king of the world was to get a joint degree—law and business—so that if saving the world didn't work out, you'd have business contacts." Recruited by Dillon Read, he came to Wall Street with a little "intellectual elitism," planning to "find out where the money is and then get out of there."

He had been attracted to Dillon Read's small mergers-and-acquisitions department, hooked by the challenge and excitement of the deal side of the business. He loved "putting the mosaic together. There are so many moving parts. And getting them lined up right so it works is really a talent." Stress was endemic. But world-class rowing competition had taught him how to handle it. "I've been through maybe a hundred transactions in the last ten years, and there is never an easy deal. There is no such thing as a friendly takeover. Whenever control shifts hands, there are tensions." Although some of Wall Street's new warriors have lapsed into amorality or delusions of grandeur, unable to question the value of what they do, Hobbs retains the capacity to look at his life's work. "I don't have any illusions that I'm making anything. If I stopped tomorrow, I would have helped a couple of people make some acquisitions or sell some companies at the right time."

Hobbs would be Brady's point man on Unocal, moving out to Los Angeles to live with the company during its time of trial. He was another Dillon Read statement of intent to join the new Wall Street. His performance, thrust into high profile beside Goldman Sachs's, would be a dramatic test of the direction Wall Street might take. Would there continue to be a place for the personalized investment banker who based his business on long relationships? The broadly skilled banker who could help a client with whatever he needed done—an underwriting or an acquisition—without turning it over to teams of specialists.

Lazard Frères and Dillon Read were virtually the only two left.
There was a small cell of like-thinking firms forming in San
Francisco, where Warren Hellman had left Wall Street and the
presidency of Lehman Brothers to open a tiny two-partner
investment firm, Friedman and Hellman, committed to
friendly deal making. Within months, Hellman would negotiate the leveraged buyout of Levi Strauss Associates by family
members, an achievement that would give impetus to the idea
of an alternative to the macho confrontational style.

Or would the deal-by-deal, meet-you-on-the-elevator-and-
sell-you-the-best-idea-I've-had-today approach Hobbs despised
prevail? "We don't want to be the storm troopers of Wall Street.
Being a gun for hire is not in our nature. In a firm like ours,
hell, what we're really selling is relationships. And trust and
faith." With an almost Arthurian purpose, Hobbs galloped in to
lead Dillon Read's quest for profit and prestige in the takeover
wars.

◆   ◆   ◆

DILLON Read would be working with Goldman, Sachs's first
team. Intense, attractive, wiry, and wavy-haired, Stephen
Friedman is "a killer, an NCAA class wrestling champion at
Cornell, absolutely brilliant," says a respectful competitor. A
more relaxed personality, it may have taken Peter Sachs a little
longer to hone the warrior instincts. But Sachs was an aggressive competitor who for several seasons in the sixties flew to
England for a month on the track racing high-performance
cars. Coming into Unocal, Friedman and Sachs were deep in
the flow. The deal flow. The place where the "deal junkies"
live—an unnatural, incestuous, addictive pool of gossip, rumor,
backbiting, and vicious rivalries where information is everything. A place where you were constantly talking to each other
and trading ideas, minds focused eighteen hours a day on
smelling out and applying every new device, every defense or
attack tactic that could help win takeovers.

Although Goldman Sachs did mostly defense, the majority of
firms worked either side of a deal, true mercenaries who met
each other again and again, working with or against each other.
The deal flow was full of athletes—marathon runners, Olympic

rowers, handball players—men compulsive about their cardio-vascular workouts. You burned out fast and young. "Thirty-five's about the upper limit," said Hobbs. Yesterday's big hitter could be kicked upstairs to corporate finance if he didn't keep the edge. As he hit forty, Morris Kramer—the compulsive deal maker at Skadden Arps who was First Boston's lawyer for Texaco's takeover of Getty Oil—an intense and sleepless week—quit smoking, bought an exercise bike, and started workouts to prevent himself from being "mailed home in an envelope at the end of a deal." Kramer carried a beeper on the Getty deal and describes with amusement the latest fad of the deal flow, a cellular telephone strapped on the hip of your pinstripe trousers like a holster.

Wearing flamboyant suspenders, Drexel Burnham deal maker Chris Anderson has equipped his office like a gym to release the excesses of energy that are his problem when he's deep in a deal. He has a Nautilus exercise machine in a corner of his office, several sizes of barbells on his desk, and uses a flexing bar while he's on conference calls for stress release. "Takeover is tremendously emotional. It's akin to your house being burned. When you're in a negotiating situation, you build up tension and your energy level comes up so high that that energy is focused in your voice," says the burly, dark-haired, ruggedly handsome Dane who submits to the confines of his office with the restlessness of a caged tiger. "If you can use something like the flexing bar, you're throwing your energy in another direction, you're calmer, your voice is less tense, and you're a better negotiator." A big bouquet of garden flowers is always on his coffee table "because a friend told me to slow down and smell the flowers," but he has the fervor of a man who has just invented fire as he describes his inventions for defense of Gearhart Industries, Inc., a major oil service company in Fort Worth which resisted a raid by Smith International by acquiring Geosource Inc. In spite of the fact that Gearhart's stock "went to hell in a hand basket," as a competitor on the deal claims, plummeting from a high of $28 to under $5 after implementation of Anderson's strategy, the virtuosity of his "springing warrants" and "Superstock" seem almost to have become an end in themselves. Boone Pickens plays long, sweaty handball matches with tigers half his age to get up for a deal, working out in the elaborate fitness center he built in the Mesa headquarters in Amarillo. It took incredible stamina and energy to stay in the deal flow, and to win. "You have to be tough to make a tender offer," cracks John Sorte, the Drexel Burnham deal maker who had seen Pickens in action on Gulf.

"It's learning from past deals and getting a feel. You start to know who are the buyers, who are the sellers, what prices they're talking," Peter Sachs explained. "You've just done the last two pipeline deals, the last Master Limited Partnership, the biggest recent oil deal." Adds Friedman, "Quality is how many you've been through, and we closed a hundred deals last year." Being deep in the deal flow was having so much of the current action passing through your hands that your judgments—the financial evaluations that were all critical to the successful pricing of stocks, debentures, tender offers, partnerships— went beyond calculations to something close to intuition. "Evaluation is an art, not a science," Friedman confirmed. It was the art Unocal had hired them for.

Scratching on yellow pads in their offices in New York in preparation for the "what if" meeting to be held in Los Angeles on March 30, Sachs and Friedman began to go through the process that would earn Goldman Sachs half of the $25 million fee on the deal they would split with Dillon Read. "We made an inventory of all the possible steps that Pickens could take, and all the responses and initiatives Unocal could take," says Sachs. Lists under A and B were changed and revised as insights and inputs flowed in. "The ground rules were that it would be cause for ceremonial hara-kiri if Pickens came up with something that wasn't on the list," says Sachs. "There were times subsequently when Steve and I spent several complete days on just *one little point,* one 'what if,' with three other people trying to destroy it." First, what were a raider's options? "As a raider, I have three basic routes: I can be bought out at a premium to get rid of me, and make money. Number two, a white knight comes in, and I get bought out at an even higher price, like

Gulf. Or if the company stays asleep, I can get control, bust it up, and sell off parts."

Second, what was Pickens most likely to do? "We looked at what he'd done in every other deal. People tend to follow their historic operating philosophy," says Sachs. The annual meeting was barely six weeks away. Sachs played with the idea of a proxy fight. "He couldn't put up a director at the upcoming annual meeting because of the bylaws. But he could put up a 'precatory proposition,' a request from shareholders which is not binding on the board. What might it be? Lever up and buy in half the stock? Sell off various operations and repurchase some stock?" What was the worst thing Pickens could do? "The worst he can do is, first, start a proxy fight with a precatory proposition, and, two, make a tender offer for half the stock, financed with junk bonds," Sachs speculated.

"There was substantial doubt within Unocal that Pickens could raise the financing for a multibillion-dollar tender offer. Big companies, generically, have the it-can't-happen-to-us syndrome," says Sachs. "When a company is raided, they haven't lived through one of these things. But for us, it's déjà vu—what they're saying now we heard the $100 million companies saying in 1975. And we felt *strongly* Pickens could get his financing."

So far, Pickens had simply bought stock as a passive investor. But at that first meeting in Washington, Long cautioned, "Boone's coming. Boone knows the game, and don't you ever think he doesn't know the game. Boone's going to tender, and he's also going to mount a proxy contest."

On February 19, Pickens quietly increased his holdings to 8.5 percent. Irwin Jacobs, the Minneapolis raider, announced that he had acquired a "substantial stake" in Unocal. Within days, Pickens would move his stake up again, to 9.5 percent.

On February 25, the Unocal board made several changes in its bylaws, fortifying the shark repellents that had been put in place two years earlier. Then, it had adopted a staggered board that elected only one-third of the board each year, making it impossible for a raider to gain control of the board all at once. At the same time, it had added the requirement of a supermajority vote of 80 percent of the shareholders, if not approved by three-fourths of the board for any bylaw changes proposed by a dissident trying to merge with the company. Now, it extended the notice period required for nominations of directors or the introduction of any new motion to thirty days before a shareholder meeting. Previously, you could propose a slate up to twenty-four hours before a meeting. It would give Pickens very little time to wage an effective proxy fight before the upcoming annual meeting on April 29. As the nation's business press reported from the front, Unocal was digging its trenches deeper.

CHAPTER 6

SAM Snyder couldn't just sit there and wait. He had to go on the offensive. Fred Hartley expected it. What Snyder was looking for was a novelty, something unexpected, but it couldn't be frivolous. There was nothing yet to litigate. Or was there? "Searching through vast documentation of Pickens's financing, my team spied the Security Pacific Bank's name." One of Unocal's principal banks. "I had seen a Security Pacific vice-president on the street and told him that if he loaned to Pickens, I'd sue him. He'd told me that Security Pacific did not loan money contrary to the interests of its primary clients." But the rascals had! Here it was, in the documentation. Security Pacific was part of a consortium that had extended a $1.1 billion credit line to Pickens to fund his bid for Phillips. The consortium was led by Pickens's principal bank, the Texas Commerce Bank in Houston. Pickens was a director of the bank. Reading carefully, Snyder discovered that Pickens could use the money to buy as much as he wanted of one company at any one time. But he could not use it to acquire more than 5 percent of any other company while he held over 5 percent of any other company at the same time. He could have been using it to acquire Unocal since last October. With the Phillips deal over, he might, at this moment, be using the credit line to buy Unocal stock for an attack! Snyder knew Pickens was dependent on getting borrowed funds for his hostile bids. And he knew that "raiders are in large measure dependent on the arbs flocking to them, buying stock, creating momentum and economic terror. They follow all litigation with intelligence networks second to none. But if you had something *new and novel* in a strange and foreign venue like California, you might puncture the arbs' enthusiasm because they couldn't predict the outcome." At last, Snyder had his "nonfrivolous novelty." He would try to cut Pickens off from his financing and confound the arbs. "I didn't figure I could shoot the snake in the head, but I could whack the body a good lick." Unocal would sue its bank.

On March 12, Hartley called the Security Pacific's chairman and CEO, Richard Flamson, and informed him of the suit. It was done so swiftly and secretly that even Goldman Sachs didn't hear about it until after it was done. As the suit was filed, the company launched a blitz of accompanying acts. A copy of the lawsuit and a letter from Hartley demanding investigation of "abuses by some banks and financiers that are feeding a takeover frenzy that strikes at the economic well-being of this country" was sent to Paul Volcker, chairman of the Federal Reserve Board. It was sent to every member of Congress and— in unmarked brown envelopes—to the directors of every bank on Pickens's credit line. The brown envelope ploy was a gimmick public relations man Dick Cheney claims to have invented, and in hindsight, it would seem to many to be embarrassing overkill. But it had impact. Delivered to homes on Sunday morning, it alarmed wives, who called their husbands at their golf clubs. Unocal had taken the offensive.

With the Security Pacific suit, Hartley had revealed the fundamental conflict between him and T. Boone Pickens. The Volcker letter was a bold statement of the direction Hartley wanted the oil industry to take. Hartley fervently believed that oil exploration and production were the key not only to a healthy oil industry, but to the United States' energy independence and its national security. Unocal's vigorous exploration, its research and development programs, were the secret to "secure oil supplies for the United States and low energy costs for the free world." The takeovers that were "cannibalizing" the industry could, he feared, leave few oil companies capable of replacing their reserves or doing the exploration needed for the long-term needs of the nation.

Born in Vancouver, a graduate in chemical engineering from the University of British Columbia and a Union Oil man since 1949, Hartley had the classic mind set of the petroleum engineer. Pickens had evolved from his engineering background to the view that the current high "finding cost"—the cost per barrel of finding oil—made drilling uneconomic as a way to maintain oil reserves. Claiming America is 85 percent energy independent, Pickens rejected the national security argument and had set a bold pattern of maintaining Mesa's reserves by buying other company's reserves until it was economic to drill again. "It's been sitting in the ground for 100 million years; it's not going anywhere," Pickens argued. Oilmen like Hartley spurned Pickens's "drilling on Wall Street" as a dead end that developed no new energy sources. This insoluble conflict would turn the struggle into a holy crusade. For to Fred Hartley, Unocal's death or survival could be read as an omen of America's energy future, its economic stability, and its security in a volatile and uncertain world.

"Hartley's act is Machiavellian! They're using us as a platform to launch their own defense, as a vehicle to attack Pickens," said an appalled Russell Freeman, general counsel of the bank, as he leafed through the complaint at Security Pacific's headquarters on Hope Street in downtown Los Angeles. "A bank exists on credibility! And on page one, they accuse us of violating everything a bank's credibility stands by: 'fraud . . . breach of contract . . . misrepresentation . . . breach of good faith and fair dealing . . .' It drives a stake in the heart." It was like suing your sister. "We've been their bankers for forty years. We manage $25 million of Unocal's pension funds; we invest those funds in Unocal stock—we hold 10 percent of Unocal's common stock in our portfolios. There's a Security Pacific bank branch right in the Unocal building."

A lean-framed lawyer of fifty, of average height, with glasses, neat thinning hair, and his gray pinstripe suit coat hung behind the door, Freeman looked right for the role of executive vice president and senior legal counsel to California's second-largest bank. In his twenty-six years of climbing from junior attorney to running the legal shop from the twenty-fifth floor, he had even developed the deliberative banker's smile. But the drab gray feathers disguised a boldness and sophistication that has made Security Pacific the strongest and most forward-looking bank in the state. As the once-mighty Bank of America became a shaken giant drained by bad loans, Security Pacific was moving confidently into a deregulated environment. On January 21, 1986, Bank of America's CEO, Samuel Armacost, would declare a loss of $377 million for 1985, cancellation of dividends for common stock, and unhappy membership in that large club of industries admitting defeat of the seventies strategies of diversification and rapid growth which had brought "a disproportionate amount of risk in the eighties." Security Pacific was buying access to other states and aggressively developing the new banking services that were chipping away at the sacred domains of the investment banker. As banks failed, Security Pacific thrived.

The lawsuit would reverberate through a banking industry already rocked by deregulation, and through a volatile California banking scene that has, in Freeman's view, "changed more in the last twelve months than in the past twenty-five years." Bank failures were beginning to undermine that faith in the strength of America's banking system. Hartley's letter to Volcker inflamed fears that encouragement of the "reckless activity" of takeovers by "stock and bond and credit schemes reminiscent of those of the 1920's" could trigger "a new wave of bankruptcies and bank failures." It hit at Hartley's deep fear of eroding America's asset base and replacing it with debt. "The market boom of the 1920's had too small an asset base to support it, and the outcome was a national disaster," his letter cautioned.

Underlying the rhetoric, the lawsuit challenged fundamental banking principles. Should your large corporate customers be able to dictate who you lend to? "It would be an easy call for me," Pickens said later. "I'd tell my board of directors and customers that I was going to have to loan money to credit-worthy customers." It was not an easy call for Freeman. Yes, the bank's general policy was not to finance hostile takeovers against its backyard customers. And, clearly, there had been a communication failure in getting word of the bank's continued involvement in the credit line to the highest levels of management. The news had probably been blocked by the so-called Chinese Wall, the honor system that forbids transfer of information between banking operations—say, corporate loans and portfolio management—where privileged knowledge of a company could give an insider an illegal advantage in buying or selling that company's stock. But even if top management had known, was the new policy a correct one? Freeman saw dangerous implications in Unocal's act, the potential for financial tyranny by corporations. A sinister entrenchment device for management.

Where could he look for precedent? Like everything in takeovers, this issue thrust them into uncharted territory. The bank's first taste of this had been last year, when Limited Inc. made a bid for Carter Hawley Hale. Should they loan to Limited Inc. when Carter Hawley Hale was a customer? There the conflict was more clear-cut; a Carter Hawley director sat on Security Pacific's board. The only useful precedent, a landmark case from ten or fifteen years earlier, was the Chemical Bank case that said there was nothing illegal in a bank funding takeovers, as long as there was *no exchange of confidential information.* "Without that rule, Unocal could get a line of credit with every bank across the country and seal off credit from anyone it wished," Freeman feared. Unocal had now accused Security Pacific of exactly that—exchanging confidential information. It was there, bluntly insinuated in the opening paragraph of the letter Hartley had written to Volcker at the Federal Reserve: "After a relationship of some 40 years, in which the Bank continually received confidential financial, geological and engi-

neering information from this Company, the Bank turned
around and loaned money to a group intent on taking Unocal
over or putting it into play as an acquisition target."

It wasn't as if the bank's chunk of the credit line was going to
halt his actions one way or the other. Of the $1.1 billion,
Security Pacific's share was only 4 percent, roughly $50 million.
But it was a moral issue that could help define the proper role
of a bank in the takeovers that would unfold over the coming
years. Freeman suspected that the subtler question of banking
principles would be lost in the headlines; to the public, it would
be an emotional black-and-white issue—to fund or not to fund
T. Boone Pickens.

Boone was a good customer. Since 1973, the bank had made
production loans to Mesa, loans in which Mesa's oil and gas
reserves were pledged as collateral. The credit line that had
caused this furor was backed, too, by oil production. It did not
specifically limit the uses to which Pickens could put the money.
It would be impossible to police all loans to possible raiders of
the bank's big corporate customers. It would require subversive
"peek and see" tactics, which were objectionable to customers—
objectionable to Freeman. But as Security Pacific and the other
banks in the consortium began to see their loan proceeds used
to invest in takeovers, they had modified the agreement to
require Pickens to get permission before going for more than 5
percent of a target period. In line with the new policy, the bank
had been concerned when Pickens had come back to renegotiate the credit line after Phillips and asked for an amendment to
go over 5 percent with another company, and it had asked
Mesa for withdrawal from the credit line even before Pickens
announced his investment in Unocal. But in that reinstatement
vote, the bank had been outvoted by the consortium by a two-
thirds vote. Security Pacific was locked into the credit line by
agreement.

But the same domino effect that was beginning to close doors
to Pickens across the country, as banks capitulated to powerful
corporate clients, gripped the executive suite of Security Pacific. On orders from its chairman, Security Pacific gradually
stepped out of the credit line, withdrawing completely by April

18. Several other banks in the credit line followed suit, joining the major New York banks that had already closed their doors to Pickens. A noose was beginning to tighten around Pickens's financing sources, evoking Carl Icahn's basic principle of war: "You've got to have your reserves stretched out in front to *know* you can hang in there and take your target." They were words Icahn would eat before the year was out.

"We've been damaged," said a dismayed Russell Freeman, as he canceled his plans for the spring and launched the massive response forced by the lawsuit's request for "accelerated discovery." In dozens of depositions and truckloads of documents, the bank would have to bare its corporate soul. Sam Snyder had his nonfrivolous novelty in spades. And he had put the nation's financial community on notice as Pickens marched on Unocal: "We sue banks."

◆　◆　◆

SECURITY Pacific reeled. But for John Kelly it was just another week in the life of a proxy fighter. Artie Long's West Coast warrior, the San Francisco–based vice-president of D. F. King, had flown to New York on Friday to meet with the firm's officers. He'd weekended in Connecticut, then flown on to Boca Raton on Sunday for a conference of mergers-and-acquisitions people, the Association for Corporate Growth. "That's how you pick up business and information," said the tall and garrulous Irishman. "I went to a pool party Sunday, ran into a Skadden Arps lawyer, and Monday morning got a call from Artie: 'Be in Los Angeles at 1:00 P.M. next day to start training Unocal executives to solicit shares for the annual meeting.'" Pickens hadn't begun a proxy fight yet. But the Security Pacific suit, filed as Kelly was flying to Florida, had heated things up. Long had warned, at the beginning, "Boone's coming." He smelled a proxy fight more strongly than ever and was preparing.

"I flew from Fort Lauderdale to San Francisco to ditch my New York wool pinstripe and pick up a lightweight suit. Usually, I go for a day and stay five, and buy button-down shirts and underwear on the road." Grabbing a few hours sleep in his apartment in the Marina district on San Francisco Bay, he tuned in the Dow Jones ticker on the cable business channel and the network news at 6:00 A.M., drank coffee, and called the King office in New York for any breaking news that might affect his clients. With phones, cable, wire services, telefax, and jets, he could stay in touch and on top of things here, and live a life that gave him a chance to see his two teen-age sons and take a date up to Sonoma for a wine country picnic. To live a life beyond takeovers.

Phillips, Gulf, Cities Service. They were already faded memories as Kelly snagged a flight to Los Angeles in time for the first training meeting Wednesday. Taking the stage in the Unocal auditorium before several hundred employees to prepare them for a telephone vote-getting campaign, he explained the mysteries of the Williams Act and the proxy process all day, then checked into the Sheraton Grande. Unocal's personnel files had been searched to find executives to assign to their own neighborhoods or boyhood homes to make phone calls to shareholders, adding a personal touch that was part of the art of proxy persuasion.

"Thursday, they put me on a company Gulfstream jet for Chicago for training all day at Unocal's Pure Oil offices, and then flew me back to L.A. the same night." He was back in San Francisco Friday, where Crown Zellerbach, a client, was heating up, too. On March 12, the same day Unocal had sued Security Pacific, Sir James Goldsmith had surfaced as owner of 8.6 percent of Crown Zellerbach's shares.

Then Kelly was off to Seattle Monday to help Rockor, a defense and development company, fight a group led by takeover specialist Norman Muller. "Eight days and four corners of the country. That's the life of a proxy fighter," he said, as he gave his sixteen-year-old son a hug and took off.

◆   ◆   ◆

CROWN Zellerbach had its poison pill in place. If Goldsmith marched to ownership of over 20 percent of its shares, the pill Marty Lipton had designed and helped the Crown board embed in its bylaws the previous summer would be activated. If, after that, he should go on to buy the entire company and merge with Crown, the pill's venom would spill forth and kill his investment. At merger, it would allow owners of the Share Purchase Rights Plan, as the pill was formally known, to buy the Crown stock owned by Goldsmith at half price—two for one. It would reduce the value of his investment by half, costing him hundreds of millions of dollars. The pill, if swallowed, would be such a devastating event that it was hoped Goldsmith would be demoralized by its very presence and halt short of 20 percent. But what if he just kept buying, and gained control by going over 51 percent? Would the pill be any defense against his buying control on the open market? And as its critics claimed, would it discourage other bids? Might it kill not only the hostile bid at hand, but the higher offer of some other bidder? Crown's poison pill, once activated, would be hard to withdraw, for the Rights would trade publicly, just like common stock. What mischief might they create out there in the marketplace for the ten years before they expired? No one knew.

It was like placing your life in the hands of an untested drug. The only test so far was John Moran's suit against Household, argued last October; there, the Delaware Chancery Court had found it legal for a board to adopt. But Household's pill had not been tested under attack; Household had only feared attack. The distinguished Irving Shapiro, a lawyer in Skadden Arps's Wilmington office since retiring as CEO of Du Pont, would be arguing against the Household appeal to the Delaware Supreme Court in May. But because there was no pending takeover hanging on the outcome, a decision from the court could take months. The poison pill, a clever invention that existed only on paper and only vaguely tested, so complex that most lawyers were dismayed by it, was beginning to run like an underground stream through the takeover wars of 1985, provoking legal challenges wherever a raider ran up against one, and consuming capital and energy resources, lawyers', bankers', and courts' time in exponentially increasing amounts. There was a growing sense that Marty Lipton's invention would be the showdown over just how far a board could go in defending itself.

Crown knew it was vulnerable. A depressed lumber market

was hurting the entire forest products industry. Crown Zellerbach's stock was down, reflecting not only prolonged recession
in the industry, but a long decline in one of San Francisco's
oldest, proudest companies. The building of its Bauhaus-in-
spired skyscraper in San Francisco's financial district had
helped anchor downtown San Francisco as a "headquarters
city." As recently as the sixties, old John D. Zellerbach, a
member of San Francisco's Jewish aristocracy and creator of
the Hanzell chardonnays and pinot noirs that pioneered the
rise of California wines to world rank, sat in the Pacific Union
Club with his handful of pals who planned San Francisco's
future over lunch. As the family pulled back from active
involvement, professional management, perhaps less caring
about Crown's destiny, had taken over, and the company had
steadily declined. The corporation CEO William T. Creson
inherited three years ago had suffered a loss of over $100
million dollars in 1982.

Yet, underneath, positive change was taking place. Creson's
vigorous efforts to turn the company around hadn't been
reflected yet in the stock price, but he was doing it. A major
voluntary restructuring was almost complete. He had rede-
ployed management, reduced personnel by eight thousand—
nearly a third—raised productivity and profit in the wood-
products and corrugated-box divisions, sold off slow-moving
pulp-paper divisions, and struck forward-looking deals with
unions. There was even talk of putting some of Crown's timberlands into a partnership that would send the value of those
2 million acres of assets directly to shareholders. He was
pursuing the lucrative markets for Crown's business and coated
paper and towel and tissue products—Chiffon, Nice 'n Soft,
and Spill Mate—and moving into computerized office products. He was deemphasizing the timber and wood that were the
industry's "disaster area," shifting lumbering and mill operations from the Northwest to the cheaper wood and labor of the
Southeast.

Gershon Kekst of Kekst and Company, hired to do public
relations for Crown, felt some frustration as he saw Goldsmith

begin his move: "Just two more years, that's all Creson needed."
Puffing big cigars in his sleek Madison Avenue office, he
watched sometime client Goldsmith's moves with admiration.
"Jimmy is very astute. He saw a job well done, but the market
didn't yet know how good it was. Jimmy knew that two years
from now Crown would have been too expensive to buy." He'd
started buying at $29. His average cost so far was $33 a share.
The stock was trading now at $35, $36.

Goldsmith's team had indeed identified Creson's efforts. "We
wouldn't want to get rid of Creson; he's a good manager," said
Fin Fogg, a front-line Skadden Arps lawyer working with Joe
Flom on Goldsmith's team. But it was the forests Sir James
Goldsmith really wanted to get, and keep. Corporations were
not sacred to him. In previous acquisitions, he had delighted in
"liberating" the values of divisions as he peeled them off like
layers of an onion to get at the assets his continental mind had
trained him to value. Although Goldsmith avoids talk of profits
by reminding that, "Profits are only known when they are
realized," the selloff of Diamond International's divisions in
1982 had given him a reported return on paper of over 200
percent in less than two years on a net investment of $248
million. His $78 million investment in two more forest products
companies, St. Regis Corporation and The Continental Group,
reportedly yielded Goldsmith's group $54 million profit in just
a few months in 1984, when the group sold back its St. Regis
stock. But why keep forests, when even the all-knowing stock
market found them uninteresting values? With the stripping of
the world's forests still outpacing reforestation, Goldsmith saw
Crown's millions of acres of forests as wood and paper products the world would increasingly need in the years to come.
These repositories of timber would be even more precious as
exports in ten or fifteen years, Goldsmith believed. Wall Street
liked to claim that, as a reflector of value, the stock market
never lied. But the market had not yet perceived the value
Goldsmith saw in Crown.

His American buying pattern had been curious and hard to
predict. Launching his fortune from sales of a $200 patent for

a rheumatism cream at the age of twenty, Goldsmith had built his empire on food manufacturing, becoming the third-largest food manufacturer in Europe, next to Nestlé and Unilever. Dismembering his manufacturing empire in six months in 1980, he had become, through acquisition of supermarkets in Europe and the United States, the third-largest food retailer in the world, after Safeway and Kroger. Entering the American market, he had clearly bought the Grand Union supermarket chain for the long haul. He was upgrading and reshaping it in the image of the emerging "American cuisine," with vine-ripened produce and fine wines and cheeses.

Forests, like food, were staples. And he remembered, says his biographer Geoffrey Wansell, "that the staples of life had often provided him with the best investment in the past." The good grocer's passion for forests made him willing to bust up a corporation to get at them. When he discovered Diamond in 1978, the old Diamond Match Company that had started making safety matches in 1882 had become a conglomerate. Underneath its playing cards, paper plates, and chains of do-it-yourself shops, Goldsmith was attracted to its 1.6 million acres of timber in the Northeast and California. After working tenaciously for two years to buy control of Diamond, he liquidated it with a decisiveness and vigor that earned him the label "asset stripper." He turned two of its companies private and independent, and sold three—one in a leveraged buyout; another to James River, which he views as "one of the most dynamic, well-managed major paper corporations"; and the third to an Irish corporation looking to establish itself in the United States. He eloquently defended his actions to a congressional committee: "We bought Diamond, weakened by a mass of heterogeneous medium-sized businesses. We liberated and we sold the pieces that would be better off independent, kept the piece we wanted, which was the forest products side and which we have not sold. . . . Each one of these companies liberated from the dead hand of a tired conglomerate has prospered," he told the senators. "The management has prospered, the new owners have prospered, and the employees have prospered. It has been termed by some of your witnesses as a hostile bustup takeover. If that is so, I am proud of it." His run in 1984 at another forest and paper products firm, St. Regis Corporation, was the first of a barrage of attacks that finally sent St. Regis into the arms of a white knight, Champion International. And now he had made his first moves on Crown.

CHAPTER 7

◆◆

THE arbitragers moved with him. Arbitrager Ivan Boesky had been so badly burned by Pickens's sellback of Phillips that he was sitting Unocal out. But Boesky had been quietly buying Crown Zellerbach shares on the New York Stock Exchange for the past week, beginning March 5.

Ivan Boesky was the Street's highest-profile arb. Listed as one of the Fortune 400's richest men in the United States, with an estimated personal fortune of $150 million, Boesky had made a reputed $50 million gross profit from Getty stock when Texaco took it over. He had made roughly $65 million in Gulf's sale to Chevron. He had lost unnamed millions in the Phillips debacle, but had gone on from that disappointment to invest a quarter billion in CBS alone. As CBS responded by suing him, Boesky said with mock shock, "I didn't think that was a very nice thing to do to their largest shareholder." The CBS lawsuit was recognition that arbitragers had become as great a threat as raiders. In fact, without arbs, raids could not succeed.

Arbitragers operated in the narrowest bands in the market's spectrum—the individual takeover deal, in isolation from the market as a whole. Taking a position in a target stock only after it has been put in play, an arb's love affair with a stock has a life span bounded by the beginning and end of a deal. Typically, three months. "You are assuming a risk based solely on the deal. If the stock market goes up or down, it will have very little effect as long as the deal goes through shortly. Most arbitragers don't want to get involved in deals that take a long time. Too many things can happen, and they are all bad—or *most* of them are bad," said one of Boesky's principal rivals, Alan ("Ace") Greenberg, since 1978 CEO of Bear, Stearns & Co. and, for a quarter century, head of its arbitrage department. Greenberg believes you must never get emotionally involved with a stock. It can cloud your judgment. The arbitrager's reputation is for having nerves of iron and a heart of steel, for he is operating on mostly borrowed money, leveraged to the hilt. But arbs still go ashen at the memory of Cities Service, another Pickens-initiated deal two years earlier, where Gulf inexplicably walked away from its premium bid to take over Cities Service, creating "the biggest bath risk arbitragers have ever taken," rues Greenberg. "Cities Service stock went from the high 40's down to 28." Upper estimates of Boesky's losses are $25 million. The last stage of a takeover was what drove the cowards out. It was always a calculated risk. If the deal went through—a takeover or major restructuring—you could make 10 or 15 percent on your money in a matter of weeks. If it collapsed, it could be a disaster like Cities Service.

It was in these last few points, or fractions of points, that macho lay. It was where arbs earned their money—the stage in a runup where institutions got fainthearted and lost their nerve, unsure that their information and intuition were good enough to dare hang in and risk pension fund money. In these last few days, hours, or minutes of a deal, where everything might be hanging on a court case, a proxy count, or a white knight coming in, the ranks of investors thinned. "You're taking a risk the public in many cases cannot take, a calculated risk as to whether the potential gain that is left is worth the risk you have run if the deal is stopped or doesn't go through," says Greenberg.

The arbitrager was often alone out there, holding most of the stock. He had become the deciding factor in the takeover wars. It was his block buying of a target stock that helped run its stock price up. Often, the way the arb tendered his stock or his proxy vote—to the raider or corporation—determined its outcome. A debate was brewing over whether institutions abandoned takeovers too soon. The "prudent man rule" bound them, by federal statute, to invest responsibly. But it also mandated them to use "skill and diligence" in making the best returns they could for the pension fund billions they managed. Why could they not develop the same sophisticated intelligence operations as arbitragers and make those last points of profit now siphoned off by the arbitragers, observers asked. The British institutional money managers had done it so well that there were almost no takeover arbitragers in the London market. But it was probably more a cultural obstacle that held America's institutions back, a certain distaste on the part of the conservative and cautious institutional money manager for the arbs' "unabashedly cutthroat" style, as *Wall Street Journal* writer George Anders described it, with their constant pestering and spying on bankers trying to weasel information, the frantic darting in and out of the market with a long-term interest in a company of about a minute, with their bloodless lack of loyalty. When you heard a trader in a noisy trading room holler, "The arbs have left," it cast the image of rats deserting a ship, or of locusts having swept a crop clean and moving on.

A major celebrity of the takeover wars by the spring of 1985, Boesky was lending his fame to a systematic effort to upgrade the image of his maligned profession. Revealing arbitrage as "Wall Street's best kept money-making secret" in his book *Merger Mania,* published in the spring of 1985, he was giving risk arbitrage a history, a pedigree. His was an art that had grown from Europe's financial markets; the earliest arbitragers had made their profits by playing the spreads between the day's closing price of currencies in two different countries—the British pound, for example, in London and in Paris, buying and selling by telephone and telegraph.

Risk arbitrage, he claimed, was far less risky than playing the stock market, far less subject to uncontrollable events that affected the stock market—"a president's earache, the price of oil, or some palace revolt." With sophisticated intelligence resources, Boesky could, he said, assess the factors that affect the outcome of takeovers so scientifically that he now made profits on 70 percent of his deals. Risk arbitrage, Boesky claimed, was not only less risky than the market, it served a high social purpose. A financial activity "that impacts 85 percent of the stocks traded on the New York Stock Exchange," risk arbitrage gave liquidity to the market by providing a place for institutional investors to sell if they lost heart and wanted to take their profits rather than ride the runup of a takeover target's stock all the way to an uncertain end.

◆　◆　◆

WHILE Boesky bought Crown stock, Ace Greenberg's arbs at Bear Stearns were sterilized. They could not move on Crown Zellerbach. The investment banking house "makes a market" in Crown stock, maintaining an orderly market in the stock and making profits trading it. Because of its power to influence the price of a stock, any firm making a market in a stock is forbidden from speculating in it.

But Bear Stearns could go for Unocal. They had done well on Pickens's deals. Unlike Boesky, they had even made money on Phillips. They had held off at first, only investing when Icahn made his bid, and sold back to the company's recapitalization at a handsome profit. And Ace Greenberg had played a dramatic inside role in Pickens's bid for Gulf Oil, helping Pickens acquire his original positions. He had committed $100 million to the deal at a critical moment, and reaped commissions for Bear Stearns in the deal that made $400 million profits realized for the Gulf Investors Group.

With a snapshot of his six young children on his desk reminding him of a saner world and other priorities as he trades, curly-haired Robert Steinberg, head of Bear, Stearn's arbitrage department, moved heavily into Unocal stock right after Valentine's Day, when Pickens filed his 13D. Steinberg and his small staff work under the eye of Greenberg, head of the investment banking house *Town & Country* recently called "one of the scrappiest and most profitable firms on Wall Street these days." Greenberg sits on a raised dais in the trading room, overseeing the trading, daily, of "billions" in stocks and bonds, municipals and governments, keeping his finger personally on the pulse of the biggest transactions. As a witness in the Household poison pill lawsuit the previous September, he had revealed a flinty sense of humor and lack of pomposity that made his power all the more impressive. An ally of takeovers, he had driven Household's lawyer mad by stubbornly referring to Household's poison pill as "the atomic bomb warrants," condemning them as devices "that destroy everybody but the pilot." And he had got the courtroom chuckling as he responded to the snide statement "You are, if I can understate a bit, very, very cynical about the good faith of boards of directors" by snapping back, "I wasn't born that way."

Eschewing all the traditional trappings of Wall Street status Greenberg has certainly earned, he chooses to stay on top of the relentless jackhammer-pounding action of the arbitrage desk he had commanded for twenty-five of his thirty-five years with the firm. With sleeves rolled up, punching up stock quotations on his terminal and calling orders, he is the very model of the meritocracy that prevails at Bear Stearns. A graduate of the University of Missouri, he scoffs at prestige degrees, and laughs, "I look for PSD degrees—poor, smart, and deep desire to become rich."

A Lou Grant look-alike with a deadpan cynicism that, one suspects, hides a soft heart, Greenberg is fifty-seven, divorced, and wealthy beyond need. He doesn't have to be here in the trading room. When he exits the elevator every morning and faces the opera-set neo-Egyptian lobby, with its squat gilt and wine-red columns, he could turn right toward the boardroom. In his private hours, he reveals the competitive strategist and hunter; he stalks African game with a bow and arrow, wins national-rank bridge tournaments, and dazzles friends with card tricks. He is hooked on the hand-to-hand combat of the trading room, where profit and loss, gratification and failure, are instantaneous and mercilessly exposed.

"Most of the deals in the last four months have fallen through," Ace said, as his arbitrage desk monitored any event that could conceivably affect the outcome of Pickens's so-far-innocent investment in Unocal. Bear Stearns had bet several million that *something* would happen. "Unocal is hard, very hard to figure," moaned analyst Nancy E. Havens-Hasty, a tall, lean women in her mid-thirties, and, as second in command of Bear Stearns's small but powerful arbitrage team, one of the few women active in the takeover wars. "We'd been watching Unocal. It had been talked about as a target for two years. We bought it immediately after Valentine's Day, and the stock went down at first." So far, it was very similar to Phillips, in a declining oil climate. "We liked Phillips. Our average price was $38—we sold out to the recap between $51 and $53." Unocal started higher. "What we basically wrote down for Unocal was, 'Buy it at $47 and sell at $50.' But the stock's been trading too high from the start. It has no business trading as high as $50. There isn't enough spread at the beginning." They were buying it at all sorts of prices, from $37 to $50, and yet they believed there was at least a $55 value in the stock. "The values are there if they can ever be unleashed," Nancy says. "But Unocal has had so much time to prepare. And you have a feisty guy who controls the board." It would only be profitable if the deal went through. And it was not at all clear, with Hartley at the helm, that a deal *would* go through. "It's a pain in the neck!" she said to Cal Crary.

As the Unocal lawsuit against Security Pacific came across the tape, Calvert D. Crary's adrenaline began to pump. The litigation phase had begun. It was the opening of the barrage of legal potshots both sides would take at each other in an intense month from March 12 to April 12, harassing and obstructing each other with every legal tactic they could devise. Now was Crary's time to get involved. He is a litigation analyst. He does not analyze oil, high-tech, or television stocks; he analyzes the outcome of litigation in a takeover—the only specialist of his kind, he claims, in a major arbitrage department. His job is to try to divine, before the judges' decisions are written, how every piece of litigation will come down. The courts are only one of half a dozen fronts on which a battle is fought. But a court decision could make or break a hostile takeover. It could send a target's stock—and Bear Stearns's investment in it— soaring or plummeting. If a decision went against a raider, killing a deal, the stock would dive, hurting them unless they had bailed out in time.

As Pickens made his response, filing a suit in California Superior Court in Los Angeles County on March 21, claiming "unlawful efforts to interfere with his banking relationships," Crary thought, Ah, that's better. They wanted to see maximum pressure on Fred Hartley. That was what would force him to restructure, or accept a tender offer from Pickens or a white knight, events that would move the stock up. When Unocal's counsel, Sam Snyder, heard about Pickens's lawsuit, he cheered. "I'm *ecstatic!* I've dreamed he would sue in Los Angeles Superior Court. I feel like Br'er Rabbit thrown into the briar patch. It's our *backyard!*" The Security Pacific suit was taking its toll of Pickens's financing. Influenced by their big corporate customers, the major banks in New York were already closed to Pickens. Security Pacific was removing itself from the credit line, and two more banks in his consortium had withdrawn—CitiBank and Swiss Bank Corp. If it became a chain reaction, the financing of his stock purchases—the life-blood of his deals—could collapse.

The ever-cool Pickens was getting close to angry. "They're trying to intimidate the banks," he allowed, as his team hustled to round up new funding sources. "Sure, we replaced them with other banks. One of them said to me, 'Boone, you're a gold-plated customer.' " But Pickens was convinced it went far beyond the Unocal deal to a vendetta by the Business Round-table, political action arm of the nation's two hundred largest corporations, to choke off his financing. "I know it's true; someone in Washington, you'd be surprised who, told me they'd all been in to see him, trying to cut me off." In late April, he would complain to a congressional subcommittee about the efforts to cut off his financing.

Pickens pushed his position in Unocal stock to over 9 percent and warned that his passive investment mode might change if Hartley made no restructuring moves.

◆   ◆   ◆

IN New York, oil analyst Kurt Wulff was waiting for Hartley to restructure, too. Instead of responding to Wulff's February 1985 newsletter, "The Last Holdout," as Wulff had hoped, with voluntary restructuring, Hartley had passed more defensive bylaws and sued his bank. But Wulff had had a preview of how Hartley would handle a fight a year earlier. After Unocal's 1984 annual meeting in Los Angeles, Hartley had driven Wulff back to his hotel, and Wulff had grasped the opportunity to tell Hartley, with his usual guileless candor, that he should make "structural changes" to enhance the value of Unocal stock. Stay independent, yes. But separate marketing and exploration operations. Create several smaller companies. Ten, perhaps. Knowing Hartley's pride in it, Wulff diplomatically avoided mention of the unproductive shale oil operation, an obsession that Pickens had condemned as "a lot like Captain Queeg." Extracting oil from shale had been a preoccupation of Hartley for decades. His shale plant, already a year late in opening, was subsidized by the federal Synfuels Corporation with low-interest loans and contracts to buy at a guaranteed high price.

Beyond shale, Unocal's debt-to-equity ratio was too low, Wulff believed, touching on the side of restructuring Hartley despised most. All around him, companies were exchanging equity for billions in debt for stock buybacks to fight off takeovers. Unocal's assets were worth perhaps $60, $70 per share by Wulff's analysis; its stock sold for $30.

Wulff had suggested in that same newsletter that the time was right for Mesa—or someone—to nominate new directors at Unocal's next annual meeting. The activist in him began to boil. Well, hell, he began to think, We can make it happen. On March 12, as Sir James Goldsmith revealed his stake in Crown Zellerbach with the filing of his 13D, Wulff revealed in a speech to the National Investor Relations Institute in Houston the "divine inspiration" he had had the night before: he himself would run against Hartley for a directorship at the annual meeting April 29. His institutional clients owned about 60 percent of Unocal. "I felt I understood better what was happening in the industry than the management of these companies." He would tap the same shareholder base he had tapped in Phillips, working for Icahn. He had already talked to some of his clients and got enthusiastic support. With their support, he'd be a shoo-in, he believed. The timing seemed right.

In his hotel room that night he placed a call to Boone Pickens, hoping Pickens might reveal whether he had the same plan. Pickens returned the call while Wulff was in the shower, and standing naked, Wulff told him his ideas. Pickens's only comment was, "Isn't that interesting." The envelope of time was closing. With Unocal's new bylaw requirement that shareholders be notified of any new issues to be raised at least thirty days before the annual meeting, any proxy effort would have to be launched immediately to rally shareholder support before the April 29 meeting. It might already be too late. He told Louise his plan next morning. She said, "Forget it. You're going on vacation."

On March 26, four days before the big Unocal meeting, Pickens attended a major powwow of the Pickens team at Skadden Arps to discuss what to do next. Unocal's bylaw changes and Security Pacific's lawsuit demanded further response. Held in the huge boardroom downstairs from the senior partners' offices, it was a full-dress power meeting, with Joe Flom, his associate Fin Fogg, and half a dozen Skadden Arps people; Pickens's longtime lawyer Bob Stilwell from Baker & Botts in Houston; Pickens's financial partners, Wagner and Brown, from Midland, Texas; and his young financial team—Sidney Tassin, and the thirty-five-year-old wunderkind from Bartlesville, Oklahoma, David Batchelder, with his handsome thatch of silver hair and linebacker's build. Skadden Arps was glad to be back working for Boone. Fin Fogg had worked on Cities Service and General American Oil, and "one of the more painful experiences was having to sit out the Phillips fight. It was the biggest takeover going at the time. Joe Flom and I were deposed on that case regarding the standstill agreement with General American and whether it applied to Phillips. But for us not to be *involved* in Phillips seemed a shame.

"We got together to just brainstorm the whole situation," says Fogg. "Boone had his investment and started us thinking, 'What shall we do?' We were not in the tender offer mode. Unocal had patched a loophole in its shark repellents with the bylaw change requiring a thirty-day notice to shareholders of new business at the annual meeting. We felt we needed more time to figure out what we were going to do." Over a day-long meeting and big spread for lunch, it was decided "simply to solicit proxies to get the meeting postponed. We did not propose any drastic corporate transactions."

Batchelder, Tassin, and Skadden Arps people started drafting proxy materials. Next day, March 27, they notified Unocal that they were about to solicit proxies for a delay of the annual meeting. It was what Artie Long had been preparing for. Boone was coming.

◆ ◆ ◆

ON March 27, the day after his big meeting at Skadden Arps, Boone Pickens flew to Los Angeles to speak to Drexel Burnham's bond seminar. He also made his next move. He bought a 6.7 million-share block of Unocal stock, moving his position to 13.6 percent of Unocal stock. It was the second-largest block trade in the history of the stock market.

The trade was made by Boyd Jefferies in Los Angeles. "It took about fifteen minutes," says Jefferies, who had been at his seat in the trading room of Jefferies & Co. on Flower Street in downtown Los Angeles, since 1:30 A.M., moving massive blocks of stock between buyers and sellers in Hong Kong, New York, Europe, Tokyo, and Amarillo, Texas. "We pursue the market all night, all over the world," says Jefferies, a tanned, fit, and handsome man with a classic chiseled profile and silvering hair. Jefferies worked through a din of voices yelling buy and sell orders over a loudspeaker. On dozens of computer screens the constantly rolling green tape of stock trades and business news from Reuters, Dow Jones, and all the exchanges, as well as their own steadily changing lists of buy and sell orders, feed into each trader's nerve ends. With maroon rep tie still tight at the neck but white shirt sleeves rolled up to his elbows, chain-smoking cigarettes he never finishes, Jefferies leaps up to yell orders and scans the action of thirty traders, each of whom sits in a plush purple chair that both rolls and rocks before a Quotron terminal and keyboard. One trader has two phones crooked in his neck, as fans installed on top of the terminals play on the sea of men. Holding a speaker close to his mouth like a rock star's microphone, Jefferies's cool voice bounces from the walls: "Hey, Chuck, if you want to make your ticket fifty, we'll make it a hundred—Pitney Bowes. . . . Larry, who's your buyer?" He thumbs quickly through a book of quotes, asking, "Does Watkins Johnson have some convertible bonds?" then snaps out, "Check the arbitragers. I think they might have some Holiday Inn."

When traffic on the freeways was just easing for the night, he had driven in from the palatial glass and mahogany house he and his wife, Sharon, built on the beach in Laguna Beach. Spurred on by a huge banner hung across the wall, JEFCO TEAM: POSITIVE PEOPLE WITH THE COMPETITIVE EDGE, Jefferies and his team became the world's marketplace while the New York Stock Exchange slept.

This trading room is the very heart of the "third market," the frontier of change going on in the buying and selling of stocks. It is a dynamic international market in which the short operating hours of the New York Stock Exchange are no longer good enough, a market in which *liquidity* has become the byword. This all-night bustle of trading is a monument to liquidity, which is the freedom to buy and sell and get your money out of investments whenever you want to shift them from one form to another. "When Morgan Guaranty wants to cash $500 million and deploy it to another industry, *that's* liquidity," says Jefferies, whose specialty, amassing and trading large blocks of stock, serves another powerful trend, the growth of the institutional investors' role in the market. "It's become a professional marketplace. They own 50 to 80 percent of the stock listed on the New York Stock Exchange, and 90 percent of our trades are created through a process of conversation with institutions and professional money managers." His customers are an insight into the makeup of the professional marketplace: institutions, arbitragers, "special situations" investors, and professional traders. Citing the dramatic increase in size of trades he has seen in the last decade, Jefferies says, "In 1962, ten thousand shares was a typical trade. Now it's two hundred thousand shares or more."

It is not only a liquid and institutional market, but, above all, "it is an international market now, and it has to be served," says Jefferies, as calls from his offices in London, Hong Kong, New York, Dallas, and Chicago boom out through the trading room, keeping everyone as involved with the action as if they were in the trading room. "The Pacific Basin is growing fast. Japan is beginning to liberalize its investment rules. We have eight men in our London office. We have an aggressive sales force that should have its finger on the pulse of every professional investor around the world. We are trying to penetrate all the countries of the world," he says, as the trader across the desk works under the eye of a tiny brass sculpture of copulating gorillas that sits before him like a mascot.

Jefferies's operation is the embodiment of changes that seriously threaten the New York Stock Exchange's domination of the nation's and world's capital markets. His round-the-clock trading is a large part of the pressure that would soon force the New York Stock Exchange to extend its hours by opening at 9:30 A.M., instead of the traditional 10:00. "The U.S. marketplace is the largest market in the world. Every part of the world is involved, and investors around the world—now and in the future—are looking for a system that provides a market for more than six hours a day. That was fine sixteen years ago. Today, it does not satisfy. We have eighteen hours the New York Stock Exchange does not have."

Jefferies prefers to bypass the New York Stock Exchange and trade through the third market's own computerized network, NASDAQ, for the National Association of Securities Dealers'

Automated Quotation, an exchange without a trading floor or
specialists. It is a fast-growing marketplace that trades 3,598
unlisted stocks, many of them gained at the expense of the
American Stock Exchange. Trading volumes that sometimes
top the New York Stock Exchange, NASDAQ is upending the
traditional route of stock listing in which a young company's
progress from unlisted, over-the-counter, third-market listing,
to American Stock Exchange, and finally the 193-year-old
NYSE was a function of growing size and financial respectability. Now, many of the entrepreneurial high-tech companies of
the 1960s, like Apple Computer and Intel, start on NASDAQ
and choose to stay on NASDAQ. Nearly four hundred such
companies have. "Eighty percent of the stocks we trade are
listed on the New York Stock Exchange, but 80 percent of our
business is done *away* from the exchange," Jefferies says. "Boyd
likes to see us trading in the third market," confirms a young
blond god of a trader who looks like a fugitive from a surfers'
calendar, as he places a third-market trade directly by punching it into the computer. Trades on the New York Stock
Exchange must be recorded by calling a special service that
does it for them. Swift, private recording of trades is one of the
reasons Jefferies prefers the third market. "You can operate
more discreetly away from the exchange—the exchange is a
fishbowl."

Discretion is one of the reasons Boyd Jefferies has become
important to T. Boone Pickens and to hostile takeovers, which
he denies exist. "I'd describe Boone as an 'asset value buyer'
who's identified assets and decided to make an investment. The
only difference between Boone and the institutional investor is
that the asset value buyer is prepared to buy 100 percent of a
company, and the institutional investor won't buy over 9.9
percent," the point at which he becomes subject to Williams Act
restrictions on short-term profit taking. Jefferies' buyers are
anonymous, known only by code numbers, such as 89M, 3N, 1.
Not even the traders know which is Pickens, Goldsmith, or
Icahn. "We never try to know the reasons why. We just try to
implement an investment decision as efficiently and quietly as
possible. It's not our job to make moral judgments." When

Pickens's order came in, it was instantly punched into the computerized buy list with his anonymous number, the order broadcast by loudspeaker through the room and around the world, and in fifteen minutes the second-largest single-block stock transaction in history had been executed. "Obviously, it's easier to put a block together when there are rumors related to a stock; arbs are a significant part of this marketplace. But the process is the same for a 7-million share order and a two hundred thousand share order, and both are equally proprietary," says a cool Boyd Jefferies, clamming up.

CHAPTER 8

◆◆

"If you can't crash a party, you shouldn't be in the game," D. F. King's West Coast proxy fighter, John Kelly, said to himself as he eased past Sir James Goldsmith at the entrance to Drexel Burnham's annual bond conference the last week in March. A celebration of junk bonds, it was an information gatherer's dream. Held at the Beverly Wilshire Hotel next door to Drexel's Beverly Hills offices just a block from chic Rodeo Drive where Michael Milken had launched the phenomenon scarcely a year earlier, the three days of lectures, lunches, receptions, and dinners with Diana Ross entertaining had attracted the Club. Superstars Pickens, Goldsmith, and Icahn were there, the CEOs and financial officers of client corporations, and all the investors—the entrepreneurs, institutional and private investors, banks and insurance companies—who had collected six- and seven-figure fees for committing to junk bonds on Gulf, Phillips, or several other major takeover battles since Drexel had invented the technique. Although most of Drexel's high-yield, low-rated bonds are used, as they remind critics, to raise capital for the small-growth companies that haven't yet earned investment grade ratings, the excitement at the conference came from takeovers. By the act of committing $100 million to a takeover bid that might never go through, a banker from Vancouver or an insurance company portfolio manager from Cleveland could collect a $750,000 fee and chat over cocktails with the legendary men who are writing the most powerful corporate story of the 1980s. In fact, a wealthy private investor in Los Angeles who watched the junk-bond phenomenon from close range as Drexel helped Saul Steinberg finance his attempted takeover of Walt Disney thinks it is the concept of "insider's club," fanned and reinforced by the glamor and access of the conference, that has lured conservative banks and insurance companies into the controversial arena of hostile raids.

As a funding vehicle for takeovers, junk bonds had moved Drexel Burnham, in less than two years, from an investment firm struggling to find its competitive niche to a member of the small, charmed circle inhabited by megadealers Goldman Sachs and First Boston. The Coastal Corporation, Drexel's first completed, consummated, "done deal" with junk bonds, was just closing as the conference began. For advice and financing on the $2.46 billion purchase of American Natural Resources (ANR) by Oscar Wyatt's Coastal Corporation, Drexel would scoop up $18.5 million in fees, inspiring a leading takeover lawyer to marvel, "Drexel Burnham is the most powerful financial institution in America today because it can raise the money to put any company into play, and I mean *any* company." What sweet pleasure for Drexel! The Coastal deal drew the takeover club—Wachtell Lipton, First Boston, Goldman Sachs, Skadden Arps, D. F. King, Kekst, the Carter Organization, Hill and Knowlton. It paid Goldman Sachs an $8.2 million fee, and First Boston a modest $3 million, a fee they received for attempting to achieve a leveraged buyout of ANR. Above all, it proved that junk bonds could not only be committed, but could be called, paid up, and used to carry through the financing of a deal. Oscar Wyatt would be flying in to speak to the conference.

Boone Pickens flew in to speak to the Wednesday luncheon. It was March 27, the day after the big meeting at Skadden Arps in New York that had spawned the proxy effort to get a delay in the annual meeting and the day of the secret block trade by Jefferies that made him the owner of 13.6 percent of Unocal stock. Pickens's poise did not betray the high excitement of events that would not explode publicly until the next day, when he refiled his 13D with the SEC, declaring that he had "reconsidered the purposes of his investment"—the red flag Unocal had been watching and waiting for.

Drexel managing director John Sorte, its principal banker-strategist on oil and gas deals, flew from New York to introduce Pickens. He had worked for Pickens on Gulf and then done a half-billion-dollar war chest financing for Mesa after Gulf. As they chatted at lunch, Pickens asked Sorte if he'd explain to Batchelder and Tassin while they were all in Los Angeles how they had done the Coastal deal. "I'd be happy to, Boone," said Sorte, as Pickens left to fly back to Amarillo. Pickens's words excited Sorte. "It was public knowledge that they owned some Unocal stock, but other than that, we knew nothing. At that point, Mesa had an SEC filing saying it was for investment purposes only, and it was clear they were trying to decide in their own minds what they were going to do, and we didn't want to push them one way or the other." Sorte speculated on the odds: "If there was a tender offer, we *could* be asked, but there is also a good chance we might *not* be asked." Drexel had not been asked to work on Mesa's financing for Phillips, although he had been subpoenaed on the assumption that they were working for Mesa. But Boone had capable people, and they acted as their own investment banker on that one.

Batchelder never showed up. Sorte flew back to New York after the conference Saturday night and left the office early Monday to go home and change into black tie for a dinner at the Waldorf honoring the fiftieth anniversary of Burnham & Co., the keystone of Drexel Burnham Lambert. "When I got home, my wife was in the new beige gown she'd bought for the dinner, and she told me, 'Fred Joseph's been trying to get hold of you and Mesa's been trying to get hold of you.' " Sorte called Joseph. "The Mesa guys want to meet you tomorrow morning in Los Angeles," said Joseph. "The dress'll look great at the partners' Christmas party, Pauline," Sorte joked as his wife took off the gown. He said goodbye to his three-year-old son and ran out the door to catch the 10:00 P.M. American flight to Los Angeles.

As he flew west to meet with Mesa, Sorte had come full circle. Junk bonds for takeovers had started with Pickens on the Gulf deal in January of 1984. Incredibly, it had been just fifteen months earlier.

Fred Joseph had come to Drexel from Shearson in 1974, a Boston-raised Harvard Business School graduate who was one of many "who were unusually good at English for a science major or unusually good at science for an English or history major, but not good enough to major in either, who have migrated very successfully into the investment banking business." When Joseph took over, "we ranked twenty-first out of twenty-one major firms on Wall Street. We were at the bottom of a bear market, and what you had here was the squish together of the old Burnham and the old Drexel investment banking operations, with no direction, no identity." Coming in committed to change, Joseph found himself heir to a firm that was a metaphor for the transformations of Wall Street over the previous fifteen years. Drexel had been one of the elegant "Tiffany" investment banking houses that reeked of old boys and respectability. It represented everything the financial world had been about since the days of J. P. Morgan, who had been a junior partner in the early years of Drexel. Founded by Francis Drexel, a Roman Catholic Philadelphian, the firm, like the Drexels, had been oriented to Philadelphia, a center of finance and industry, of railroads and oil refining, of coal, steel, and iron.

"A new era began after World War II, the beginning of the information-based investment process," says Drexel vice-chairman James Balog, who was swept into Wall Street on that tide of change in 1961 as a trained chemist with a Rutgers MBA.

Balog came to Drexel in 1976, when the research-oriented firm
he had helped spearhead into the new era in 1969, Lambert
Brussels Witter, merged with Drexel Burnham to become
Drexel Burnham Lambert. He has become the firm's Herodo-
tus, informally chronicling Wall Street's revolution as Herodo-
tus had chronicled the Persian wars. "Drexel was moribund
when it was acquired in the early seventies by a small but
opportunistic firm founded in 1935, Burnham. Burnham was
primarily an institutionally oriented trading and international
brokerage firm that needed to become a prominent investment
banker in order to get the major bracket underwriting. And so
it bought Drexel.

"When I arrived on Wall Street in 1961 to do financial
analysis of the drug industry," says Balog, "I was on the frontier
of a revolution in research. Until then, analysts had done
statistical analysis and financial statement analysis, but always
combined that with information from members of the board.
. . . In these old-line firms, boards of directors were close to the
companies and they knew much-sought-after pieces of information—today it's called 'insider information.' When I arrived,
it was important to know someone on the board." But as
technology spread, research became the Street's new pet.
"Groups of young men were coming into Wall Street, forming
what were called research boutiques—Donaldson, Lufkin &
Jenrette was one of the first. Most of the boutiques were totally
institutional." For, spewing out highly specialized information,
the new breed of research analyst served another fundamental
change in the marketplace. Ownership of stock was going into
the hands of institutions handling billion-dollar pension fund
portfolios, and they needed sophisticated research to perform
their fiduciary duties well. "But the big firms didn't see it. If
they had, research boutiques would never have thrived. We
grew like hell," says Balog. But deregulation of commissions
hurt research boutiques, and as big firms "began to dance" for
survival, they gobbled up the research boutiques. Lambert
Brussels Witter and its cadre of analysts was taken over by
Drexel Burnham, because they needed more research horse-
power to capture institutional business. "But humans resist

change. We become captives of our vested interests. Even when I came," says Balog, "an analyst still had to know someone on the board."

Fred Joseph had joined Drexel Burnham knowing "Wall Street had changed. We couldn't just be an also-ran saying, 'We can do that, too.' We weren't going to get any orders. I very quickly came to the idea that we had to differentiate ourselves." But how? "You could differentiate yourself geographically— you know, the premier investment banker in San Antonio. You could differentiate yourself by product, the kinds of specialized things you do for clients—mergers, LBOs, and so on. At that time, I didn't even care. I just said, 'I want a niche, whatever it is, because nobody is going to select us as a transaction firm unless we have a bona-fide edge in doing business that would stand analysis by an intelligent executive officer asking a lot of advisers." While a major investment banker by name, the firm was still having an identity crisis. "When the telephone company was looking for people to advise them on the breakup, all sixteen of the major firms made proposals except us, because I didn't think we had an edge."

By 1983, Drexel Burnham had climbed to a rank of sixth in investment banking. Fred Joseph continues: "I kept hearing that we had this brilliant guy, Michael Milken, trading high-yield bonds—he was here when I got here. I spent some time around his desk trying to get to know him; he'd bring me a good idea or I'd call him, but for the first year or so we didn't find much that we could do together." Milken had become preeminent in what Drexel still prefers to call "high-yield bonds," offering less-than-investment-grade financing unsecured by specific asset pledges to companies, often the young and growing "rising stars," that needed capital and, in Joseph's eyes, more corporate debt. They were also held by troubled older companies whose credit ratings had been lowered, their bonds demoted to junk—"fallen angels" as Balog termed them. High-yield bonds were serving that massive niche, the 95-plus percent of American corporations that do not qualify for investment-grade financing. Of the nineteen thousand U.S. companies with assets of $25 million or more, only six hundred of them have an investment-grade rating. Joseph and Milken developed a dialogue on the telephone, exchanging ideas, problem solving. But *the* idea had not yet come.

"Then in late 1983, one of my mergers-and-acquisitions guys came in and said, 'Freddy, I've done great, my revenues have gone up 70 percent,' and I said, 'David, that's okay, but it's not great, and the reason it's not great is that as a percent of our total investment-banking-fee income you are only up 10 percent, and all the other departments are up 30 to 40 percent.' He told me I was a jerk." After both agreeing that David was, in fact, the real jerk, Joseph said, " 'Well, David, let's see how we can make a quantum jump in our presence in the merger business. Let's have a seminar.' So we went out to Beverly Hills to brainstorm." In Drexel's offices, above the old W. J. Sloane store now occupied by Gump's, a block from Rodeo Drive and next door to the Beverly Wilshire, a powerful idea was about to tie California even more tightly into the takeover network. "There was no magic to it, except that we're a little different because we won't reject an idea. In most companies, new ideas are met with 'What's wrong with it?' and put right back in its jug. We've developed a kind of cultural willingness to do something new."

As they brainstormed, Fred Joseph asked, "So, okay, we want to get our merger activity to be as important as our finance activity. How do we do that? What's our edge?" The questions and answers began. "Well, we can do financings. In fact, we can do difficult financings. . . . So all right, where in the merger business is it tied to finance? . . . It's tied to finance on friendly takeovers." And then the question that gave birth to a better idea: "Well, why is it that we have to stick to friendly takeovers? Why not use high-yield bonds to finance hostile takeovers?"

Mike Milken already had his team of salesmen in Beverly Hills. He had a network of investors all over the country and Canada who had been putting money into the high-yield corporate bonds he had been selling to raise money for companies—a network of sophisticated investors who had experience with high-yield bonds, who knew their low default rate and had profited from the high interest rates they paid. The difference in applying the bonds to hostile takeovers would be that, instead of buying the bonds and putting their money up, the investors would simply make a commitment to buy X millions of bonds, but would not have to pay up and actually buy the bonds unless the takeover went through and the money was needed to buy the target company's stock. Meanwhile, for "standing by," committed, the investor would be paid a fee, usually ³/₄ percent of the total commitment.

And Milken had another idea. What about making the high-yield bonds even more attractive by giving them that most desirable of qualities—liquidity? These bonds did not trade in established markets. By setting up an in-house trading department for the bonds, money managers could move in and out of them as freely as they could with other corporate bonds.

Until now, only huge corporations had the resources to fund a billion-dollar merger or takeover. For individual raiders or smaller companies with ambitions of taking over a giant, no bank credit line would stretch far enough. Was it possible that, with aggressive marketing and the lure of liquidity, Milken's network of investors would back a billion-dollar takeover? The Los Angeles seminar had invented the fire Boone Pickens needed to set corporate America ablaze.

◆   ◆   ◆

IN its first trial runs, the daring new financial device didn't fly, Sorte recalls. "We tried to generate interest in some transactions, but they never went anywhere." But as the idea was being born in Los Angeles, Boone Pickens was making an audacious move on Gulf Oil. Discovering undervalued assets in Gulf's annual reports, Pickens had organized the Gulf Investors Group, which was trying to force a restructuring of the company through a proxy fight that would culminate at a special shareholder's meeting in Pittsburgh on December 2, 1983, with Pickens's group continuing to buy Gulf shares up to and during the meeting. They had a voting block of 21.3 million shares— 12.9 percent of Gulf—as Pickens made his first nationally televised stand as the shareholder's champion, and only narrowly lost.

"We heard that Mesa was working with Lehman Brothers,

trying to raise additional financing for a possible purchase of
more shares or a tender offer for 50 percent of the company,"
says Sorte. "Several members of the Gulf Investors Group were
Drexel Burnham clients, and when Lehman seemed to be at a
point where they could go no farther, they suggested to Boone
that he meet with Mike Milken. Mike met with Boone, called
me afterward as head of the oil and gas group, and said, 'I
don't know if this makes any sense, but why don't you and Mike
Brown from our mergers-and-acquisitions department go out
there to Amarillo and have a real look?' "

Sorte flew to Amarillo and met Pickens in the handsome
Mesa headquarters downtown, a square bunkerlike building
colored the same dun-tan of the Panhandle soil. Halls, walls,
and lobby were filled with a superb collection of Western
paintings and sculpture. But it was in the wood-paneled and
elegantly appointed executive offices, the top-of-the-line computers and electronic communications equipment, the conference calls and Quotron terminals, in Pickens's pinstripe-wear-
ing young aides—a polite, sleek, smart troop of men and
women who worked out in Mesa's fitness center and dressed
for success, Wall Street style—and in the air of precision and
efficiency that pervades Mesa's headquarters that the sophistication of Pickens's operation revealed itself. If Diane Sawyer
had visited Pickens at 1 Mesa Square, she would never have
tried to cast him in a mythic western mold as she did on the
"CBS Morning News." "We didn't just get off the watermelon
wagon yesterday," Pickens loved to say, with an air of absolute
control of any situation.

As Sorte studied the financial models Pickens's financial team
had developed for Gulf, he knew this was the transaction they'd
been looking for. "We saw that Gulf was very undervalued; it fit
all the parameters we had laid out. It made sense as a leveraged
buyout. We told Boone we could raise the financing." Drexel
would try to raise $1.7 billion, and get it locked up with
commitment letters, before the tender offer was launched.

Sorte had sold *his* client, Pickens; it was time to hand the ball
to Milken and see if he could sell his clients, the investors who
would commit to the bonds. "Gulf was the first transaction

where any investment banker was going to be arranging high-yield bonds to help support a tender offer." Clearly, corporations would fight it as they fought anything that encouraged hostile tender offers. There would be concern about generating large amounts of unsecured, low-grade debt in a deregulated environment in which the collapse of major banks was creating general uneasiness about the nation's rising levels of debt. "We had a lot at stake," Sorte said.

Milken began his blitz of potential investors in a shroud of secrecy, trying to keep Pickens's plans from the market. He achieved "verbal expressions of interest" for $1.7 billion. It was encouraging. "We didn't have the papers signed, but we were confident we could arrange the financing," says Sorte. They appeared to have found the means to raise over a billion dollars—and why not $3, $5, $10 billion?—for T. Boone Pickens, a bootstrapping oilman from the Panhandle who hadn't been able to come close to raising those amounts in his previous run at Cities Service.

But before they could get the commitment letters signed, there was a leak. Pickens's cover was blown, and the package had to be abandoned and replaced by a minitender for only 20 percent of Gulf stock. People cannot keep secrets. A dozen commitment letters from investors would mean the potential for a dozen leaks. But Sorte could see promise in his new tool as Drexel raised commitments for $700 million of high-yield bonds to finance Saul Steinberg's raid on Walt Disney. They got commitment letters, but Disney, taking Steinberg's financing seriously, bought back Steinberg's shares.

"Those two transactions led us to try launching a tender offer without firm commitments for financing, but with a strong statement that we *can* raise the money," said Sorte, replaying the genesis of the "highly confident" letters that have become one of the most famous devices of the takeover wars. "It was a gray area. Lawyers told us that, to launch a tender offer, we'd have to have firm financial arrangements." But Carl Icahn had appeared, proposing a friendly leveraged buyout of Phillips Petroleum, and if that didn't work, an unfriendly tender offer. He would need $4.5 billion worth of financing. "Carl wanted us to commit before he launched. There were a number of reasons why we knew we couldn't and shouldn't. We spent a weekend trying to come up with how to say that Drexel *could* raise the money without having raised it yet." Sorte and his team felt confident, from their aborted trial runs with Gulf and Disney, "but up to that point," says Sorte, "we had never *demonstrated* that we could raise commitments at that level." To prove that he was serious about his offer. Icahn knew he needed to have Drexel raise at least part of the $4.5 billion, but unwilling to pay the entire commitment in the early stages, Icahn asked Sorte and associate Leon Black to raise $1.5 billion—in forty-eight hours. Phillips's lawyer, Marty Lipton, who had just sold Phillips the poison pill that would be triggered if anyone bought over 30 percent of its stock, would be looking for ways to discredit Icahn's financing with the courts and the SEC.

"Then someone came up with the words *highly confident,* as in "we are highly confident that we can arrange the financing . . ." Fred Joseph joined the word search, and that weekend "it was decided at the highest levels of the firm that we would go with a 'highly confident' letter. We knew we had better be able to deliver."

All hell broke loose when Lipton and Morgan Stanley's Joe Fogg saw the "highly confident" letter. Joe Fogg, then head of Morgan Stanley's mergers-and-acquisitions group, spotted an inconsistency in the letter. Drexel had said, in its letter to Icahn, that it was "highly confident" it could arrange money for the leveraged buyout, and then went on to say it was "confident" it could raise money for the tender offer. Ah ha, merely confident! Smelling an opportunity to attack Icahn's financing, Fogg picked it up and ran. He called Icahn's aide, Al Kingsley, and confronted him with the inconsistency, claiming, "We investment bankers *know* there's a big difference—Drexel is *not* as confident they can finance the tender offer." Says Kingsley, "What did we know about 'highly confident'? We hadn't even noticed the difference in the letter." A cause célèbre had been launched by an oversight.

Drexel treated the issue with a leavening of humor, stating in their next letter that "we are highly confident it was an oversight." But the *Wall Street Journal* picked it up. For the Phillips defense the words became an issue in litigation, in appeals to the SEC, in indignant statements to the press. Sorte was deposed, and as Sorte was being grilled by lawyers trying to establish that Drexel was violating securities laws—that launching a tender offer with the mere words *highly confident* was fraudulently misleading, that Drexel could not, in fact, raise the money—the sweetest moment of Sorte's professional career occurred.

"We were taking a break in the depositions." Sorte grins at the memory. "I was in the hall, and it was whispered to me that, within minutes, good news was going to be put over the broadtape." He returned to depositions and waited. A paralegal came in, whispered to one of the interrogating lawyers, who went pale, called a break, and exited swiftly. Sorte felt the deepest sort of pleasure. He knew that the lawyer had just been told that Drexel had raised the money. Mike Milken had got commitments for the entire $1.5 billion!

The lawyers reentered the deposition room, trying to keep their composure, and with bravado that made Sorte laugh inside, launched an aggressive new line of questioning: "Well, we know you have commitments. We want you to tell us now *who* those commitments come from." At which Drexel's lawyers jumped in: "That's proprietary and confidential, and we will *not!*" The depositions drifted off into academic inconsequentiality.

Ultimately, Icahn sold back to Phillips, Phillips held its independence, and Drexel never had to call on the money. A consortium of private and institutional investors, including such active raiders as the Canadian Belzberg family, Saul Steinberg, and Leucadia National Corporation, had, for committing to $1.5 billion for about two weeks, received $5,625,000 in fees and never had to put up a dollar.

With the news on the tape, Drexel Burnham and their junk bonds had become the hottest vehicle in takeovers. After flailing about in search of an identity, they had carved one of the most potentially profitable niches in the history of Wall Street.

And overnight, two little words had entered the takeover vocabulary. From that moment, the words *highly confident* would be awaited and searched for by every arb and analyst on the Street as clues to the success of Drexel's financing efforts and the outcome of takeover deals.

The outcry against the dangers of junk-bond debt raised by Fred Hartley in his letter to the Federal Reserve Board when he first heard of Pickens's investment in Unocal was rising as Drexel's share of the takeover financing market swept it, in 1984, to second-largest investment banker in the industry. A bill to curb junk bonds' use in takeovers was moving through the New York State legislature. The Federal Reserve Board was studying restraints. Felix Rohatyn and corporate officers were condemning them before congressional hearings in Washington. Milken had walled off the press and would have no contact with reporters. In that climate, they had just raised $600 million in commitments for Coastal, a deal that had turned friendly and given Drexel their first test of the stuff their commitments were made of. "We raised the money, the transaction closed, and we had proved that we could not only get the commitments, but that people would put their money up." As Sorte arrived in Los Angeles to meet with the Pickens team, he was confident that "by the time of Unocal, nobody was trying to make the point that we were launching fraudulent tender offers." This one would be important to them and to Pickens. Pickens hadn't got one of his target companies yet. He had steadily claimed he wanted to, but there were growing numbers of cynics.

♦   ♦   ♦

DREXEL hadn't been hired yet. Sorte was flying to Los Angeles simply for a talk. Pickens had apparently not yet decided what to do. Joined by his colleagues, Mike Milken and Peter Ackerman, they met at Drexel's Beverly Hills office with Mesa's Batchelder and Tassin. "David and Sidney walked through their evaluation of Unocal with us. They had a computer model, and do excellent analytical work." If Drexel got the assignment, Sorte's role would be different than what investment bankers usually do. "Typically, you're hired to do evaluations and strategy as well as financing, but Mesa has a team of people that plays investment banker. They do not look to us for mergers-and-acquisitions advice, and we wouldn't be paid a fee for that. The way we were going to make our money was for arranging the commitments and then arranging the subsequent financing." Sorte flew back to New York that afternoon, while Mike Milken flew to Hawaii for a rare event, a vacation.

Next day, Wednesday, at Drexel's New York offices, Sorte and Ackerman put one of the few bearded men in Wall Street to work punching Mesa's numbers into their own computer model as they started playing with the structure of a junk-bond buyout of Unocal. "We were asking questions like 'How much debt can Unocal support? How much should we pay for the company based on our valuation of what the company is worth?' We were looking at cash flow, repayment schedules, and whether some of the securities would have to have interest deferral, which is often the case in these highly leveraged deals where the Pickenses of the world, in this case, can't afford to pay cash interest on all the securities at the beginning."

Sorte worked from an office that radiated memories of his pioneering days with Boone. Like most deal makers, his office was laden with mementos of successful financings—small plastic cubes encasing miniaturized pages from financial prospectuses, framed "tombstones" from the *Wall Street Journal,* a bronze pumping rig commemorating Templeton Energy, a toy twelve-wheeler truck from Gelco. A reminder of the first deal with Mesa sat on his desk, a can of Gulf Super Premium oil, Gulf's best, embalmed in plastic like a fly in amber, memento of the $300 million they raised for Pickens from Penn Central to do his minitender offer for Gulf after the big deal fell through. On a side table sat a handsome teak cigar humidor with JOHN F. SORTE engraved on a bronze plate, souvenir of the $500 million war chest Drexel raised for Mesa right after Gulf, in July 1984. Responding to Pickens's obsession with fitness, "both David and Sidney gave up smoking at the beginning of our involvement with the Gulf deal, but they both chew cigars just to have something in their mouth. We thought that if anyone needed humidors, they did," Sorte said, chuckling.

Within hours of putting their computer man to work, Sorte's team had a preliminary financial structure. "We called Amarillo by Wednesday afternoon and fed our structure into their computer model—a very sophisticated model of Unocal from an operating point of view." There could be no more vivid example of the difference between the new financial world and the clubby deals that used to be worked out with slide rules and golf-club friendships. As the computers in New York and Amarillo talked to each other, the next priority was to play with the price of oil—the main determinant of an oil company's cash flow—as well as with marketing and refining factors to see if Unocal could carry the debt. For if Pickens borrowed the money to buy Unocal by issuing junk bonds, he would be paying back both the interest and principal on that debt primarily from Unocal's cash flow and, perhaps, by selling of some assets. Although non-OPEC countries were ignoring the quotas set by OPEC and beginning to flood the market, prices were still relatively stable. The price of oil did not have the same urgency as in the Phillips deal in December when the fears of declines were compounded by the approaching pressure season when use of heating oil declines. The benchmark price was $27 for Texas intermediate crude.

"That night, Mesa telecopied us with what their output looked like. Over the next few days, we had them run two models with two scenarios—a $20-a-barrel case and a $25. And to make sure we had debt coverage, we ran a worst-case scenario of oil falling to $15 a barrel. . . . The deal had to be attractive to our buyers, the guys Mike Milken would be selling it to. The $20 case was projected to get a 25 percent rate of return. We knew that would be very salable to our buyers. Even at $15, the debt would have been all paid back, though it would not have been a real good investment for the common shareholders of the new Mesa/Unocal." The buyers of these junk-bond securities were, Sorte knew, "sophisticated investors who depend on us to do a lot of the homework for them. They depend on our analysis." He also knew that if the numbers were very wrong, and these investors were badly burned, the junk-bond movement could be damaged just as it was gaining momentum. A "comfort factor" was established of $15 a barrel, allowing for a wide margin of play in oil prices.

Sorte knew that junk bonds and, in fact, the whole takeover wave, could be damaged, too, by the two-tier tender offer they were going to propose. There would be a cash offer, up front, for 50 percent of the stock, to go to the first shareholders who tendered. It had two advantages for the raider: with the offer expiring in a tight time frame, it spurred institutional share-holders into tendering swiftly to take advantage of the more attractive cash at the front end. And with the shares of the back 50 percent to be bought out with securities, basically junk bonds, Pickens could acquire the whole company by borrowing cash for only the front 50 percent. Devised to serve cash-short bootstrapping raiders, the two-tier tender offer had served them well. But it was being attacked in courts and congres-sional hearings as coercive, panicking shareholders to rush to the front end, and discriminatory to the "Aunt Minnie" type of individual shareholder who might not read her mail and even know about the front-end cash offer until it had expired, leaving her to sell her shares for the often lower-priced paper securities at the back end.

Working through the night, Sorte and a growing team at Drexel sent their response the next morning and got the critical call from Amarillo. As Sorte recalls, Tassin said, "John, we're coming to New York today. We'll be meeting at Skadden Arps. We want you to tell everybody what you propose to do." Mesa's key men and legal counsel flew by Mesa Falcon to New York to meet in the late afternoon. With the air beginning to be charged with that electricity of an incipient deal, nearly forty people crowded a Skadden Arps boardroom. Flom was there, and Fin Fogg. "We're comfortable we've got this thing down to a well-oiled machine," Sorte told the group, as he and his four-man team from Drexel's corporate finance department walked the meeting through the transaction they had devised. They talked about their successes in the Phillips and Coastal transac-tions. "We believe," Sorte summed up, "that as a result of

Phillips you can launch a tender offer based on a 'highly confident' letter." Batchelder's response: "We'll get back to you later tonight."

With a decisiveness and speed of action a Los Angeles federal judge would never believe possible without premeditation, Pickens decided to launch his tender offer. He intended to get the benefits of both surprise and momentum by doing it faster and larger than ever before. It would be done over a weekend; $3 billion in junk bonds would be raised. Batchelder in New York called Sidney Tassin, who was just preparing to take his family for an Easter picnic in Amarillo. The amount of work to be done over a weekend was more than one could bear thinking about. The Mesa Falcon had Tassin in New York a few hours later.

Takeovers have added a caveat to Murphy's Law: if a deal *can* happen on a holiday, vacation, or weekend, it will happen on a holiday, vacation, or weekend. The next day was Good Friday, the beginning of the three-day Easter weekend. "They called me at home, and we met at noon next day at Skadden Arps to hammer out terms, fees, price of the tender offer, explain a 'highly confident' letter," says Sorte, hearing the drums of battle. We talked $55 per share as the right price for the tender offer, and by Friday night we were pretty close to an agreement. I slept for a couple of hours Friday night, spent Saturday talking with Milken in Hawaii and Fred Joseph here, making sure there was a consensus on our analysis of how much we could raise, on what terms, over what time period, what fees we would charge, and so on." The entire buyout of Unocal would cost $9.4 billion. Mesa needed to raise $3.5 billion to buy the $64 million shares it did not already own. "That day, we basically signed off on being able to raise $3 billion," said Sorte.

In Amarillo, Boone had not made the final decision on price. But through Saturday and Easter Sunday, Sorte swelled his team as if made of infinitely expandable elastic and lit the burners for twenty-hour days all weekend, preparing the tender offer documents for the SEC and the private placement documents for the investors. "The Jewish people got a couple of hours for their seder Friday, the Christians came in a couple of hours late on Easter so they could go to church or have Easter egg hunts with their kids," says Sorte. "We were going to have an outdoor hunt at our place in Connecticut, but my wife hid eggs around the living room, and that was just fine by my three-year-old son."

As the computer staff worked feverishly to get final numbers integrated, they had to leave blanks for the price per share. "Boone made a last-minute decision on Sunday—the tender offer would be for $54 per share." A classic front-end-loaded two-tier tender offer—cash for the front 50 percent, junk-bond securities for the back 50 percent. Feeding that into the computers, speeding back and forth to printers in the south Village, they completed a crash printing of several hundred information books that would go to all the prospective investors before dawn. An inch-thick, 200-page document produced in a weekend, these books became critical in defense of junk bonds. As attacks on junk bonds grew, they would be given, says Sorte, "to congressional committees to show people that even though we did it quickly there is a lot of detailed background information in this—that we don't just call up a guy on the telephone and say, 'Hey, would you like to buy some junk bonds to back Boone Pickens?' "

Batchelder had the Mesa jet standing by. Sorte bundled a junior associate up with several hundred of the books, and they took off for Los Angeles at 5:00 A.M. Several dozen of Milken's salesmen were waiting for them before lifting their telephones, as one, to begin a blitz of their investor list. A smaller team of salesmen in New York would do the same. The deadline to deliver commitment letters for the entire $3 billion was two and a half weeks. The first half, $1.5 billion, had to be committed in writing, with telexes in by 9:00 P.M. that Friday night.

◆ ◆ ◆

ON Easter Sunday, April 7, Unocal's PR office got a call from a New York reporter saying that Pickens's tender offer would be announced in the *New York Times* Monday morning. With his Easter dinner blown by exploding events, Sam Snyder called Artie Long to pick up an early edition in New York Sunday evening. It was searched for the dread black-bordered tombstone announcement, but it wasn't there. Snyder breathed easier, for just a few hours. "I had a call from Artie Long in New York before 6:30 A.M. telling me it was in the later edition," says Snyder, who placed a call to Fred Hartley.

Peter Sachs, in Stamford, Connecticut, for the Easter weekend, had received a call from Brinegar telling him of the reporter's rumor, and made contact with Friedman, who told him to prepare to move out to Los Angeles. In a climate of crisis, the whole team converged on Los Angeles for a major team meeting on Monday, April 8. Peter Sachs and Fritz Hobbs were in the air even before the *New York Times* edition that carried Pickens's tombstone hit the streets. "So cute to put it in the second edition," said Friedman, as the tombstone appeared.

◆   ◆   ◆

ONE of the first investors to get a call was Edgar Kaiser, president of the Bank of British Columbia and grandson of industrialist Henry Kaiser, whose empire had spanned steel and aluminum, automobiles and aviation, housing and health care. It had created the revolutionary Victory Ships and popular Willys jeep. Edgar Kaiser had spent most of his youth in the Northwest, where his father ran operations that, since 1956, had been part of the family conglomerate, Kaiser Industries Corporation. Kaiser had run the Canadian coal operations, Kaiser Resources Ltd. Milken hoped to attract the pools of capital that sat in Canada. While Canada's own takeover wars were just beginning, following the same pattern and techniques as the United States, the entrepreneurs were pouring their money into the already rolling game in the States. The most powerful were two tight-knit families at opposite ends of the country. In Montreal, the Reichmanns were about to add Gulf-Canada to their empire, in Chevron's rigorous divestment of assets to try to pay down the debt it took on to buy Gulf. In Vancouver, the Belzberg brothers were already so well known in the United States that the media had dubbed them "Canada's first family of raiders." Led by brother Sam in Vancouver, they had leveraged their financial company, First City Financial into an empire that had family members posted in Los Angeles and

New York. They had initiated their own takeovers and joined Pickens in his bid for Gulf and both Pickens's and Icahn's investing groups in Phillips. Through their development company, Olympia & York Equity, the Reichmanns had made the rebuilding of American cities a major Canadian export, and now Reichmann money was moving into takeovers.

Kaiser was bringing not only his own personal capital to an increasingly international game, but the resources of the Bank of British Columbia. As Drexel called, he was fast becoming one of the most colorful bank presidents in Canada's history. With the Hudson's Bay Company and the British crown having laid law and order and a bureaucracy over pioneer Canada from the beginning of its settlement, the entrepreneurial spirit had not flourished there as it had on the American frontier. The crown's tax collectors had even been there to count heads and levy fees as miners rushed up the Fraser River to the Cariboo gold rush in the 1860s. Kaiser was helping erase the image of the gray Canadian.

A Canadian citizen, he had run Kaiser's Canadian division until three years ago, when the Kaiser holdings were finally dismantled. With internal management conflicts that verged on bloody war, Kaiser, as heir, had the emotional job of overseeing the liquidation of his grandfather's empire. What was not liquidated was the enterprising spirit he inherited or absorbed from Henry Kaiser, with whom Edgar had close contact as a child. Unlike many sons of the rich, the blond and wiry Kaiser became a high-stakes entrepreneur who pilots his own twin-engined jet, bought and sold the NFL's Denver Broncos, and knew most of the takeover club before he bought the Bank of B. C. in 1984. The bank was on the brink of bankruptcy. He swiftly revived it with a bold recapitalization that included selling off its debts. He stabilized and increased the base of depositors, bought out a chain of failing banks in neighboring Alberta, and started investing aggressively in the Pacific Basin. At a time when banks were suffering from prolonged recession in Canada, the ripple effect of bank failures in the United States, and, soon, the shock of bank collapses in Alberta,

Kaiser's turnaround of the Bank of B. C. was celebrated in Canada's influential newsweekly *McLean's,* as "The Little Bank That Could."

Kaiser was part of the swift and secret creation of Drexel's financing for Pickens. He flew to Los Angeles, met with Milken's team, and agreed to do more than commit the Bank of British Columbia to $100 million, for which the bank would receive a $750 thousand commitment fee. He agreed, for a fee, to help Drexel place the money in Canada. Kaiser got on the phone and achieved commitments of "much, much more" than the $250 million of Canadian money that would be easily identifiable on the list of investors filed later with the SEC.

Kaiser prided himself on being aggressive, but prudent. "These are not unsecured loans," he claimed. "We do our homework. I want to know *which* barrel of oil—or if I'd gone into a TWA deal, *which* 727—is backing our investment." Sorte clarified: "No, the high-yield bonds he committed to were not secured like a house mortgage. Assets are not specifically pledged. But the bonds are backed by a general pledge of the entire god-damned company. We give very senior position to this debt; it's ahead of all common stock. If Kaiser had a claim, he could look to the entire assets of Mesa for satisfaction of his claim." But the growing worry outside was that perhaps the investors—banks, insurance companies, fiduciaries—relied on Drexel's research with blind faith, and caught up in the excitement of riding the junk-bond wave, might not have done their homework as well as Kaiser.

When word of the Bank of B. C.'s investment in the Unocal tender offer became public, Vancouver newspapers went wild, appalled that the bank founded by the provincial government should be underwriting the corporate marauding of T. Boone Pickens. Although Kaiser reduced the bank's stake to $70 million, he had touched the same chord of concern resonating south of the border that America was "leveraging up" to dangerously high levels. That banks, especially, were inviting vulnerability to collapse by lending money to go-go high-risk deals. The 1920s were being evoked. So far, Coastal was the only consummated junk-bond deal in which investors had had to pay up. So far, most had collected six- and seven-figure commitment fees simply for being on standby. But what if several of the takeover deals went through, and weak banks committed to two or three financings had to pay up, all at once? What if banks in Texas or California with large oil-production loans to Mexico or Venezuela were hit simultaneously with paying up and a decline in oil prices? Could they meet their commitments? Kaiser believed he was risk-free: "First, I didn't think Boone would get Unocal. I knew Fred Hartley—he'd destroy the company rather than let Boone get it. Second, the bonds were backed by Mesa's oil reserves. Third, if he did get the company and we had to pay up, we had the money to do it."

They would know by 9:00 P.M. Friday if the largest junk-bond deal ever attempted would succeed. Sorte and his team had moved to the offices of their lawyers, Davis Polk, because they had a bank of six telecopiers. Secretaries raced around New York in limousines delivering revised documents and, by Friday, picking up commitment letters. Now the commitment letters started coming in from around the country. They quickly overwhelmed the telecopiers' capacity. "We'll never write a three-page commitment letter again. We'll reduce it to one page," moaned Sorte, as the letters took forever to print through. Some of the letters were coming in incomplete, their text lost somewhere in the circuits of the overloaded machines. Commitments were flooding in. From the Bank of B. C., the Belzbergs, and the Reichmanns, north of the border. From the American Lutheran Church, from pension fund money managers and insurance companies. From the private pools of predatory capital. When Unocal's team acquired and studied the list later, Goldman Sachs's Peter Sachs would see the names of Minneapolis raider Irwin Jacobs, in for $40 million, and the Belzbergs' $100 million, and say, "This is a regular rogue's gallery of raiders!"

Sorte could feel success even before they had tallied the final commitments. "Everything was just coming together. Our institutional buyers knew Boone Pickens. This was now our third transaction, right on the heels of Coastal, which had been successful for our buyers. And we had turned our entire attention to it that week. In total bodies, we had nearly forty people working on it full time," Sorte said, preparing to make a triumphant call to Amarillo. The last letters had clicked in at three o'clock in the morning. Their goal for that date was $1.5 billion. "By about 4:00 A.M. Saturday morning, we knew we had $3 billion worth of commitments." They had not only swept over the goal and raised 100 percent of their target. When the commitments were all tallied, they were $400 million oversubscribed.

CHAPTER 9

With the Easter weekend launch of Pickens's tender offer, "we were in the trenches with no furlough, from Easter right through to the end," says Sam Snyder. "My wife considered herself a widow." Skirmishes swiftly developed into the full panoply of war. Intensity and critical mass in terms of bodies and resources reached a peak on both sides. For a proxy fight was being waged, too. Just after launching the tender offer, Pickens mailed the proxy materials to shareholders asking for a sixty-day delay of the annual meeting.

Boone was no longer coming. He was here. In Los Angeles, the "number-one anticipation" from the earliest scenarios they had scratched on blackboards had come to pass: a joint tender offer and proxy fight. Sam Snyder instituted twice-daily conference calls that tied in all the principals around the country. The two war rooms, Sam Snyder's office and room 437 on the executive floor, became the central hives from which the teams came and went. Room 437, with its long rectangular table, telephone at one end, and whiteboards on the walls, was also called "the boiler room," after the hot, noisy, crowded, window-

less securities trading rooms that are a symbol of the financial
excesses of the 1920s. Snyder commanded "legions of bodies.
At one time, I was running fifteen law firms and two hundred
lawyers." D. F. King's Dan Burch headed a three-man team that
moved out from New York to head up the proxy fight, preparing the seven hundred employees, trained earlier by John
Kelly, to begin their telephone blitz for proxy votes. Legal
action—litigation and petitions—were soon flaring on many
fronts, with Uncoal running 19 actions simultaneously in eight
states and Washington, D.C. by late April. Coordinating the
legal circus, Snyder's assistant counsel Jasmina A. Theodore
was having the test of her career. Wild cards were liable to
erupt in any court, anywhere either side could claim a forum.

Young lawyers were sent wherever bodies were needed to
shepherd litigation through the courts. "It's terrible, *terrible*,"
fighting from the boondocks, getting only glimpses of the
larger war, says a young lawyer who had been introduced to the
takeover wars by deposing Sir James Goldsmith on his
Diamond International takeover. "You're working eighteen-
hour days, trying to write creative, lawyerly briefs at four in the
morning, racing to courthouses all over the country to file
something by the deadline. And all the time you know that
what you're doing is just obstructionary stuff. It probably won't
determine the outcome."

At the highest levels—Fred Hartley and Claude Brinegar—it
had been determined that Unocal would not relinquish control
to Wall Street, nor would the war be lost for lack of coordination and information exchange. At the heart of communications were the morning and afternoon conference calls at 10:00
A.M. and 4:00 P.M. New York time, a device Sachs had found
useful in the Marathon deal where it was christened "the four
o'clock follies." Brinegar and Snyder were usually the anchor-
men. At 7:00 A.M. Los Angeles time, a secretary connected all
the offices for the call and ran down the names for a sign-in:
"Ted Levine and Lou Cohen here in Washington. . . . Art Long
and John Cornwell here in New York. . . . Gil Sparks here in
Wilmington. . . . Andy Bogen at Gibson, Dunn in L. A."

The troops were many. The strategy was in the hands of a few—the privileged handful of insiders who met in the boiler room to devise the game plans that would win or lose the war. "Every idea had to meet the litmus test of judgment of each member of the team," says Sachs. "There was no monopoly on bright ideas." With deal makers like Friedman and Sachs in the room, the strategies that emerged from the team came from deep in the deal flow. There could be no one grand plan. Strategies were revised daily, hourly, in response to the unpredictable events that flowed in from the other side. "Before Pickens surfaced with his tender offer," says Goldman's Friedman, "we had made an inventory of all the possible steps that he could take, and all the rebuttal steps we could take. Column A. Column B. But, like chess, there are only so many moves you can think ahead." Friedman, with Sachs and Dillon Read's Fritz Hobbs, was focusing on the financial evaluations that had to underlie Unocal's response to Pickens's tender offer. Perhaps as important were the psychological evaluations of the enemy that went on steadily in the war rooms and hotel rooms that were the boundaries of the team's world. It was a dimension in which Sachs, who had been introduced to strategic thinking by Henry Kissinger as an undergraduate government major a Harvard, reveled. Facing Pickens's two-pronged attack, the one thing they did not do was search for a white knight. "We thought Unocal was the best white knight for Unocal," says Friedman. The team tried to prioritize. What's most important to stop—the tender offer or the proxy fight? They were both critical and intertwined. For the first few weeks, the tender offer dominated thinking.

There was broad consensus that the proxy fight must be won. "We couldn't allow Boone to get adjournment of the meeting. It might have given him time to elect his four nominees and have one-third of the board," Long declares, "then at the *next* annual meeting elect four more and gain control of the Unocal board. With two-thirds of the board, he would have effective control of the company and its assets. . . . If we elect our board one more year, with our *staggered* board, it would be *two* more years for Boone to gain control. And that would make it more difficult, I believe, for Boone to keep his financing in place."

Did Pickens have the resources to hang in there for two years, with his huge investment tied up, paying interest? When he didn't have the cash flow of the company to service it? "He might have the resources to hang in," says Fritz Hobbs, "but I don't think he has the *patience*. He has other things on his agenda." Hobbs believed the proxy fight, as a shareholder referendum on Pickens's plans for the company, was "*the* most important." A two-year wait would strip Pickens of his momentum, sharply reduce his staying power and stamina, Sachs believed. "There's a dramatic difference in terms of uncertainty—questions of falling oil prices, interest rates, Unocal diluting him down. But it's not even a difference of interest rates. It's that when you have an investment so *big* it lacks liquidity, yet too *small* to give you control, it's a dangerous situation.

"But if he buys 51 percent of the stock, the proxy fight is a nonissue," said Sachs, raising the specter of the tender offer, as he made a presentation to the board at a ten-hour marathon meeting on Saturday, April 13. The length of those meetings would play well with the judges in Delaware, who would see them as proof of the board's "due diligence" in exercising the Business Judgment Rule. They might lose the company while they focused on the proxy fight, he warned. Examining the recent history of takeover wars, Sachs and Friedman had looked at Pickens's proxy fight with Gulf and concluded, "Gulf focused so much on the proxy fight they didn't realize it was a big cloak hiding a takeover. Don't forget Newton's first law: large companies tend to remain at rest. We *have* to take care of the takeover threat." Rumors that Pickens was getting ready to tender for 80 percent of Unocal's shares had reached the war room. "We don't know what's bluff," says Sachs. "But say this offer goes forward and you guys do nothing. The day the offer closes, 80 percent of your stock gets tendered to Boone Pickens. He buys 52 percent. All that other stock is sitting there saying, 'Hey, what about me?' He comes back next day and does a junk-bond-financed exchange offer for the balance. The market says, 'The ball game's over,' and he gets 90 percent, and he throws the whole board out and owns the company." Sachs reminded them, "If he gets across 90 percent, he can do a 'short form' Delaware merger without the consent of the board—and after that you guys are in Paducah! A staggered board is useless at that point. So you *have* to stop step one." The tender offer.

But how?

After every deal there is debate over what the most important and decisive piece of strategy was. In Unocal, it unquestionably was Unocal's response to the tender offer. Introduced jointly by Hobbs and Sachs, it became one of the most controversial acts of the 1985 campaigns and a landmark in takeover law. On April 17, Unocal made its riposte to Pickens's tender offer in the form of an offer to buy back up to half of Unocal's shares—approximately 80 million shares to be bought as the back end after Pickens's tender. A self-tender. At a price far, far higher than Pickens's $54. The self-tender would require Unocal to take on more than $5.8 billion of new debt, a painful act for Fred Hartley. Sachs knew that "he did not want to leverage up this company. Fred does *not* like exchanging equity for debt."

The offer was for $72 per share, a price so high it inspired Drexel's John Sorte to brand it "overkill." The number was arrived at after days of constant consultation by the investment bankers with their own arbs in New York, Goldman's Bob Freeman and Bob Rubin and Dillon Read's Alan Curtis. "We asked them to give up their Saturdays and Little League baseball—Freeman was the coach!—because it was incredibly important," says Steve Friedman. "They spend all their time living with these things—how much stock will we get if we self-tender? How would an arb act? Can we count on the greed factor?" The arbs from the two firms met in New York, again and again, resulting in a synergy that was the product of the Goldman and Dillon Read collaboration on the deal. The air was electric with competitiveness and tension. The two firms ran their evaluations separately, giving Unocal a double opinion. But their findings and strategies were almost always closely aligned. "They pulled their weight," says Sachs. "We felt that the two firms worked together better than anyone had ever experienced in a co-managed situation. In this deal we acted as one firm." It confirmed Hobbs's conviction that, though a boutique, Dillon Read was indeed in the same game as Goldman Sachs.

Hobbs had been waiting for a year to try it out. In his playing with "what ifs" at Dillon Read's offices in New York in the first weeks, Hobbs kept coming back to an idea he had developed a year earlier for a client. He had discussed it with Sachs on the flight to Los Angeles April 8. It was a leveraged buyout concept that had never worked out. But it might work for Unocal. The heart of the concept was a self-tender—an offer by Unocal to buy X millions of its own shares. You'd let Pickens buy his shares on the front end, and even gain a controlling 51 percent. But the company would come in at the back end and make a very high premium offer for the rest of the shares, loading the company with debt to buy them back. But here was the beauty of it. Shares that are bought back by the company are canceled. They don't exist anymore. Pickens's 51 percent would become 100 percent of Unocal's outstanding shares. All the new debt would be his. "The theory went that Pickens's buying 36 percent in his tender would trigger the purchase by the company of its remaining stock at $72, resulting in an effective blended cost to Pickens of $64.50 a share," Sachs explains. "The borrowings by Pickens and the borrowings by the company equate to that blended price." The price would be too high, it was hoped, to make the deal profitable to Pickens. And it would leave him carrying a massive burden of debt. Added to the billions of debt he'd have to assume to buy the shares at the front end, his financial resources would be stretched too far. In theory. But Hobbs did not underestimate Boone Pickens. With a self-tender for the back end, you'd be inviting Boone to buy the company. It was high risk, as were Pickens's bids for the giant oil companies. But as Sachs said, "Often the boldest and most effective strategies are high risk."

The strategy of self-tender was finally presented by Hobbs and Sachs directly to Hartley in the boiler room. "In that little shit-hole room," Hobbs recalls, "Hartley asked with interest, 'Who thought up that idea?' It was the only compliment I heard him give." By that time, input from the team had carried the idea so far from its genesis on the flight west that Hobbs did not feel sufficient pride of ownership to speak up and claim it as his own, and there would never be consensus.

A self-tender was chosen as the course of action. And Unocal went out to borrow money from the banks, planning to make a cash offer. But, like Pickens, Unocal found itself cut off by the banks. "The banks should be held up by their thumbs," said Hobbs, as the team watched efforts to "go out and get a bank line," as Goldman had been urging, fail. Even Unocal's clout could not transcend fear of the raider. "We went to two of the biggest banks in the country to raise cash, and they turned us down," says Hobbs. "The fact is that none of the banks would lend to any company that might be owned by Boone Pickens," says a team member.

Unocal would now be forced to create its own securities, an "indenture"—a piece of paper Unocal would issue to its share-holders in exchange for tendered shares. Ricardo Mestres, the Sullivan & Cromwell lawyer who became known as "Mr. Inden-ture," constructed a document so elegant that rejection by the banks became a blessing. For into the indenture could be woven the controls and the protections of Unocal shareholders and the company's assets and cash flow that would never have been achieved in the conditions of a bank loan. Above all, the indenture would put "our customer first in line," says Hobbs. Hartley might hate $5.8 billion new debt, but at least Unocal's would be the senior debt, Pickens's the junior, placing anyone who held the indenture above those who held Pickens's junk bonds in getting satisfaction of their claims, if it came to that. For the entire assets of Unocal's single operating subsidiary, and the source of 100 percent of its cash flow, the Union Oil Company of California, would be pledged as collateral. As he watched Dillon Read's Frank Murray help Mestres fashion a document that combined boldness with impervious rings of protection, Hobbs marveled, "Very, very dicy work."

"It was a critical decision to make our own debt senior," says

Steve Friedman. He personally doubted, though, that the junk-bond commiting group would hold together. "I don't think he had any chance of taking that 51 percent and having that junk-bond financing hold up. I don't think those people had done any real credit analysis when they signed their commitment letters or knew how much debt was ahead of them. I think they were a bunch of people who would say, 'I'm selling my name for three-quarters of a point. I'll never have to put my money up. What's the last company Pickens took control of?' If every time you'd followed the Pied Piper you'd found a basket of money at your doorstep, and he came again and said, 'Follow me' . . ." If they did have to pay up under these circumstances, Friedman believed many would collapse.

The two strategies—the high cost of acquiring the whole company and the senior debt—were the deterrents that stood between an independent Unocal and Pickens in the chairman's seat. It was consummate brinkmanship. Running their "shadow tender"—or "phony tender," as Pickens called it—conditioned on Pickens completing his first held the risk that Pickens could "break through the barricades we've erected by raising more financing from Drexel and doing an offer for 80 percent-plus," speculated Sachs and Friedman. "If it was *that* big, he might attract enough stock to squeeze down the amount tendered to us, and then we wouldn't have raised his cost above the 'choke point.' " And there was concern that shareholders saw the conditional offer as a defensive gimmick to defeat Pickens rather than a serious offer to buy stock. "We finally arrived at the judgment that unless we were willing to buy some stock *unconditionally*, not wait until he bought, we ran a substantial risk of not getting enough stock to stop him." Friedman argued for strengthening the self-tender. "We knew Pickens could say, 'Yes, they have something that's better, but you're not going to get it.' We have to convince them that they *would* get it if they came to us. We had to have credibility. We *had* to buy a certain amount of stock."

They had a "nonfrivolous novelty" at hand. Embedded in an indenture document so exquisitely complex that Mestres may be the only one who fully understood it was a provision that was overlooked, at first, while focus was on "the bizarre conditional aspects of our tender," says Sachs. Unocal had the option of altering its offer to exclude Boone Pickens from the $72 company offer. It was there, in the small print. And it held the option to go unconditional on any or all of Unocal's shares.

The self-tender was revised, and it reemerged as an unconditional offer—a *guarantee* to buy 50 million shares. And a daring wrinkle was added to the offer, an element that would make it a killer to Pickens if it worked, a disaster if it didn't. They would exclude T. Boone Pickens, Unocal's largest shareholder, from the offer. Like the self-tender itself, there probably never had been a consensus on who originated the idea. But Sachs says, "The whole idea about excluding Mesa from the self-tender was an idea we and Mestress originally had," a financially driven idea that had sparked "tremendous discussion and dispute."

"It drove an ironic wedge between Pickens and his constituency—he wants to get in the tender offer, and they would just as soon see him excluded," Sachs smiled. And excluding Pickens from the tender offer hurt him in the proxy fight because voting for Pickens's economic package would not be in the best interests of shareholders. But fiduciaries found it attractive. With Pickens out of the proration pool, there was more for them. It forced Pickens into the confusing position of encouraging shareholders to tender to Unocal's offer, rather than his own, while urging them to vote for him on the proxy issue—the delay of the annual meeting.

"There was risk," Sachs admits. "It had never been tested. The closest had been Phillips where Icahn was excluded from the poison pill. We just didn't know. We thought the SEC was a greater worry than Delaware." No matter how daring, the exclusionary self-tender was still a reaction, a defensive move, some in the war rooms worried. There was a dangerous tendency, they feared, to focus on defensive tactics. "A Maginot Line complex builds up around shark repellents. Managements often believe what they want to believe," Friedman and Sachs emphasized. "The key to winning the fight is *positive* steps, creating *value* rather than just 'supporting your management.' " The next step in Unocal's restructuring was just such a move: the creation of a Master Limited Partnership (MLP). They would put 45 percent of Unocal's oil reserves into the partnership, with 5 percent to be sold to the public. The Partnership sent profits directly to shareholders and avoided double taxation, corporate and individual. Units of the partnership would be distributed to shareholders as a dividend, a gift to the shareholders that would make all of Unocal's stock look good. "We want to use the MLP to close the gap between the stock price and liquidation value. If we can raise the price of the stock in the market with this device, it's going to be very helpful in the proxy contest," Sachs argued in the war room. In urging its creation, they drew on deep experience in the deal flow; they had just finished creating a large MLP for ENSERCH.

Supporting the strategy, Dillon Read's Fritz Hobbs expanded, "The partnership focuses on the worth of the assets. The idea is that if the investment community says, 'Gee, this part is worth *this* much, the rest is worth that much more.' It's a showcase for the company's larger value." The Master Limited Partnership emerged as a device to win the votes of the institutional investors in the proxy fight, Pickens's constituency—the group Friedman and Sachs had identified as "in the middle of the spectrum between the purely financial men like Boesky and the individual investor who is a more natural supporter of management—the fiduciary who's taking a longer view. You aren't going to win by just saying you're a nice guy. Arbs don't care; individuals don't need it. You win the centrists by creating value."

The success of the strategy would depend on how accurately they had read the institutional money managers' attitude toward T. Boone Pickens. Friedman had watched Pickens testify in Washington. "I thought he had a certain contempt for the people he was talking to, and in many cases it was justified. But a bright Washington person said to me, 'Jimmy Goldsmith is candid. He's in it for the bucks, and the quicker the better.' There is an almost irresistible wish to cloak what you're doing in some social purpose. If the guy had said, 'Hey, I'm a throwback to the aggressive, free-enterprise capitalism, laissez faire guys of last century,' okay. But when you start being treated adoringly and you're on the cover of *Time* magazine . . . I think you begin to believe your own public relations." Fred Hartley had begun calling Pickens the "pious piranha" when they discovered, as Friedman says with a chuckle, "that there was probably no one who had erected a more fantastic web of shark repellents than Pickens. Talk about perks and bonuses!" Snyder concurred. "I'll take my golden parachute off if I get a premium-to-market offer for Mesa," Pickens often said, claiming that his own corporate defenses were not for entrenchment and would never stand in the way of a takeover bid for Mesa itself if it was in the interests of Mesa's shareholders. "Pickens is a highwayman masquerading as Robin Hood," Friedman retorted. "It's our job to expose him." If they had read the money managers correctly, "We thought many of them had the sense that Pickens had gone too far—his mantle was frayed." Says Sachs, "We had this feeling that if you could give the institutions an excuse to support the company—the value in the MLP—that, coupled with the disenchantment, we could win."

The Master Limited Partnership was another arrow in Unocal's swelling quiver of counterattacks as both sides prepared for the first decisive court tests of their strategies. "We called it 'the soft landing,' a vehicle to kick the stock price up after the self-tender and keep it from plummeting so that Pickens could steal it at the back end," says Sachs. They all knew that the effect of Unocal's exclusionary self-tender, if it was permitted by the courts, could be to kill Pickens's bid and send the stock skidding. But Pickens did not intend to be excluded. In devising the strategy, the Unocal team had tried to put themselves in Pickens's shoes in Amarillo and imagine his reaction. "We didn't think he'd like what he saw. We knew we'd see him in court on that one," says Sachs. And of course they did. Cries of "discrimination" and "exclusionary self-tender" went up from the Pickens camp; court tests were scheduled in a Los Angeles federal and a Delaware state court for late April. The Delaware courts and the SEC would, the Unocal team believed, be the self-tender's severest tests.

They had all combed the Williams Act to see if an exclusionary self-tender was legal. Remarkably, "self-tender rules are silent on the point," said Peter Sachs. "Baloney!" was the response of Gregg A. Jarrell, the SEC's chief economist, who was shocked by Unocal's act when it was revealed in mid-April. "You've got a federal statute out there that precludes it. It is clearly inconsistent with the Williams Act." Called personally by Skadden Arps's Mike Mitchell to ask the SEC to intervene on Pickens's behalf, Jarrell challenged, "It's long been an interpretation of the Williams Act that you *can't* make these kinds of discriminatory tender offers or self-tender offers. The problem is that it isn't actually a written rule. It's an interpretation of a bunch of rules. A very *solid* interpretation." On two prior occasions the SEC had proposed rules that would prevent exclusionary self-tender, and both times withdrawn the proposals.

Jarrell was the spearhead of a new activism within the SEC. With Jarrell's prodding, the SEC had filed a "friend of the court" brief in the Household case in Delaware. Jarrell had thrust himself to the front lines of the 1984 battle between Carter Hawley Hale and the Limited. He was eager to take on Unocal's exclusionary tender. "The things I consistently object to are unilateral actions by management that are not in the shareholders' interest," says Jarrell. A disarmingly boyish-looking, high-energy thirty-three-year-old who set the University of Chicago Graduate School of Business record for shortest time to get a PhD, he was a professor at the University of Rochester at twenty-five, junior colleague there of Michael Jensen, and a member of the University of Chicago's influential "club" of economists whose laissez faire writings and teachings provide the theoretical underpinning for the Reagan administration's economic policies. Philosophical sons of Adam Smith, their scholarly advocacy of free markets gives credibility to takeovers.

Jarrell is the antithesis of the cautious bureaucrat. "Unlike the lifers, the professional economists who come on board here owe their primary duty to the profession," says Jarrell. "Lawyers come in and say, 'Who's my boss? What will advance my boss's interests?' We come in and say, 'Who's my boss? My boss is getting published in academic journals. My boss is Nobel laureate George Stigler, my professor at the University of Chicago. And Milton Friedman.' People like George and Milton say, 'Go, have a ball. Don't stay more than two years, but go. Don't get frustrated, and pick your battles carefully.' It's a badge of honor for us to get fired and thrown out on our ear because we won't take a certain position. Our staff is filled with that kind of independent people."

Hired because his views matched the ideology of the Reagan administration, Jarrell says, "Most regulations hurt more people than they help. They thrive because the beneficiaries of the regulations are very effective politically. They have concentrated interests, well organized and well represented in Washington. Agencies stay in business by knowing where those interests are, and we are flying in the face of that."

In Carter Hawley Hale, "the SEC went in in a new role," says Jarrell, who had unsheathed his sword against the retail giant in the interests of shareholders. "Carter Hawley was being attacked by Limited Inc., and defended itself by a massive buyback of stock which the SEC contended should have been called a tender offer. They snubbed their nose at the SEC and went out and bought the stock brazenly in four hours. I contended that it was a front-end-loaded, quick self-tender that beat the hell out of the individual shareholders, because, when the arbs and the smart money saw that with every hour of the buyback Limited's takeover deal was dying, they dumped their stock and the stock price fell. The average investor didn't even learn about it until next day in the *Wall Street Journal*. The lawyers who pulled it off were Joe Flom and his boys at Skadden Arps. They did it brilliantly. Goldman Sachs was their investment banker. Marty Lipton and Felix Rohatyn represented Limited. The SEC came in and asked for a preliminary injunction to stop everything.

"We had a meeting with Joe Flom and Goldman at the SEC building in Washington on a weekend. I wrote a declaration that weekend, and Judge Tashima read it in federal court in Los Angeles, and said, in effect, 'I've been influenced by

Jarrell's declaration.' " For Jarrell, it was an exhilarating moment. "All of a sudden this uppity academic kid was in the middle of the thing, and Lipton and Flom were freaked out. We got a preliminary injunction, and an order to be back in court in five days. Now we had about five or six guys eating donuts and living in this ratty motel, preparing the SEC's brief.

"As we went back before Tashima, the courtroom was packed. Tashima had said earlier that he might bring me to the stand, and I was in the back of the courtroom absolutely terrified. Six feet away from me was Joe Flom sitting next to Philip Hawley. Hawley sat there and listened to that argument, and I just watched him. I never felt so sorry for an individual in my life. That man was dying a thousand deaths. He was an older guy, but very attractive. Fit. The model of success. But you could see where he'd been crying, and the bags under his eyes where he'd been up all night. You could see this took eight years off his life. Here he's worked all his life. People are trying to take over his company, claim it's undervalued. He tries to defend himself and the government comes in with this young whippersnapper, Jarrell. What the hell's going on here? What are these people doing in my store?"

The judge listened to both arguments, went back into his chambers, came out and raised his gavel. "When he hit his gavel and ruled, Mr. Hawley would be either a winner or a loser," Jarrell said. "The judge's gavel went up. I couldn't take my eyes off Hawley. He had hold of Joe Flom's hand as that gavel went down—the judge was a master at keeping you in suspense—and all of a sudden he said, 'We rule with the defendants and against the SEC.' Hawley had won. He had absolutely won. He just went 'Aaaaahhhh' and closed his eyes and looked up. Then he turned around and he hugged Joe Flom, hugged him as hard as he could. It was just him and his investment banker."

Jarrell was deeply affected. "As an academic you're divorced from the emotional side. You're looking at data, you're not involved in the individual case. And you often fall into using a shorthand of 'entrenched, inefficient management.' But when I was watching that scene, and saw the color of Hawley's face, his jaw muscles clenching and unclenching, I felt such compassion.

I could feel how painful the whole process must be. I saw that, for him, this was a referendum on his life effort. Since that day, I have not used, without qualification, the phrase 'entrenched, inefficient management.' "

Jarrell could feel the activist's energies rising again as he argued for intervening against Unocal's exclusionary self-tender. "The SEC threatened to sue us, but twice we got them to back off," says Peter Sachs. Overruling Jarrell, the commission had decided this was not the time or place to fight.

Timing was now everything. And the clock was ticking in Unocal's favor. "The timing rules for self-tenders are shorter than for third-party tenders like Pickens's," says Sachs. "Even though Pickens had launched his tender on April 8, and Unocal's self-tender was launched on April 17, ours would expire three days ahead of his, on April 30; his closed on Friday, May 3. People would have to decide whether to tender to the company several days before Pickens would be able to buy. We seized on it early and it gave us a great advantage. If Pickens is promising you something that's pretty good, and I'm promising you something that's terrific, but you've got to come to me first, and if I can hold you to your commitment, he's never going to get a sniff of your stock. . . . We had to be first. We had to be able to lock you up," Sachs said. That tiny envelope of time would force shareholders to act, or risk losing the $72 offer. "If there was one absolute article of faith," says Sachs, "it was that our tender had to close before his, and it had to be filled with stock locked in, prior to his time to buy. Because that would stop his tender offer."

◆　◆　◆

FOR two consecutive Easters and birthdays, Juanita Crowley had been in Los Angeles working on deals. The special occasions helped her remember events that began to merge after having been sent to so many takeover battles in California. "Boone Pickens's tender offer—April 8, my birthday. Last Easter, writing a brief for Carter Hawley Hale in their fight against The Limited. This Easter, writing a brief for Unocal." She'd been in California in 1983, defending Kaiser Steel as it fell to the Frates group, which was about to launch a bid for

Kaiser Steel's sibling, Kaiser Aluminum; and again last August, working for Irwin Jacobs in the Disney fight.

A partner in Unocal's Washington law firm, Wilmer, Cutler & Pickering, she had been sent, as before, to coordinate the deposition-taking phase of "discovery," the fact finding that equips lawyers to prepare their briefs and arguments for court. Discovery, at first, was for the Security Pacific lawsuit, but it was swiftly expanded and intensified as lawsuits proliferated, and the courts ordered "accelerated discovery" to accommodate an ever-tightening time frame. Her equal number at Unocal was also a woman lawyer, Jasmina "Jazz" Theodore, Snyder's assistant. But there are few women on the front line. In responding to the question "Why aren't there more women in the takeover game?" First Boston's Joe Perella explained, "We're actively looking, searching. But you won't find any women leaders in the merger business. It's very intense and demanding, and it appears to be more demanding of their personal time than they perhaps are prepared to give." Forthright, good-humored, and articulate, with the sporty look of a young woman who might have been captain of her school's field hockey team, Crowley has come to terms with the lifestyle. Grabbing her briefcase and packing a suitcase to rejoin the troops at the front, she said, "I couldn't do this if my husband, who's a lawyer, didn't support it. He even sends me solution for my contact lenses because he knows I never have time to shop."

Unocal had begun for Crowley on a midafternoon of the week following Saint Patrick's Day. With Wilmer Cutler heavily involved in Unocal, she had watched the action build as she cleaned up some projects, any of which could be back-burnered. "I'd skipped the firm lunch to watch Georgetown play the opening round of the NCAA basketball tournament. When I got back, an associate came into my office and said, 'Why aren't you on the Unocal team?'" She responded, "No one ever asked me," and was on an airplane next morning with associate Jim Robertson. "Jim and I got on a plane March 28 and with the exception of two weekends, I didn't get back to Washington again until May 17." Jazz Theodore invited her over for Easter, but that was broken up by a call that Pickens was launching his tender offer. Booking into the Sheraton Grande in Los Angeles, her days began with the 7:00 A.M. conference call in Sam Snyder's office. "We'd stay until 8:00 or 8:15, as long as it was useful to us, then go over to Gibson, Dunn's law office, about five blocks away up two huge hills. And Unocal sits on a hill. So with two big litigation bags, we *drove*." Gibson, Dunn's principal lawyer on Unocal, Andrew E. Bogen, was usually in the war room at Unocal; "He was omnipresent," Sam Snyder says. But there were always teams of lawyers back in the law offices, working on brief writing, issue development, deposition lists. "There were many nights when we worked so late I'd get back to the Sheraton Grande too late for room service. There were all-night sessions preceding every brief. But about a quarter of the nights, people would be done by seven or eight and we'd eat at the usual assortment of Chinese, Japanese, and Italian restaurants. We saw two Dodgers games. The previous year was the Olympics, but I didn't go. I was offered tickets to things like Graeco-Roman wrestling. . . ."

In the trenches, Crowley was in touch with a human dimension of takeover those closeted in the war rooms rarely saw. "If we'd been working in the Gibson, Dunn offices all the time, we might have isolated the emotion. We might have been able to argue in court without feeling. But when you go into the Unocal building every morning, and ride up the elevators, you sense it. It's a big company, but they know a corporate fight is going on. They feel threatened. And we worked closely with Unocal employees who were to give depositions. Depositions are frightening, especially for people who are not members of the board or executives, who go through it a lot. You spend a lot of time preparing your witnesses, you ask questions that are likely to be asked. You want to know what their insecurities are, what they're worried about. It is a very personal process."

In this intimate contact with employees' anxieties, Crowley touched the most emotional issue of takeovers and one of the disquieting issues of industrial America—the human damage done by the dislocation and uncertainty of change, by the "major restructuring and redeployment of assets required by changes in technology and consumer preferences," as pro-

takeover economist Michael Jensen has described them. The
agonies hit, too, at the executive level. Crowley had been in the
courtroom when the same judge who would hear the Unocal
case made the decisive ruling in favor of Carter Hawley Hale
that saved that company from takeover by Limited the previous
summer. She had witnessed the event that had so powerfully
moved the SEC's Gregg Jarrell and awakened him to the pain
and emotion of takeovers as elegant economic theories from
the University of Chicago had not—the sight of Philip Hawley
streaming tears of relief, hugging Joe Flom for saving his
company.

Fear and uncertainty grew with distance from the war
rooms. Removed from the buzz that bounced off the elevator
walls and halls at headquarters, employees in Santa Paula, two
hours north of Los Angeles, hungrily scanned press releases
and bulletins as they were posted, and ripped open their pay
envelopes to read the messages Fred Hartley sent along with
their paychecks, decrying the damage of takeovers. With employees the second largest block of shareholders next to Pickens, they read the mountains of shareholder information that
poured out. They ordered and wore Boone-busters T-shirts
and tractor caps. Santa Paula did not rise up to cry collectively
for salvation as Bartlesville had; it did not have the cohesive-
ness of a company town.

And yet in Santa Paula attachment to the company was
strengthened by history and by direct, physical contact with the
black stuff that drives the world, a contact those who worked in
the freeway-wrapped Holiday Inn–style high-rise in downtown
Los Angeles did not have. Santa Paula is Union Oil's birthplace.
Employees work in the same quaint Victorian building in which
the company began. Employees climb stairs to offices that sit
above the oil museum. They work in high-ceilinged rooms
embellished with Victorian woodwork in which computers
share space with drawers of tightly rolled archival drilling and
production plans. Driving home after a day at the office, they
pass the oil seeps that still ooze like lava from a fault in the 10-
million-year-old Miocene formation in the hills behind Santa
Paula, blackening the roadside and reminding them of the

feverish, wildcatting days of strikes and gushers that gave rise to a great corporation and the California oil industry. "I admire Mr. Hartley so much. He's been telling us what happens when Boone Pickens comes through and how bad it is for our country," said secretary Barbara Mayfield, who had just ordered more Boone-busters T-shirts. She wore her T-shirt like a talisman and prayed she would have a job when it was all over.

◆   ◆   ◆

As the litigation grew, so did the "wish lists" of people both sides wanted to depose. "They were constantly taking Mr. Hartley's depositions," says Snyder. "It was part of the wear down. What they will destroy they will first make mad."

"You don't take Boone Pickens's deposition fifteen times just because you've thought up a new lawsuit," said Crowley. Deposition taking became a vast interwoven process in which coordination of information was vital. "You're talking time pressure. There were up to twenty depositions on any given day, often in three or four cities. The more lawsuits and the bigger the team, the more time you have to spend sharing information. If you have your Texas team down in Amarillo taking depositions from some of Pickens's people and they get some information in a deposition on Monday that could be useful to the deposition of a bank that's taking place in New York the next day, you have to be sure the information gets from Amarillo to New York."

Nita Crowley was the switching station. "The depositions were available to us almost instantly. They were put onto a computer disk by court reporters, transmitted by modem, and were on-line to us in a couple of hours. I read every deposition instantly. I'd know who was deposing next day and would call those lawyers to tell them what lawyer X had got in Amarillo, or whatever could help them." With the burgeoning information flow threatening to overload even her seasoned mind, Crowley had to constantly hold the larger goal before her: to write a brief that would convince the judge of Unocal's points. As the Security Pacific suit, the first shot fired, folded into more urgent issues before the courts, the first brief was being prepared for an April 25 hearing before Judge Wallace Tashima, in the central district federal court. The brief was due April 18.

For Crowley, the 7:00 A.M. conference call became a vital part of the sophisticated communications network created to turn back T. Boone Pickens. "Nothing could be isolated. We couldn't make litigation judgments about how we wanted Judge Tashima to rule unless we knew what Lou Cohen found out at the SEC yesterday, or what Artie Long could tell us about the proxy contest. Jim and I would attend these 7:00 A.M. calls in Sam Snyder's office. There would be ten or twelve people in there for up to two hours, a lot of Type-A personalities on the phone, all brainstorming, and there were some inefficiencies. But they weren't really inefficiencies. You had to have that information flow.

"Everything is ultimately working toward one result—to win," said Crowley. One day, after they had filed their brief, a gem of information came in from Texas. "It was one of the turning points on the legal side," said Snyder. "We learned that Pickens made a speech April 19 in Galveston to a group of lawyers at a bar meeting of some sort. Susman, the Texas law firm working with us on Unocal, sent a paralegal to hear the speech. It had been taped, sent to Susman's law offices in Houston, and transcribed." Hearing it, the lawyers called Crowley: "I think this will be of interest to you." It was dynamite. "Pickens had essentially talked about destruction of files as a standard practice." What words to have said to a roomful of lawyers: "What I'll do on anything that is . . . that I feel should not . . . we, we, we have a shredder in my secretary's office and I shred anything that is not going to be of any use. . . ." It could strengthen the credibility of their "false and misleading" charges against Pickens's 13D material to be argued in Tashima's court April 25. Back in Washington for one of two brief weekend visits with her husband when the call came in from Houston, she and her colleagues integrated what they hoped would be an incriminating weapon against Pickens into their brief, and flew back to California.

❖   ❖   ❖

As Ricardo Mestres's indenture document was structured around Unocal's self-tender and new debt "to build a ring fence around Unocal's assets and cash flow," Snyder was trying to tighten the ring around Pickens.

"The SEC had begun a formal investigation of his activities and another formal investigation into insider trading," says Snyder. "We were also proceeding with the feds to restrict junk bonds—we had instituted formal proceedings before the Federal Reserve Board. Within a week of the Security Pacific lawsuit, it was disclosed that the Texas Bank of Commerce, of which Pickens was a director, was in trouble with loans to some of its directors. Moving on that, we made sure regulators knew about it. The cumulative effect was building." Pressure on his financing was so bad that Pickens complained to a hearing of the Judiciary Subcommittee in Washington in late April that his banks were being cut off.

And the harassment Pickens hated most had begun again. "They hired private investigator Jules Kroll in New York to try to dig up dirt about me," Pickens complained. "They'd bother my family and friends, ask them intimate questions about me and Bea. They called a former employee and said, 'Do you want to spill your guts about Pickens?' " Pickens had endured it "on every deal since Cities Service," as hiring private eyes had become a basic corporate tactic against raiders. In the Phillips deal, Pickens had demanded $10 million damages and got an injunction against Kroll's man, Bill Kish, in an Amarillo court, charging "a well-orchestrated and concerted campaign of harassment and attempts at intimidation aimed to destroy the reputation of Plaintiffs through a variety of surreptitious acts, including . . . attempts to determine the identity, background, and whereabouts of close relatives and family members of Plaintiff Pickens in order to further harass and intimidate Pickens, and making knowingly false statements concerning both the business and personal habits and conduct of Plaintiff . . . such an unreasonable intrusion into his private life that has no other purpose than to inflict mental distress, outraging the normal and ordinary sensibilities of society." But a Delaware judge had given the opinion that "very frankly, I can't see where anybody is sacrosanct in an investigation. I don't know that anybody ought to be stopped from calling somebody else up and saying, 'Will you talk to me?' " Jules Kroll, in effect, came with the territory. And the spying, to Pickens's distress, continued.

Adding to the pressure, Kurt Wulff gave his deposition on April 23, just two days before the hearing before Judge Tashima. Unocal lawyers, through their questions, insinuated a premeditated conspiracy between Pickens and Wulff's firm, Donaldson Lufkin & Jenrette, in Pickens's swift and secret acquisition of the huge block of Unocal stock that had preceded his tender offer. "Do you know anything about the source of the 6.7 million shares of Unocal stock that Mesa bought through Jefferies or from Jefferies on March 27?" lawyers demanded. They had searched for connections with Boesky, Jacobs, and Icahn in the genesis of the Unocal takeover attempt. Wulff refused to name the institutions who had expressed support for his candidacy for a seat on the Unocal board, saying, "I am prepared to bear any of the consequences." One of them was the loss of business. He would later reveal in his July 2 letter, entitled "Blackball," that Unocal had blackballed Donaldson Lufkin from its usual, profitable role in the underwriting group that would bring Unocal's new Master Limited Partnership to market.

As the ring tightened and his resources were stretched ever thinner, the Pickens legend, as well as hundreds of millions of investment dollars, were at stake.

Mesa's responses emanated from their war rooms at Skadden Arps's New York offices. "Mesa and Baker & Botts people, the whole cast, *lived* in our office in New York. They took over every conference room on this floor. For *weeks,*" says Fin Fogg, who was enjoying being back in a Pickens deal, after being sidelined in Phillips. He relished the ceremonial occasions that pulled everybody together. "One night, after Mesa made its tender offer but before the final court decisions, Boone was coming in and we planned a big dinner for everybody working on the deal, Kekst, Carter, Mesa, Baker & Botts people. Boone gave a talk. It was terrific. Then we all went back to the war rooms after dinner."

The Unocal team was feeling the pressure, too. They were playing the endgame. Down to the last decisive moves. The proxy fight. The litigation. But the team never stopped running the "what ifs." They never took anything for granted and flayed themselves with "worst case" scenarios. What if we used a poison pill? What if we lose in federal or state court? Or both? Hobbs was still talking up the idea of Unocal buying Mesa. Goldman was still evangelizing the Master Limited Partnership. Encapsulated in a Union corporate jet en route to California during the last wave of litigation, the "what ifs" were regurgitated to a point where Fritz Hobbs felt like punching out a window. You could escape from the boiler room when you couldn't stand it anymore. "But here you can't get away from it." With "the bonsai squad"—Sachs, Friedman, David Luschen, Mestres, and Doug Pitts, Dillon Read's senior vice-president of corporate finance—munching "god-awful sandwiches," this was the pressure of the boiler room intensified to the point of explosion. "Stale food spread everywhere. You're feeling whipped. Five hours of talking. The Socratic Mr. Friedman chewing on it and chewing on it. Oh, my God! You don't get anywhere," Hobbs grumbled to himself. Yet he would remember that flight as one of the classic moments of Unocal.

◆　◆　◆

CAL Crary, Bear Stearns's litigation analyst, was in Judge Tashima's courtroom on April 25. The deal was coming down to the wire, and as the institutions dropped out, leaving the final risk and profit to the arbs, Bear Stearns's large arbitrage position was at its greatest risk. The federal court in Los Angeles would rule on both Pickens's requested delay in the annual meeting, and the claim and counterclaim by Unocal and Pickens that both had filed "false and misleading" 13D's and proxy materials. Pickens's exclusion from the tender offer would be tested in the same court after the weekend, on Monday. That same day a major opinion would come down from the Delaware chancery court on the same issue. Crary hoped the judge would grant Pickens his sixty-day delay of the annual meeting. "The more pressure you can put on Unocal, the higher the eventual value of the takeover or recapitalization," his colleague Nancy Havens-Hasty had said.

Nita Crowley knew this courtroom. She had been in the same room, before the same judge, at almost precisely the same time the previous year playing the same role for Carter Hawley Hale. "He's been around the barn before in a big takeover," she said, relieved. "He was stellar. Understood the issues in a very practical way." Her colleague Jim Robertson would do the argument. She would do "second-chair arguing," sitting beside him as a second brain, giving him ideas as the hearing unfolded. Skadden Arps's Mike Diamond argued for Mesa.

After hearing the arguments, Judge Tashima ruled from the bench. "We won two and they won one," Crowley said with relief. The judge had found both Pickens and Unocal guilty of "false and misleading information" in their printed filings, and Pickens's tender offer material flawed in its description of his financing and his intent for the company, if he achieved control. Reference to Pickens's Galveston speech in Unocal's brief had had telling effect. Reading Tashima's memorandum decision handed down next day, the Unocal team delighted in Page 11: "The fact that Mesa executives systematically destroyed notes and other documents together with habitual inability . . . to recall discussions concerning the subject of intent strongly suggests a studied effort by Mesa to conceal its true intent. . . ." Pickens won a partial victory; Tashima delayed the annual meeting two weeks, rather than the sixty days Pickens had wanted. He also routinely moved the closing of the two tender offers along to coincide with the changed date.

But suddenly the whole game almost came apart. "Following the oral argument, Tashima took a short break, then came back and ruled." As he read his oral opinion, Crowley was horrified at what she heard. Christ! "He had ruled from the bench in a way that flip-flopped the order of the annual meeting and the closing of his tender." He had ruled that Mesa's tender would close *before* the annual meeting. "I knew he hadn't intended that." He'd just confused the dates. But it was said. "And if Pickens's tender offer had closed before our annual meeting and he had taken down 36 percent of the shares, he could vote them with his own at the annual meeting, and vote in his slate of four board members." If it wasn't corrected instantly, it would destroy the strategy. It could lose the company.

Crowley drove her fist into Robertson's arm. They looked at each other with shocked recognition, and Robertson leaped to his feet to protest: "Your Honor, this ruling is a big disaster for us." Before he could complete his statement, says Crowley, "half the press runs out of the room with Jim's quote. Meanwhile, Tashima hears Jim, says 'Okay,' and changes it." The reporters filing their stories had not heard. The *Los Angeles Times* published it. But Tashima had restored the vital order. Unocal's self-tender would still close before Pickens's tender offer closed. The annual meeting would now be held May 13.

That Monday, Judge Tashima ruled on the exclusion of Pickens from Unocal's self-tender. He ruled for Unocal. Tashima could find no specific prohibition to an exclusionary offer in the Williams Act. "But at the same time that Tashima was ruling for Unocal, Judge Carolyn Berger was ruling just the opposite in Delaware," Crowley says. "She barred Unocal from proceeding with its exchange offer unless it included Pickens. They were applying different laws." Now it was Unocal 3, Pickens 2.

"It was never a federal matter. We *knew* it would have to be decided in a state court," said a confident Cal Crary, delighted that he had called every court decision accurately in the Delaware cases now before the chancery court. Judge Berger had issued a temporary restraining order against Unocal. That was good for the arbs. Unocal's counsel immediately asked for swift review by the Delaware Supreme Court. And then, in a move some see as "a slap in the face to Berger, who, don't forget, used to be a lawyer for Skadden Arps," two of the Supreme Court justices ordered Berger to reconsider her opinion in the context of broader issues. Judge Berger would rule on the matter again May 13, the day of the Unocal annual meeting that would decide the proxy fight. The proxy fight went into its fiercest phase.

The seven hundred Unocal employees trained by John Kelly weeks earlier now solicited proxies by phone from big boiler rooms set up with banks of telephones. Biographies of employees had been scanned, and, to add a personal touch, callers were assigned lists of shareholders from their hometowns or schools. "We used the Chinese army approach, throwing bodies at the problem," says Goldman's Peter Sachs. Big tacked-up sheets of paper recorded every contact. "The bankers got involved with the D. F. King guys in the campaign because the basic argument to the institutions was a financial one—that the self-tender and the Master Limited Partnership was doing more to create value than Pickens was," says Sachs. Fred Hartley hurled himself into the fight. "Every institutional investor got a call at the top level of the department. Anyone who was going to vote for Pickens got a call from Fred or Brinegar. Every director of the banks who managed Unocal money—and the CEO and directors of every corporation whose money those banks managed—got a call. Bankers Trust had 2.1 million Unocal shares; at the end of the day, they voted 1.6 million for the company. Pickens started calling these people, too, but he started too late," Sachs said. "Fund managers had already been called and told how to vote."

"They put up a good fight, a very heavy contest," marveled Nancy Havens-Hasty, whose colleagues in Bear Stearns's risk arbitrage department did not get called. "They know how we're going to vote," she said, knowing that more profit for the arbs' probably lay in Pickens getting a delay of the annual meeting. "Hartley put pressure on the pension fund managers—anywhere he could find people beholden to him, such as suppliers and banks, threatening to yank Unocal's pension funds from anyone who wasn't voting for him. We know he did. He'd call up a money manager who's managing Unocal's money and tell him, 'You want to vote with management and not for Pickens's proxy.' I'd never heard of it done before. He pierced the veil of the money managers."

Lobbying for the vote of the powerful California state pension funds, Hartley had lunch with Jesse Unruh in Los Angeles. "I may not be a real fan of Fred Hartley's, but we voted for management," Unruh says. "We thought Unocal was a good corporate citizen, and Hartley had done a pretty good job." Sam Snyder says, "Unruh helped us a lot. He called people for us and won us some votes." Pickens ran his campaign on both coasts, staging big meetings of institutional shareholders in both Los Angeles and New York. Pickens called Unruh, too, hoping Unruh would get the Council of Institutional Investors to swing to Pickens's camp. "It was Pickens's lieutenants who called me," chuckles Los Angeles County treasurer, Richard Dixon. "Jesse had five times as much Unocal stock as I had."

Results would not be known until after the annual meeting May 13. The campaign for votes would go on, unabated, until the moment the gavel went down. Although both sides predicted victory, press polls of large shareholders indicated that the tide was running for Fred Hartley.

But everyone knew that the next decision to come from the Delaware courts could well be determinant. Most litigation, in Nita Crowley's experience, is "a side show to the corporate strategy." But there was a collective sense that the issue of excluding Pickens from an offer made to all other shareholders would give litigation, in this case, "a bigger role than it has had in most cases in the last four or five years." In New York, Fin Fogg observed, "Now, just about everything is riding on Delaware," as several hundred heads turned eastward to the courthouse in Wilmington.

◆ ◆ ◆

Pickens was fighting the Unocal battle on the Hill as well, commuting all spring to testify at the series of Senate and Congressional subcommittee hearings exploring the need for legislation to control takeovers. He was in D.C. on May 2, the day after a Gregg Jarrell editorial piece most pleasing to T. Boone Pickens had appeared in the *Wall Street Journal*. It had revealed data that indicated that hostile takeovers were not sacrificing corporate research and development and long-term planning, as critics had claimed. Jarrell was back in his office May 2, having flown in the night before from Dallas and Chicago. Over morning coffee he was telling his deputy chief economist, Ken Lehn, of an experience the day before that had tickled him. On the flight from Chicago he'd sat beside an

executive with a major oil company. The man was reading
Jarrell's *Journal* story, punctuating his reading with groans and
mutterings of "Goddamn garbage!" Jarrell identified himself as
someone interested in takeovers, but not by name, and was
treated to a colorful indictment of the *Journal* piece, its theories, and the SEC's role. "The guy was feeling threatened. His
company was vulnerable, and, in fact, he was on his way to New
York to meet with takeover defense lawyers. When we got to
Washington, he asked me for my card, and I gave it to him. He
looked at the card, looked at the byline on the story, back at the
card, and said, 'Oh, my God, no! You're not going to hold this
against me at the SEC, are you?' " Lehn was just laughing over
Jarrell's punch line, "You bet your life I am," as the phone rang.

"Gregg, this is Boone Pickens, and I'd like to congratulate
you on that story in yesterday's *Journal*. I'm just delighted with
the study. You've done a real service to American shareholders." It was Pickens. Jarrell composed himself and teased his
caller, "I appreciate your kind words, Mr. Pickens, but don't get
the wrong idea. If this research had shown just the opposite,
we'd have written it up, and it would probably be Andy Sigler
calling to congratulate us." CEO of Champion International
Corp., Andrew Sigler was spokesman for the Business Roundtable, political action arm for the Fortune 200, which was taking
a bold antitakeover stance.

Pickens, who relishes a sense of humor, said, "I'd like to talk
to you some time about your views."

Jarrell was delighted, and said, "When can we meet?"

"Now's real good," said Pickens.

"Now? Well, where are you?" Jarrell asked.

"I'm outside and I guess I'm looking up at your window,"
Pickens replied.

Lehn and Jarrell crossed the room at a run and leaped up on
the sofa like kids to look out the window. Below was a long
black limousine. "Boone came right up, and stayed for two
hours talking to Ken and me."

With the bruising Pickens was taking from corporate America, Jarrell's words must have been music. "What a shame it is,
Mr. Pickens, that a businessman in your line of work has to

spend 50 percent of his time in Washington because so many people are trying to legislate you out of business," Jarrell told Pickens. "It's remarkable how much hostility can be created toward someone who is willing to pay shareholders a 60 percent premium for their stock." Jarrell explained his provocative theory. "I look at raiders as inventors who are responsible for creating large value. They're the ones with the ideas and with the money, and they put their money where their idea is. They say, 'I'm willing to gamble that I can make these resources worth 70 percent more than they're currently traded for under this management. To prove it, I'll pay a 60 percent premium. Does anybody want to top me? It's an open market. Let's go.' " Pickens was interested. "They're inventors creating information, new ideas, new structures of business," Jarrell went on. "With most inventions, we go out of our way to make sure the inventor gets the monopoly on his information. In takeovers, disclosure and regulatory delays assure that the person with the idea will have to tell everybody his idea; there is plenty of time for the target to defend, and for other bidders to bid the price up."

And Jarrell played racquetball, too. From now on, Pickens's trips to the Hill would combine a spin in Jarrell's yellow Corvette to the racquetball courts for a good talk and workout.

◆ ◆ ◆

APRIL 29. Unocal might be looking east to Delaware for deliverance. Robert O. Anderson was looking within. From the splendid art-filled executive offices on the fifty-first floor of his headquarters in the ARCO towers in downtown Los Angeles, sixty-nine-year-old chairman Bob Anderson took off the stained and battered cowboy hat he wears to work and glanced out his glass wall of windows. Across a formidable tangle of freeways, the Unocal building's twelve floors looked squat and flashy, a corporate signature that bespoke an oilman with little sense of the bravura. Compared to the sleek, soaring glass towers Bob Anderson had built for ARCO, Unocal looked like an airport motel. Within a few days, steamrollers would be laying a strip of black asphalt in the street that ran between Unocal's headquarters and the auditorium where the annual meeting would be held on May 13, sprucing up for the nation's press, who would be there for the showdown between Fred Hartley and T. Boone Pickens. Anderson had been watching the hostile siege across the street. It was not the kind of news Anderson intended ARCO to make. By the end of the day, ARCO, he hoped, would be immune to predation.

He had built ARCO over forty-five years, bootstrapping it up from a tiny refinery in New Mexico to the sixth-largest oil company in the United States—the twelfth-largest industrial corporation, by sales, on the Fortune 500. ARCO's assets reached a peak in 1983 of $22.9 billion. Able, like all great entrepreneurs, to ride comfortably with risk and debt, he had started with a borrowed $50,000, a stake he leveraged into a company with assets of $24 billion. Perhaps his comfort with debt came from his banker father, who pioneered loans to the oil industry, looking on "the inventory on nature's shelves" as good collateral. Anderson spent a quarter century as a wildcatting independent, focusing on exploration just as Pickens had done with Mesa. In fact, he says, "We run our company very much the way Pickens would see himself running a company if he were able to gain control of it. We are very much oil and gas producers." Aggressively merging and acquiring, Anderson merged Atlantic Refining in Philadelphia with Richfield Oil of Los Angeles in 1966—the same year ARCO made the sensational strike in Prudhoe Bay that made Alaska the core of the company. He filled in the geographic gaps in the mid-continent by acquiring Sinclair in 1969, a move that gave him gas stations from coast to coast. ARCO's self-service stations were pioneers of the breed.

Yet even with the fierce preoccupation it takes to build a huge integrated oil company, Anderson had managed to keep his scuffed boots firmly planted in several worlds. He was as comfortable meeting with European industrialists or addressing the Aspen Institute as he was flying to Ruidoso, New Mexico, with Joe Mims, the manager of his ranching empire, to negotiate a breeding program for his cattle herd. For beyond ARCO, Anderson is a working rancher whose sprawling southwestern ranches make him the nation's largest individual landowner. In the leather-and-longhorn setting of one of his hand-somely decorated ranch houses, an empty jeroboam of Château Lafite Rothschild signed by a group of friends—two ambassa-dors, a movie star, several CEOs and politicians he had flown in by corporate jet for a weekend of hunting and riding—spoke of the exhilarating mix of elements that flows through his life. He wears well-cut navy blue suits with his boots and stetson. His executive floor combines masters of contemporary art—Louise Nevelson, Frank Stella—with kachina dolls, the traditional folk art of the Southwest.

He is both a wildcatter and an internationalist. The thing that allies him most with Pickens—and separates them both from the men who worked their way up the ladder in one of the "elephants" of Big Oil—is the wildcatting spirit they carried with them into more sophisticated corporate activities. It was the wildcatting spirit that drove Anderson's rise from a mod-estly bankrolled entrepreneur with a University of Chicago philosophy degree to a leader of industry. "Wildcatting is risk taking. I've been in on most of the big strikes—Prudhoe Bay on the north slope in Alaska. But as an old wildcatter, I can honestly say that there aren't any good wildcats left in the United States. We've been reducing our exploration budget substantially here. But, hell, the wildcatting spirit is not yet dead! Lots of areas in the world are still wide open. We made the first discovery in China offshore."

A wildcatter, yes. But the international oil business has made Anderson a world citizen of the dimensions of Sir James Goldsmith. "There is no isolation. Every market in the world is interlinked," he says, his robust body and broad ruddy face exuding virility, warmth, and confidence as he relaxes into a leather sofa. Tufts of white hair pushed out into wings at his temples by his cowboy hat give a hint of the leprechaun to this rugged man. "I check the prices every day, and the price in the North Sea is just as important as the price in Houston, Singa-pore, the Far East. I check the water level in the Rhine; if it's too low, prices of petroleum in the interior of Europe will go up because you can't use barges. If something impacts heavily on the Rotterdam market, I know it's going to impact on the

California market shortly." Unlike many oilmen, he is not afraid to project into the twenty-first century, and the fading of the Age of Oil within the lifetimes of his seven children. "There will never be a day it just ends. It will phase out, becoming shorter and shorter in supply. But oil may never be replaced for lubrication. At a price, there will be oil available where it's needed. I think petroleum will remain our source of automotive power well into the next century.

"We're a contracting industry, and the consolidation that's been forced by takeovers is a healthy thing. You consolidate for higher efficiencies. I don't think the hostile takeovers have been as damaging as a lot of people think." Anderson sees the contraction of oil as a broader "deindustrialization of America" that could turn us into "a big England," while production continues to move abroad. It is a point Irving Shapiro argues, for Shapiro sees the transforming impact of takeover as a "reindustrialization" that is returning vigor to corporate America. Anderson is really talking about the end of basic resource industries as the backbone of the American economy and culture, a transformation so alien to America's historic image of itself that it is hard to look at directly, as Anderson does. "When you drive down the Ohio River and look at the number of giant plants that are shut, with weeds growing in the parking lots and windows knocked out, you realize that industrial America as we knew it will never come back. In the oil industry, it means that any activity that can be done abroad will move out of the country. The gas you'll be buying a few years from now could have been refined anywhere in the world." For several years, plans to contract ARCO have been a very closely held secret between Anderson and his senior executives.

A bird flashed past the window and Anderson's eyes narrowed to twinkling slits, like a cowboy's scanning for stray cattle, as he searched the glass-and-steel landscape for another glimpse. "It's a peregrine falcon!" he said, excited. "He nests in that building over there and feeds on pigeons from that park," he said, pointing to the small green plaza on the roof of a parking garage at the base of the ARCO building, where a noontime party was being set up with balloons and festive tablecloths. "He takes them on the wing. You know, peregrines dive faster than any bird on earth." He was supposed to attend the party, a kickoff for a new YMCA facility to be built there. But today there were higher priorities.

In a sensational move, Anderson had just lifted himself above predators. That day, ARCO had announced a massive restructuring that had made its stock leap. It had been trading in the mid-40's; by mid-May it would be trading at $60. In 1984, ARCO "bit the ultimate bullet" and started divesting itself of its unprofitable mining acquisitions—taking a write-down that would reach $785 million as it sold its aluminum holdings to Alcoa, dumped its disastrous Anaconda copper division, and got out of mining. Total writedowns for the entire restructuring package would be $1.5 billion. It would sell all gas stations east of the Mississippi, eleven hundred of them, and buy back a $3.4 billion block of ARCO stock, dramatically increasing corporate debt. The buyback would begin in two days, on May 1. To help retire new debt, the restructuring would even include putting up for sale ARCO's 48 percent of its headquarters, the oval towers that are the most striking piece of architecture in downtown Los Angeles.

Anderson was performing elective surgery on his own baby, doing the things that would make ARCO a less attractive target. It would leave ARCO a leaner, more efficient company with a higher debt-to-equity ratio. A company better equipped to face the difficult decades ahead for the oil industry, he hoped, if it survived the new burden of debt. And if the price of oil didn't fall too far. OPEC, in increasing disarray, was a wild card out there. As the news of ARCO's restructuring hit the Dow Jones tape, another great wave of change was launched from the oil industry, where the hostile megamergers had begun. ARCO's bold act would trigger an epidemic of voluntary restructuring in America's industries. Born out of fear of takeover, by the end of the year restructuring would be as powerful a wave as hostile takeovers. It was Kurt Wulff's dream.

◆   ◆   ◆

IT was 3:00 A.M. on April 9. The night after Pickens announced his tender offer. Fifth Avenue was dark and almost still as a solitary man cut in at Ninety-third Street and ran purposefully down the center of the street. Moving with rhythmic grace, Fin Fogg darted quietly down through the Eighties and Seventies, past Saint Patrick's Cathedral and Rockefeller Center, Saks and Tiffany, across Forty-second Street and Thirty-fourth, toward Greenwich Village and the arch in Washington Square, the World Trade Center towers framed within it growing larger as he ran. He ran through the park and west to Hudson Street. Fogg had run three New York marathons, one Boston, would celebrate April in Paris by running through Paris end to end and back again, and, in June, would participate in the International Veterans Games marathon in Rome. The night run to Pandrick Press was more than training. He had come to "buck up the troops" as half a dozen paralegals and lawyers worked round the clock to complete the preparation of Sir James Goldsmith's formal tender offer for Crown Zellerbach. It would hit the tape next morning: a $42.50 per share offer for up to 19 million shares—70 percent of the company. Drexel Burnham would be raising junk bonds. The offer was conditioned on withdrawal of the poison pill, which Goldsmith was fighting as vigorously as he had, for the past twenty years, fought against shackling restraints on the free play of the capitalist system in his two homelands, England and France.

As he ran to the printers April 9, Fogg was fully engaged by Crown Zellerbach. For months, he had been yo-yoing between Unocal and Crown Zellerbach, working with Joe Flom on both. But as litigation had begun to take center stage in Unocal, he started throwing his energies more fully into Goldsmith's developing drama. There was lots of depth in Unocal. Flom was involved in all aspects, "and when Joe Flom is involved, he tends to orchestrate," Fogg said, smiling, as he began to pull back from the Unocal war rooms.

It was strategy he loved, and Crown was all strategy. Mainly, how to maneuver around the poison pill. Fogg had been involved in the Crown deal from the beginning. He had worked with Roland Franklin, Goldsmith's man in America, to file the 13D in March that announced Goldsmith's 8.6 percent stake and $78 million investment in the San Francisco–based forest products company. He had been a participant in the endless debate over what Crown's poison pill could or could not do, the pill Lipton had embedded in Crown's bylaws the previous July. Nine months later, it was still an unknown quantity. Its biggest test case, Household, was still pending in the Delaware Supreme Court where Fogg's colleagues, Irving and Stuart Shapiro, had argued against it.

"I am convinced that Goldsmith had no intention, at first, of going for control of Crown. I've seen these guys buy and sell stock. They were buying Colgate at the same time, and they weren't going for Colgate," Fogg observed. But Sir James had been growing increasingly restive. On April 1, after one of the "literally hundreds of meetings" that would be held through the spring, Flom and Fogg had drafted a letter for Goldsmith making a $1 billion offer to buy the company *if* Crown would remove the pill. The informal offer was rejected out of hand, and the pill was not withdrawn.

Goldsmith, who spends roughly four months a year in each of his homes in Paris, London, and New York, came to New York for the month of April. The idea for the tender offer had come from one of the many meetings between Flom, Fogg, Goldsmith, and Franklin at the Eightieth Street townhouse, which was, as Fogg wryly observed, "a very nice facility." Removal of the pill was still the condition of the formal tender offer, a $1.4 billion cash offer for the majority of Crown's outstanding shares. Crown had, of course, rejected that, too, as "inappropriate" and remained intransigent about removing the pill from its bylaws. Both sides had started lobbing lawsuits at each other, prolonging the struggle. Sir James was eager to bring the thing to a conclusion. He had been at it since last December.

Suddenly, on April 24—the day before the critical federal court hearing before Judge Tashima in Los Angeles that would sway the balance of power in the Unocal fight—events began to break explosively in the Crown deal. Fogg got a call from Sir James at the office, early in the morning: "Come to the house. *Immediately.*"

"It began the night before, actually," Sir James recounts. "I

got a telephone call from Joe Flom saying that Mead Corporation wanted to talk to us, with the encouragement of Crown,
and I said, 'Fine.' " Fogg raced to Eightieth Street, where, over
breakfast, he met a new character in the drama: a lawyer from
the very large paper products company, Mead Corporation, "a
very charming man from one of the big law firms, Cravath, I
believe," as Goldsmith describes him. He had arrived to formally propose that Mead acquire Crown Zellerbach at $50 a
share, a substantially higher price than Goldsmith's $42.50-per-
share offer, and to buy out Goldsmith's shares at that price.
Well! Sir James had wanted the forest lands, but a possible $80
million profit on his shares would be a pleasant consolation. "I
didn't welcome it. It wasn't my original purpose. But I had no
choice. You had to face the facts. They'll pay $50. I'm not going
to pay $50. The deal took about ten minutes. And the charm-
ing man stayed for lunch."

Gone in a stroke was all the worrisome debate about the
poison pill. The Crown deal appeared to be ending for Goldsmith in the most civilized way, with good talk, wine, and food,
which Goldsmith wolfed down with surprisingly little sensual
involvement for a man of such worldly tastes and a large stake
in food stores. "It was delightful," says Fogg. "The Mead lawyer
had run their Paris office. He and Jimmy talked French politics
and had a *lovely* time."

The Mead man left the table during lunch to call the company to tell them of the successful conclusion of the deal. He
returned in a few minutes in a state of shock. "The deal's off.
The Mead board of directors turned it down." He excused
himself, leaving Sir James perplexed. The transaction had
come and gone within the space of a few hours. Euphoria, and
now confusion. Why had Mead changed its mind?

The day's drama had only begun. Says Goldsmith, "Within
five minutes, Bill Creson, Crown's chairman, called me from
San Francisco, and said, 'Will you work together with us on a
restructuring, help us maximize shareholder values, and join
the board?' I said, 'Yes, subject to some conditions we have to
agree on,' and hung up." Goldsmith had just made his second
deal of the day. "Jimmy was real happy," says Fogg. "It was

several weeks before the annual meeting and he was not at all sure that his proxy effort would achieve any seats on the board. Now he would get some board seats, buy some more shares, and have a significant say in Crown Zellerbach. Wonderful, wonderful."

Then Creson called back. There was a small caveat to his offer. "Jimmy, we would like a standstill that you won't go over 15 percent for five years." The plug was being pulled again. "We want the freedom to go over one-third," Goldsmith replied, and the whole thing broke down. Next day, Crown would announce the breakdown of the Mead deal and a major restructuring. From the little Creson had told Goldsmith, they apparently planned to split the company into three divisions and put the forests into a limited partnership. But no one knew any details. It was fast becoming what Goldsmith would term, with British understatement, "an *enormously* significant day."

"Jimmy has quite a range of emotions, and I saw most of them that day," Fogg says. "By now, it was time for dinner, and Jimmy was getting a little upset. Flom and Bob Pirie of Rothschild, Jimmy's principal investment banker, had come by, and we all sat around before dinner and tried to analyze what had happened.

"Mead had come and gone, but why?" asks Fogg. "We began to wonder if they had found out something about Crown that we didn't know. Perhaps we were overpaying. The thing was getting very confusing, and we weren't sure that the company was worth it." And then, over dinner, the idea was generated by Goldsmith and Franklin that perhaps they should pull—summarily cancel!—their tender offer for Crown. This was the point, in Fogg's view, where Flom gave a classic demonstration of the skills that make him the most sought-after takeover lawyer in the United States. "He analyzes all the issues involved—legal, business, strategic—and discusses grand strategy. Yet he makes specific suggestions, and is very good at getting everyone to come to a decision."

As dinner wound up, the decision was made. They would terminate the tender offer. But they would continue to press on with the proxy fight for seats on the board. "We would let the stock settle in the market for a while and then buy more stock," says Fogg. The collapse of the Mead deal and the tender offer could send the stock down, and it was looking very possible that Goldsmith might buy control at an average price per share less than his own tender offer. For all his continental glamor, Goldsmith had the halfpenny consciousnesss of a British grocer, a trait Nancy Havens-Hasty at Bear Stearns had seen to her disadvantage: "We never make money on Goldsmith's deals, because we only make money when someone overpays, and Goldsmith never does."

Flom and Fogg went back to the Skadden Arps office to write the press release. It was the end of the most tumultuous day of the entire deal.

Just to keep a little sly pressure on the board and the proxy contest, Goldsmith went back in the market on May 8—the eve of the annual meeting—and increased his stake to 19.6 percent. He was now within less than half a percentage point of the 20 percent that would trigger the poison pill. "There was still a lot of sense of risk involved," says Fogg. No one—not Lipton, Flom, Goldsmith, or Creson—really knew what the pill would do if Goldsmith marched over 20 percent. It might well be the Valley of Death. But for whom?

♦   ♦   ♦

As Crown moved toward the hard in-fighting of the endgame, Sir James was preoccupied with a seductive project. An invitation to testify before a Senate subcommittee hearing on takeovers. An outspoken critic at home of the "ossification and decay" he had watched drain Europe of its competitive vigor, this would be his first opportunity to praise and lecture the nation that made folk heroes, albeit controversial folk heroes, of its corporate raiders.

As he flew to Washington, Sir James joined the chorus of discordant voices rising from the Hill in one of the most spirited national debates in the nation's economic history.

CHAPTER 10

◆◆◆

"DIANE, will you set up a lunch with Morris Kramer," Joe Perella called out to his secretary from his corner office on First Boston's forty-second floor. "Is he the one with the frizzy hair and the gold chains?" Diane called back. "Yeh," laughed Perella, looking forward to lunch with the lawyer who had shared the Getty-Texaco deal with him.

Leaning back in his chair, his six-foot-four frame stretched out, and legs crossed up on the desk, he eyed, through his polished black shoes, images of another world. The photographs of Yellowstone Park, Arizona desert and Utah he had taken on his eighteen-thousand-mile journey through America before joining First Boston in 1972. Just out of Harvard Business School, a former CPA shedding the "shiny pants, reactive image of the accountant" for the front-line action on Wall Street, he had determined that, "A lot of people in the East know more about the back streets of Rome and London. I don't want to be one of those provincial New Yorkers." He may also have sensed that the project ahead would leave little time for drifting America's blue highways.

That trip had given him his first, somewhat simpler, contact
with Texaco. "I went down to the Texaco touring office and got
maps and sat down with a guy there and told him, 'I want to see
this country.' " Thirteen years later, he kept the framed pictures before him, humbling reminders of nature's grandeur in
an office that breathed Wall Street success. A corner office with
walls of glass and sleek steel and leather furniture. Framed
double-page tombstones from the *Journal* announcing dozens
of First Boston's completed mergers and acquisitions. A Lucite
forest of tiny plastic cubes commemorating the giant deals. The
magazine for Ferrari buffs on the coffee table.

It was so easy to go beyond confidence to arrogance when
you'd helped negotiate the world's biggest mergers. He mused
on the seductions of power. "So many of these toreadors on
Wall Street get carried away with 'les limo, les club, les weekend.' They begin to think *they* have the power. But we're not the
ones who change the world. There are few true giants."

And yet, in early summer, 1985, Perella sat at the summit, a
star among deal makers, earning $5- to $10-million fees that
would put him, before year's end, on the cover of *Fortune*
magazine. As 1985 was tallied up, Perella's team would have
made an estimated $200 million in fees, handling mergers
valued at $60 billion. They would have done more deals over
$100 million than anybody—seventy-five of them, with Gold-
man and Morgan Stanley just a deal or two behind.

Perella had been at the epicenter since the hostile takeover
wars took fire in the late 1970s. With Bruce Wasserstein, co-
head of the mergers-and-acquisitions team Perella had built
from scratch since 1973, he had played in most of the major oil
mergers, the landmarks. Marathon–U.S. Steel, Cities Service–
Occidental, and Du Pont–Conoco, which had been affirmation
for Perella "that First Boston was in the top, top tier" of the
takeover game. They had gone on to co-manage all of Du
Pont's subsequent long-term financing, a client that had been
almost exclusively Morgan Stanley's for fifty years. Du Pont,
Perella sensed, put to rest "criticism on the Street that we're
deal-by-deal operators who never build relationships." The

storm-trooper, deal-factory image. "One or two things could be a flash in the pan; years of success means you've got a system, a collection of people, which is superior. You have a discipline and a fanatical attachment to preserving reputation." There had never been a $7 billion deal. It was too big for the arbs to control, like they'd controlled the $600 million Pullman deal that first gave us recognition." Representing Du Pont, they had triumphed over Seagram and Mobil with an unprecedented offer of cash and paper for 100 percent of the company. "Du Pont came down in August '81, the beginning of the big oil wave. Then in November of '81, the $5 billion Marathon takeover by U.S. Steel."

The Texaco-Getty deal two years later, surpassed in size only by Chevron's takeover of Gulf, revealed the power shifts on Wall Street that, by the end of 1985, saw First Boston confirmed as head of a new hierarchical order. "The special bracket in mergers used to be Morgan Stanley, First Boston, Goldman Sachs, and Lehman. Now, on any given day, we and Goldman are running neck and neck, we're gaining market share at the expense of Lehman, and Morgan Stanley is coming up fast from seventh last year." Morgan Stanley's new mergers-and-acquisitions head, Eric Gleacher, was driving hard to regain Morgan's old stature.

Wasserstein had taken the leadership role on Texaco-Getty. But as Texaco's investment bankers, Wasserstein and Perella had both played pivotal roles in arranging Texaco's $10 billion-plus acquisition of Getty Oil, a bravura coup launched in the last week of 1983, in which Getty made an eleventh-hour switch from the arms of Pennzoil to Texaco. First Boston had played the deal by Wall Street's rules. Perella felt confident that Texaco would win a jury trial that was just getting under way in Houston, challenging the legality of Texaco's move on Getty. It was ancient history now: Getty and Pennzoil had announced an "agreement in principle" that Pennzoil and Getty Oil would joint-venture a buyout of all outstanding stock for $112.50 per share, an agreement forged with a handshake, celebrated with champagne, but never signed. At issue before the jury was whether or not it had been a binding agreement. If it had not, First Boston's acts were aggressive, perhaps, but a model of resourceful deal making. If the jury determined that it had been binding, Wall Street's most basic way of doing business would be disqualified. For, in claiming $7.53 billion in damages, Pennzoil was challenging the principles that governed not only Wall Street but the whole vast realm of contracts in American law and business, including how people buy and sell their homes. It challenged the basic tenets: a deal isn't over till it's over. The opera isn't over until the fat lady sings. Until the deal is signed.

Like witnesses to an accident, each of the insiders on the Texaco-Getty merger would remember the flashes and balls of fire a little differently. To Perella, to members of the Getty Oil board, to Pennzoil's Hugh Liedtke, and to Gordon Getty, the individual experience of the deal *is* the deal. As Perella replayed it in anticipation of his lunch with Kramer, his candor still uncolored by the shock and caution that would follow the Houston jury's decision, he revealed the process by which the Street's most successful "deal factory" does its work. It is the stuff of case studies at Harvard Business School, Perella's boot camp. Only later would it take on the dimensions of history.

"At least six months before Getty Oil surfaced as being up for grabs when Pennzoil raided them Christmas week 1983, we had begun to pick up a lot of rumblings about friction occurring internally," says Perella. "Our energy group picked it up— they're out in the oil patch all the time. The rumblings told us that Gordon Getty was out to make trouble for Getty Oil. A clue: he had insisted that the company hire an investment banker to 'evaluate what their options were,' a banker who had never done one stitch of work for Getty Oil—one that was totally independent and not beholden to the company. We were rejected because we had advised them on a small acquisition. Getty hired Goldman Sachs.

"By now, we had identified Getty as 'something is going to happen,' and said, 'Well, fellows, since the company didn't hire us, we better get intelligent because something may go down,

and when it does we need to be in a position to take advantage
of it. In addition, we might want to go out and see if we can
align ourselves with someone sooner, someone who might want
to take advantage of what's going on.' "

They had been getting intelligent for months before the
rumblings. Early in 1983, Perella's group had identified Getty
as "an interesting acquisition opportunity" and tried to get
something going. In simplest terms, Getty was a strong company whose asset value was far higher than its stock price, and
the controlling blocks of stock were concentrated in just a few
hands. "We brought it to the attention of one of our accounts,
Santa Fe International, a wholly owned subsidiary of Kuwait
Petroleum. They said, 'Fine, but we aren't big enough to do it
ourselves. We want a partner.' 'Fine,' I said, 'we'll find a partner.' " His group contacted a major American oil company,
whose name Perella will not reveal, and developed a joint
venture to explore the acquisition of Getty Oil. "For months
and months, we studied Getty Oil from A to Z. We studied all
the trust instruments set up by Jean Paul Getty, principally the
Sarah Getty Trust, which controlled 40 percent of Getty Oil
stock, and of which Gordon Getty was the trustee. The Getty
Museum held around 10 to 13 percent. The stock was in the
hands of fiduciaries. We identified early on that anyone who
could lock up the museum and the trust stock controlled Getty
Oil."

Ivan Boesky was scrutinizing Getty also. Casting "the restless
eye of the arbitrager" over the oil company, as he describes in
his book *Merger Mania,* he, too, identified the elements that
could make it an attractive arbitrage play. "In mid-1983, Getty
Oil stock was selling in the sixties. Earlier in the year it had been
trading in the fifties and total value of the company at that
price was about $5 billion. It was rich in domestic reserves of oil
. . . and by the fall of 1983, oil prices were beginning to steady.
Getty Oil shares were worth nearly three times what they were
selling for in 1983, according to one widely quoted estimate by
Herold and Company. That fact could not have escaped Gordon Getty's attention." As Getty picked the brains of people like

Kurt Wulff and Boone Pickens, it became known that Gordon
Getty was getting restless to realize some of that value for the
shareholders, especially the family members.

"The joint venture died on the vine," continues Perella, who
consoled himself with a $250,000 fee, "and then, free of any
conflict, we began to dialogue with oil companies around the
country. What became clear was that none of the big oil
companies wanted to make the first move. It was more than
protocol. They're part of the same industry. The only one who
ever really raided was Mobil, who always behaved like a maver-
ick. In fact, Mobil may have shown that it was a bad thing to
raid because it had tried to take over both Conoco and Marathon, unsolicited, and didn't win either one."

In October 1983, the squabble between Gordon Getty and
management went public, a struggle revealed more by the
announced armistice that ended hostilities than by an overt
sign of the fight. To Boesky, "it read like a for-sale sign,"
proving that there was a fight going on that would lead to
something happening. He speculated that the fight had broken
out over Gordon Getty's pressure to increase stock value to
shareholders by some of the devices he had explored—stock
buybacks, royalty trusts, and divestment of assets. All avenues
that could threaten the jobs and power of the incumbents, they
had been rejected by Getty Oil's board and management. In the
standstill announced in October, Getty Oil promised not to pass
antitakeover measures or to dilute Gordon Getty's or the museum's controlling interest by issuing new stock. Getty would
have the right to appoint three new board members, but he and
Harold Williams, head of the museum, agreed not to sell their
shares to an outsider. No one believed the truce would last its
appointed year.

Within days of Getty's appointment of the new board members, the trouble First Boston's team had identified early in the
year escalated into a major media event. In December, Getty
and Williams formally banded together, bringing the joint
force of the Sarah Getty Trust and Getty Museum against Getty
Oil. And then, several days after Christmas 1983, came the first
move from outside. J. Hugh Liedtke, the oilman whose wildcat-

ting ambition had surfaced in the early 1960s when Artie Long had helped him wage proxy fights, seized the opportunity. Eager to acquire cut-rate reserves for his prospering Pennzoil, Liedtke launched a partial tender offer. He offered to buy 20 percent of the shares at $100 a share.

"Cute trick to choose Christmas week, when a lot of investment bankers, lawyers, and corporate executives are away," said Perella, who himself was just beginning a week-long visit to his parents in Florida. The communal Italian family life he'd known in Newark with his uncles, aunts, and grandparents had been diluted with time, but he valued the holiday get-togethers. "While all the 'big elephants' were sitting around looking at each other wondering what was going to happen, Liedtke decided he was going to make it happen." Perella reached for the phone.

Wasserstein was on an island in the Caribbean. Perella called Art Reichstetter, head of his energy group, and they ran over the list of all the companies with whom they had discussed a Getty deal. With the confident assumption that they *would* be involved, Perella said to Reichstetter, "We've got to finalize *now* who we're going to work for, who's going to hire us. I can make calls as easily from Florida as from my office." He had no intention of missing what would clearly be the biggest oil deal yet. The First Boston machine had been preparing for a decade.

◆ ◆ ◆

PERELLA had entered a Wall Street on the eve of transformation. "In 1973, people ignored Wall Street as an industry. Now it's covered as an industry the same way chemicals, oil, and airlines are." As he spoke in 1985, investment banks were going public, their stock traded on the exchanges like any other: First Boston, Salomon, Donaldson, Lufkin & Jenrette, and Bear Stearns. "Going public" gave them the capital base that was critical to keeping a competitive edge in the environment of multibillion-dollar megadeals. By the end of the year, even Morgan Stanley would be going public; of the leaders, only Goldman would still be private. "But in '73, people didn't yet realize that the industry was going to go through a transition—

that there was going to be a profound shift in influence within
the firms. The account people had functioned on all questions
a client had; you'd be given part of an account, work on it for
years, and finally the account would be yours. But I could see in
the first three months at First Boston that, as the world got
more complicated and specialized, firms were going to have to
rely more on specialists. Mergers and acquisitions were beginning to be a business at Goldman and Morgan Stanley, but *not*
at First Boston. They were still being done as golf club deals;
they were not created in a predatory environment."

When Perella arrived, First Boston was still run in the style of
George Woods, former head of the World Bank, and, to
Perella, "a signature of the old-style American banker who,
with a phone call, could make things happen anywhere in the
world." First Boston had begun its reform by 1975, when
George Shinn was brought in to replace Emil Pattberg, retiring
as chairman. What was wrong, said Shinn, was that First Boston
was a white-shoe firm, but the white shoes were scuffed; the
firm had not been aggressively recruiting at business schools
during the 1970s. Perella was among the first of a flood of
Harvard Business School graduates who would create a new
Wall Street elite. Felix Rohatyn had helped focus Perella on the
potential in mergers and acquisitions. "He was my inspiration.
The month I joined First Boston, he was on the cover of
Business Week, and when I saw the list of all the fees, I said, 'My
God, look at all the money you can make in this area for your
firm, and you don't use any capital.'" In an article in the
Institutional Investor, Perella dared to characterize Rohatyn's
emergence as a critic of takeovers, while still making million-
dollar fees representing the attack side, as "a pot calling the
kettle black"; but he admires Rohatyn as "a person of presence
and authority" in the financial revolution they both pioneered.

The most basic element in that revolution, as Perella identified it, was "the basic shift from waiting for a client to call to
initiating client contact." Marketing would be his focus. His
team would market "custom-tailored products." The goal
would be to be in every major deal.

First Boston's team had cut its teeth on the giant takeovers that evolved in the oil industry, landmarks of the larger hostile wars Perella traces back to 1973, "the days of the 'blue chip raids' when one major corporation went for another. The '80s saw the beginning of the era of what I call 'private pools of predatory capital.' And *that* really began with Marathon being taken over by U.S. Steel in 1982; what most people don't remember is that the Bass brothers were accumulating Marathon before the Conoco deal closed. Then came Conoco-Du Pont with the Seagram family, and the emergence of Boone Pickens in Cities Service."

◆ ◆ ◆

FROM Florida, Perella had directed the response to Liedtke's bid. They divided up the list of oil companies and began to call. "I had concluded from my calls that four of the five companies were definitely not going to be doing anything. I wasn't discouraged. That's part of the game. Most people say no. It's very interesting to get excited, but most of the time it doesn't get you anywhere." Reichstetter and Perella compared notes. Reichstetter had called his list, and come up with Texaco. Perella had done the same and come up with Standard of California. "It was very clear that we were down to Standard of California and Texaco." They kept working.

As the last few days of 1983 ticked by, Liedtke's bid was still the only visible event. Then, at 9:00 A.M. on Wednesday, January 4, the "agreement in principle" was announced. If he can pull it off while the giants are asleep, what a brilliant coup for Liedtke, Perella thought. "It was, in effect, a leveraged buyout of Getty Oil that would take the public out, but let the Sarah Getty Trust remain as a shareholder. Pennzoil and the Sarah Getty Trust would jointly own the company and Liedtke would run it. It was a great deal for Pennzoil because, in the trust, they got a money partner, and Pennzoil would get to run a $10 billion oil company with only half of their own money in." In Boesky's view, the deal satisfied Liedtke's need for reserves and Gordon Getty's desire to control his father's company. "But we were dumbstruck by the deal," says Perella. Why had the

Getty board taken it? Why would one of the premier oil companies, "a high-quality company with one of the best records in the industry at finding oil," give working control to Pennzoil? And at a price lower than their advisers, Goldman Sachs, were telling them they could get outside if they wanted to sell, as the rumor mill was saying. "Word we were getting back," says Perella, "was that the board sessions were stormy, that they had recessed and reconvened, that Pennzoil had sweetened the deal slightly, and the directors had approved, in principle." But it meant approving a deal created by Gordon Getty as an end run around the Getty Oil board, on the heels of a recent drama in which the board had tried to remove Getty from power by secret coup while Getty was out of the boardroom. The machinations of the board during this period, if ever fully revealed, would be a gold mine for corporate historians.

On the strength of the clues that had surfaced, Perella felt "there was an opportunity for a company that wanted to move fast." For as Perella, Wasserstein, and the entire First Boston mergers-and-acquisitions team gathered back in New York after New Year's, they discovered a hole in the agreement so wide the entire takeover army could march through. The agreement had not yet gone to contract. "The standard procedure is that a deal isn't a deal until it's inked in, and even then it has outs: outs for antitrust, outs for shareholder votes, outs for fairness opinions of bankers. In a multibillion-dollar transaction, it would appear that you ought to reduce the agreement to writing so that people agree." It was a principle so accepted that Boesky had hunted hard to find proof of a signed contract and, finding none, bought more Getty Oil shares on the belief that the unsigned agreement would fall before a higher bid from a third party. The principle had been upheld in a recent law case, *Reprosystem, BV* v. *SCM Corp*, which stated that in big, complex deals there is "a practical business need to record all the parties' commitments in definitive documents." Pennzoil and Getty Oil had not. "For some reason, this thing was announced on the tape as an agreement in principle, and not put to writing," Perella said. Pennzoil had had the sophisticated advice of Lazard Frères. He couldn't understand it. But there it was. And with opportunity laid before him, Perella determined "to get that high ground first and keep it."

The consensus was: "We need some intelligence. Let's try to find out what's going on." Perella had a friend on the Getty Oil board. Laurence Tisch, head of the family-owned financial conglomerate Loews Corporation. Tisch was one of the three new members just appointed by Gordon Getty, who, by joining forces with the Getty Museum's Harold Williams, had gained controlling power over the board. It was Tisch's appointment that encouraged Ivan Boesky to buy more Getty Oil shares in his growing arbitrage position, for he knew Tisch as an activist and "renowned takeover specialist." Perella and Wasserstein called Tisch now on connecting telephones, putting into play the network of contacts the First Boston team had adroitly built over the past decade.

"I first called on Larry in 1974, part of a recognition that if we were going to just rely on the First Boston client base we would never have a dominant market position." Perella began to build his team. "All that toreador crap—the capes and trappings—they're just a distraction. The toreadors can't do the creative, reflective thing. They're the trigger pullers. It's the brain power—the understanding of the process, the market, and how to get the deals done—that wins. It's a game of subtleties, not a game of hammers and macho. It's a game of numbers and judgment." Perella remembered from college biology that in the plant and animal world "hybrid vigor" came from mixing a diversity of talent—"sameness does not bring out the best in people. It's a mixture of people with different personalities, backgrounds, and strengths that generates new thinking." It was the basis of the "hothouse concept" that became his underlying philosophy. The group Perella built—luring his superstar and co-head of the mergers-and-acquisitions group, Bruce Wasserstein, from the law firm Cravath, Swaine & Moore in July 1977—was not of traditional First Boston men. "Joe met me in Corvettes the day he hired me, I had cut myself shaving and had blood on my shirt. Here's this guy with blue jeans, beard, blood on his shirt, and a jacket that's twenty years old," says Bill Lambert, a managing director whose client- and deal-development skills led him, the year he joined First Boston in 1978, to snag a Morgan Stanley client and create a $240 million takeover deal for them and a $1 million fee for First Boston. Lambert and Wasserstein had gone to McBurney School at Sixty-third and Central Park twenty years earlier and had kept in contact through the years. "We were not part of the country club set, and I say this with a little bit of envy—we couldn't do the golf club deals. So we decided to do business the best way we could." They were outside the establishment, like so many of the new Wall Street warriors.

Perella himself had carved and shaped his life by the empirical method, evolving from the dream of being a center fielder for the Yankees, through false starts in engineering at Lehigh University, and six years as an accountant, before going to Harvard Business School in his late twenties. "Looking around, I'd noticed that a lot of the so-called leaders who were making a difference, good or bad, in business and industry were graduates." At Harvard, he had found an egalitarian climate where the quality of faculty, students, and ideas was valued over the old school tie. "I did not care too much about being a member of a club. I got my money's worth. I got insight into my strengths and weaknesses. And more than anything else, it gave me a practical approach to everyday business life." He had tried the World Bank for a while, but found that nonprofit was not for him; "when there's no bottom line, the goal is not well established." He had abandoned accounting because of its reactive nature. And he finally gravitated toward investment banking as a place where he could play an active role in shaping corporations' futures. His team had changed the way Wall Street does business. But the values haven't changed much. "On weekends, we go home, we don't go to the golf club," says Lambert. "Joe's in his garden on his knees on weekends hurting his back growing tomatoes."

Bill Lambert joined the team as Perella was launching his "outreach program" to develop new relationships for First Boston. A shaggy-bearded iconoclast, Lambert developed "the List," the core list of one hundred companies from the Fortune

500 Lambert has identified "as companies that have the capability of doing major transactions within twelve to eighteen months." Running down the list he's written on a yellow legal pad, checking "this is a client" or "this is a prospect," Lambert says, "The key factor I look for is the company's financial flexibility to do the transaction. I look at the balance sheet—the price of the stock, the multiple of the book value, the cash flow. What's interesting is all the companies that have the financial ability to do these transactions—to initiate—are *also* targets. . . . I've called on them all. Maybe a third will never do business with us. Some may be in industries where the wave is just beginning to hit—banks, food products. Perhaps a third on the list are already our clients. But you must continue to run and run and run. There's a paranoia aspect to this business. There are clients on that list where we think we're very comfortable but we're being replaced. You have to assume that this one stops tomorrow, and keep calling and calling, bringing them new ideas. Drexel Burnham's junk bonds can take a lot of business away. They haven't yet, but . . . you can't afford to let your competition get a leg up on you. The first time you fail, you bet your life your competitors are in the door saying, 'I could have done it better.' That's how we targeted people to begin with; any time a deal went bust, we'd go out and say the same thing." Lambert ran his finger down the list. "We cracked ten of these companies in the first half of '85. It's almost like being at a roulette wheel. You know you're going to play and play and play, but you never know when you're going to win. But you know if you're not at the table, you're never going to win." He let his finger stop on two clients and grinned through his beard. Baxter and Allied. The payoff of persistence and the systematic process. With Wasserstein as architect, Baxter, the health services corporation based near Chicago, and Allied Corporation, a New Jersey–based company ranked high in the Fortune 500, had initiated two of 1985's most important deals. "Baxter-Travenol and Allied-Signal—they're classic examples of how First Boston works. I like 'em."

Perella had worked on building capital sources. Talking with the repetitive speech pattern that gives a rhythmic cadence to the takeover language, Perella describes the building of the network: "I said to myself, 'Joe, there are people around this country that are very wealthy that we should get to know because it might come in handy someday.' I didn't just camp on their doorstep, but whenever I had an interesting idea, I brought it to their attention. I got to know Pritzker, I got to know Sid Bass, I got to know Larry Tisch. They always wanted to listen to a good idea." He did some business with Loews, learned to value Tisch's market judgment. As the Getty deal broke, Larry's brother, Bob, had just invited Perella to sit on the board of NYU's Tisch School of the Arts.

Now Perella and Wasserstein jointly talked to Tisch, trying to "dramatize that we had a serious interest in trying to do something, and thought we might have a client that was interested. Neither Texaco nor Standard of California had said who they'd hire or even whether they were going to do something. 'But we're out there trying to come up with something,'" Perella told Tisch. "I don't know how much time you have, because this deal could be signed up. The lawyers are working on the papers," Tisch told them. Perella could envision armies of Pennzoil, Getty Oil, trust and museum lawyers feverishly preparing documents to seal the deal. Perella and Wasserstein pressed: "Larry, we just want some insight, we just want you to know we're out there trying real hard."

They then called Marty Lipton, the man whose testimony later in the Houston trial sounded the death knell for Texaco's cause, according to several jurors at the trial who felt Lipton had wrongfully kept open the doors to options while working to finalize the Pennzoil deal. "Marty was the lawyer for the Getty Museum, and we said, 'Hey, Marty, we're trying real hard to come up with somebody. How much time do we have before the deal is signed up?' and he said, 'I really don't know, but you've been through these things many times before, and you know that it's not a matter of weeks—it's usually a matter of hours or days. I'd say you have about 24 hours.'"

The juggernaut rolled. Perella met Wednesday morning in his office with Standard of California's vice-president of finance Sellers Stogh. Stogh asked Perella, "What's going to happen?" Perella shot back, "What's going to happen is if you guys are all sitting here staring at one another—if one of you doesn't do something—Pennzoil is going to own this company!" Standard of California was paralyzed, it seemed, because chairman George Keller was in Mexico on vacation, and the company had not yet made a decision as to who they would hire, Stogh revealed. It was a marketing opportunity Perella could not resist. "I'm going to tell you how to do the deal. They don't have a contract. You're going to lay a big number on the museum, and you're going to lay a big number on the trust, and you're going to crack that alliance, and because of their fiduciary duty, they're going to have to take the higher offer. Without the museum, the trust doesn't have control, and the whole thing breaks apart. And what you're going to do, you're going to contract to buy the museum stock and the Sarah Getty Trust stock. You are not going to announce an agreement in principle like these bozos at Pennzoil did."

The deal could die during the time it would take for Stogh to try to get back to his boss, George Keller. Trying to infuse him with a sense of urgency, Perella said, "As I sit here and talk to you right now, I don't have a conflict. I hope when you decide to make a move we still don't have one. But one never knows. . . ." He recognized that Stogh was a victim of circumstance, at a great disadvantage based in San Francisco with his chairman in Mexico. "They were a West Coast company logistically three thousand miles away from the scene of the action. The action was in New York. That's where Marty Lipton was. That's where Larry Tisch was. That's where Gordon Getty was holed up. By this time, we had determined that Getty was at the Pierre Hotel.

"By Wednesday night, we thought we were running out of time. Art and Bruce had flown to Texas on a deal they thought would break but didn't, and had talked to Texaco. I went home that night very discouraged because all of a sudden the people at Standard of California stopped returning my phone calls." Uh-huh, thought Perella, they've decided to go with their traditional banker, Morgan Stanley. You couldn't let your feelings get hurt. "You don't win 'em all, and you don't lose 'em all

either," says Perella. "You just have to go out and compete
every day for business." But if Art and Bruce didn't come
through with Texaco, he mused, "we're hurting."

The phone rang at 8:00 P.M. in Perella's Upper East Side
apartment. It was Art and Bruce calling from Houston. "Joe,
Texaco wants to hire us." First Boston was in the game, and
with a client they had never worked for before. All the months
of "getting intelligent" on Getty had paid off, for "what had
sold Texaco was our prior analysis of the Getty situation, the
fact that we had a team that had studied Getty backward and
forward, ready to roll on the project."

Now, as adviser to one of the largest of the Seven Sisters, he
would help orchestrate what could well be the largest corporate
takeover in history. From Houston, Wasserstein said, "We'll try
to rent a jet and get up there as soon as we can, but get
whatever team you can together and get out there to White
Plains," Texaco's headquarters in New York.

Like a director calling onstage a cast that's been waiting in the
wings, Perella mobilized the team. "Get in a car and drive to the
Texaco headquarters," he told Jim Elliott in New Jersey. Jim
would cover oil and gas. "But it was more complicated than
that. We pulled together the team that had studied all the
disparate elements of the company—Chuck Ward for media
and John Lathrop, my insurance specialist." Elliott, Ward, and
Lathrop leaped into their cars and converged on White Plains,
as Perella called Morris Kramer at Skadden Arps. Texaco's
traditional counsel was Marty Lipton, but with Lipton tied up
working for the Getty Museum, Texaco had indicated they
wanted to hire Joe Flom's firm.

Perella had been hiring Joe Flom and his partners at Skadden Arps since 1974. It had broken tradition when he first
hired Flom. First Boston had always hired Sullivan &
Cromwell, one of the most prestigious and elegant of Wall
Street law firms. But as the new leader of First Boston's
mergers-and-acquisitions effort "muddled along making $3 to
$5 million a year in fees," Perella had met Flom, and earned
respect for him the hard way, in the 1973 deal in which Perella
had worked for Cargill Inc., from Minneapolis, the biggest

grain-trading company in the world. For Perella, it was Cargill that had initiated the current merger era. "Because of its high profile, a lot of people think it was International Nickel, but the first hostile deal of the whole wave was Cargill's December '73 raid on Missouri Portland Cement. With Cargill, people began to realize that it was now legitimate to raid, and advisers like Joe Flom were going to play a more important role. In '73, tender offers had ten-day lives, courts would often use their power to delay things to give the target more time to pull himself together, and so legal tacticians were becoming very important." Just out of Harvard Business School, and with no training program in takeovers, Perella had had to teach himself how the game was played and who the players were. "Flom was the Missouri–Portland Cement lawyer who had got an injunction against our client, Cargill, and devised legislation that slowed us down for six months. I learned that he was an important guy to have on your side." Hired as adviser by Perella just months after the Cargill deal, Flom "helped me refine my thoughts as to how to build a merger and how to sell the concept here at First Boston. He was a very important person in the evolution of my thinking."

Ironically, the trend to the breakup of friendly deals that brought Perella and Flom together on Cargill would bring Perella and one of Flom's lawyers, Morris Kramer, together in another Cargill deal in late 1978. Cargill had hired First Boston to help it break up a signed deal between Missouri Beef and Conagra. A farm belt nickels-and-dimes deal compared to Getty, Cargill had won Missouri Beef with a $3 million bid over Conagra's $64 million offer. Like an angry Pennzoil five years later, Conagra was still carrying its lawsuit against Cargill and Missouri Beef, now MBPXL, through the Nebraska courts as Perella joined another effort to break up a love affair. The final Supreme Court appeal decision would not come down until March 1986, in time to be used as precedent in the legal battle which would be raging then in another test of an agreement—Texaco-Getty.

◆　◆　◆

SKADDEN Arps lawyer Morris Kramer took Perella's call at home. "I'd gone home to ride my exercise bike, and just got off for a meal of pear, cheese, and salad when Joe called and said, 'Morris, are you involved in the Getty affair? We represent a client; *maybe* the company is Texaco. Do you have a conflict working with them?' " Kramer would have to check with his partners, but said no, and ran to shower and dress. Shunning limousines, Perella had called a Dial-a-Car, and would be picking him up in half an hour. The adrenaline began to pump. "I wasn't involved, but I'd been watching. This was a very major transaction, with one of the five largest companies in the U.S., a transaction I knew was many, many billions of dollars."

He felt physically ready. "It's very much like the bell goes off and the boxer gets in the ring. The sound of the bell . . . the charge . . . !" With a small, wiry body topped by a mop of very curly hair and eyes of fiery intensity, Kramer is one of the classic deal junkies who dreads the moment when he might have to face the desk he abandoned at the start of the last deal. But it was incredibly exhausting. "Five months earlier, on the Northwest Energy deal, they had to pack me up and mail me home after two days of negotiations." But not this time. "I'd been going to a gym."

On the drive to White Plains, Perella briefed Kramer. Kramer called from the telephone behind the guard station, trying to reach Flom or Peter Atkins to see if they, or any of the partners, were involved in the deal. They were "out of pocket"—couldn't be reached. By 11:00 P.M., the team was converging on a boardroom on the third floor, Texaco's executive floor. Through the night and early morning, they talked values and strategy. By 2:00 A.M. Wasserstein hadn't arrived yet from Texas. An assembly of about twenty senior Texaco executives challenged Perella: "And if we do the deal, how do you propose we get it done?"

Both Texaco and Perella ran down the list of possible suitors for Getty Oil—Shell, Mobil. "But fundamentally," says Perella, "it got down to Texaco versus Standard of California. It made sense for Standard of California, I told them, but I thought we could beat them logistically because of our geographic advantage. But we had to move fast."

Perella unfolded his scenario for action to Texaco: "Here's how you get the deal done. First, you go and see the museum and tell them you're willing to buy their shares at a price that is significantly higher than the Pennzoil price. You contact Marty Lipton and say, 'We have someone to buy your client's stock at a price.' " Perella believed $125 was where the price should be, but didn't say so yet. "Second, we call Larry Tisch and tell him we want to have a meeting with Gordon Getty and make him a proposal. We sign up both blocks, the trust and the museum, and we announce to the world, 'Mr. and Mrs. America, we own 53 percent of Getty Oil under *contract,* and we will make the same offer to all the public stockholders.' That's the plan, to take advantage of the fact that the other guy hasn't signed up his contract."

The Texaco team expressed worry about the competition. Quite rightly. Closeted in the White Plains boardroom they were only peripherally aware of the aggressive barrage of "courtesy calls" being made by Getty Oil's investment bankers, Goldman Sachs, searching for counterproposals to Pennzoil's offer from outside suitors. In fact, Goldman's Geoffrey Boisi had already placed a call to John McKinley, part of "a shopping spree, that would look sleazy to the jury," as the *American Lawyer* would describe it. And McKinley had called Goldman's CEO John Weinberg to talk it over. "If you keep worrying about the competition," Perella told them, "they're going to gain on you. I'm telling you, you're way ahead of them logistically." He didn't want to tell them that Standard's chairman was on a beach in Mexico. "You can't be distracted by competition. You've got to seize the ramparts first!"

It was the next phase in which First Boston made or lost its reputation, in Perella's view. The evaluations of the Getty Oil assets that would determine the price Texaco would bid, if it made a tender offer. "We're here to listen. We've done our own evaluation, but we'd like to vet it against yours," Texaco's group said. Calling on his specialists to give specific values for the divisions—the cable TV network ESPN, a billion-dollar rein-

surance company in Kansas City—Perella built up an overall
value for Getty Oil, with the Texaco men listening with particular attention to evaluations of the nonoil and gas assets. Perella
knew that if their evaluations were too high and rosy, First
Boston would be accused of goading Texaco into making a bid.
"I knew we were being tested and that Texaco would always
remember our behavior and advice in that midnight hour as
either being sound or full of bull. In the service industry, it
takes years and years to build up your reputation as a leader,
and you can lose it overnight by screwing up on a deal."

By two in the morning, evaluations completed, Perella
named a number. "If you could buy this company for anything
like $125, $130 a share, you would be buying oil in the ground
very cheaply."

The Dial-a-Car drivers were still sleeping in the parking lot at
4:00 A.M., when Wasserstein, Reichstetter, and their senior oil
analyst Thomas Petrie arrived from Houston, having rented a
jet. "As they entered the room, Al Decrane, president of
Texaco said, 'Okay, Joe, you stop talking. Bruce tell us how to
do this deal.' Then Bruce went through the entire process,
repeating what I'd said, confirming the strategy." For Kramer,
these first hours of the first meeting were when the bonds were
struck, or not struck, between strangers. The advisers came in
with an advantage. "We're brought in as brain surgeons, and
you don't usually argue with your brain surgeon because he's
there to do a very serious operation on you." But trust had to be
gained, and there was always a "crisis of confidence," which,
once passed, cemented the relationship. Client and lawyer.
Client and investment banker. By 9:00 A.M.—thirteen hours
since Wasserstein's call from Houston—that crisis had been
reached and transcended, and Perella and Wasserstein were
taken to the office of Texaco's CEO, John McKinley, to review
the strategy ideas.

McKinley had been hunting in Spain with Fred Hartley and
Bill Douce when word came of Boone Pickens's raid on Phillips,
but he had so far avoided the attacks that had so drained
Unocal and Phillips. Perella was not introducing McKinley to a
new idea. Getty's record of finding oil was better than Texaco's,

and Texaco needed Getty's oil reserves. Petrie's presentation of graphs showing the combined reserves of Texaco and Getty declining much less rapidly than Texaco's alone were a powerful argument for acquisition of Getty. "John, here's how the deal should go down," they told McKinley, as they brought the scenario down to specifics. McKinley must offer $125 a share. And he must strike a deal with the museum first. If they could get the museum to agree, then the power of the 40 percent Sarah Getty Trust block would be diminished and might make Gordon Getty easier to convince. The trust, together with the museum, held over 50 percent. McKinley must get on the phone to Marty Lipton and tell him, "Marty, I'm calling a board meeting this afternoon. I wouldn't be calling it if I didn't have something very attractive to offer the museum." With Perella and Wasserstein in his office, McKinley called Lipton and Tisch. He set up a board meeting for noon, assembling the board with such swiftness that Perella could only guess that, anticipating events, McKinley had put the board on alert.

Wasserstein and Perella left the meeting with orders to try and get the deal done. The contingent piled into Texaco cars and raced to New York to meet with Marty Lipton and, later, Gordon Getty. They carried the mandate to negotiate what Kurt Wulff had believed was unthinkable to Gordon Getty when the two had talked several months earlier—selling the entire company. Removing the family from the corporation that held its name. But there may have been a general underestimation of the financial sophistication of Gordon Getty. While hung with the public image of an absentminded giant of a man who preferred composing music to the financial responsibilities forced on him by an accident of birth, he had quietly prepared himself to deal with Getty Oil's destiny. He had screened the ideas of many, but relied on only one adviser, former undersecretary of the treasury Marc Kaplan in Washington. And he entered negotiations now with far less emotional attachment to Getty Oil, the creation of a cold and distant father, Jean Paul Getty, than most imagined.

Texaco played a strong hand. An offer of $125 per share for the entire company was such a premium over Pennzoil's sweet-

ened bid of $112.50 for a portion of the company that fiduciary
duty to the shareholders would virtually force acceptance from
even the Pennzoil deal's architects, the museum and the trust,
or risk a challenge in court. As the implementation phase
began, the center of action shifted to the Wachtell Lipton
offices, where the powerful pair, Marty Lipton and Jay Higgins, head of Salomon's mergers-and-acquisitions group, were
preparing to represent the interests of the museum, which
stood to receive a bonanza for its endowment from a high
Texaco offer. It was now Thursday night, scarcely twenty-four
hours since Perella had received the call from Wasserstein, and
the deal was swelling in logistical complexity and momentum.
"You couldn't tell without looking out the window if it was day
or night," says Kramer, who had gathered several of his associates from Skadden Arps to the meeting at Wachtell Lipton.
Wasserstein and Lipton were playing cat-and-mouse. As Perella
recalls it, $125 per share finally came from Lipton as the price
at which the museum would sell. The museum committed its
stock. The first vital step of the strategy had been achieved. At
Skadden Arps, Kramer began the frantic preparation of documents that is, as Kramer says, "what lawyers *do* in deals," the
contracts that, that very night, would be signed, locking the
museum's block for Texaco.

But Gordon Getty held the trust's far bigger block. "For that
step, we split up," says Perella. "Bruce went with Lipton to meet
with Larry Tisch, who left a black-tie dinner to meet them in
the lobby of the Pierre, then McKinley went upstairs to see
Gordon Getty. I called Goldman. I got Geoff Boisi and told
him, 'I think we're going to have a deal to work on, and I think
you should come up to Wachtell Lipton with your team.' I knew
damn well Boisi was looking for a deal because he'd called me
before the board meeting. He was very nervous. 'I can't tell you
what's happening, Geoff, but if I were you I would relax.' I told
him they'd talked at $125, McKinley's seeing Getty right now,
and we'll find out shortly."

They had not slept since Tuesday night. As McKinley negotiated with Getty for the trust shares he controlled, a California
court was passing an order prohibiting Getty from doing

anything with the trust's stock. But on Thursday night, as the deal with the museum was signed, Getty, too, signed a letter saying that if he was not prohibited, he would sell the stock to Texaco. McKinley came out of the meeting with a commitment.

On Friday, the final piece of the artful construction Perella had been shaping in his mind since identifying Getty as a target was hoisted into place. The Getty Oil board met, confronted by the signed commitments of the museum and the trust, and agreed to a marriage with Texaco. Convinced, by now, that no sub-rosa dealing with Pennzoil was going on among the principals, Kramer's team had drafted a "hell or high water" agreement, an agreement that says, "If we sign up with you there is definitely going to be a deal, not lots of conditions," Kramer explains. Deal makers were still cautious after the multibillion-dollar deal between Cities Service and Gulf had inexplicably collapsed, costing arbs and investors many millions. "No one wants that to happen," says Kramer, as he directed his growing army at Skadden Arps in the preparation of final documents. The $125 deal was struck with Getty Oil on Friday, and news of the largest merger yet was announced and moved across the Dow Jones tape.

"Great, but we haven't signed anything yet," said Kramer. "Pennzoil went out and celebrated, and they didn't have the deal." It wouldn't be *signed* until Saturday morning. And Gordon Getty was still restrained by a court order. Until he signed, Texaco would not have commitments for a controlling block of stock. "We were worried about Chevron. McKinley had received a call from Chevron Thursday asking if Texaco wanted to be a partner in acquiring Getty. We didn't know if they were just fishing. We figured we had at best a twenty-four-hour lead on Chevron because of the differential of time," Perella said.

Kramer knew the fragility of deals. "What you see in the newspapers is only the tip of the iceberg. Thousands and thousands of man-hours and investments of time and serious money go into a deal, and maybe only one-quarter or a third work out. They fall apart because of ego, personalities, timing, third parties, and fears." That night, the deal started to unravel. Getty Oil CEO Peterson was called as he boarded his flight home to Houston and raced back to Skadden Arps's offices as disputes over some of the hard issues of the deal threatened the agreement. "It's the old story," says Kramer, "the businessmen shake hands and then leave it to the lawyers. You can make or break the deal at that time. There's a lot of raw emotion. A major oil company is going out of existence. It is the demise, the rebirth, the reincarnation. There's a lot of macho in this thing—a winner and a loser. There is always some unhappiness, not said openly, but it runs as an undercurrent in the negotiations." In this environment, Kramer saw himself as more of a brain surgeon than a psychologist. He felt he practiced law on a different planet from his lawyer father, "a general practitioner who works for *people*. He does adoptions, murder cases, accidents—he's a humanist." Relegating corporate law to a lower level in terms of compassion, he says. "The corporation is a substitute for real people." Yet in the cold gray dawn of any deal, it is clearly sensitivity to the human factors that keeps it breathing with life. It is what puts this small man whose intensity trips up his speech pattern and whose wiry body seems one electric nerve end on Joe Flom's front line. At 3:00 A.M. Saturday morning, after hours of massaging by Kramer and the other advisers, the principals for Getty Oil and Texaco finally shook hands, the abrasive subissues that had almost scuttled the agreement resolved. Just hours earlier, the court order restraining Getty from committing the trust's shares was lifted in California. Perella felt the first bit of relief as Gordon Getty signed later that morning.

"If the fat lady hasn't sung, she has opened her mouth already. She is definitely warming up," mused Kramer, permitting himself a moment of satisfaction before girding for the next stage. The documents were signed that Saturday morning. But it would not be over, a done deal, until Texaco had made its tender offer for all the publicly owned shares and had paid $10.6 billion for, and physically possessed, all the stock of Getty Oil. Under the tender offer rules, they couldn't buy stock for at least three weeks and would have to keep the offer open for a minimum of four weeks. Regulatory delays could extend that. During that tense envelope of time, lawsuits, court and regulatory approvals, and crises would pepper the deal. Higher bidders could appear. Tender offer materials were being printed up for immediate launch. But Kramer knew that anything could still happen.

The squabbling between beneficiaries of the trust that had triggered the court order against Gordon Getty was spitting and boiling again before the ink was dry. By Sunday, the day after the signing, McKinley ordered a contingent led by Al Decrane out to California to deal with it, and within days would raise his bid from $125 to $128, mollifying the beneficiaries. Perella stayed in New York. New deals were developing; Texaco would be Wasserstein's to carry. And it was Perella's tenth wedding anniversary. "I begged forgiveness of all the team members and went out for dinner with Amy." The largest deal of his career, Texaco had spanned only six days. First Boston's fee would be $10 million.

As the locus for the weeks ahead shifted to Skadden Arps, Kramer became ringmaster, as deep in the deal flow as it is possible to be. "A buzz begins. You try to isolate it, but everybody knows what's going on. Everybody's pace quickens. Everybody's running. You have thirty or forty people gathering in your office and it's a three-ring circus. But it's actually easier at the epicenter than on the fringes. The winds are fastest on the outside."

For the child raised in middle-class Brooklyn, the epicenter of the takeover wars seems an unlikely destiny. A brainy child, Kramer seemed a better candidate for cloistered academia. "But I had wanted to be a lawyer since I was five or six—it always appealed to me from a philosophical point of view. I was a very academic child, and for the first eight years, I had a traditional Jewish education, with school six days a week and Hebrew studies on Sunday. At Fort Hamilton, a big public high school, I was president of the debating club and the academic society." Then the pain began, as he tried to grab hold of the American dream. Kramer went to Dartmouth. "I chose it because there was a picture of a bunch of guys playing touch football on the lawn. To me, it was the metaphor for the all-Americanism of college. I'd had none of that. I was a city kid. I

was not athletic, but I had a dream," he says, slightly embarrassed at the poignant search for his niche that is a common
thread in the lives of so many of the most successful takeover
warriors. "I was not happy there. There were a lot of preppies,
a lot of football, a lot of fraternities. Sure, I wanted to be, but I
was not a frat person. It is a very good school, but not a good
school for me. I like being *from* Dartmouth."

From his office in New York, Kramer orchestrated activity in
New York, California, Oklahoma, White Plains, and Washington. The twenty working days the tender offer must be open
was his official envelope of time. But with delays, weekends and
holidays, it could stretch to two or three months. "Buying stock
is the last act," he said, as his army fanned out to fight their
individual skirmishes. Before that, peace must be achieved
between the warring family factions in Los Angeles. Court
approval must be gained to lock up the Getty part of the
transaction. Litigation had erupted in Delaware and Oklahoma. And on Capitol Hill and the White House, they had
"substantive antitrust" issues to clear with the Justice Department and Federal Trade Commission (FTC).

"We had document production from anywhere Texaco has
facilities. I had units of lawyers and paralegals who went
through their Houston building from top to bottom looking at
every file drawer, pulling out documents that we had to hand
over to the government. We had tens of thousands of documents. When we made our second submission to the FTC, we
sent down two corporate jet planes filled with documents from
all over the country. We were always moving bodies around. An
advantage we had—the only way we could *do* the transaction—
was access to the Texaco air force. All its airplanes. At one
point, we had to have one of our lawyers in court in California
and Oklahoma on the same day. A Texaco jet picked him up at
some airport in California after he'd done his thing and had
him arguing before a judge in Oklahoma the same day."

The possible "what ifs" that could kill the deal haunted
Kramer. "What if Texaco gets through antitrust and then
Exxon decides to take over Mobil tomorrow? That'll blow us

out of the water because the government will step in and say, 'Absolutely, *no,* that can't happen.' " What if a new bidder came in? Everything had to be cleared. If there was even one injunction in some obscure court, they could not legally close and buy the stock. "If we get notice we're okay, and *if nothing new happens* . . ." Kramer didn't dare leave the telephone. He started carrying a beeper for the first time in his life.

When fifty days had gone by and no third party had shown up, Kramer's anxiety began to ease. Tendered shares and letters of commitment of shares from banks and brokerage houses were pouring into a bank depository. They were down to planning the last question: How do we buy the stock? "We spent days developing strategies of how, when we got the notice that we're okay and it was 'go,' who goes where, who calls who, who makes sure the check gets in the mail and checks registration in our name," says Kramer. "We spent literally *weeks* planning the last twenty-five minutes of this game." There was a last-minute wild card. A pressure tactic from some independent gasoline retailers in New England to enjoin the merger. It failed. When clearance came, the deal was done in a minute, and Texaco owned Getty Oil.

"You've put the peg in the last hole," Kramer said. "You've put in sixty days. You're too tired to celebrate. At that point, happiness is the absence of pain. We did have champagne. We went over to the Four Seasons—Wasserstein, Perella, and my-self," says Kramer. Across the street from First Boston, the Four Seasons is a favored spot. Perella and his party are always seated in the Barroom, which is quieter and less festive than the main room by the pool where the out-of-towners and birthday and anniversary crowd dine. "But you don't really celebrate," says Kramer. "As soon as the deal is over, you go on to another deal." "It's not like a *high five* in football," said Perella, savoring his Roederer Kristal champagne. "It's sort of a quiet kind of a great feeling."

While champagne popped in New York, rage was building in J. Hugh Liedtke, outrage over the destruction of a deal that would find its expression in a lawsuit filed in Texas state court in Houston. Finally tried before a twelve-man jury sixteen months later, the case that would lay the elegant complexities and principles of corporate contract law against the most fundamental American folk ethics rumbled quietly, like distant guns, through the summer and early fall of 1985. The headlines followed other battles.

CHAPTER 11

Its huge jet fleet still roared into the sky, on schedule. Its thirty-three hundred pilots still marched, full of pride, to their airplanes. Its operational and maintenance hubs in Missouri were still a rock of stability and employment in the nation's heartland. But while ARCO stripped down to a lean, debt-burdened entity no raider could love, TWA sat as fragile as a butterfly. In New York, Carl Icahn prepared to make his move. On April 29, the day of ARCO's highly public act of restructuring, he quietly crossed the 5 percent level of stock ownership that triggered the ticking of the clock. Within ten days, he would have to file his 13D with the SEC, revealing his stake to the world.

"If you thought we'd just stand by and do nothing while you try to take over our company—think again!" the full page ad would blast out from the *Wall Street Journal* two weeks later, livening morning coffee for millions of Americans as TWA launched its counterattack against Carl Icahn's raid on its stock. "You have to be proven 'fit' to operate an airline. . . . We think it's a

commitment you just can't handle," the ad went on. Anyone
who had seen the disheveled pack-rat's nest of an office where
the analysis that led to the choice of TWA as a target was done
would probably have emphatically agreed. He would probably
have been wrong. Young business students may one day genu-
flect before Al Kingsley's office at Icahn & Co., Inc., at 1370
Sixth Avenue.

Hired for summer work while he was still in the Wharton
School, Alfred D. Kingsley is Icahn's most loyal and trusted
aide. The two men share the same broad New York accent and
contempt for the white-shoe establishment. Al Kingsley evalu-
ates companies as potential investment targets for Icahn. Evaluations are what takeovers are all about. What's the stock
selling for? What's the book value? What *might* it be worth with
a little creative massaging of the assets? What price should we
pay? It is what investment bankers are paid $15 million fees for.
Icahn trusts Kingsley's evaluations so much that, he claims, "If
Al doesn't like a company, I pretty well forget it."

It is hard to believe that some of the most sophisticated and
creative financial analysis in the business comes from this room
Al dignifies with the name "library." Behind his desk, Kingsley
is barely visible above a two-foot-high mountain of paper. He
appears to have kept every business journal, proxy statement,
legal brief, dogeared letter, annual report, computer printout,
and telephone memo that has touched his fingers since the day
he started with Icahn in 1965. It's a corner room. But the light
level has been substantially reduced by the drifts of paper piled
on the counters behind his desk, and what the desk and
counters cannot hold has spilled onto the floor. Yellowed
papers and fat file folders stacked against the walls on three
sides give the room the look of a bunker surrounded by
sandbags. Here it is, a monument to takeover, a paper grave-
yard of the deals that have been profitably put to bed.

Curly-haired, with a friendly, boyish-looking face and blue
business suit hung on his chubby body like an unimportant
afterthought, Kingsley runs his library like his family living
room. His dad, Herman, drops in, a small, neatly dressed

retired lawyer who ran a quiet little practice in New York—
wills, taxes, divorces—and goes to Florida for the winter. They
chat and drink coffee, while Kingsley also works over material
in his hands and diverts his eyes every few seconds to scan the
terminal, which has somehow staked a claim to a position on
the left side of his desk. "Whadda ya watching, Al?" his dad
asks. "Everything," says Al, keeping his nerve ends open and
alert to the flow of the market. Who knows how many million-
dollar positions they're holding out there at any given minute?
Al's wife, Temma, calls, "What's up? Yeah, she went in a cab. I
took her. Where are you . . . home? What're we going to have
for dinner? Anything there? Want me to bring something in?"
A secretary hurries in while he's talking to Temma, anxious for
him to find a particular letter Ichan wants to see. He cradles the
phone in his neck, keeps talking—"Yeah, yeah, I'll be home
reasonable"—swivels around, shuffles a stack of papers with
pudgy fingers, and finds the letter in seconds.

Is it even conceivable that Icahn's legendary memory—his
ability to press his fingers to his forehead as if punching in a
computer program and call up the data on any number or fact
he has ever heard or seen in discussions, contracts, or research—may be, partially, compensation for the chaos in
Kingsley's library?

Is this any way to run an office? The scalps on the entrance
lobby wall—neatly framed covers of fourteen annual reports of
Icahn's targets and source of at least $200 million profit over
the last few years through sellbacks or takeover—say *absolutely*.
They are a road map of Icahn's daring raids: Bayswater Realty,
Tappan, Simplicity, Dan River, Hammermill Paper, Chese-
brough-Pond's, Baird & Warner, Saxon Industries, American
Can, ACF, Anchor Hocking, Owens-Illinois, Marshall Field
and, finally, Phillips—Icahn's first taste of the really big time.
As decor, they are far less quaint than the prints of nineteenth-
century Wall Street that hang above a red leather sofa, a Wall
Street with top hats, cobbled streets, and horse-drawn car-
riages. But they are a revealing document of the distance Icahn
and Kingsley have come together from the hustling arbitrage

days and nickel-and-dime deals to membership in the very
small club of entrepreneurs who go for billion-dollar corporations.

When he heard that Icahn was stalking the airline, Captain
Harry R. Hoglander was sure he knew what triggered Icahn's
interest. "We had the premier airplanes, the premier routes,
carried on our books for nothing. Icahn probably saw Pan Am
sell off its international routes to United for a good price—
$750 million. And they aren't worth *half* the value of TWA's
routes," growled Hoglander, watching over the pilots' interests
from his small, utilitarian union offices in the Pan Am Building
a few blocks east of Kingsley's library. "Pan Am just confirmed
our thinking," says Kingsley, "but long before the Pan Am sale
to UAL, we saw the value of the international routes. The
reason is they're limited. Domestic's been deregulated, but
international has not. There's no way American Airlines can fly
New York to Paris. TWA has it. It's locked in by government
agreements, treaties, presidential approval." But that was only
the beginning of their hunt for value. Kingsley and Icahn stalk
values with the sensitive eye and intuition of the most cunning
hunter. It is the eye of the rancher who sees the water in his
creeks and rivers as an asset to manipulate and whip around
like a jet from a garden hose and raise the productive value of a
scrubland a thousandfold. It is a view of virtually all things as
assets that can be manipulated, leveraged, transformed, spun
off or consolidated, shrunk or expanded, to extract their greatest possible value. Most businessmen, Icahn believed, tripped
over unpolished gems without seeing the fortunes that lay
inside.

Night people whose creative juices flow best at two and three
in the morning, Kingsley and Icahn poured over TWA's numbers and assets for months before they made their first purchase in September 1984. Working at the office until eight or
nine, eating together at Icahn's favorite restaurant, Christ
Cella's on Forty-sixth Street, phoning each other at home at
any post-midnight hour, they developed an evaluation of
TWA's assets. As their view of TWA's values unfolded, TWA's

lead lawyer, Jim Freund, would say with considerable respect, "Nobody sees values the way Icahn does."

"What I look for in these companies," claims Icahn, "are *hidden* values, values that are not apparent. Analysts look at numbers. They don't see these nonapparent values." Pickens had been masterful at identifying and releasing value in the oil industry. But oil reserves were more readily quantifiable. Spanning all industries, Icahn's was a subtler game.

They explored what's in a name. "If you asked anybody on the street, 'What's TWA,' they could tell you," Kingsley said, "Just those *initials* hold all the value of fifty years of advertising and good will. You couldn't put a value on that. If we started buying TWA stock at $8 per share, that means the company's common stock had less than $300 total market value. Compare that to just the *name* of TWA!"

As they had searched TWA's assets, Icahn observed, "A lot of these companies are undervalued because of poor management. You can *replace* bad management, right. So that's one big hidden value there." It was one of his most passionate themes. "Mediocre managements kill a lot of industries. Look at steel. It was such an establishment industry that nobody could ever *touch* them. But in this decade there are guys like *me* around, for *this* industry." For airlines. "The airlines are badly managed. TWA is an excellent example of terrible management—terrible! Meyer is probably a nice guy, but he's a classic example of an executive who is way, way over his head." It was the theme he would lay on the CEOs at the Diebold seminar in July, his belief that, to keep competition away, CEOs surround themselves with mediocrity and suppress the best men. But management, like any other asset, could be made more efficient. His anger flared when Kingsley uncovered the "golden passes," the kind of perk that confirmed the worst Icahn had ever said about arrogant, entrenched boards and managements. The golden passes flew directors and their families free anywhere in the world. When a director retired from the board, he kept the pass for as many years as he had served. If a director died, his widow retained the pass—for life! The company even paid the income tax assessed by the IRS for the personal use of passes. The golden passes would be one of the first cuts, if he got control.

They uncovered another unexploited gem. PARS. TWA's computerized reservation system. Some of its value was obvious. "It's the third largest in the business," said Icahn, "after Apollo and Saber, the systems of United and American. They have a captive market—all the other airlines have to use them for booking flights." Then he exulted, "Here's the undervalued asset—the *travel agents*. PARS goes into fifteen-thousand travel agents' offices! The tendency is for travel agents to book the airline that owns the system." But Icahn loves to play with the possibilities. PARS had potential far beyond the booking of flights. "It's a computer system that does a lot of things other than making reservations. Scheduling flights. Fuel consumption," Kingsley speculated. "But it could be expanded to add things like travel services. Anything you can think of. This is the world of computers, and once you have a system in the agent's office, it could be used for other things. Hey, Carl, that data base is a valuable asset." Icahn's intensity was rising as he grabbed hold of the system's potential. "Yeah, yeah, you could use it as a planning tool, or for travel packages. Say a fifteen-year-old is going to Europe and you want to lay out a whole education package for him. You punch in your need, and up on the terminal comes a whole printout with travel, hotel, schools, places to stay and see . . ."

But how would you market it? "Perhaps you could separate out the reservations service. Keep it for TWA, but franchise it to other airlines," Icahn proposed. "We'd have to lure some of the business away from American and United," said Kingsley. "It would take a lot of marketing. You'd have to keep fighting for those agents. But you *have* all those agents out there."

There was an even more valuable asset languishing unmaximized. The real hidden vlaue here at TWA is the high price you pay the unions, Icahn believed. Labor costs, they discovered, were 35 to 40 percent of an airline's expenses. "If you could negotiate that out, it becomes much more valuable." Kingsley added, "You can't have two airlines leaving New York for Chicago and one is paying $80,000 for a pilot and the other $40,000. Both planes take off at two and arrive at three. They offer the same services, the same Marriott food." Kingsley scrutinized the annual reports of fast-growing airlines like Frank Lorenzo's, whose Texas Air had just gobbled up Continental. The labor cuts he'd achieved were stunning. Where the hourly cost of an American Airlines DC-10 crew was $703, the equivalent crew at Continental cost $194. Where TWA's average pilot pay was over $87,000, Continental's was under $30,000. Massive concessions from labor would have to be the basis of any strategy for maximizing value. Icahn liked pilots. But let's face it, they were just another asset. Or so the two thought, as they refined their own findings at meetings with a consultant, Sanford Rederer. They had not yet met Captain Harry Hoglander.

One thing both Icahn and Kingsley realized from the research: they'd have to *control* the assets to work the magic. They would have to own the airline.

While Kingsley and Icahn played with scenarios and bought stock, complacency reigned at TWA. No one would dare attack it. And why would anyone want to attack an airline? The industry was too high-risk and volatile, and—except for a few of the new budget airlines—too unprofitable to attract a raid. For in spite of all its prestige and coveted international routes, TWA was having a turbulent trip through the deregulated age that engulfed the industry in 1978. In 1984, it had eked out a profit of $60 million, but took a heavy loss for the fourth quarter—a gloomy omen for 1985. Its stock price was far lower than its book value—the market's blunt measure of lackluster performance. A few blocks away from TWA's corporate headquarters in New York, Carl Icahn had passed the 5 percent mark.

Now he had just ten days to continue buying quietly at a bargain price before filing with the SEC, and he intended to exploit them aggressively. Icahn was entering that controversial window of opportunity many in Congress were trying to close because of the advantage it gave raiders, allowing them to buy stock cheaply before the runup triggered by their filing of a

13D. It was a window of time, too, that invited insider trading by arbitragers and investment bankers, a growing issue for those concerned about the integrity of the market. But the window was still wide open as Icahn reached 5 percent. As Icahn likes to say, he "strapped on his six-guns" to sweep the Street.

When Icahn filed his 13D on May 9, he had acquired 20.5 percent of TWA's common stock. He was by far the largest single shareholder.

His attack would shock, as attacks on Walt Disney and CBS had shocked. TWA was the third-largest airline in the United States, after American and United. An institution that had been flying Americans for nearly sixty years. Unlike oil or paper companies, which seldom touch the emotions, TWA had carved a sentimental niche for itself in the national psyche. It was the airline launched, in 1929, by the *City of Los Angeles,* a Ford Tri-Motor with Charles Lindbergh at the controls and christened with temperate grape juice by Mary Pickford as it took off for its first scheduled flight to the East Coast. TWA had helped Ibn Saud set up an airline to replace the thousand-car cavalcades that had moved his royal retinue across the Saudi Arabian deserts. Its flights to Bangkok, Nairobi, Paris, and Madrid had opened an exotic window on the world for a nation hungry for travel after World War II. Its first-class flight to Europe was still the glamor act of the air, with the cuisine and service that had largely vanished from commercial air travel.

And Icahn's attack shocked because an airline was a repository of public trust; with the purchase of your ticket, you voluntarily gave control over your safety to the airline. TWA had not had a crash for ten years. It was still a "pilot's outfit," as it had been from the beginning, with enormous pride in its professionalism. Its pilots still reveled in a life-style second to none. A pilot could leave his home in Napa Valley, fly to New York, and settle into the seat of his 747 for his flight to Athens confident that he was one of a superbly trained elite with skills and standards as high as any in the industry. Terrorist hijackings had brought a new hazard to the routes he flew. Within two months of Icahn's filing, a TWA flight for Athens would be taken hostage in a hijacking that would grip the world. And all around them TWA pilots saw pay and status eroding under tightening economic pressure on the industry. But TWA's thirty-three hundred pilots had been pretty well buffered from the ravages of change by a strong union, and even junior captains like Harry Hoglander, their union head, still made $125,000 a year. The pilots looked to Hoglander, a 727 captain elected chairman of the Master Executive Council in 1982, to fight to make the revolution in the cockpit as painless and dignified as possible. There was no doubt that it was revolution. Or that, if the storm of takeover broke over TWA, Hoglander would be leading TWA's pilots into turbulence that would largely determine the survival and quality of the unique culture of America's commercial airline pilot.

As Icahn put TWA in play, he set in motion the most fascinating of all of 1985's sensational megadeals. The struggle would encompass a sixty-year sweep of aviation history, and the great merger wave of the 1960s. It would be a decisive clash between the government-controlled environment in which TWA matured and the reigning laissez faire, free-market climate in which takeovers have thrived. It would be a telling view of the impact of deregulation. And it would be a classic showcase for the Byzantine mosaic of deals, men, and issues that give the takeover wars their distinctive pattern. Familiar players, firms, and strategies would weave through the drama. Other deals—Phillips, Unocal, Household, and Crown Zellerbach—would influence decisions.

But its uniqueness lies in being the deal that reveals, more than any other, the human side of takeovers. Unlike Unocal or Crown Zellerbach, it would matter to many millions of Americans. It is the deal that demonstrates that although takeovers may be cold-blooded asset plays driven by balance sheets, they are still unmapped frontiers in which the behavior and personalities of individual men determine the shape and outcome. TWA became a crucible that tested three of the principal players—Icahn, lawyer Jim Freund, and Captain Harry Hoglander—as they had never before been tested. It saw the historic evolution of the employees of a company caught up in

takeover from hapless pawns trying to save their jobs and life-
style with prayers and cookies—as Phillips employees had done
in Bartlesville—to front-line warriors and, indeed, linchpins in
the deal.

♦ ♦ ♦

TWA did not welcome Icahn as the agent of its destiny. "Mr.
Icahn's presence is uninvited and undesirable," said TWA's
formal press release on May 9, when Icahn filed his 13D. But it
was not a surprise. TWA had discovered his activity in the stock
just ten days earlier, although they had no idea how large his
stake was. In fact, there had been an urgent behind-the-scenes
effort to halt Icahn from a hostile bid, an effort led by TWA's
lawyers at Skadden Arps and by Drexel Burnham. "We monitored the activity in TWA stock in late April," says Jim Freund,
the Skadden Arps lawyer who would be TWA's principal legal
adviser, "and when the rumor that Icahn was buying was
verified, our first thought was to try to keep him from making a
hostile run at the company."

It was Drexel Burnham's goal, too. Drexel was very embarrassed by Icahn's move. Both Icahn and TWA were clients.
Drexel had helped Icahn with Phillips just months earlier, and
had done $100 million worth of financing for TWA within the
year. Both Icahn and TWA executives had addressed Drexel's
annual seminar in Los Angeles in March; Icahn had shown a
lively interest in an optimistic speech on TWA's future by
TWA's chief financial officer, and that might, Drexel feared,
look like the genesis of Icahn's growing interest in TWA. With
congressional hearings and regulatory and legislative action to
discredit and restrict junk bonds gathering momentum from
New York State to the Federal Reserve Board in Washington,
Drexel didn't want one client going after another, and thought
that a hostile bid by Icahn on a beloved institution would give
Washington a focus for its arguments. Drexel first tried to talk
Icahn out of going for TWA. "They suggested that we meet
with him, and two meetings were held," said Freund. The first
meeting, put together by Drexel's president Frederick H. Joseph, set the stage for the second, larger one.

It was held in Skadden Arps's large conference room. Icahn's airline consultant, Sandy Rederer, had prepared a summary of recommendations for action Icahn would take if he got control. TWA's team recoiled as they heard it. Clearly, Pan Am's big sale of routes to United had not gone unnoticed. Icahn was proposing, in effect, to close down or sell the domestic routes and run only the profitable overseas routes. He talked of selling off facilities and leasing out planes. In other words, a bust-up. "We knew that the whole key to the overseas routes were the domestic routes that fed into them," said Freund, "and we tried to tell him, 'Don't come after us thinking that you'll be able to close down domestic routes, sell off excess airplanes to reduce expenses and raise cash flow, because it just *won't work*. The feeder routes are the key to TWA's prosperity.' We told him we needed to expand domestically to compete with United and American and to generate increased passenger load for the international routes."

It was an airline, damn it. An integrated system. An institution. And in the chaos of deregulation—as airlines were being created, gobbled up, and going bankrupt, planes and pilots leased, and ruthless competition replacing the gentlemanly, subsidized days of regulation—the established airlines were clinging with increasing ferocity to the concept that survival lay in the very things the oil industry was now abandoning: in the integrated system and in expansion. And, of course, in cutting labor costs; TWA's were among the highest in the industry. The company was negotiating right now with two of its unions, the machinists and flight attendants, and was about to begin with the pilots, trying to bring that cost down. "But guys like Icahn look on companies as asset plays," said Freund, convinced, as everyone else was, that Icahn had no interest in running an airline. "He behaved himself at the first two meetings. He was very low-key. But we disliked his game plan because it would bust up the airline," Freund observed. An anti-Icahn feeling took hold that would only need a little fanning to become explosive.

Icahn needed a lawyer to prepare his 13D for filing, and on

May 7 he called Stephen E. Jacobs, of the New York law firm of Weil, Gotshal & Manges. Steve Jacobs had helped him in his acquisition of ACF. "It would be wonderful if your client didn't start the accumulation process without first talking to you," says Jacobs, with the sense of humor that would serve him well in the next few moments, as Carl asked him to be his lawyer for TWA. " 'Why on earth would you want to invest in TWA?' I asked, which shows how much I know. 'How much stock do you own?' " Jacobs asked next. " 'Twenty percent,' said he. I gulped. 'When did you cross over 5 percent?' 'Eight days ago,' said he. Why didn't you call earlier? thought I, but instead I shot back the cryptic comment to Carl, '16(b).' " It was a caution that Icahn's 20 percent could cost him some tax on his profits. "I know," said Icahn. "Draft up a 13D."

Freund had hoped Drexel's influence would be enough to hold Icahn back. But when Jacobs, sent the "Purposes of the Transaction" section of the 13D over to Freund for comment just before he filed it with the SEC, Freund knew Drexel had failed. On the up side, the 13D showed that Icahn had listened and perhaps learned at the two meetings. What Icahn had told Jacobs in their first phone call was expressed in the 13D—that, as Jacobs paraphrases it, "he had been initially interested in TWA by the consultant Rederer, who had led him to believe that TWA could eliminate some domestic routes and sell off a bunch of planes, but that TWA in these meetings had convinced him that that strategy was a terrible idea." The tone of the 13D was still relatively friendly. But Icahn's lawyers hadn't sent over the section with the numbers—the size of Icahn's stake. "How much stock has he got?" Freund asked Gary Duberstein, Icahn's inside lawyer. "I can't tell you," Duberstein replied. TWA guessed he had under 10 percent. "Then it came across the tape," says Freund, "and, Christ, it was over 20 percent! All the talk of Carl holding back went out the window. Once we saw the numbers, we knew he would go for control. Everything else was wishful thinking. The fat was in the fire."

Freund found himself standing squarely on the front line. He had been advising TWA on an entirely different matter when the Icahn thing began to bubble. Hostile takeovers were not his primary focus. Of all the lawyers who would be involved, he was probably the only one who had studiously worked *not* to get caught in the hostile deal flow. He had left a sleepy firm in 1966 to join Skadden Arps, then a little fifteen-lawyer firm few had ever heard of, because he wanted action. "I had action from day one. But as the firm grew, Joe Flom developed such a terrific reputation in the contested area, that it was clear to me I'd always be a bag carrier in that field. Flom was just larger than life."

So Freund had veered away from hostile takeovers and created his own niche in the area of negotiated mergers. "All of us have egos to express. I knew that in hostile deals the client would always want Joe Flom. I wanted clients to look to me for advice." From the late 1960s onward, friendly acquisitions were one of the most fertile fields of lawyering. "I found I was good at it. I also found it was a field ripe to write about." He wrote a book on the subject of negotiated mergers, *Anatomy of a Merger;* Marty Lipton gave it a great review. Although his merger work was less sensational than the deals Flom took, his clients—Dun and Bradstreet among them—were top drawer. And friendly deals still vastly outnumbered hostile deals, even in the mid-1980s. "It's still the grist of the mill," says Freund.

Freund's professional profile had been shaped by more than the need to escape Flom's awesome shadow. Freund believed he had more a bargainer's than a warrior's temperament. It's not that negotiated deals were a love fest. It was hard confrontational stuff. But the parties had a common goal. "And I didn't like the idea of forcing my will on someone else. I like a win-win situation. . . . Flom was the fighter; I was the lover," Freund said, as he faced the most significant hostile deal of his career with Skadden Arps.

And yet he'd been increasingly attracted to hostile deals. After twenty years, Jim Freund was restless for change. "I was no longer so stimulated by straight negotiations. The intricacies of mergers no longer fascinated me." He'd begun to nibble at the edges of the hostile action, serving as counselor to companies that feared attack. In a few cases, he'd represented companies like National Can that were under siege. It was part of a broader transformation of his life. He was fifty-one, divorced after a long marriage, and had just married a woman in her mid-thirties. Barbara Fox, his new wife, ran a residential real estate business, was excited about her work, and he loved that. They ran together in Central Park, and he was feeling fit and operating on a new energy level. A muscular five feet eleven inches, with rough good looks, heavy dark brows, and an attractive thatch of graying hair, he was increasingly active. As he had neared fifty, he had intuitively begun to strip passive activities from his life. He rarely read a novel anymore. "But I *write* books and articles. I *play* music and tennis. I *take* pictures." His fathering was anything but passive. His two boys, seventeen and nineteen, would come over; they'd put together a trio, playing jazz and rock, Jim at the piano and the boys on bass and drums. Sometimes they'd tape their trio and then feed in an extra track of Jim on the vibes and son Tom on guitar to make a quintet of songs such as "Angel Eyes." Playing it back, Freund would grin and say, "Hey, we're not bad."

Joe Flom was busy with Unocal and Crown Zellerbach. Freund was delighted to be on his own. He had feeling for TWA. It was TWA Super Connies that had carried most of Freund's generation on their first flights to Europe in the 1960s. He had discovered in the several hostile deals he'd done that he could handle it without Flom. But as the crises came thundering into the boardroom over the next weeks and months, would he have the decisiveness and judgment all-out war requires? "In defending a takeover, most of your clients have never been here before. They've had little preparation. They don't just want you to spell out the options and alternatives," he said. "They want your *views*."

A strong point of view had come hard for Freund. "We were the silent generation. We missed all the wars—World War II, Korea, and Vietnam—and the activism of the 1960s. We matured in the fifties during the Eisenhower years. The Age of Conformity. We were noncontroversial and I was always uncomfortable with strong opinions." He had vivid recall of a moment during his navy service when his captain had called him up to the bridge on their icebreaker as they entered an

Antarctic ice field, and asked Freund, as the only veteran of that icy route, "Okay, mister, what do I do now?" Freund had forced himself to recommend some minor maneuver, and the ship had slithered safely past an ice floe. As the ice got heavier, the captain had called him up again, and Freund had managed to devise some slightly more complicated tactic. But as they abutted thick blue ice, unable to budge, he balked at making any more seat-of-the-pants decisions. "Well," demanded the captain, "is that your whole bag of tricks?" "Yes, sir," said Freund weakly, as he slunk back to the wardroom.

An absence of strongly held views had been the story of his young adult life. "I went through Princeton acutely aware of shades of gray. And that was compounded at Harvard Law School, where you argued fifteen points of view and professors who were models for *The Paper Chase* turned us into judgmental eunuchs. I went through my entire three years of law school without forming a view on whether any of the court opinions we had read were right or wrong. I just focused on the issues." While others effortlessly leaped chasms of ignorance and arrived easily at firm conclusions, lawyers, he observed, often got stuck at the cliff edge shackled by caveats, concern for nuance, and the desire, always for more raw facts. Entering law, he cautiously qualified his opinions with "subject to a number of other relevant considerations," "one might think," and "it can be argued that."

He had treated the issue of his own lack of strong views lightly in columns he wrote for the *Legal Times*. He had recounted the story of a friend who had deftly vivisected a movie he had thought was rather good, condemning the star as a disaster and the director for losing control in the middle scenes and for leaving a better ending on the cutting room floor. He had wondered how one could ever, in personal or professional life, have sufficient control of the facts to make unqualified judgments. But there was, he knew, "definitely something heady about going for broke, particularly when your clients are nodding their heads in emphatic assent." With experience, he had become increasingly decisive in his profession. Still, when someone at a cocktail party pushed him for his position on an issue of world politics, he would deflect the question with "I don't have enough facts."

◆   ◆   ◆

Now there was no time to be indecisive. With Icahn's 13D, events were exploding. "Up to that point, there had been telephone briefings with the board. After the 20 percent, we had board meetings in person or by conference call every few days." A frantic search for defensive weapons in TWA's charter and bylaws came up empty. TWA had no corporate defenses. None of the usual shark repellents. No poison pill. No special voting stock. And most important, no staggered board. TWA had been spun off in 1984 by Trans World Corporation, as TWA's parent conglomerate cast the airline unceremoniously adrift and held on to its more profitable divisions—Hilton Hotels and Century 21 realtors. That was the time they could have put defenses into the charter. But, as the board explained to Jim, they hadn't expected to be the target of a takeover. Why would anyone want an airline?

By the early 1970s, airlines had lost much of the financial glamor they had gained in the sixties during the expanding early years of the jet age, which began in 1958. The oil shortage of 1973 and 1974 drove fuel costs up, adding to the expense of already high fuel consumption by jet aircraft, And with OPEC having taken control of the world oil market, fuel prices continued to be volatile. Jet fuel that had cost 12.4 cents per gallon in 1973 had broken the $1 gallon barrier by 1979. Meanwhile, a vigorous pilots' union allied with the powerful Air Line Pilots Association, kept driving wages and benefits up to the $150,000-a-year level for senior captains; pilots were one of the highest-paid professions in the nation. The Deregulation Act of 1978 issued the coup de grace to profitability for any airline that did not swiftly adapt. Deregulation tore the large established airlines from the protective bosom of government and thrust them into open competition in the marketplace, exposing inefficiencies as brutally as it was currently doing in banking, trucking, and telecommunications.

Competition was nothing new for TWA. It had been born out of the barnstorming capitalist spirit that made America the

pioneer and early leader in commercial aviation. Its predecessor companies were three of the small regional airlines that
erupted by the dozens in the 1920s. From the beginning, mail
had been the basis of profit. In a frontier nation with a
compulsion to adopt the trappings of order and civilization as
swiftly as possible, delivery of the mail has always been as
motivating a force in building America's transportation system
as settling the land. And in 1930, the postmaster general forced
a merger of the three airlines to consolidate mail and passenger
service into Transcontinental & Western Air, Inc., TWA, bringing the infant airline under the protective wing of regulation.
The Air Mail Act of 1934 forced the merger of the two into
TWA, and TWA matured and flourished in an environment in
which routes, fares, and competition were tightly controlled.
The Civil Aeronautics Board (CAB) allocated routes, regulated
fares, and subsidized ailing carriers so that each airline could
make a profit. Fares had been based on industry averages, not
on competition in the marketplace. As hard-bargaining pilots'
unions got increases to match the culture-hero status they had
acquired since World War II, the CAB simply raised passenger
fares to pay for them. In this environment, TWA, like an
animal taken from the wild and domesticated, had lost much of
its survival instinct.

Suddenly finding itself competing for routes and customers
with aggressive young cost-cutting airlines like People Express,
TWA was now forced to join price wars that reduced revenues
even further. The airline still sat on a fortune in hard assets—a
huge jet fleet, rich transatlantic routes, state-of-the-art maintenance and training facilities in Kansas City and operational hub
in Saint Louis, and its computerized reservation system, PARS.
And it contained less tangible assets—superbly skilled flight
crews, an excellent safety record, and sixty years of goodwill.
But as in the oil industry, its assets were not being maximized.
The company was barely breaking even, and growing union
unrest could lead to devastating strikes, like United's. In January 1985, *Fortune* magazine had awarded TWA the ignominy of
being the third-least-admired major corporation in America.
As Icahn began to buy, that view from the marketplace was

summed up in the price of TWA's stock: it was trading at $8 and $9 per share.

And now he was at the doorstep. Without defenses, how could they deter Icahn? "We couldn't do a stock buyback like Unocal because that takes economic muscle we didn't have. We had cash flow, but we needed the cash for the winter. TWA does better in the summer," Freund said. And even if they *had* the money, a stock buyback would be suicidal; by reducing the number of outstanding shares, it would make Icahn's block an even larger percentage of the remaining shares. "Twenty percent could become 30 percent! It would do his job for him," Freund said.

A poison pill was considered. Jim had real doubts about it, what with the pill's uncertain legal status. Household was coming up for appeal to the Delaware Supreme Court in a few weeks, but it could be months before a decision came down. "Our firm was on the other side of that. It would be a little hard to advise a board to do something you were simultaneously arguing was illegal." They were all watching Goldsmith. He appeared to be marching right over Crown Zellerbach's pill. On May 9, as Icahn filed, Goldsmith was just four days from passing the 20 percent mark, which activated the poison pill. Even then, its effect would not be known for some time. Freund had to act now. "The most threatening aspect of a poison pill is the flip-over provision—that if somebody acquires you in a merger, your shareholders can buy the other guy's shares cheap. With Carl, there was nothing to buy. No real company there. No stock. No assets." No, the TWA board would not adopt a poison pill.

The board was glaringly vulnerable. Without a staggered board, Icahn could remove all nineteen directors at one time without the need to assert cause. He could achieve it simply with written "consents" from the shareholders, which he could solicit by an ad in the *Wall Street Journal* or by a proxy mailing. All he would need was a controlling majority of the stock. For there was a provision of Delaware law that says that unless the company's charter provides otherwise—and TWA's didn't— anything that can be done at a meeting can be done by consents. If Icahn collected consents on 50.1 percent of the shares for the removal of the directors, and presented them to the company, the board would be out on its ear.

How could he be stopped? Buy him off with greenmail? No. Greenmail had been roundly condemned as an odious if not yet illegal practice. Since Pickens's sellback to Phillips, any act that even smelled of greenmail could kill your credibility in ensuing litigation and with the media. And greenmail was precluded here by the sheer size of Icahn's block of stock. When he went over 10 percent, he fell under the 16(b) provision of the Securities Exchange Act of 1934 that would force him, if he sold his 20 percent within six months of the purchase, to return to TWA any profit he made on the sale of his stock in excess of a 10 percent holding. Icahn was smart. "When he crossed 10 percent, he was giving out another message," Freund said. "He was in this for something other than the quick sellback." Freund had glimpsed other goals when Icahn had hung in and bought ACF in 1983, and then operated it. "Perhaps, after all the flak Icahn had taken as an evil, greenmailing raider, he wants to show us and the world that he is serious, that he isn't just in it for the greenmail," Freund speculated. But if he *was* out to acquire the airline, how likely was it that he would keep it intact? His record and his statements at the first two meetings suggested he would buy it for the bust-up. Freund searched for ways to buy some time so the board could come up with a plan to stop him.

CHAPTER 12

WITH a trained legal mind under a tough New York accent, a captain's air of authority, and combat experience in Korea, Harry Hoglander had the right stuff to lead his union through the hell of the mid-1980s. He was just beginning a gritty round of contract negotiations with the company when Icahn's presence set off an alarm in late April, and he had hardly noticed. "Like the rest ot the employees, we were wondering what the hell was going on. But there had been passes made at TWA before." In the late seventies, Frank Lorenzo of what was then Texas International had bought 4 or 5 percent, but his approach had been rebuffed by management. In 1983, the Odyssey group had bought 7 to 10 percent and were trying to get seats on the board. Fearful that Odyssey intended to sell off Trans World's divisions and dismember the airline, Harry had taken the kind of action that gave clues as to the kind of fighter the pilots had on their side. "I and another guy bust into Odyssey's offices to demand to know what the hell they were going to do with the company, and we were thrown out by the police." As head of TWA's Master Executive Council, Hoglander had been kept informed of the meetings with Icahn before his 13D filing. But he was consumed by the contract negotiations. He had drawn a firm line beyond which pilots could and would not go, and he was not above strike threats.

Since deregulation, negotiations had become a story of concessions, not gains, for pilot salaries had been clearly identified as the area where the greatest cost cuts could be made. And the company was pushing for the hated new two-tier pay scale, which hired new pilots at half the regular pay scales. Part of the supply and demand of a free market, two-tier had been pioneered by American two years earlier, adopted by United, and the trend was spreading. Two-tier was what United's pilots were striking about, a particularly inflexible and abusive two-tier, in Harry's view, and was the issue that could permanently destroy the unions. TWA's council was affiliated with the Air Line Pilots Association (ALPA), and in an impassioned letter Hoglander was preparing to write to his pilots urging them to give to the war chest that was sustaining United's striking pilots, he would caution, "Make no mistake about where we are in labor relations in this country. The United Air Line management wants to throw the pilots union and its contract completely off the property. Others will seek to follow that effort."

For Hoglander, deregulation was "the greatest antilabor legislation ever passed by this Congress." And two-tier was one of its most threatening manifestations. It thrust the brutal competitive realities of deregulation into the cockpit—a captain making $130,000 sat beside a highly qualified junior pilot making $30,000. It created a class structure that could only breed resentment. And it bared the wage disparities so blatantly—the fact that qualified young pilots were willing to fly for a fraction of the pay and conditions the union had fought since 1938 to achieve—that somebody would have to give. He knew it would be, as always, the high-paid pilots.

Hoglander's hatred of deregulation was focused on one man. Frank Lorenzo. Chairman of Texas Air. To the Reagan administration, he was the darling of deregulation. To Hoglander, he was the archenemy of all pilots. Applying the spirit of free market competition with ruthless purity, Lorenzo had built Texas Air into a major carrier by aggressive cost cutting and acquisitions. Starting as Texas International, he had expanded northward into the profitable East Coast corridor by merging with New York Air, and nationally by merging with Continental, and he had achieved miracles of profitability. Creating a holding company into which he dumped the aircraft of the three carriers, he achieved efficiencies of operation. He had made Continental a model of cutting labor costs, reducing the hourly cost of a Continental DC-10 flight crew to $194 and the average pilot's pay to less than $30,000.

But Lorenzo had achieved those stunning reductions by an act that had shocked the industry and earned the hatred of every unionized pilot: he had thrown Continental into bankruptcy court and used bankruptcy laws to break the union and, as union men described it, "throw it off the property." Its pilots had been summarily stripped of seniority, benefits, and bargaining position, and reduced to less than house painters' wages. "It's *immoral* to use bankruptcy rules to break union contracts," Hoglander angrily argued, as he saw Lorenzo's undisputed financial success turn momentum for concessions into an irresistible tide. He could accept that the glamor days were over. But this was a tide, Hoglander believed, that ran roughshod over dignity and that would sweep away the culture of the commercial airline pilot as he knew it by the end of the decade. It was a culture that, to the guys his age, meant high standards and pride and safety in the air as much as it meant high salaries.

For twenty years his life had beat to the airline's rhythms: the step-by-step climb up the seniority ladder to no. 5558—a precious number that determined his pay, his bidding for routes and schedules, his prestige within the company. His life had beat to the monthly bidding rounds, to training and check rides, to step jumps to new generations of aircraft, and the patient progression in the cockpit from engineer's seat to right seat to the lefthand seat of the captain. It beat to steady stepups in pay, and to the routine of thousands of takeoffs and landings that thrilled him every time he began his roll down the runway.

The airline was his lifeblood. It commanded total loyalty and commitment from Harry Hoglander. "Our stake in the success or failure of the company is much higher than the machinists or attendants," he said. "We have an older work force. Pilots can't relocate very easily. If they move to another airline, their seniority goes to square one." If Hoglander lost the seniority number he'd earned by joining on March 8, 1965, it would mean starting at the bottom of the list and for less than half the pay. If, at fifty-two, he could even get another job.

It was the airline he loved. But his loyalty was locked in to a management he had no reason to believe gave a damn about employees. "In thirty years, they've never asked our opinion. I've been in this job three and a half years, and I've only been to our president's office three times. In each case, I invited myself." The company had just scheduled, then summarily canceled, two meetings to discuss a leveraged buyout/ESOP (Employee Stock Ownership Plan) scheme that would give TWA's employees participation in profits and stock ownership—the union's goal for years. The third was scheduled for June 5, but he wasn't holding his breath. Hoglander had no idea whether the company was sincere about the ESOP, or had contrived the meetings just to keep the unions pacified while they looked around for other merger candidates now that Icahn was sniffing around.

"I think it stems from Meyer and Smart," said Hoglander, referring to C. E. (Ed) Meyer, vice-president and CEO of TWA, and L. Edwin (Ed) Smart, chairman of TWA's board and chairman of Trans World Corporation, the conglomerate created from the nucleus of the airline in 1979. Hoglander had disliked a comment Smart made then to *Business Week* that revealed the diminishing importance of the airline in management's eyes: "Our company is Trans World Corp. One of our subsidiaries is an airline." Not pilots, but professional managers with backgrounds in law, accounting, and airline finance, Meyer, Smart, and their predecessor, Charles Tillinghast, represented a profound change in the personality of TWA, one in which pilots had become increasingly alienated.

The tradition of TWA as "a pilot's outfit" had been embodied in the presidency of legendary pilot Jack Frye in the thirties, under whose management TWA had been described as "the most technically proficient airline of them all." Charles Lindbergh had piloted its first transcontinental flight and had championed the infant airline so vigorously that it became known as "Lindbergh's Line." Wiley Post had set round-the-world records in its planes. Amelia Earhart was just another pilot employee. From the earliest seat-of-the-pants mail-plane days, TWA had attracted talented and daring pilots who had made their planes flying laboratories, pioneering high-altitude flying, pressurization, navigation, icing, weather, computers. A terrible midair collision between a TWA airliner and a United DC6 over the Grand Canyon in 1956 was the catalyst for the creation of the Federal Aviation Administration (FAA) and a positive, radar-controlled national air traffic control system. By 1964, TWA pilots, standing in smart trench coats beside their dolphin-sleek Super Constellation before takeoff on the inaugural flight to Paris, were at the pinnacle of one of the most admired and envied jobs in America.

Pilots were not always good managers. The vastly wealthy Howard Hughes was a celebrated pilot, too, when he bought control of TWA through a secret purchase of 46 percent and a coup that threw out the board in 1939. But he was an eccentric disaster for the airline. As he grew reclusive and uncommunicative with his own key executives, he refused to commit to purchasing the jet fleet TWA had to have if it was to compete. As exasperated pilots watched Pan Am's 707s steal domination of the Atlantic routes from its competitor, TWA, a consortium of banks and insurance companies forced Hughes out of the company and replaced him with a man "eminently respectable to Wall Street," Charles Tillinghast, as their condition for the loan of $165 million for a jet fleet.

With a background as Wall Street lawyer and Bendix Corporation executive, Tillinghast sent TWA hurtling full-throttle into the jet age, buying thirty-six planes in ten days, building a soaring Eero Saarinen–designed terminal at Kennedy International, making TWA the most profitable airline in 1965, and earning himself the honor of being the first airline executive on the cover of *Time* magazine. "We have redefined our business scope," he said in 1969, after buying Hilton Hotels and launching an aggressive acquisitions program that, by the time Ed Smart took the reins of TWA in 1977, had transformed TWA into a conglomerate. In 1980, Trans World Corporation had revenues of $5 billion, with the airline providing two-thirds of that. But uncertainty and volatility were making the airline industry less and less attractive to the market. Beyond the industrywide factors, Hoglander blamed management: "Management has always been mediocre. When the airline almost went broke in '74, they sold half the fleet off to the Shah of Iran. And '83 was bad times. That's when they decided to sell us off." In February 1984, the Trans World Corporation spun off TWA.

Hoglander had moved into union work in the midst of the expansion in the 1960s, as the "pilot's outfit" became a professionally managed company which viewed pilots more as assets than folk heroes. "We were the young guys leaping into the 1960s to make our mark and change the system. I saw a lot of unfairness. Flight scheduling is the lifeblood of pilots, and lists were getting conveniently lost, or changed. And seniority! That's religion for me. I believe it's the *only* system that keeps favoritism and vindictiveness out of the cockpit." Seniority gave pilots the same sense of order and stability as rank in the military. In a rigidly standardized job with no place for prima donnas, it motivated pilots to high performance. There were ways of getting rid of bad pilots, and to be stripped of seniority was to be sent to Siberia. Hoglander would go to the wall for seniority.

Seniority had been stripped from the airlines owned by Texas Air's Frank Lorenzo, symbol of Hoglander's worst nightmares. "We knew we were in for a period of readjustment. We're not *blind* to the possibility of deregulation being a path to lower transportation fares. There's always been a recognition that it would occur, that it was necessary. But we thought there was a less brutal way than being run over with Lorenzo's steamroller. We lulled ourselves into thinking that perhaps increased efficiencies through aircraft acquisitions, or lower fuel prices, or marketing schemes would preserve TWA's market share and the yields they needed. It never happened." The blunt truths were: fuel was 25 percent of an airline's costs; labor was 35 to 40 percent. No matter how special their skills and responsibilities, no matter how elite they felt compared to factory workers in the rust belt, pilots—like other strongly unionized industries from steel to trucking—had priced themselves out of the market. "We began to take severe wage cuts years before deregulation. In 1972, we gave the company a $60 million concession package—10 percent of our salaries. We took another pay cut with the spin-off. We got a little profit sharing with the company and separated off our retirement fund from other unions." Now management was trying to impose two-tier.

And the raiders were closing. As the Icahn rumors swept the airline, Hoglander had tried to remain an observer. It wasn't the pilots' role to get involved. But with the filing of the 13D, Hoglander had called Tom Barr, the lawyer with the prestigious New York firm Cravath, Swaine & Moore. Harry needed advice.

"Once you're in play, there's no way out," Barr told him. Icahn's 13D had put TWA irreversibly in play, he explained, "and somebody's going to have to pay." It was usually the employees, Hoglander had observed. Examining the Phillips deal, he saw that the company had paid a high price for independence, and a large part of that price was being paid by the workers. "They laid off something like twenty thousand employees, and for all their prayers and 'I Love Phillips' cookies, the employees had just watched it happen. They were the ones who suffered the most." An idea was forming in his mind. TWA pilots were a different kind of union man. Many had been fighter pilots who had seen combat. They were smart, mature men in their forties and fifties. They were not the kind of men to stand by and be cannon fodder, if Harry read them correctly. Of course they couldn't stick their heads in the sand, he knew. The gravy days were over. But they could try to negotiate some fairness out of the chaos. "If we are going to have to pay, *we are going to play*," he resolved, banging a fist on his desk in the Pan Am Building that made his secretary, Diane, jump.

He had resisted hiring an investment banker. It would cost millions. The Air Line Pilots Association (ALPA) war chest came from the pilots' paychecks, and it was already being drained by the United strike. But if they were going to play, they had to start learning the game. He authorized Barr to set up a meeting with a Lazard Frères banker who was a protégé of Felix Rohatyn, Eugene Keilin. He met him and felt instant trust. ALPA's legal counsel, Bruce Simon, would be the third member of a team that would soon be bonded like the Three Musketeers. In public, the pilots were forming a united front with management against Icahn. They were being issued "Stop Icahn" buttons. But Hoglander hoped to get the machinists and flight attendants to join him in a unified employee effort to control their own destinies. No union had ever before resolved to defy its own management, if that's what it took, and move to the barricades of a takeover battle to protect its interests.

The pilots watched as closely as the Icahn camp as TWA prepared to respond to the 13D. There was strong suspicion the company would turn to Washington for help. "Under regulation, they learned very well how to talk to Washington. They were not good at running a company—they didn't *have* to be good in a regulated environment. But they were good at lobbying—it's what they did for forty years," said Al Kingsley, Icahn's close aide, as he placed the buy orders that moved Icahn's stake in the airline up to 23 percent.

◆　◆　◆

TWA's lobbying blitz, when it hit Washington, was so intense that Icahn's lawyer, Steve Jacobs, joked to Freund, "When we tried to hire a lobbyist for Carl, we couldn't, because you'd hired everybody. They were all on retainer." To cries from Icahn that its actions were "horrendous," TWA, on May 16, made a frontal attack against Icahn's moral and professional fitness to run an airline. It filed an appeal to the Department of Transportation (DOT) for an investigation that would test the airline's continuing fitness to operate under Icahn's control. On the same day, the appeal to the DOT was echoed in a full-page

"Open Letter to Carl Icahn," a challenge to his fitness published in the *Wall Street Journal* and major dailies throughout the nation: "You see, Mr. Icahn, running a major airline is a big job, one that we don't take lightly. It's not like speculating with paper on Wall Street. You have to be proven 'FIT' to operate an airline—'FIT' to manage; 'FIT' to raise the vast sums of money needed to maintain equipment safely and invest in new, modern aircraft; 'FIT' to comply with the many important rules and regulations that the various federal, state, municipal and international agencies demand of an air carrier. . . ." The DOT had never before been asked to rule on the fitness of a potential owner.

TWA's open letter to Carl Icahn commanded more attention from the public than most of the takeover letters and ads that appeared daily in the national newspapers. Fitness hadn't been an issue in oil companies. But it was becoming a significant issue in industries where the public's money and safety, or influence over their ideas, was at stake. Banks, airlines, and television networks had a controlling and intrusive power over the most intimate aspects of people's lives. And although fitness tests could be exploited as defensive ploys and delaying tactics, the issue had substance. It touched chords in the public consciousness. Children were climbing aboard TWA flights for summer vacations. It did seem to matter who ran an airline.

TWA had many friends in Washington, and now the board cashed in all its chips. TWA appealed to Congress and to the Reagan administration to stall Icahn until the DOT ruled. It waved the red flag of job loss and damage to the economy of Missouri, where TWA employed ten thousand people; and Missouri Senator John Danforth, chairman of the Senate Commerce Committee, introduced legislation to halt Icahn from selling off international routes if he got control. A longtime and vocal supporter of deregulation, Danforth sidestepped an embarrassing conflict by claiming, "I could not stand by and seriously see a major airline liquidated." In the House, influential lawmakers James Howard of New Jersey, chairman of the House Public Works and Transportation Committee, and its Aviation Subcommittee chairman, California Representative

Norman Mineta, whipped together and introduced bills to bar anyone controlling more than 20 percent of TWA's stock from voting their shares for ninety days.

Within two weeks, CBS would be making an almost identical assault on the Federal Communications Commission, the Justice Department, and Congress to challenge cable network mogul Ted Turner's fitness to run a major network, as Turner's hostile bid for the network reached its fiercest phase. As he geared up to defend Turner before the FCC, Justice Department, and Congress, lawyer Bruce Sokler of the firm Mintz, Levin & Cohen observed with amazement the same phenomenon that, with TWA, had just struck airlines: "It's only very recently that anyone thought it was even feasible to attempt to make a hostile run at a communications company. In fact, most of the companies have not even bothered to put in the normal shark repellents."

As the Washington effort rolled, Skadden Arps had already launched litigation on behalf of the airline. The American way. On May 15, TWA filed a federal court action in New York's Southern District, the principal issue being, Freund said, "that Icahn planned to dismantle the airline and hadn't disclosed it. We felt we had a valid claim. But even if a lawsuit isn't ultimately successful on the merits it can be helpful in other ways." If they could get temporary restraining orders against Icahn's stock purchases, it would help gain time. And through the process of discovery, they could gain information. Documents and depositions could reveal gems.

In depositions, Icahn revealed that he had telephoned Frank Lorenzo of Texas Air even before surfacing with his TWA stock; as reported in the *Wall Street Journal*, Icahn's evasions in questioning seemed to confirm suspicions that his goal was to dump or dismember the airline. TWA's laywers pushed Icahn hard to explain a memo on a scrap of paper on which Icahn, talking to his airline consultant, Rederer, by phone had allegedly scribbled, "Let 2,000 people go." Icahn never admitted he'd played with the notion of firing two thousand employees. But the memo would be incriminating stuff in Missouri, where TWA employed ten thousand people.

On May 16, the airline filed a state action in St. Louis, alleging violations of Missouri statutory and common law, implying that Icahn was out to loot and cripple the airline, then callously take his profits and go on to his next victim. "Missouri was the hub, the state with the most to lose if the airline was dismantled." Missouri, Freund hoped, would rise as Oklahoma had against Pickens when he threatened Phillips.

The federal suit in New York bought TWA its first tiny breathing space. To prevent the judge from issuing a temporary restraining order, Icahn voluntarily agreed to buy no shares for a week, until May 28—the same day as a major TWA board meeting.

But the litigation had subtler strategy, in Freund's mind. TWA was accusing Icahn of having plans for liquidation, layoffs, and dismantling of routes. In order to gain credibility in the eyes of the courts, Congress, and the DOT, Icahn would be forced to take positions committing himself to the long-term interests of the airline, commitments that would lock him in to the things that mattered to the board. Freund had been trying to sense the gut feelings of the board. "They saw TWA as a national institution. They wanted the airline to survive."

As TWA filed its suits and hoped for the best, Freund mused, "Lawsuits in takeovers very rarely stop the takeover completely. But they *can* be the key decisions." His comment was more prophetic than he knew, for the very day after TWA's filing in Missouri, the decision that would bring Pickens's bid for Unocal to an end would come down from the Delaware Supreme Court, a warning to raiders that would not be missed by Carl Icahn. For while TWA was gathering momentum, Unocal was moving into the endgame.

◆   ◆   ◆

THE court action in Delaware hung over the Unocal annual meeting, which finally convened at 10:00 A.M. on May 13, charging it with a special tension. Polls would be open until 12:30 but results of the proxy contest would not be known for several days or longer. As Fred Hartley took the podium in Los Angeles, Gil Sparks and Charlie Richards were winding up their arguments before Judge Carolyn Berger in the Delaware

Chancery Court in Wilmington. It was the second test in that court of whether Unocal would, or would not, be allowed to exclude Boone Pickens from its $72 self-tender offer. The first ruling had been in Pickens's favor. Berger's opinion would probably come down while the annual meeting was in session. With the proxy fight still unclear and with every institutional vote still being fiercely contested, the decision from Wilmington could decisively tilt the balance of power.

But that tension did not dampen the day for Fred Hartley. The annual meeting was to be an affirmation of oil, the mighty black stuff that would continue to drive the world throughout his lifetime. The Pickens group sat near the front, in a sea of hostility. For conservative Hartley, it was a Cecil B. De Mille production. Stirring music played, and a rich and sonorous male voice boomed out, "This is *Uno*cal '85!" Then, on a big screen behind the dais flashed lusty images of the powerful, bright-painted industrial trappings of oil: shiny steel refineries, offshore drilling rigs, pipelines, signs for Union 76 (Unocal's logo) glowing like beacons by the roadside, and the human pageant of muscle, of dedicated, perspiring faces and hardhats. Was this Pickens's industry in liquidation? "Unocal has been profitable every year since 1901," Hartley told the crowd, "and exploration is the key to continued success." The meeting was a challenge to Pickens's way. Was it really smarter to drill for oil on Wall Street? Maybe you could buy it there for $5 a barrel, but all you were doing was trading existing reserves; how would that help the nation when oil ran short again in the 1990s? While, in speeches, Pickens cited "Mukluk"—the billion-dollar dry hole in Alaska that had become a symbol of the decline of good drilling prospects—as proof of his argument, Hartley beamed, "Unocal has some of the brightest exploration prospects in the history of the company . . . from the frigid regions of Alaska to the turbulent North Sea and the jungles of Southeast Asia . . . the kinds of plays where a company has a chance to hit a billion-barrel field!"

"Heartless Hartley," as he was nicknamed, had never pretended to be the shareholders' champion. "He put a piano in the company jet, for chrissake!" a fellow CEO had cracked. He

was still living down his remark about oil-killed birds after
Union's disastrous Santa Barbara oil spill. And he put his foot
in his mouth at the meeting as he searched for a folksy analogy
for the belt-tightening Unocal would have to do to pay back the
debt they'd be loaded with after their stock buyback: "It's like
anybody who's behind on their mortgage payments. They have
to eat rice and leftovers for a while." He lost, with a sentence,
the goodwill of Asians and every woman who has ever served
reheated Thanksgiving turkey.

But he was a committed oilman. And the shareholders
cheered.

It was only at the press conference afterward, as he was
forced back into breaking events, that the gruff, commanding
energy that had carried the meeting began to drain off. A
stressed and aging man began to emerge. Hartley heard just
minutes before the press conference that Unocal had lost in
chancery court. Gil Sparks would appeal to the Delaware
Supreme Court within hours, but Pickens was gaining momentum in his fight to be included in the company's $72 offer. And
here was Hartley, with better things to do, having his statements and delivery orchestrated by public relations man Dick
Cheney, who hovered at the side of the room whispering to
Hartley's aides. The reporters were pushing him. When *Wall
Street Journal* reporter Fred Rose asked Hartley if Unocal's
1963 buyback of shares from a speculator had been greenmail,
he went on the defensive, like a cornered bear: "Fred, you have
a nice way of putting things so I feel like a crook." As his
command of the press conference became more tenuous, a
naive female reporter from a Long Beach paper asked, "You
said earlier that if Mr. Pickens got control, he would fire one
person from the board. Can you tell us who that would be?"
Hartley gripped the lectern with both hands and said with a
wan smile, "Me, my dear. He doesn't know value when he sees
it," and strode back to his office.

Results of the proxy vote would not be counted for some
days. But a confident Fred Hartley announced at his press
conference that he had swung a massive block of votes the very
morning of the meeting. As most guessed by then, the proxy

contest would be a triumph for Fred Hartley. He would ultimately win the individual shareholders vote by 8 to 1, and the institutional vote less decisively. "The company won in a virtual landslide," said Peter Sachs, delighted that his stubborn championing of the MLP as an argument to the big shareholders had apparently helped win the day.

But with the outcome of the proxy vote and the Delaware courts still uncertain, the first round of secretly planned settlement talks began later that day, but failed. Pickens and Hartley could not negotiate in the same room. Pickens walked out "without even shaking hands or saying goodbye," said Sam Snyder, and flew home to Amarillo. It was the ultimate gambler's bluff. "Walking away is the worst strategic decision Boone Pickens ever made," a close observer said later. "I was overconfident; I thought it was all academic after the chancery court ruling," Pickens would admit a few weeks later. But Pickens is a consummate card player, and he held good cards. He was winning in Delaware. Unocal's appeal to the supreme court would be heard in a few days. "Going into the appeal, I figured we had a fifty-fifty chance of getting the company."

◆　◆　◆

MAY 16. At his home in Wilmington, Andrew G. T. Moore II, justice of the Delaware Supreme Court, swiftly adjusted his black tie for a bar association dinner, absorbed by the legal issue he must resolve in court the next morning. Unocal's appeal had been accepted within three hours of Judge Berger's decision Tuesday; it had been briefed—elegant, inch-thick briefs by both sides—argued, and would be decided by Friday, the next morning. Since the argument this morning, Moore had written a twelve-page draft, circulated it through the court, then rushed home to change into his tuxedo.

A suave and handsome forty-nine-year-old, with a courtroom lawyer's poise overlaying the gentle manners of a Louisiana upbringing, Moore had, until three years ago, been one of the tight-knit club of Wilmington lawyers who have become the Swiss gnomes of American business. But now, as a supreme court justice, Moore was one of a handful of high priests in the temples of U.S. corporate law. In fact, he had decided so many landmark cases in his first three years on the bench that he was rumored to be eyeing the seat of the chief justice, soon to retire. His decision tomorrow would clearly be another. It could shape the fate of a huge oil company four thousand miles away; it could slow, speed, or divert the mighty tide of corporate takeovers that, in 1984 alone, swelled nearly 70 percent over the year before. In almost every takeover struggle, at least one, and sometimes five or six, lawsuits would land on Delaware's doorstep. For wherever their home or headquarters—New York, Dallas, Detroit, or Los Angeles— over 50 percent of the Fortune 500 companies were incorpora- ted in Delaware, the state that had shrewdly created the most desirable body of law and corporate climate of any in the union.

It was exciting to be here, deciding landmark cases where "people's lives, futures, *fortunes* are involved," Moore said. But it was demanding. "We used to have twenty cases a year. Now we have four hundred. Not all hostile takeovers, of course, but they demand by far the most time." The clock was always ticking, for takeovers were compressed by federal regulations into a tight time frame. *Accelerated* was the operative word as Delaware courts and lawyers worked feverishly to hold their lead in an increasingly sophisticated and competitive field of law.

At the dinner, he spotted the two lawyers who'd argued the case that morning, Charles Richards of Richards, Layton & Finger for Pickens and Morris Nichols's Gil Sparks for Unocal. "Hi, Charlie, you look more rested than you did this morning," he teased Richards. "I took a nap," replied Richards, who, for two months, had been maintaining the adrenaline rush re- quired for war. Five days later, he would be back in court, arguing the appeal on the landmark Household case, going against the most formidable opponent Skadden Arps could have put up—Irving Shapiro.

"You can think of it in terms of the Battle of Britain," says Richards, "where British pilots had to go up on mission after mission in a very short, intense period of time. I'm not liable to be shot down and killed, but you need to manage your own physical resources, as well as those of your troops." The Phillips litigation had tested his energies more than any other. He had represented Mesa on that, too.

"One day, I argued for two hours in federal court and won, walked three blocks and got up and argued it over again. When you argue something significant for which you've prepared, you get an adrenaline rush, like an athlete, and it gives you energy, the power to be interesting and exciting. After the excitement is over, you feel very tired, more tired than you otherwise would. I could feel that starting to happen as I was walking across the street, and I knew I had to get myself up. It was the hardest thing I've ever done." Now, Richards shifted his total concentration from the issues of Unocal to the issues of Household, trying to get himself up as he must to go against Shapiro on Tuesday.

If Pickens lost here in Moore's court, it could end his bid for Unocal, making it too expensive for him to go on. At his own press conference at the Sheraton Grande after the Unocal annual meeting, Pickens and Batchelder had stated that Mesa Partners had already paid $60 million in fees, and that interest payments would add an additional cost of $7.5 million every forty-five days. If Pickens gave up the fight, it could shatter the market's belief in his golden touch, in his will to gain control of his targets, and in the sincerity of his role as shareholder champion. For if he bailed out, it would almost certainly hurt both Mesa and Unocal stock. Mesa's cost for its billion-dollar investment, he said, had been between $45 and $49 a share. "If Mesa goes away, this is a stock that trades at $35," Batchelder said. Analysts were estimating that Pickens would lose, on paper, $300 million, if the deal failed.

If Pickens won here, he could well go on to control, and snuff out Unocal as an independent company. And he would finally get to run an "elephant." On the eve of the decision, Pickens was closer than he'd ever been before, he claimed. No friendly white knight had surfaced to snatch Unocal from him. "If it went in our favor, the odds were three to one we had 'em; if it went against us, we'd fold our tent and steal off into the night."

Heading to the courtroom to hear the decision the next

morning, Charlie Richards was worried. The judge, he
thought, had sent out ominous signs. After Judge Berger's first
decision in Boone's favor, Judge Moore had sent Berger, a
former Skadden Arps lawyer, what Skadden lawyer Fin Fogg
and his colleagues saw as a "very strong order to reconsider her
decision in the light of four questions. It was clear they were
slanted against Boone. Questions like, Does a corporation have
the right to defend itself against predators?" We were gathered
in a conference room here in New York—Joe Flom, David, Sid,
Bobby—when Charlie Richards called and read the order to us.
We could all pick up the tone," says Fogg. "We still thought we
could brief and present the thing well. But Wilmington is a
small town. Charlie knows all the judges. And the tone was
clear. We realized it was all riding, right there." When Sam
Snyder read the same four questions, he said, "Those questions
are, I would say, most comforting."

By 8:45 A.M., the courtroom was filled with a classic assemblage of the takeover club—Unocal and Pickens people, reporters, investment bankers, observers from Congress, regulatory agencies, and lawyer-observers for the arbitragers. Cal
Crary was there for Bear Stearns's arbs, for Bear Stearns was
still sweating out its big investment in Unocal. Cal was feeling
good. "So far, we've called every piece of litigation, including
Justice Berger's rulings, exactly right!" He had replayed yesterday's hearing a hundred times in his mind, debating it with the
Wilmington counsel Bear Stearns had hired, and last night "I
had come to a table-pounding conclusion about how Moore
would rule—he would *reverse* the rulings." He hoped he would.
If Pickens were excluded from Unocal's $72 per share offer,
Bear Stearns would be able to sell more of their shares back to
the proration pool. The portable cellular phone was still a few
months away, and Cal was ready to run from the courtroom to
call Nancy Havens-Hasty in New York. "He had lots of quarters
in his pocket," says Nancy.

As he delivered his decision, Moore ordered the doors
locked and forbade anyone—especially the arbs' men—from
bolting for the telephones.

He drew from one of his own landmark cases, *Pogostin* v. *Rice*, which had established that "the Business Judgment Rule . . . is applicable in the context of a takeover." And with an eloquent caution that "the boards of Delaware corporations do not have unbridled discretion to defeat any perceived threat to corporate control by any draconian means available," he affirmed the Business Judgment Rule. Cautioning any future raiders against using "coercive two-tier tender offers" and greenmail, he slapped Pickens's hand with a sledgehammer. He reversed the decision of the chancery court. Pickens would not be allowed to share in the $72 bonanza with other shareholders. Unocal had won. Sparks and Richards shook hands. They would be seeing each other here again, and again, and again. Then Richards called Pickens.

Cal Crary ran for the phones. Ace Greenberg's arbs had done it again. Now, they would get more stock off in Unocal's self-tender. And even though, with this decision, Pickens's takeover would surely fall through, there was the ongoing restructuring that strengthened Unocal's stock price—the stock buyback and the Master Limited Partnership. *Something* had happened. "We made a nice little profit," said Nancy, as they crunched the numbers on the transaction, "but it's more fun when you make a *lot* of money."

Fin Fogg was working with Goldsmith when he got the news. "It wasn't like JFK being assassinated. But that was a dark day," said Skadden Arps's Fogg in New York, expressing the mood of dashed momentum that swept the Pickens team. "Everything had been very upbeat going into Delaware. Pickens had his financing lined up. I think he could have made it. But when the Delaware decision came down, that was it." As a lawyer, he was indignant. "I think the Delaware Supreme Court came to the wrong result and there's no appeal. Should a transaction of such great significance to so many people be decided in a state court somewhere, based on some totally unpredictable theory that the court enunciates? I wouldn't favor a federal Business Judgment Rule, but should some judge in Utah or Alaska decide the outcome?"

The "if onlys" were always more painful than the "what ifs." At Drexel Burnham, John Sorte dealt with the aborted hope that this could be Drexel's second major completed junk-bond deal. "We had a number of ideas of what we'd do if it went in our favor. One scenario would have been that we'd tender our shares to Unocal and use that cash to give people more than 50 percent—perhaps two-thirds—cash and one-third securities. . . . There had been big criticism of Pickens's 50 percent front-end offer, with securities in the back end of questionable value," said Sorte. "In fact, we were seriously considering, if we'd won here, to refile our offer as a 100 percent offer of cash plus securities, packaging the whole thing so that people would see exactly what they were going to get and avoiding constant attack on the back end. It would take longer. It would have to be approved by the SEC. . . ." It was now academic.

But Drexel Burnham, like Boone Pickens, thrives on "learning experiences." The judge's message reverberated from New York to Beverly Hills. "Delaware upheld that it doesn't matter what the form of the financing is—U.S. government or junk bonds—as long as the shareholders all get cash," Sorte said. It was the end of the front-end-loaded two-tier tender offer with junk bonds at the back end. "From now on, all our offers will be cash offers."

◆   ◆   ◆

As the decision came down, Pickens was in a suite at the Hay Adams Hotel in Washington to attend the President's Dinner, a fund raiser for the House and Senate races in 1986. With him were Joe Flom, Dave Batchelder, and old pal and Mesa board member Wales Madden, who'd flown in with Pickens from Amarillo.

Batchelder took the call from Richards. Pickens says, "I saw David's face, and turned around and looked at old Joe Flom, and said, 'Goddamn, I can't believe this!' " Bea Pickens heard the news from a phone in an adjoining bedroom. "I was devastated. So disappointed that the courts could be so discriminatory. I couldn't believe this could happen in America." She ran into the room, "but by the time I got in there, they were already picking themselves up." Calling on the sense of humor that has sustained the Panhandle through drought and dry holes, Pickens's old friend Ed Watkins managed to drawl, when he heard the news by phone, "Well, it's back in the stanchions."

"There isn't anybody yet who's said I'm not a big boy," Pickens said later, remembering the moment. "Hell, yes, I mean I *hated* that decision. But long ago my mother taught me, 'Play the hand you're dealt.' " Within ten minutes of the news of the loss in Delaware, Flom had placed the call to Peter Sachs that would initiate settlement negotiations. "It was time to make a deal."

Fifteen minutes after the call from Richards, Flom called Peter Sachs in New York and said, as Sachs recalls, "Can we still settle this?" "I think there may be an opportunity," Sachs replied. "What shall we do?" Flom asked. "Have Stilwell call me," said Sachs, as he prepared to call Sam Snyder. Sachs directed Stilwell to call Snyder, too, and flew to Los Angeles for the negotiations that should end the Unocal deal. By the time Sam Snyder arrived at the company headquarters in downtown Los Angeles, Stilwell had already called and was flying in to begin settlement negotiations. Armistice was near. "But Hartley didn't really want to settle," said Snyder. He had won a holy war in which, Hartley claimed, "our economic system is at stake." Said Snyder, "I think he wanted to savor the victory. He'd gone to Armand Hammer's eighty-seventh birthday that night, and Armand had announced that he should get the Nobel Prize."

Yet they had to settle. Pickens might havé taken a $300 million paper loss by being excluded from the tender, but he still owned 13.6 percent of Unocal. If Unocal's stock plummeted, which it well might with the deal falling through, Pickens could still buy the company at a bargain price. It was the doomsday scenario they had dubbed the "black hole theory" during the early days of brainstorming with the Goldman Sachs and Dillon Read teams. It could happen. "It's like having a raccoon in the house. By law, you can't kill him. You've got to leave an opening for him to get out," said Goldman's Peter Sachs, urging a settlement that would include at least some of Pickens's stock in the $72 offer.

Too drained for small talk, the teams negotiated through the weekend. "You should see those Mesa guys smoke when Boone's not around," Snyder chortled. "Batchelder was puffing on big black cigars!" Drexel's John Sorte, however, claims Batchelder and Tassin just chewed on cigars to get rid of nervous energy. With Snyder and Andy Bogen facing Stilwell and Batchelder for the final rounds, they had, by Sunday, hammered out the last points. Pickens would have roughly a third of his 21 million shares included in the $72 offer, a smaller percentage than the other shareholders. They had found a way to get the raccoon out of the house. But his shares would be locked in for at least a year, to be sold only under controlled circumstances. It would be his first loss since he started his campaigns against Big Oil. Hartley finally agreed to settle and called a board meeting for the next day. It would be a working lunch with sandwiches, suggested Claude Brinegar. *"No,"* Hartley bellowed, "we are not barbarians!" The despised raiders might lack "all manners, morals, or integrity." But Unocal would sit down to a proper lunch.

On Monday, May 20, the settlement was announced. The struggle for Unocal was over. And its people would sleep soundly, and secure, for the first time since Valentine's Day. Sam Snyder fell asleep on top of the bed still in his business suit.

◆   ◆   ◆

IN Delaware, the courtrooms scarcely had time to cool. That same day, May 20, the takeover club flowed in by car, train, and plane to Dover, the state capital. Next morning, in the courtroom of the Delaware Supreme Court, Irving Shapiro and Charlie Richards would argue the Household appeal. The highway looked like a mafia convention. "Every limousine in Delaware had been rented," says Stuart Shapiro, who drove down with his wife, Noreen, and his father and mother. Noreen was superstitious about watching Stuart in court; she never had. Although Stuart would not argue the case, he would sit at counsels' table with his father. But the family decided they would all go to Dover. It would be a landmark judgment on the poison pill and on the rights of a board to defend itself within the Business Judgment Rule. It was a moment of history. For Irving Shapiro was reentering a courtroom to argue a case for the first time in thirty-five years.

He had fought being here. After Stuart had lost the first hearing in chancery court in a protracted trial the previous October, Stuart and his associates had debated over who should argue the appeal. Discussion circled but always led back to one man: Stuart's father, Irving, a partner in the Skadden Arps Wilmington office since his retirement from Du Pont. "He'd been CEO of a company involved in two takeovers. He had sat through the entire trial in October, had read all the transcripts and briefs. He'd been one of the best oral advocates in government when he was in the Justice Department. He'd argued before the U.S. Supreme Court before he was thirty," Stuart explained. Irving Shapiro had been a founder of the Business Roundtable and one of its former presidents. His arguments for accountability to society and for dynamic involvement of corporations in government in his book *America's Third Revolution* had made him a corporate statesman.

It was his father's ability to see the case from the boardroom's point of view that had helped Stuart prepare his argument for the chancery court. Stuart had been planning an confrontational line of questioning for their witness, John Whitehead, who is one of the most distinguished men in the financial world. Senior partner at Goldman Sachs before becoming undersecretary of state in the Reagan cabinet, Whitehead and John Moran had been the only two members of the Household board who had voted against Marty Lipton's Share Purchase Rights Plan. "My father had read our brief, and he went for a walk with me around a football field for about an hour and said, 'There's something missing here, Stuart. It seems to me, in cross-examining John Whitehead, you should treat him as a statesman. Build his credibility. Show that the most knowledgeable man on that board voted against a plan that was presented by people from his own firm, Goldman Sachs. A little honey will work better that the usual lawyer's technique.' " That advice had transformed Stuart's approach to Whitehead, and had made him a powerful witness against Household, even though Moran, the plaintiff, had ultimately lost the case.

Stuart knew his father would refuse if he asked him to argue the appeal. Stuart took his suggestion to Flom. "I got a phone call from Flom saying will you please take this on," says Irving Shapiro. And it was obviously a command. "Father was white-hot angry," says Stuart. "He said, 'I don't really expect my son to blindside me that way!' I let him cool off for about a week." And then Shapiro senior got to work. "There was an enormous vacuum that had to be filled with factual information. I had to educate myself on old Delaware court decisions." But a confidence began to come back. "All the little work habits, things I did thirty-five to forty years ago, suddenly came to the surface."

The courtroom was packed and charged with anticipation. Shapiro's appearance had made it a media event, and spawned a delightful joke. When Wachtell, Lipton figured out Irving Shapiro was going to argue the case, a lawyer called Stuart and said, "I just want you to know that Bella Katz will be arguing for us." Stuart said, "Who's Bella Katz?" The Wachtell lawyer said, "That's George Katz's mother. If you're going to have your father arguing, we're going to have his mother." The odds that father and son would ever sit as coleagues in a courtroom had been remote. "I went to university in the Midwest to get away from home. I didn't want to work in a large corporate environment and work with the same people all the time." Stuart had planned to become an English professor, and had finally been turned toward law by a professor who told him, "The world is full of English lit professors, but there are very few literate lawyers." He had married a girl raised in Boston's Irish ghetto—a background ethnically alien to his own Jewish upbringings—and had gone to work for Joe Flom in New York over his father's objections. "I tried to convince him to stay here in Delaware and practice law, and he just said, 'No, I've got to be my own person. I don't want to be just your son.' "

"Father had never heard of Skadden Arps," Stuart adds. Nor had Stuart when the firm called him to interview for a job. "I called the professor at Georgetown who had recommended me, and he said that Skadden Arps, though small, was the best securities law firm in the country." And New York was appealing for another reason. Clerking for a federal judge in Wilmington, Stuart worked with the young woman he later married. She was going to New York to practice law with Dewey, Ballantine.

The growth of Flom's firm in both size and stature brought Stuart Shapiro full circle back to his father. "When Father was retiring from Du Pont at sixty-five, a lot of firms were coming after him, and I said, 'Why don't you come with us?' He said he didn't want to interfere with my career. Joe Flom talked to him, and let him understand that if he went to any other firm, it would be considered a great insult. He came in as a full partner and has been working like crazy ever since." Shapiro senior, who lives in the same three-bedroom house he had lived in as CEO of Du Pont, joined the Wilmington office. It had all come together several years ago. Shapiro senior had taken Stuart and Joe Flom to an Alfalfa Club dinner in Washington, an event that begins with a blood-stirring military band and is a "meeting of the power brokers of the nation all in one room—the president, Supreme Court, businessmen, bankers, people from all over the country. There are 150 members, no more, and it's only function is to have one big dinner a year." It may not have been Flom's milieu in the sixties. "But it turned out that Joe knew a lot of peole in the room and they knew him. He had a great time."

Irving Shapiro stood before the Supreme Court to begin his argument. With his well-prepared notes in hand, he "had a feeling of controlled tension." He was a courtroom veteran. His first court experience had been at the age of eleven, when he had testified before a grand jury in Minneapolis against a hoodlum he had seen beat and shake down his father, Sam, in the family's dry cleaning shop, a case that was preamble to a 1931 landmark U.S. Supreme Court First Amendment case. Shapiro had argued before the highest court in the land before he was thirty, but his last argument before the U.S. Supreme Court had been in 1949. "I spent literally weeks just trying to get up to speed. It's a good, very exciting kind of stress. But I had a lot to lose." A man of compact build and average height in navy pinstripe suit, with an air of both warmth and toughness and the same deep rich voice that made Stuart so effective in court, he knew he also presented "the rather quaint picture of a retired CEO making a case for shareholders." Beyond that irony, "I was putting my reputation at stake. The significance is so personal it's hard to explain. Here is a younster who had never seen me in action as a lawyer seeing his father under the gun for the first time. . . . In my view, Stuart was a more proficient lawyer at that time than I was."

Stuart was tense as argument began. "I was very nervous because I had dragooned him into doing this." Shapiro argued first. He addressed the three judges, "I rise this morning, may it please the court, to present a case which I think is of great importance to the corporate community . . . a matter unique in our experience." As his father continued talking, Stuart felt relief. "He had prepared far more thoroughly than I would have. He was very smooth and low key, but there was a lot of humor. He was articulate, calm, sensible, and quick."

First, Shapiro defined the case "as one where the board's conduct served to accomplish a shift in the internal structure of Household in such a way as to transfer power from the shareholders to the management. The instrument for accomplishing that transfer was a document called a Rights Plan adopted by the board of Household on August 14, 1984. Even though there was and is ample time to take the matter to the stockholders for approval, it was not done."

Then he moved smoothly into the basic issue of his argument, the issue of power. "I want, first, to set out the crucial questions of power which . . . are at the heart of this case." The Unocal decision, which, just a week earlier, had allowed Unocal its exclusionary self-tender as a defene against Pickens, would not help him. Judge Moore asked, "In the case of Mesa versus Unocal, didn't we hold that the board had power to deal with the perceived threat?" Shapiro replied, "Yes, indeed, Your Honor, but we are challenging a specific exercise of power that goes beyond the corporate governance of the corporation." And then he went on, exploring the actions of the Household board on August 14: "The board took two actions essentially. First, it decided it wanted to adopt a policy of opposing take-overs and staying independent. We don't challenge that in any way. We think that was within the exercise of their business judgment. Second, the board accepted the advice of its outside counsel that the Rights Plan would accomplish that result. We can't find any statutory provision that says a board acting on its own has the freedom to deny the vote to the shareholders . . . and that's what this plan does . . . and one has to keep asking, and I'm going to keep asking all morning: Why did this board choose not to go to the stockholders? That's what corporate democracy is about." The Household board had adopted Lip-ton's poison pill, a pill that would trigger when a raider ac-quired 20 percent of Household's stock, killing the possibility of successful proxy contests for control, Shapiro argued, and a raider or shareholder needed a block of at least 20 percent to mount an effective proxy contest.

"It was a hot court. A lot of questions from the bench," Irving Shapiro noted, exhilarated. "But Justice Moore was climbing all over me with questions. I quickly interpreted that as saying, 'We'll show this guy that he's just another lawyer when he comes before this court.'" Shapiro was going to have to work for it.

He directed his most intense attack against the Pill's contro-versial and confusing "flipover" provision which its critics claimed would make tender offers prohibitively expensive and reduce the shareholders' options for a tender offer. "This plan says that if there is a merger that the board hasn't approved, and if the rights haven't been redeemed, then the acquiring company not only pays for the corporation at its value, but it pays a penalty of a hundred dollars a share in addition." He emphasized that "someone buying Household would have to pay somewhere in the range of $2 billion and then an addi-tional $6 billion to manage this flipover. The penalty is so enormous that there could be no merger. What it's designed to do is say, 'The risk over here is an atom bomb, so if you want to talk about a merger, you better do it on terms that this board finds acceptable, otherwise go away.'" The Share Purchase

Rights Plan, Shapiro argued, shut down the free market process. And with boards free to keep extending the plan past its ten-year life, its poison could be released forever.

"This is going real well," Stuart whispered to him as he finished his opening statement and prepared for rebuttal. "In rebuttal, he's even better," Stuart thought, as his father went on. "He's masterful!"

Shapiro summed up, "What are the values that are important here? In our society we expect corporations to be held accountable. The stockholder has been assigned the function of performing that job, and so far the system has worked pretty well. I would make the argument that corporate management . . . would recognize that keeping the shareholders in an active role in the corporation is absolutely vital to the health of corporate America." He added words that he was sure would reach Delaware judges: "When you deny the shareholders an active participation, what the corporation is doing is inviting the Ralph Naders and Senator Metzenbaums . . . to opt for government regulation of corporations as the best way to hold managements accountable." To Shapiro, "accountability is the ball game."

He finished up, turned, and walked back to counsels' table as the University of Chicago Law School professor Geoffrey Miller, and then Charlie Richards, stood to make their arguments. As he sat down, he thought he heard Stuart say, "It was just a superb argument. It's one you ought to be very proud of." He *knew* he heard great respect in Stuart's voice.

Because Household was not part of a tightly scheduled takeover battle, they might have to wait for months for the decision of the judges. But, for Irving Shapiro, there were more important values here than Household per se. "I have no doubt in the world that my son's perception of his father has changed. Household is important, but that will disappear in time. We go on for the rest of our lives."

CHAPTER 13

MAY 20 was one of those watershed days in the takeover wars when the action is punctuated and slowed by ceremonial events, and the fraternity pauses for breath before plunging on. On that day, what may be T. Boone Pickens's last great hostile battle, the battle for Unocal, formally ended with the signed agreement. The tarnished devices of two-tier tender offers and greenmail were displaced, that day, by the issue of the poison pill, as the Household battle climaxed and took on landmark status—whatever the outcome.

◆   ◆   ◆

For Carl Icahn, May 20 was the eve of the declaration of war. Next morning, he would deliver his merger offer to the TWA board, formalizing his quest for control. And, that day, he gave TWA its first tiny pocket of time, its first respite from scrambling from behind. He agreed to stop buying stock until a ruling from the federal court in New York on the preliminary injunction. That ruling was due to come down on May 28, the day of a full board meeting at TWA. It gave TWA an eight-day breathing space.

275

Icahn did not choose the route of a hostile tender offer bursting on corporate America over its morning coffee from a full-page tombstone in the *Wall Street Journal.* He threw down the gauntlet with a hand-delivered letter to the board. His invitation to merge had the flavor of courtlier days. It was the first of a series of letters that would pass back and forth, as they had in the Phillips affair, between the principals in a battle fought, on the surface, largely by the written word. "There was a lot of communication by letter and by press release," Jim Freund would comment. But Icahn's first billet-doux to the board was no love letter. He made it clear that he was playing from strength: he spoke, he informed the board, as owner of roughly 24 percent of TWA's outstanding stock. His offer was for $18 a share, all cash, in exchange for all of TWA's common stock that he did not already own.

The Unocal decision had helped shaped Icahn's bid. It had come down from the Delaware Supreme Court on May 17, just four days earlier, and Steve Jacobs had swiftly got a copy. "I read relevant portions to Carl, who said, 'Wait a minute. A court might think that Boone is a greenmailer, but if they reviewed my record they wouldn't think I was one, would they?' Well, it didn't take a rocket scientist to conclude that Carl was within the universe of people whose prior activities might give rise to some inference that he was seeking greenmail from TWA." The Unocal decision made them nervous, too, that Trans World might provide some cash to TWA to do a discriminatory tender. And how to avoid the two-tier tender the court had condemned? "Carl was in the enviable position of having enough available funds to pay cash for over 50 percent of TWA, but not 100 percent, without access to TWA's assets," says Jacobs. "Carl thought of a partial tender offer to go over 50 percent, but decided against that approach because of Unocal. We decided to do what we thought was our only course to do. First, to declare his determination to seek control. Second, to make clear that his proposals would be all cash, with no junk bonds. Third, to take the high road and disclaim any intention to be greenmailed. Fourth, to affirm his intention to operate the airline and not to dismantle and ruin it. Fifth, to pressure the TWA board to put the company up for auction to the highest bidder, including Icahn." Learning from Pickens's bruises, Icahn had made himself unimpeachable.

A negotiated merger! Freund felt right at home. It was his specialty. It had a civility hostile tender offers lacked, offering a chance for dialogue and compromise rather than the crudeness of bypassing the board and going directly to the shareholders. "But," Freund reflected, "for TWA, this was almost worse than a tender offer, because once you make a tender offer, you can't buy shares in the market for at least twenty business days. Carl didn't want to be out of the market, and with a merger proposal he didn't have to be." He could continue to rampage toward a controlling 51 percent. But there was risk also for Carl. The board could reject his bid. To counter that, his letter bristled with threats. "He starts out as such a straight guy, saying, 'I won't take greenmail, and if other shareholders don't like it, I won't do it,' " Freund observed. Then he unleashed the thunderbolts. "We have this day," Icahn warned in his letter, "commenced the consent procedure to, among other things, remove the TWA Board of Directors" and replace them if they did not permit shareholders to vote on his offer. His financing, he claimed, was in hand. He would, from his own ACF Industries and other companies he controlled, raise $400 million of the $600 million cash he needed to buy out the balance of the shares he did not already own. Icahn was so confident he could raise the remaining $200 million from equity investors and financial institutions that he volunteered, "We would be prepared to agree to a . . . two-year standstill agreement . . . if commitments for the $200 million are not obtained by the time proxy materials for the cash merger are ready for mailing to TWA's stockholders."

As a parting shot, he reminded TWA that his $18 offer would be, for shareholders, a "substantial premium" for a stock that, since the spin-off of the airline from Trans World Corporation, had traded at an average monthly price of just over $10. It was an offer few shareholders would refuse. Any board that did not take it to shareholders would probably be sued. Carl Icahn was turning the screws.

Salomon Brothers, TWA's investment bankers, ran the numbers and came up with an evaluation on the $18 offer: it was inadequate. Salomon managing director Michael Zimmerman, who was handling the deal along with Ira Harris, the banker who had shared so many takeover defenses with Marty Lipton, did not believe $18 reflected the true value of TWA's assets and would recommend that the board reject it. "But we knew that if we didn't do something more than label it 'inadequate' it was a winner," Freund said. "If we put the $18 to the shareholders in the absence of any alternatives, they would have voted for it because it was at a much higher price than the market had been before Carl came on the scene. There were plenty of institutional investors out there who would leap at the profits. Hell, these shareholders weren't exactly Aunt Minnie; they were *arbs!*"

And, yet, if they didn't put the offer to the shareholders, Icahn would probably have been able to throw out the board with the consent procedure. Icahn was already in the process of clearing his proxy materials with the SEC. He was poised, ready to solicit. The TWA board didn't like the prospect of being thrown out. But it wasn't for entrenchment reasons, Freund honestly believed, as Hoglander and Icahn never would. "The board wanted to stay in place until a deal was done to make sure that the shareholders got taken care of. And the fear throughout was that if Icahn removed the board and took control, he could drop his $18 offer and say, 'Look at the books, this company is in terrible shape. I can't pay $18.' " They would then have lost not only the company, but the chance to get a better offer. Freund and Michael Zimmerman of Salomon Brothers—who brought the investment banker's perspective to all the major strategies and decisions—had begun to think that the only real alternative to Icahn, the only way to maximize the value for shareholders, was something boards found most abhorrent, something that would force them to make the most painful and significant transition a management under siege can experience: the shift from defending the company to accepting that perhaps it cannot be defended. It is a subtle but very real transitional moment in takeover wars that would be identified by a judge in the Revlon takeover, a few months later, as a psychological event that transforms strategy. Freund and Zimmerman had begun to think the unthinkable—*that the company must be put up for sale.*

Three days after Icahn's $18 bid, a possible buyer surfaced. Frank Lorenzo of Texas Air, the embodiment of deregulation, made contact with TWA. On May 24, Lorenzo flew to New York from Houston and met with Meyer and Freund. Lorenzo talked about paying $20 a share, $2 higher than Icahn's offer. He wasn't a perfect suitor. The Continental bankruptcy proceedings that had freed him of union contracts were still pending as he approached the airline, encumbering him with financial uncertainty. Texas Air wasn't exactly a giant among airlines, Freund knew. But Lorenzo made a very good impression when he flew in to meet the board. This was the villain of deregulation? "He was quiet and polite. A dark-haired, lean-faced guy. He was strictly here in friendship, taking a very gentlemanly approach." And he'd said, as Freund understood it, "I'm here, I'm willing to pay $20 for the company. We can raise the money. It will be a terrific fit. But I'll only do something if you invite me in. I'm not going to write any letters." But so far, Lorenzo's $20 offer was only an idea, not a formal offer. Icahn's proposal was. His $18 offer would have to be dealt with at the board meeting coming up on May 28. TWA must come out of the meeting with a response to his bid and a strategy, Freund was convinced, for the clock was ticking fast. Icahn's brief halt in buying could end when the decision from federal court came down. If Icahn won, he could go back in the market vindicated and stronger than ever.

TWA's president, C. E. Meyer, had earlier made a futile attempt to talk Icahn out of buying any more TWA stock. In a deposition taken just five days before the May 28 board meeting, and still sealed by the federal court, Icahn told of calling Meyer on the phone, and Meyer being "upset. He said, 'I don't want to talk to you anymore unless you stop buying stock. . . .' I said, 'I won't stop buying stock, and I won't talk to you.' " A few days after that first call, as Icahn's voluntary halt in buying was within hours of expiring, he and Meyer met in the almost-deserted bar of the Waldorf-Astoria Hotel in midtown Manhattan and, as Icahn described it, the talk turned bitter. " 'All you want is a fast buck. That's all you've ever done in these corporate raids, go for a fast buck,' said Meyer. I said, 'If we are psychoanalyzing each other, why don't you admit what you really care about is your job, and you are afraid I am going to take it away from you.' " They glared at each other, and the meeting ended. Icahn learned later that Meyer had already resigned to go over to Trans World's Hilton Hotel subsidiary. Knowing would probably not have softened his convictions about management.

In preparation for the TWA board meeting May 28, Freund and Salomon's team hammered out a strategy and reached a consensus. If Icahn wasn't halted by the federal court, the company would have to be put up for sale. As they gathered in the boardroom at the TWA corporate headquarters at 605 Third Avenue, Skadden Arps and Salomon Brothers presented a unified front to one of the most impressive corporate boards in America. Fourteen of its nineteen members were outside directors, all extraordinarily accomplished, strong-minded individuals. Most were famous. Here for one of his first board meetings was Peter Ueberroth, commissioner of baseball and masterful boss of the Los Angeles Olympics, facing a takeover his first time to bat. There was Robert McNamara, former secretary of defense and president of the World Bank. Brock Adams, former transportation secretary. Jack Valenti, president of the Motion Picture Association of America. Arjay Miller, dean emeritus of Stanford University's prestigious graduate school of business. Andrall Pearson, a Harvard Business School professor. Lester Crown, the largest stockholder in General Dynamics. And a powerful handful of former or current chief executives of major corporations—AT&T, National Intergroup. It was what Carl Icahn called a white-shoe board. They held one of the choicest board assignments in the nation. They received not only a five-figure a year fee, but the precious golden passes that flew them free.

Tension was electric in the boardroom as they waited for word of the decision from the federal court. A lawyer stationed

in the courtroom would call the moment it came down. Bob
Zimet of Skadden Arps, who had handled the litigation, left the
boardroom briefly, then returned. "I've got bad news for you,"
he reported. "We lost." The odds had been against TWA all
along. They were poised men. But recognition that a raider
could disrupt and possibly derail a national institution swelled
to indignation. There would be no injunction against Icahn
from the federal courts. Icahn was no longer just an upstart
raider; he was a federally certified, credible contender. This
could hurt them in Washington with their fitness test, for the
New York court had found him fit. And free of the brief
restraining order that had halted him for two weeks, Icahn was
now free to buy stock again. Carl was out there buying, Freund
was sure, while the board meeting was going on.

"Michael Zimmerman and I made major presentations, and
we told them straight," Freund said, "in the absence of doing
something, the company's lost." The only move that made any
sense was to sell the company. That concept, Freund sensed,
would not be an insurmountable obstacle. "The board's highest
priority was never staying independent. They were willing to
merge to expand. But they didn't want the airline dismantled,
which was what they feared from Carl." There was no obvious
white knight; nobody felt terrific about Texas Air.

"We must actively look for a better deal than Carl's," Freund
told the board. "Then we'll submit the best offer we get to the
shareholders." But simply putting the company up for sale
wasn't enough, Freund knew. Carl could just keep buying stock
while TWA was looking; he could just solicit consents and
throw out the board, contending that the search for a merger
partner was just a smokescreen and that TWA wasn't really
interested in being acquired. So now Freund presented to the
directors the strategy he and Zimmerman, and Freund's partner Rich Easton, had formulated prior to the meeting. "If
within sixty days, there's nothing better than Carl's—and if Carl
gets his financing commitment, the DOT doesn't object, and
there are no legal restrictions—we'll submit Carl's proposal to
the shareholders, and we'll give our view at that time on the
merits of his offer." It could put Icahn on hold for sixty days.

And it would get Carl's offer before the shareholders, but still leave the door open for the board to condemn it if it deemed it to be bad.

Freund knew that some on the board would resist anything that seemed to validate Icahn. Some would fight it. To sell his strategy to the board would require a formidable display of decisiveness. A loaded gun was at the company's head and they were still woefully unprepared for war. They must expand their options and buy more time, and as Freund presented his ideas, he found himself increasingly convinced that the correct route for TWA lay in his strategy. He found himself making strong statements, expressing his personal *views,* with all the force and confidence he had feared he might lack in the heat of war. As the vote was taken, Freund glimpsed the shaking off of an old albatross from the Age of Conformity, and he began to feel confident that he could handle the hostile arena.

The board voted unanimously to put the company up for sale. It approved Freund's entire package. If Icahn stuck to his word, TWA had bought sixty days of time in which to find an alternative to Carl Icahn. There was one more bit of strategy: to stop Icahn from soliciting the consents that could throw out the board. "As Zimmerman and I wrote the press release right after the meeting, we added the fillip that we expected Carl not to use the consent procedure because it might thwart the best interests of the shareholders. We sent out the press release and held our breath." Then the Salomon team flew from the room to start hunting for white knights.

"Icahn didn't reply directly," Freund recalls. "He sputtered to the *New York Times* about level playing fields and 'I don't know if I'll be here in sixty days' and all that crap. He did buy some more shares, until he was restrained by the Missouri court a few days later. But he never did the consent thing," Freund said later with deep satisfaction. "That strategy is one of the things I'm proudest of in the whole deal."

Vigorously beating the bushes for a white knight, Salomon Brothers talked to nearly a hundred potential suitors in a two-week period. "They talked to every airline, every major hotel, and other companies that might be interested. We explored leveraged buyouts with Kohlberg, Kravis Roberts & Co., but they didn't think it could be done," says Freund. Talks with Lorenzo were stepped up. A company called Resorts International stepped forward. They had big casino resorts in the Bahamas and Atlantic City. They flew to New York and said they were prepared to make a $22 offer, 60 percent cash and 40 percent Resort debentures—junk bonds. It was less cash than Icahn was offering. They had a strategy for playing hardball with Icahn to get him to support their deal. They would sign an agreement with TWA, then give Icahn an ultimatum: take our merger deal, you have an hour to decide, or we'll do a front-end-loaded cash tender offer you can't accept because of your 16(b) problem. Freund feared they were underestimating Icahn's response to coercion. But the Resorts deal seemed to be real, and talks intensified.

As the dust of the hunt settled, the only two real prospects were Lorenzo and Resorts International. "There was some question about Resorts as an appropriate owner because they were in the gambling business," Freund admits, "but TWA wasn't flooded with suitors. With the high-cost union and rate structures, and tough competition from United and American, it was not a desirable acquisition. Who, except Icahn, would want to run an airline?"

Litigation and legislation were not stopping Icahn, as Freund had hoped they would. On the heels of the loss in federal court in New York, the state of Missouri rammed through an amendment to the state takeover statute that favored TWA, a large employer in the state. Five days later, that amendment was declared unconstitutional, killing help on that front. But almost simultaneously, there was good news from the Missouri state court, which, on June 3, temporarily restrained Icahn from buying more stock or soliciting consents until at least June 17. That news came the very same day that a flurry of buying by Icahn raised his ownership level to almost 33 percent—steadily moving toward control.

The court order was another small gift of time in a climate that increasingly favored Icahn. For whatever happened in other courts, the loss of the federal court case in New York the day of the board meeting had given Icahn the respectability he needed going into congressional fitness hearings next week— June 7. "New York had the effect of validating him on credibility," says Freund. "We were saying, in effect, that Carl was a liar. Carl said, 'I changed my mind,' and the judge said, 'I believe Carl.' " Freund knew that TWA's Department of Transportation challenge to Icahn's fitness, so ingenious at the time, was seriously undermined. We may be dead in Congress and dead in the Department of Transport, Freund worried.

◆ ◆ ◆

As heads of the pilots' and machinists' unions, respectively, Hoglander and John Peterpaul had no love for each other. But bonded by greater enemies, they met over drinks at Gary's in Washington a couple of days before the hearings. "There's a lot of bad blood between the machinists and the pilots," Hoglander said with regret. It was kind of a class war, really. Pilots were educated, sophisticated men. "And the machinists aren't all jet technicians; they're also the guys who sweep the ramps and clean the toilets," Hoglander explained. The machinists accused the pilots of being overpaid elitists. Pilots resented always being the ones to make the biggest concessions. As they met, both he and Peterpaul were flirting secretly with Icahn. Peterpaul had already met with him, Hoglander had heard. And making his first bold play in the game, Harry had called Icahn. Hoglander had had lunch with some of his Master Executive Council guys, and when he'd urged getting involved with the man who owned a third of their company, they had directed Harry to pursue Icahn and find out what his intentions were. But mellowed by a few drinks, Hoglander and Peterpaul commiserated now like lovers jilted by the same woman. Rumors were flying. Management apparently was talking to everybody. Resorts. Even Lorenzo. But the company had never talked to them. There had been no contact. Ed Meyer, TWA's president, was going to be a witness at the hearings. "It will be the first contact I've had with Meyer since Icahn surfaced!" Harry fumed. "That goddamn management cares more about its own selfish interests than about its employees." Could Icahn be much worse, they wondered. "Going back to Hughes, we have a history of unusual guys running this company, so why not Icahn?" Harry speculated.

Hoglander and Peterpaul were suspicious of Icahn's motives. But loosened by scotch, an obsessive hatred of Lorenzo erupted that made any dislike of Icahn pale. "Lorenzo is vicious, reneging, and calculating. He's reneged on every promise he's ever made to the unions, and thrown them off the property," Hoglander fumed. They needed to talk strategy, to form a consortium of the three unions—pilots, machinists, flight attendants—he felt. He and Peterpaul agreed on a loose sort of strategy: Hoglander would try to keep Icahn on the hook while they fished for alternatives. Hey, Western or Northwest might be a nice fit. Or maybe Eastern. There was one thing they could shake on. They would never, never go across to Lorenzo.

◆　◆　◆

JUNE 7. As he ambled in to the hearings room where Icahn's fitness would be scrutinized by a congressional committee, Hoglander's eyes were riveted by a young black woman sitting near the front of the room. It was a pro-company crowd, orchestrated by Gershon Kekst's public relations guys. The woman was wearing her TWA uniform and "Stop Icahn" button, but you could see incredible feeling in her face that had nothing to do with public relations. Harry went up and talked to her. She was twenty-two, maybe twenty-three, and had driven all night from North Carolina. TWA was her first airline job. She loved the job and the company, and her mother had told her Icahn was a scoundrel and Mr. Meyer was going to put him away. She had driven five hundred miles to stand behind her president.

Meyer was the third to testify. Icahn listened, and as he talked, he was distressed that "Meyer's making this a personal attack on me. He is not dealing with the issues."

Hoglander listened. "I watched Meyer testify and as he responded to the questions, he became unraveled. I watched him stammer and screw up his answers as the congressmen zeroed in on him. Then they went on to his golden parachute, and how he was going to make millions of dollars, no matter what happened to TWA. The congressmen ripped him apart,

and it came out that, just the week before, the board of
directors had voted about thirty of the key company officers
severance pay and parachutes, and golden passes to everybody." Harry felt embarrassed to be a TWA employee. "It was
the self-serving, the *greed*." He looked at the young woman and
winced as disillusion transformed her face. He saw her later, in
the hall, in tears.

Icahn testified next. As the lanky, brown-haired Icahn
walked to the microphone, Harry was surprised that he was
such a tall, attractive guy. He spoke in a coarse New Yorkese,
but then so did Harry. It was *what* he was saying that gripped
Hoglander. "His answers were straightforward and deliberate.
He said that it was his money, and that he didn't intend to break
up the airline. He'd said it before a federal judge, and he said it
now before a congressional committee: he intended to run it as
an airline. Despite all the propaganda, my impression was that
he was a very shrewd and intelligent individual." Hoglander
was wearing his "Stop Icahn" button. But at the two o'clock
break in testimony, Harry went up to him and said, "Carl
Icahn. I'm Harry Hoglander. I think that you and I, at some
point, should have a talk."

To please the courts, Congress, and press, Icahn had, it
seemed, indeed become a respectable "man of commerce," as
he liked to style himself. He had handled himself so well,
Freund guessed, when he heard later about Icahn's performance, that the still-pending ruling on his fitness by the Department of Transportation would be moot, and might never be
completed. On June 10, the DOT canceled TWA's request for a
test of Icahn's fitness; they declined to pass on the issue.

But Freund also sensed, with tentative but growing certainty,
that a side effect of the lawsuits and the fitness test was that
Icahn was being forced to commit himself to the "long-term
interests of the airline." In his letter to Senator Danforth, who
had introduced legislation to stop him, Icahn had stated, "We
are deeply committed to and concerned about the future of
TWA. . . . We would expect to operate TWA in such a way as to
maximize the long-term interest of TWA, its employees and the
travelling public." He had said it in court. He had said it to the

board. He was saying it here. The more Icahn was forced to publicly state his commitment to keeping the airline intact, Freund hoped, the more he would be bound up in a net of promises he would be forced to honor.

◆　◆　◆

FOR those involved, the TWA hearings filled their world. But in the context of the rounds of takeover hearings that had engaged Congress and its regulatory agencies all spring, they were simply part of the final round before summer recess. As the TWA crowd packed its briefcases and left the Hill, Boone Pickens and Fred Hartley were preparing to testify before the Senate Banking Committee's subcommittee on securities, and preparing for their first sight of each other since the agreement a month earlier.

It was a bonanza day for takeover groupies, for as Pickens and Hartley came face to face in the subcommittee hearing room, they were joined by Sir James Goldsmith, who was close enough to control of Crown Zellerbach to be taken very, very seriously. The senators were still vigorously investigating takeovers, trying to establish whether legislation was required to curb excesses and, more to the point for politicians, to protect the nation's shareholders and their own states and constituencies who might be wounded by the takeover wars. California's treasurer, Jesse Unruh, one of the nation's savviest politicians, had warned that legislation would be futile. He got laughs and cheers from a hotel ballroom full of county pension fund managers in Santa Rosa, California, with his witty tribute to the raiders' boundless ingenuity: "Boone Pickens is smarter than Tip O'Neill and *a lot* smarter than Ronald Reagan. In fact, if he becomes governor of Texas, I'm going to buy stocks in Oklahoma, New Mexico, and Kansas." The administration did not want antitakeover legislation, and just about everyone agreed it would take about five minutes for Pickens and his colleagues to do an end run around it. But the hearings—like a takeover deal once put in play—had taken on a life of their own.

Hartley's head was down, his arms crossed on the table, as he studied his testimony. Scanning the room for opportunity, Pickens moved smoothly toward the senators on the dais, and as he passed Hartley, stuck out his hand and said, "Hello, Fred." Pickens was always, no matter what the pressure or emotions inside, a Texas gentleman. Hartley looked up gruffly, angry to be interrupted, stuck out his hand, submitted to a handshake he clearly hated, and turned back to his work.

Then, flanked by two of the handful of men who have knocked the complacency out of corporate America, Hartley unleashed a diatribe. Addressing himself to the subject of the $3.6 billion debt forced on Unocal by the raid, he lashed out against "a highly engineered conspiracy . . . that has the whole world laughing at us. And may I say, sir, especially the Japanese. South America is a mess today because it's leveraged damn near 100 percent. But we had to do it . . . or let the barbarians do it. We had to exchange the warm blood of equity with the cold water of debt. . . ."

Pickens stayed cool and impassive as Hartley called him a barbarian. As Pickens gave his brief speech, he presented the panel with a few performance figures for the two companies that showed Mesa the superior performer. And as always, he kept his message simple. Repeated in speeches, on TV, and in hearings, this message was as plain as the Panhandle, one that should be understood on the Hill: "In the five deals we've been involved in, there were 950,000 stockholders that actually made a pretax profit of $16 billion; out of that, about $4 billion was paid in taxes." Pickens delighted in barbing Congress with the fact that he, and takeovers, were helping to reduce the national debt. Pickens put his arms back over the chair, a gesture of relaxation, as Hartley went on, under questioning from the senators, to flail him with the serious decline in the price of Mesa stock since the Unocal settlement. "It was at $20 and fell to $13.50 June 10—a loss for Mesa of $115 million. Looks like Mesa needs to be restructured," Hartley exulted.

Keeping cool, Pickens politely tried to correct him. "Fred, it may not be that much. . . ." Through careful and creative reading of dividend provisions in the federal tax code, Pickens's team had uncovered a way to offset some of the losses on their Unocal stock. In fact, Pickens would soon be declaring an $83 million profit for Mesa Partners from the Unocal transaction, after taxes, "capitalizing on adversity," as a Pickens aide said. He had quietly held this ace-in-the-hole even while they negotiated with Unocal, and he held it now while Hartley lay down his storm of abuse. Jesse Unruh's comment on Pickens's ingenuity could not be proved more true.

Excused by the senators to catch a plane to London, Hartley left in a bluster for a globe-circling visit to Unocal's oil exploration and production projects. Hartley was back in his world.

♦   ♦   ♦

IN a week in which raiders were showing well in Washington and Ivan Boesky had paid tribute to Pickens in a speech to an analysts conference as "a great gentleman who has led a revolution in corporate America," it was now Goldsmith's hour. His appearance before the senators came at a moment of grace in his quest for Crown Zellerbach. He had gained a seat on the board at the annual meeting in San Francisco May 9, an event that had opened a dialogue with the company. He had struck a truce with Crown and was in a phase of friendly collaboration with the company, trying to work out Crown's proposed restructuring in ways satisfactory to Crown and to its largest shareholder. And to the heightening interest of Wall Street and distress of Crown Zellerbach, he had crossed the critical 20 percent mark of stock ownership on May 14, triggering the poison pill. Since that date, his march toward control had an aura of excitement and suspense; it surrounded Sir James as he appeared before the senators.

Until now, he had been just another of the headline names marching in and out of Washington during the friendly inquisition. He had been the elusive Sir James, an "asset stripper." But as he stood, six feet two, elegantly dressed, and read his prepared statement, he commanded attention. With a voice of Shakespearean range and timbre, he delivered an eloquent ten-minute summary of the decline and fall of Europe, a speech of international dimension, scholarly erudition, and wry British humor. Frustrated by an England "stripped of vitality by gentrification," and an oppressive France, whose personal liberties had been smothered by "a civil service mandarinate," he had sold most of his European assets to invest in

America. He was tiring of the fight, in England, against an upstairs/downstairs class society in which "admiration was reserved for amateurs, dilettantes, and a somewhat effete set of values . . . and adventurers, risk takers, tough and ambitious professionals were considered rather uncouth and vulgar. . . . The cultures of Athens, Florence, and Venice were founded on prosperity from commerce," he lectured. And yet he despaired that, even with Margaret Thatcher's "awe-inspiring courage," England "might prefer to lie down and die slowly rather than to muster the vigor needed for survival." The system of meritocratic capitalism that had driven his remarkable life seemed to thrive, now, only in America.

Like a pilgrim who has finally reached his spiritual home, he described America's "entrepreneurial revolution" to the senators in terms that could have been intended specifically to describe the TWA struggle. He saw America's "new industrial revolution" as a fundamental shift that "reduces the role and power of the megacorporations and the trade unions . . . and creates a truly competitive economy. And in a truly competitive economy either you do it right or you get eliminated. Mega-companies either get it right or they get taken over. Trade unions have to agree to competitive practices or unionized companies perish and trade union membership is correspondingly reduced." He had said almost the same words at the Drexel Burnham seminar in Los Angeles in late March. Icahn had been there, too. In fact, his words might well have been an exhortation to Icahn as he girded his loins to take on TWA's unions.

In summarizing "the national debate about hostile takeovers," he said, "the question really being asked is whether or not large corporations should be treated like institutions and should be granted special protection from the marketplace. . . . Who would have believed a few years ago that conglomerates, created at the time by freewheeling entrepreneurs, today are described by some as sacrosanct institutions which should be protected from the marketplace by special legislation. All that has changed in many of these companies is that the flame of the founder has been replaced by the complacency of the bureaucrat. And because the members of such bureaucracies control the disposition of vast amounts of other people's money and the power and patronage that accompany it, they feel they are part of the establishment and therefore deserve special privileges."

The senators were disarmed, and as they pursued him further with questions, they treated him with the respect of visiting royalty. It was his first public appearance of this kind in America, and Goldsmith would write about the experience in a privately published book of his speeches several months later as "an unusual pleasure."

It was a forum he relished. He was coming to America with a respect for its systems that came from disillusion with France and England. His belief that, in the world today, this was where commercial opportunity lay was borne out by the fact that he was here, in the marketplace, investing billions. After being picked to pieces by the press in England and France, and having his reputation seriously damaged by the sensation of the *Private Eye* criminal libel suit in England, it was gratifying to be treated like a statesman. "Since an early age, I've rejected the prevailing cultures in England and France, which seemed to me to be the cultures of decay," he would soon write. "The hearings were one of the first times in my life that I was not counterculture and that I found myself in fundamental agreement with many of the members of the panel." As he responded to questions, he let a little of the passionate intensity he had suppressed during his statement escape, making him even more engaging.

But he remained an enigma. His brilliance was undisputed, his intensity apparently real. But was there any warmth and feeling behind it? Even the men who worked most closely with him didn't really know. But he had lifted the image of raiding from the cellar and put it somewhere much higher as he wound up his appearance to delighted laughter. To a question from Senator Chic Hecht of Nevada, "If you think America's so great, why didn't you come earlier?" he said with a droll smile, "Stupidity, actually." Hecht couldn't contain himself. "Boone," he said, "this guy does a better job of talking than you do. You

ought to take him with you," and then broke into the laughter
to add, "Sir James, personally, I would like to invite you to
become an American citizen and join the Republican party.
You could be one of our top spokesmen." With the gallantry
and mutual respect the raiders tend to show each other, Goldsmith responded privately to Hecht's comment, "I don't really
think Mr. Pickens needs my help."

But Pickens was nagged by the issue of Mesa's declining stock
price. Back at his suite in the Hay Adams the evening before
the hearings—and just after a joint speech with Ivan Boesky to
a conference of investment analysts—it dominated his
thoughts. "We'll figure it out. We'll show them a white blackbird
yet," he said, raising his legs and flexing them as he leaned back
on a sofa, keeping fit even on the road. "We're working on it."
His team had gone into intensive reevaluation and soul-search-
ing after Unocal. Even the ingenious $83 million paper profit
from Unocal he would soon announce would probably not
bring Mesa's stock price back up as far as he, and the shareholders, would like it. Typical of the dissatisfaction, a Baltimore
money manager, David McCallum, president of Adams Express, checked his portfolio of oil stocks and noted the slide in
his hundred thousand shares of Mesa stock. Pickens had visited
him personally on the Gulf deal, trying to win his proxy vote.
McCallum had liked Pickens. But what's he going to do about
his own stock, he wondered. It was embarrassing for the man
whose corporate stationery said "Mesa: The Shareholders'
Company." But the resilience that had marked Pickens's life,
which had let him look on all setbacks as "learning experience"
and bounce back to fight again, was being brought to bear. No
one doubted that he would come charging back with a solution.

Resilience seemed to be a family trait. Bea Pickens, with her
husband in Washington, even *looked* uncrushable. She sparkled
with the chunky gold jewelry—choker, earrings, pins, brace-
lets—she often wore, and her striped dress was of a cotton so
crisp and heavy that it withstood the steamy Washington heat.
Her silvering hair was as crisply coiffed as ever. Her voice
steady and pleasant, she was enjoying a brief visit with her
daughter, Liz, who worked now on the White House staff after

running the national Youth for President Reagan effort in November's campaign. So often on the road with Pickens, Bea relished moments with her four children whenever she could snatch them, and savored the pause since Unocal.

Right after Unocal, Bea Pickens invited a group of her artist friends from Santa Fe to Amarillo, and she took them by helicopter to the floor of nearby Palo Duro Canyon to see the rust and ochre cliffs painters always loved. It was a shock to see it from the air, a mini–Grand Canyon of cliffs, trees, and color cleaved from the flat, bleak Panhandle rangeland. It was a place that pulled Bea back to her childhood on an Oklahoma ranch, and back to the region's pioneer days. Panhandle ranching had started there, on the canyon floor. Heroic cattle drives that had linked the Panhandle to the rest of the cattle culture had originated in the Palo Duro. And the cliffs bared the ancient Eocene structures that held oil, spur to so much of the Panhandle's history. Bea had also taken the group to the Pickens ranch north of Amarillo, and to her favorite woods for a day of riding, painting, and a chuckwagon barbecue. The ranch staff had set out tables and lounge chairs in the woods, and while the group painted, Bea had just enjoyed being in the place she so rarely had time to visit. She'd named the woods, with their magical cottonwood grove and wildflowers, "Sen-Tosa," a phrase she'd heard in Singapore on one of their foreign trips. She was told it meant "peace and tranquillity."

◆   ◆   ◆

For those embroiled in TWA, a tranquil grove of cottonwoods was an unimaginable fantasy. The pace had accelerated to a full gallop. Life, for the principals, had shrunk to a very narrow range of offices, streets, and coffee shops. For Freund, "Resorts had started to waver. They talked about financing problems, but I think they just felt they could buy the company cheaper. We fought to hold them to their original deal and keep our problems with the deal secret from Lorenzo when—the timing was beautiful!—Lorenzo got in touch with Salomon and said he was willing to go higher than $20. Just as we were losing Resorts."

And then, on Saturday, June 9, there was an unexpected

signal from Icahn. "It was a weak signal, and I didn't respond at first," says Freund, "but it was a signal that he was a seller.

"It was Sunday, June 10. I was at a dinner party in New Jersey. They held dinner while I took a call from Steve Jacobs, Icahn's lawyer. It was clear that he was saying that if there was a deal with Lorenzo that didn't discriminate against Carl, and if there was a merger that he could participate in and not have a 16(b) problem, he might not stand in the way." It was the first time Icahn had said that he might be willing to sell his stock rather than go for control. But it confirmed what Freund had always thought about Icahn: he doesn't get emotionally involved with the property. He is either a buyer or a seller. Excited and preoccupied, Freund left the dinner as soon as he politely could and raced back with Barbara to New York.

"By Monday," Freund continued, "we stopped negotiating with Resorts and entered into nonstop negotiations with Texas Air. As word filtered out to Resorts, they contacted us to say they would go back to $22, half in cash. But we said, 'Sorry, we're doing a better deal.' Zimmerman was doing a good job of raising Lorenzo's sights up to $22.50 . . . $23, and mostly in cash." On June 3, Lorenzo had hired Drexel Burnham to raise the financing through junk bonds.

"At that point, we preferred Lorenzo to Icahn. And the fit between Texas Air and TWA would have been terrific." What had to be negotiated was the fee Lorenzo would pay Icahn to back off, as well as the price Lorenzo would pay for Icahn's stock.

The night of June 12, the teams for Lorenzo, TWA, and Icahn met at Wachtell Lipton's offices, Lorenzo's lawyers. One of Lipton's protégés, Richard Katcher, was handling it for Wachtell. Drexel Burnham's Leon Black was handling the financial side of the negotiations for Lorenzo. But Lorenzo wasn't there. "He was in New York but not there," which struck Freund and Rich Easton—his "right hand" throughout the deal—as very odd. But Katcher and Black were speaking for him. Icahn had been invited, too. "But he was on an evening cruise. It was absurd. We needed him and he was on a boat. He didn't arrive until about 2:00 A.M." But his presence was there, the relentless threat of Icahn going into the market and buying control. That day, the Missouri court had dissolved its temporary restraining order, and Icahn was free to buy again. "When Carl finally arrived, he got into the negotiations, and by daybreak we'd reached this tentative agreement." It is the agreement that could have wound up the deal and made Lorenzo chairman of the nation's second-largest airline system.

The deal would buy Icahn—and all other TWA shareholders—out at $23, giving him roughly $79 million profit on his stock. And it would pay him an additional $16 million to walk away. The package of approximately $95 million would be the largest profit he and his partners had ever made. "Carl agreed to it. Black and Katcher left the room and called Lorenzo—woke him up—and told him the deal," Freund recalls. "I'm told Lorenzo said, 'Carl's a pig. Let him have the airline.' We didn't tell Carl. We hoped Lorenzo would calm down after a few hours, so Leon and Katcher rushed over to see him.

"It was now 6:00 A.M. We went to the Brasserie for breakfast. We were all dragging, but Carl was ebullient—feeling terrific. He won't get the airline. He's a seller. But he's perfectly satisfied. I'm listening to Carl reminiscing about other deals, and I'm feeling a sense of dread because I know we have a problem with Texas Air," says Freund. On the way back to Wachtell Lipton's offices to get a report from Black and Katcher, Freund dashed into a couple of stores to buy a shirt and razor so that he could clean up before the TWA board meeting later that morning. He shaved and changed in the Wachtell bathroom, and then waited anxiously for Black and Katcher to return from their talk with Lorenzo.

"They come back, we go into a private office, and they tell us, 'Frank won't buy the deal.' " Freund looked at them in dismay. "He won't buy the deal." The night's work—the chance to buy Icahn out—was gone. "That was the night a deal should have been struck. But it wasn't. There was a gap—and it wasn't closed. If they had communicated, it might have been settled. But you were dealing with two massive egos, and there was an awful lot of macho wrapped up in this," Freund said. Icahn was still a loose cannon on the deck. Whatever deal was struck with

Lorenzo would be haunted by the fact that Icahn was still the largest shareholder.

"Carl predictably blew up. He felt Lorenzo had reneged, which he hadn't. I think his advisers had just got too far out in front of him." Freund and Zimmerman had to go to the board meeting in a few hours and report. They sat down with Icahn and Steve Jacobs and reached an informal understanding: Carl would not be a spoiler. He would not buy more shares if he didn't have the best bid on the table. *Unless*—and that unless would haunt the next month and a half—unless Lorenzo started accumulating stock himself, or unless TWA changed the status quo, such as issuing some kind of lockups to Lorenzo. Icahn agreed to put out a press release to that effect.

Freund rushed to the board meeting, described the events of the previous forty-eight hours, and told the board he thought the deal with Lorenzo was the best they could do. They signed an agreement with Texas Air and issued a joint statement: "Trans World Airlines, Inc. and Texas Air Corporation jointly announced that their respective boards of directors have unanimously approved a definitive merger agreement providing for TWA to become a wholly owned subsidiary of Texas Air. In the merger, each share of TWA common stock would be converted into the right to receive $19 cash and $4 of a new issue of 14.5 percent cumulative nonconvertible preferred stock of TWA. . . ." The agreement also gave Lorenzo an option to buy over 6 million TWA shares at $19.50, the then current market price for TWA stock.

Icahn's brief statement hardly expressed the drama of the night: "Carl C. Icahn stated that he is currently reviewing the $23-per-share bid for all of TWA's common stock by Texas Air and is not presently taking a position on the offer. Consistent with his philosophy, Mr. Icahn stated that he does not intend to be a 'spoiler' and will not use his TWA common stock interest to prevent TWA stockholders from taking advantage of the best available bid." He owned 33 percent—over 11 million shares. He would not now, he stated, make a counterbid, but "Mr. Icahn reserved the right to do so."

"Icahn had the best of all worlds," Freund mused. "He had $23 locked in on the downside. And yet he was free to do what he wanted since he hadn't actually *agreed* to the Lorenzo deal." That nagged. "But at TWA we were pretty pleased. We had done a wonderful deal for shareholders, saved a national institution. What a powerful competitor—Texas Air and TWA."

The media greeted the announcements as a done deal. The *New York Times* celebrated "the $793.5 million deal that would create the nation's second-largest airline network, after United Airlines" as well as profit Mr. Icahn, "who stands to reap . . . $50 million."

"What we didn't anticipate," said Freund a few weeks later, "was the depth of union feeling against Lorenzo."

CHAPTER 14

JUNE 12 was Harry Hoglander's fifty-second birthday. He was supposed to testify against Icahn in Washington, but that had been canceled. While the all-night meeting raged at Wachtell Lipton, he was out celebrating his birthday and was feeling good. "Next morning, June 13, I went out to pick up a *New York Times*, and there was the story on the front page.

"I was flabbergasted! I was shocked and sickened—as if someone had hit me in the stomach." Lorenzo's footprints were rumored to be around, but he had known nothing about it. As the reality set in, anger took over. "Those first-class bastards! They've betrayed us without giving us a chance to participate. They've sold us out to an immoral guy who deals only in absolutes, and that absolute is victory—unconditional surrender of labor."

A grim memory flashed. "I remembered the Texas International and New York Air runway shop episode in 1980–81, when we picketed at La Guardia in the dead of winter. Lorenzo's scab pilots came through our picket lines to go to work for New York Air, flying repainted Texas International airplanes, while a cocktail party was going on over at the Marine Air Terminal at JFK where Frank Lorenzo was being toasted as the hero of deregulation and the darling of the Yuppie Right. He was being praised for being able to knock labor on its ass." What enraged Hoglander most was Lorenzo's exploitation of the bankruptcy laws, laws that "foster and encourage people to declare bankruptcy and then seemingly have the wherewithal *while still in bankruptcy* to buy a billion-dollar corporation! It's legal. But it doesn't seem right to me. It's a question of morality, and Lorenzo's morals are supported by the administration."

United's pilots were still on strike, trying to negotiate a two-tier pay scale they could live with. If they failed, and if Lorenzo got TWA, the Air Line Pilots Association would be crippled. "I was numb over the whole goddamn thing. We're not professional negotiators, or businessmen, or bankers, or people who haggle in the marketplace. We are *pilots!* How could we possibly win against a TWA/Lorenzo combination? I didn't know how we were going to handle it." Events were happening so fast, and the stakes were so high. It was like a phenomenon of New England winters that never ceased to surprise him. "When you live where lakes freeze over, you can go out in December and it's been 25 degrees for the last seventeen days, then it goes to 20, then 18, and the lake still has no ice on it. Then one morning you wake up and a little ice is forming. The next day, it's frozen solid. That's damn near where we're at." He had made a few moves. He had talked to ALPA's lawyer, Bruce Simon, and made contact with Gene Keilin, the investment banker at Lazard Frères. But he was still an observer of events. Now, he determined that it was time to play. He would call Carl Icahn.

He believed—he hoped—the Master Executive Council and ALPA would stand behind him. A union had never before collaborated with a raider against its own company. He would be putting his career at risk. If they fought Lorenzo and he got the airline, Hoglander knew he'd be fired. Even with a union, there were ways to fire a pilot. They could fail you on a check ride. But if Lorenzo took over, he would kill the union and do anything he wanted. "Lorenzo takes no prisoners." On June 14, he called Icahn.

◆   ◆   ◆

ICAHN wanted to meet him right away. But first Harry had to clear his mind, and flying always did that. He flew to Saint Louis for a weekend with the National Guard. He'd flown National Guard since he left the air force in 1965. "I guess I am a patriot, like my dad," he mused. "He's a superpatriot. He quit his job at the stock exchange in World War II to work for a shipyard in New Jersey." But it was more than patriotism that inspired Hoglander to climb into his T-bird, the little T-33 jet trainer, and streak to twenty thousand feet. He had always been able to put things into perspective up there above the clouds. He was fighting for survival of his union. But he knew he was fighting, also, for the survival of the idea that airlines and aviation were about more than assets and profitability.

He wasn't supposed to fool around and do aerobatics, but he did. Every time he rolled the T-bird into an inverted dive and pulled Gs in a 15-degree climbout that took him screaming almost straight up—or even when he strapped into the cockpit of his 727—he felt the same thrill he had felt the first time his father rented a ride in a small plane for him and his brother when Harry was ten. Following jobs, his dad had moved them to Queens, Brooklyn, and Staten Island. "I went to fourteen grammar schools, so I got used to fighting early," he says with a laugh. But in the air he had found the habitat where he felt most at home. He'd promised his mother he wouldn't fly when he quit high school twelve days before graduation to enlist in the air force during the Korean War, but he became a gunner flying combat in B26s and B29s. "I thought it was going to be like a Gene Kelly movie. I didn't even shave yet. But you mature rapidly when you're evacuating wounded men." Even that horror hadn't deterred him from wanting to fly. He'd stayed in the service for eleven years, flying four-engined B47s.

The work ethic was strong, and had finally driven him out of the service and back to New York, with his pregnant wife, to get an education. He drove a truck while he took business courses at college at night. But two years later, with the second of his four children on the way, he was yearning to get back in the service. He was hungry to fly. "You had to have a commission to fly and the only way I could see to do that was to finish college in a school that offered ROTC. It was Christmas. I was in a library. My wife and I were both working a couple of jobs to keep food on the table. I looked up on the wall, pulled the Florida State College catalogue down, and found it had an ROTC program."

He got his degree and commission at Florida State, learned to fly single-engine jets, and rejoined the service as fast as he could, in 1959. He moved up to multiengine jets and ended up, in 1965, flying B47s at a Strategic Air Command base in New Hampshire. It was the year he was hired by TWA during the huge expansion phase in the early years of the jet era. Since then, he had made his home in New England. And flying has transcended any other love. Divorced from his first wife and remarried in the late sixties, he had been eager for more school, and was intellectually attracted to law.

The first in his family to go to college, Hoglander had work and motivation deeply imprinted. "My father had worked in the Horatio Alger concept of capitalism since he was fourteen." A first-generation German-Scandinavian, he had worked his way up to a prosperous job with a New York Stock Exchange firm, but when the company lost its seat in the thirties, his father "went back to selling things" and to a pattern of mercurial swings in the Hoglander family's fortunes. "We weren't poor. We got a car every four or five years, but we'd all struggle and chip in whatever we earned. I was sweeping floors at fourteen, carrying boxes in the five-and-dime, and selling newspapers. We got the first television in the neighborhood in 1950, and it was a total family effort."

On his days off from flying Hoglander started studying law at Suffolk University in Boston, the country's largest law school. After earning his law degree, he was accepted by MIT for a business degree, but couldn't ethically do both. The choice to stay with TWA, the "pilot's outfit," was easy. He flew out of New York on the international routes for twelve years, as co-pilot on 707s and 747s. But he wanted command of his own aircraft. To be captain, he had to start back at the junior domiciles again. They weren't Paris or Cairo. "In fact, I fly the shitty trips. New York to Cincinnati, St. Louis, and Kansas City, a layover and back next day via Kansas City, St. Louis, Louisville, and Cleveland. It's not exotic, but I love every minute of it." He commands the flights. And he gets to do four or five takeoffs and landings a day. He gets to fly! As he rolled the T-bird back to the air force base in St. Louis, he knew that it was flying he was really fighting for.

◆ ◆ ◆

THE game had begun. Hoglander flew from St. Louis to the White Plains Airport, where Icahn picked him up in his silver Mercedes and drove him directly to his estate in Westchester. It was Hoglander's first glimpse of the life-style of a multimillionaire raider. They drove through acres of immaculately manicured lawn to a handsome stone mansion decorated with the comfortable trappings of an English country house. Icahn was casually dressed in sweater and slacks and, Harry noted, no socks. They had work to do. TWA was only as valuable to Icahn as the concessions he could get from the unions. Icahn was the only alternative to Lorenzo the pilots had at this point. At that first meeting "we didn't negotiate. We formulated ground rules. It was the beginning of our dialogue."

That night, the Three Musketeers—Hoglander, Keilin, and Simon—had their first meeting at Harry's apartment, the furnished flat ALPA rented for him at the Avenue of the Americas and Fifty-fifth Street. "It became our headquarters. We'd meet there and have conversations about conversations, examining every word like the entrails of a goat." He had thought Gene Keilin would be in it just for the $1 million-plus fee Lazard would get, but he saw Keilin get involved, almost as much as himself. The three started working out together. "I would get to love those guys." Next day, the pilot's team drove to Icahn's estate for the first formal talks. "That guy is amazing," Hoglander said with a laugh on the way back to New York. "We work all afternoon, he's going to give us dinner. And he goes to the freezer and gets frozen pizza. The guy's *cheap!*"

Westchester estates were not the daily reality of the takeover wars, Hoglander swiftly learned. Nothing he had done, not even flying jets, could prepare him for the speed and urgency of events in a billion-dollar battle for corporate control. The war rooms were in New York, at the law offices of Weil Gotshal and Watchell Lipton, and at the ALPA offices and Hoglander's apartment. Just as Icahn kept pressure on TWA by threatening to buy control in the market, Icahn found the pilots' pressure point, and threatened, constantly, to sell his stock to Lorenzo. One of his first acts with the pilots was to demand a deadline of June 30 for negotiating concessions and signing a contract.

The pilots still preferred to merge with another airline—Northwest, Western, Eastern—or even a hotel chain rather than Icahn. It would be a more natural fit. While Salomon Brothers was doing its intensive hunt for white knights, the unions initiated talks with anyone who was interested. They were talking to Crosbie at Western, to Borman at Eastern, to Resorts, which was still flirting with the airline, to the financier Jay Pritzker, and to a mysterious Mr. X, whom Hoglander would not identify. And a revolt within the ranks of the employees was creating internal pressures. An employee committee had formed to organize an ESOP (Employee Stock Ownership Plan) to buy the company and was raising its own funds to hire lawyers. For Hoglander, they were a pain in the neck. Not only were they undermining the union effort, he feared, but they were using space in his offices in New York, diverting him from his principal assigned task—to stall Icahn while the rest of the union team hunted for better candidates. To keep him on the hook.

Hoglander had been working way out ahead, on his own, with no time for the usual calls and letters to the union guys and pilots. He kept in touch with daily reports to Henry Duffy, head of ALPA in Washington. But he felt he had to get approval from the Master Executive Council (MEC)—the eighteen senior pilots who shared the running of the union—before he negotiated away what could be huge chunks of pilots' pay. "Pilots," he knew, "are conservative—financially and politically." He feared that he had stepped too far beyond the job he'd been elected to do and committed the pilots to millions of dollars they might not want to pay. Two days before the June 27 negotiations, he went through four hours of grilling in a closed session with eighteen members of the MEC, convinced he would be fired. Instead, he was given a unanimous vote of confidence. At least he had support as he headed into the negotiations with Icahn. "I was going to have to say a lot of things to keep Carl on the hook, because we were running out of players at that time." The unions were finding, as the company was, that there weren't too many suitors for TWA.

On June 27, the entire coalition met in Weil Gotshal's offices for the beginning of negotiations. It was like a great sprawling play that gets dumped on the stage with the curtain up before the principals have had time to rehearse their lines or get their roles coordinated. "Nobody trusted anybody. I suspected Peterpaul was talking to Lorenzo, making a deal at the pilots' expense. The attendants wouldn't negotiate with anybody. We were talking pay cuts of 20/20/20, 20 percent from each union, with as few 'hard' dollars and as many 'soft' dollars—working conditions dollars—as possible." Icahn's presence in the hurly-burly of the union negotiating arena was unprecedented. "Carl went down in the pits with the workers," says Al Kingsley. "The white gloves of the previous management—and most managements—*don't* discuss, they don't go down to the workers and talk to them and find out what the real problems are. They do it through layers and layers of hierarchy. How can they really understand the problems?" Hoglander winced as they went at it. "The machinists promptly told Icahn to shove some heavy demands in his ear, saying, 'We goddamn don't need you, and we'd sooner strike Lorenzo, you lousy, greedy fucking . . .'" They started making demands about work rules. "What do we know about work rules?" said Kingsley.

Icahn and Kingsley had been through some rough moments in the past, but this was obscene. "These guys, they bang on the table and they stand up and scream. It was more like a circus," Kingsley commented. Hoglander admits, "It was rough, a terrible night. It was constant profanity and almost physical violence." For the mechanics' negotiator, a big, feisty Irishman, Timothy Connolly, who loved a good fight, it was the usual way.

But the pilots' four-letter words were more the profanity pilots use in the cockpit when they're fighting to avoid a crash. "When a guy is trying to take something away from you, and you find yourself in a helpless and hopeless position, and the guy puts demand upon demand and, when you concede, adds more demands, you feel like just striking out," Hoglander explained.

Kingsley admits that Icahn's determination to negotiate and achieve agreements with the speed of light—to achieve in six hours what normally takes six months of negotiations—may have intensified the brawling style. "I mean, Carl doesn't know from these long, protracted negotiations," Kingsley says with a shrug. "He knows, 'Do you want to make a deal with me? You better do it now, because I've got Lorenzo, who calls me every day, he wants to buy my stock, you wanna make a deal, this is it, you've got a deadline, *do it*' . . . and the style develops from there."

Icahn's style was driving Hoglander crazy. "The reason he's a master negotiator is his ability to never say yes or no, but offer so many alternatives that he covers everything. He'd say, 'I would if I could, and I will, but maybe I will, but I can't do it right now, but then if I could, I really shouldn't, so I won't.' " How could you pin him down? How could he explain it to the guys at the MEC?

"We met for two nights, and he'd start the meetings at eight, nine, ten o'clock and go right through to morning. Keilin had been in crisis situations for the last twenty years, so he could sleep, but Simon and I had never been through this kind of intensity where we were dealing with so many groups, and making so many decisions and trying to apply them so rapidly that I was getting by on maybe three, four hours sleep, and it seemed as if my mind never slept at all. We were driven by the fear of the domino effect knocking the pilots down. Always Icahn kept threatening that if he didn't have the deal by June 30, he was going to Lorenzo."

Joking around helped. At an impasse, Hoglander would say, "Icahn, your problem is you have a terrible New York accent," and Icahn would snap back, "Whatta you talking about? Your accent's worse than mine." At breaks, they talked about their childhoods and high school basketball, and how Icahn and Bruce Simon went to the same high school. Icahn talked about how the Irish kids beat up on the Jewish kids all the time in Far Rockaway and how Icahn found anti-Semitism at Princeton. Except for occasional meetings with Davis Polk lawyers, who made Hoglander feel "as if I were on a tennis court with white socks and tennis shoes," he was virtually the only gentile in the inside team, and it was a tension-cracker when he'd say, "A guy with prejudice could find himself at a real handicap here, but you guys never make me feel discriminated against."

War was hell. But Hoglander recognized that, for the first time since deregulation, there might be an alternative to the company's benign neglect and Lorenzo's brutality. Out of the tantrums and profanity, Icahn was forging something no raider, and certainly not TWA management, had ever even tried to forge before.

"It was three or four in the morning; we'd been negotiating for two days when we reached the deal breaker," says Hoglander. "It was over the two-tier. United had gone on strike for twenty-nine days for it, and we would not budge off the United two-tier, which brought the low pay of the new hires up to parity with the old tier within five years. Even though Carl agreed that, eventually, the two tiers would have to merge, Carl wasn't going to budge off the American two-tier. Everybody was getting excited, so we threw his advisers out, and I said, 'Carl, I want to talk calmly to you. Do you understand what religion is, and what tradition is? Seniority is religion to me. *This* is religion to me. I'm not backing off this. Watch my lips, Carl, I don't give a *fuck* about the new guys, but I *do* care about tradition. We're not going to budge off this. If it breaks it, it breaks it.'"

To Hoglander's amazement, Icahn backed down, and out of the tantrums and profanity, an agreement was struck. Icahn had what he'd come for. He had forced concessions from the unions the company had never achieved. In "hard" and "soft" concessions, the pilots had agreed to give up roughly 20 percent of their salaries. But in exchange Icahn had committed to keeping the airline intact and not to sell to Lorenzo. "It's what they wanted—their jobs and their planes," he said. And he had achieved reductions in labor costs that could save the airline $300 million a year, and make it profitable again.

But Icahn would never again meet jointly with the unions. "They hate each other worse than they hate Lorenzo," he said to Kingsley, throwing up his hands, as they waited to see if the pilots would get the agreement ratified and back to them by the June 30 deadline.

Hoglander had one day to get it ratified by the MEC and ALPA and back to Carl. The MEC guys were all in Miami at an ALPA meeting. "We flew down on the thirtieth—the plane wasn't working and we got in late afternoon, exhausted, and explained it to the whole MEC group. We didn't even have the documents. The lawyers at Weil, Gotshal in New York were still putting them together, and they were having trouble with the word processor. The machine wasn't as tough as the firm was." The thirtieth was almost over and they'd never make it. They cajoled an extra day out of Icahn: midnight of July 1 was the new deadline. "We were flying paper back and forth by jet express. I think Carl staged it that way to add to the drama." Hoglander met with ALPA for eight hours on July 1, hours before it had to be back in New York, and had the group ready for a vote, when one man said, "I can't vote for this." Hoglander yelled, "Christ, we don't have time for this," and ordered, "You leave the room and go to the men's room. I want this *unanimous.*" They took the vote, and the agreement was ratified 17 to 0. Later, Hoglander would say, "I don't think those deadlines ever meant anything."

But now Hoglander had some breathing time. Icahn would have to come to terms with the mechanics and the flight attendants before final ratification of the deal. He had at least a week in which to pursue the other possibilities. With the agreement on its way to New York, Hoglander collapsed upstairs in his suite in the hotel in Miami and took a telephone call. "Hello, Captain Hoglander. This is Colonel Borman at Eastern Airlines." Says Hoglander, "I thought it was some guy joking around, so I told Bruce Simon to go in the can and get on the bathroom extension. And I'll be damned if he didn't say,

'I want to tell you, Captain, I'm deadly serious about this
proposal to buy TWA. Keep all options open and we'll put this
together. Think about it, and see me when you can.' "

This was getting heady beyond Harry's dreams or experience. Here he was, a 727 pilot, with Mr. X on the hook,
Borman begging to be let in the door, and the Icahn deal on
the table.

Hoglander, Simon, and Keilin went over to Borman's office
in Miami the next day, July 2. Harry had never met Borman
before, never met an astronaut before, but he was predisposed
to be impressed. He wanted to be impressed. They still preferred an airline to Icahn. "Borman was a fighter pilot. A West
Pointer. He was a very small guy—about five foot seven. But he
gave the impression of a very nitty-gritty guy. To everybody, he
is always 'Colonel.' At first he seemed straightforward, and then
he got vague about how jobs were to be handled. And how he
was going to finance it." But Borman proposed a major meeting in New York on July 13.

Next to flying, horses were just about the best tension re-
liever Hoglander could think of. His daughters used to show
and jump horses when they lived in New Hampshire. His office
walls are covered with racing posters, and he keeps race horses
in Ocala, Florida. He spent July 4 with his horses in Ocala, but
he couldn't get rid of the anxiety. He had to take a check ride
next day in Kansas City. He knew he was a damn good pilot.
But a Continental executive had been brought aboard TWA to
check things out for Lorenzo, the prospective owner, and his
presence made Hoglander nervous. The thought hit him regu-
larly. He was leading a hostile takeover against his own company. They wanted to get rid of him. He thanked God for the
National Guard, where he could still climb in the cockpit of his
T-33 and wring it out. Flying the line for TWA was no longer
relaxing. "Every time I went to the ramp, fifty guys would
surround me and want to know 'What's going on? What's going
on?' I was dealing with their lives and future."

The meeting with Borman was set for July 13. Borman was
talking frequently to Icahn, trying to get him to sell his stock to
Eastern, but he'd made Icahn angry. As Icahn told Hoglander,

Borman had said, "Carl, what do you want an airline for? You probably don't even know how to drive a car." Icahn burned, and thought, Just because he's a frigging astronaut, who the hell's he think he is? then snapped back to Borman, "I don't *need* to drive a car. I have guys doing it for me."

The Borman meeting July 13 was one of the great set pieces of the entire affair. It was a 96-degree day on the streets of New York. The drought was on, and air conditioning was turned off as thirty to forty people trooped into the offices of Eastern's lawyers, Sullivan & Cromwell, an aristocratic old-line law firm that has moved successfully into mergers and acquisitions. Borman opened the meeting with a show stopper, as Hoglander recalls it. "I welcome you with particular enthusiasm, ladies and gentlemen, because today you are about to take the first step in making aviation history—putting together the largest airline in the world."

But he didn't have a second act. "The only problem was they were broke," Hoglander shrugged. "Borman was going to get back to us in a week. But we never heard much more from him." For Hoglander, it was another plunge into despair. "Eastern was going to be our savior. If they could just raise a billion four, what the hell! Even if Frank Borman was the worst manager in the world, it would still take him four or five years to waste all of that money. And even then, if the largest airline in the *world* was teetering on bankruptcy, it would be another Chrysler deal because national security would be involved, and the government couldn't let it happen."

◆   ◆   ◆

"THROUGH July the pressure was getting intolerable. I'd never known anything like it in combat," Hoglander said grimly. "I was going against my own company, and the results of mistakes would be catastrophic. I was leading the pilots out on a limb that would kill us all if I fell. Lorenzo was dedicated to grinding down wage scales and degrading the profession, and word was coming back that Lorenzo was close to having his financing. Drexel should have $800 million circled by July 25." Hostility and suspicion still bristled between the three unions. The machinists were moving toward agreements, but the flight attendants weren't agreeing to anything.

His daughter's wedding July 18 was a brief escape. The Hoglander family converged on Phillips Exeter, in Massachusetts. His daughter had graduated with the first class of girls to go to Exeter, and he was proud of that. Although he was divorced again, he kept the family home in Magnolia, Massachusetts, and was as close as he could possibly be to his four kids and four grandchildren.

He took Judith Linquist with him. "My name's *Judy*, not Judith," she said, laughing, when he introduced her to his family. He seemed to prefer the formal sound of it. And he liked to introduce her as "an opera singer," even though vocal cord problems had forced her to stop serious singing in her early twenties. She looked more like a ballet dancer, small and slim, with her black hair pulled up into a chignon. Judith had a sophistication that didn't necessarily fit the image of Kansas City, where she lived, or Hoglander's style. The obvious bond between them was that she was a pilot, too. She flew aerobatic airplanes, just for fun. But he seemed to appreciate their differences most: the trained modulation of her voice compared to the rough accent Harry had picked up in three boroughs of New York, her delicacy and chic. It was as if she was a reminder of the sensitive side of himself that tended to get lost in the hollering and crudeness of union negotiations.

The wedding was fantastic. "My mother and father are seventy-nine and eighty-two, and they danced till two or three in the morning. They're athletes. Mother used to be a competitive swimmer and father used to be a six-day bike racer in Madison Square Garden during the twenties. That's why they're still alive and kicking." Harry hoped he had inherited a large legacy of that energy and endurance.

By July 22, he was back in New York, still trying to stall Carl. How much longer could he keep it going? He was running out of excuses.

◆   ◆   ◆

WHILE Hoglander was watching the horses run in Ocala, Florida, on the July 4 holiday, Sir James Goldsmith was cruising the

coast of Turkey, anticipating the end of his nine-month struggle for Crown Zellerbach. The truce Goldsmith and the Crown
Zellerbach board had reached late May was bearing fruit.
Goldsmith had lost the proxy fight. The day John Kelly had
marched into CEO Creson's office with the proxy results had
been a proud one for Crown and for D. F. King—a three-to-
one win. But Goldsmith's huge stake in Crown had earned a
spot on the board for Goldsmith's key man, Roland Franklin.
He had been working with Crown on it restructuring and, by
early July, had struck a deal. Goldsmith was relaxing in the
Mediterranean sun, satisfied. "They would spin off the assets I
wanted—the forest lands—and we would exchange our stock. I
would get out of Crown, which would continue. . . . It was the
end of a major battle. I'd flown in to San Francisco for a
number of board meetings. I'd fly in for a day from Paris by
Concorde and private jet, and it was exhausting." When Crown
had wafted greenmail before him, with offers of "*huge* profits,"
he had been, he admits, "vaguely indignant but vaguely
tempted. I was starting to get tired. We'd been in it a long time."
But Crown had stated at the annual meeting that they would
never pay greenmail. "I was rather angry at their self-righ-
teousness. And I wouldn't accept it anyway. I refused."

As he and a party of friends cruised the Turkish coast,
dropping in at small ports and ancient ruins, the battle seemed
within days of being over. "I thought we'd done a deal. It had
been unanimously voted on when I was in San Francisco. Then,
suddenly, it was the nightmare of the Mead day all over again.
Over a weekend it collapsed, for reasons which I have still not
been able to fathom. The principals had changed their minds
and would not sign the agreement." The yacht became a war
room. "I had a satellite telephone and was in constant contact.
We even had a board meeting by satellite." The deal was gone.
Sir James went back in the market. And as his lawyer, Fin Fogg,
said as he watched Goldsmith march on to 50 percent, "The
rest is history."

◆   ◆   ◆

To Brian Hunter, standing by his specialists' station on the
floor of the New York Stock Exchange, Crown Zellerbach was

not an institution or an assemblage of assets. It was a stock symbol. ZB. The green symbol that moved across the ticker on the dozens of terminals scattered round the floor of the exchange every time a trade was done. It was one of the stocks in his book, the list of stocks he, and only he, was permitted to trade on the floor. A specialist was known by the size and prestige of his book. It was the source of his income, the measure of his skills. Your book was built, over the years, by the annual evaluations of each specialist's performance by all the investment banking houses who trade with the exchange; those rankings are what earned you a good book. Hunter had often ranked in the top five, and over his twelve years on the floor, he had built a solid book. To stand in his specialist's coat at his station on the floor of the New York Stock Exchange, watched from the gallery by a daily flow of visitors from all over the globe to the world's financial center, was a pride to him. He had not gained the wealth of the deal makers, but the floor of the New York Stock Exchange had given him a very good life.

It was shrinking with takeovers. With every merger, or whenever a company was taken private, a symbol vanished from some specialist's book. Just months before, he'd lost Houston Natural Gas (HNG), a terrible blow, for the pipeline company had been a large and very profitable part of his book. He'd handled the chaos well, as Internorth went on a blitz of buying HNG stock. In two days in May, the stock leapt from $46.8 to $67.1. He had not had to ask for a halt to trading in the stock, as many specialists did when things got hot. His obligation was to maintain an orderly market, and he did, even when he had to step in as buyer or seller himself to keep the price in balance, committing his company to millions of dollars for minutes, hours, or sometimes overnight—events fraught with risk and stress. Houston Natural Gas had been like a train wreck, with traders lined up ten deep, yelling at him, frantically trying to buy and sell. It was only after the rush subsided that he realized HNG would vanish from the ticker. He'd lost 25 percent of his book.

Now Crown. Goldsmith's tenacious battle for Crown Zellerbach was in its drive to the finish. While Marty Lipton argued that Crown's poison pill had never been intended to stop takeover by open market purchases like Goldsmith's, Goldsmith had continued to march to 25, 30, 33 percent. The week of July 15, the takeover fraternity watched, as an apparently helpless Crown Zellerbach was overrun. The final stock blitz began on July 15. The stock had shot up to the most actively traded for two consecutive days, and although it was nothing like the frenzy of the HNG takeover, Hunter had worked with furious concentration to keep an orderly market. But there had been a curious lack of chaos, considering the volumes. There was basically one buyer, and a steady stream of investors ready to sell. As the transactions clicked across the tape, he feared he was watching another major chunk of his income vanish. If Crown Zellerbach merged, or Goldsmith took it private, ZB would be gone from his book. Damn takeovers!

On July 22, Sir James Goldsmith went over 50 percent. He had taken control of Crown Zellerbach.

◆   ◆   ◆

THE settlement meetings that would lead to an orderly transition of corporate control began in lawyers' offices—Skadden Arps and Wachtell Lipton. Covering for a lawyer who was on vacation, Stuart Shapiro sat in on one of the meetings, and fascinated to watch Sir James in action, observed that he handled a large, unpolished piece of amber in his hands, like an amulet or pet rock. Shapiro, a lover of objets d'art picked up on his travels, had a string of very old amber he often ran through his fingers like worry beads during tense meetings, but today he was handling a carved piece of jade he'd picked up in Japan. He had been transfixed by the huge glob of amber and played with thoughts of how appropriate amber was to Goldsmith's temperament, with its opaque surface screening the internal fire that had made the ancients think amber held the sun. He asked Goldsmith where he'd got it, and when told the name of a gem dealer in London, Shapiro smiled knowingly. He knew the shop. He'd banged on the door, been permitted entrance, and tried to talk the jeweler into selling him a piece of old Baltic amber very like Goldsmith's. But the man had refused to do business with him. He obviously wasn't important enough. For Shapiro, the golden glob in Sir James's fingers was as good a measure of Goldsmith's power as 51 percent of the stock.

On July 24, the day before Icahn joined Joe Perella and Stuart Shapiro at John Diebold's estate for the seminar on hostile takeovers, Goldsmith flew in on the Concorde to take formal command as chairman of Crown Zellerbach, its great forest lands finally within reach.

◆　◆　◆

"THE role of the bidder is not for everyone," Icahn's lawyer Steve Jacobs would say several months later to a seminar audience in New York. Documenting the obstacles a raider faced, he said: "It is certainly not for those who aren't prepared to gamble lots of money on their judgment that the target is undervalued; not for those who are intimidated by the adversary process or heavy litigation; not for those who are afraid to have their past lives and deeds undergo microscopic examination; not for those who shudder at adverse publicity; not for those who wish to take extended time off with their families for the pleasantries of life; and not for those who have a passion to know with certainty 'How can I get out of my stock position once I get in.' "

It was dilution that was plaguing Icahn now, in his quest for TWA.

The issue that had reared its contentious head at the Diebold seminar was plaguing him. Icahn had attacked management then for trying to dilute his holdings by defensive schemes—by offering lockups of key assets to white knights that reduced the value of the company to him, or by issuing more stock or, more commonly, stock with more votes per share, watering down the percentage and value of his holdings.

Specifically, lockups were plaguing him. Icahn had just fought back lockups that would have damaged his big investment in American Hospital Supply (AHS), which had just lost a three-week battle for control with Baxter Travenol. Baxter's assault had been led by Perella's partner, Bruce Wasserstein, and Icahn had written a letter urging AHS to accept Baxter's bid and reject the lockups its board, advised by Marty Lipton, had given to a preferred suitor. AHS's July 15 agreement to merge with Baxter had protected an investment in which Icahn stood to make $50 million. Wasserstein had declared the deal "the death of lockups." But most of the headlines were appearing in the Chicago press, where the corporations were based.

Back in New York, lockups would soon be at issue as another American institution, Revlon, struggled for its independence. And Lorenzo had been pushing for lockups of certain assets from TWA since June. Nervous since he'd heard Icahn was talking to the unions, he was trying to strengthen his position with TWA and discourage Icahn. "Lorenzo had lots of suggestions for lockups and dilutive kinds of things," says Freund. "He wanted to buy the option stock that was part of the merger agreement for a note, rather than cash, freeing the $125 million it would have cost to buy TWA stock on the market. He suggested selling Texas Air a preferred stock with special voting rights to dilute Icahn's."

The TWA board was not eager to grant Lorenzo lockups, and Freund took the lead in making them conditional on a number of things: Lorenzo would have to have his financing in place and make a substantial bump in price from his $23 per share. The debate over lockups built through July as Icahn continued to work with the unions. The agreement struck after the bruising negotiations with the pilots and mechanics and filed with the SEC at the beginning of July had been a valuable first step. But Icahn needed more concessions. Drexel Burnham was out raising Lorenzo's financing, and Lorenzo was preparing to merge. Icahn was still bound, by his word, not to be a spoiler as long as there was a better offer than his on the table, and he had still not raised his bid from the original $18. Lorenzo's was $23. If he genuinely wanted to buy the company without enraging shareholders and being challenged by everybody, he would have to raise his bid. And he would not raise his bid until he had even bolder concessions from the unions to justify paying more. Drexel's deadline for having the junk bonds committed was July 25. TWA would be getting its merger materials out to shareholders as soon as it was cleared

by the SEC, bringing the TWA–Texas Air deal that much closer
to a done deal. Putting pressure on the man who was so skillful
at putting pressure on everyone else. Icahn needed contracts
signed with all three unions by the end of July or early August.

There was still silence between the company and its pilots.
"We had almost no contact with the pilots," says Freund. "They
were conducting negotiations with Icahn and not talking about
them."

◆   ◆   ◆

ICAHN walked cautiously through the lobby of the Lexington
Hotel at Forty-eighth Street. He told Hoglander he believed
Ivan Boesky had spies in the lobby, mapping his moves. It was
July 31. Icahn and Hoglander were about to begin the critical
second round of negotiations in which Icahn would try to
wring more concessions from the pilots. And yet the guys
didn't know this man who came closer, every day, to controlling
their airline. They had reopened negotiations on the agreement signed at the end of June, and Icahn was pushing now for
a two-tier pay scale and for cuts that, for the older pilots, would
be almost as severe as a two-tier. There were still nagging
doubts about his motives. Hoglander and Carl and their lawyers and bankers had logged days and nights in the trenches,
but Carl had never met with the eighteen members of the
Master Executive Council. "I'd relate these incredible stories to
them, but how could you explain Icahn?" The MEC was meeting on July 31 at the Lexington, and Icahn had agreed to come.

In a dingy meeting room, he confronted roughly four hundred years of flying experience. For Carl Icahn, the room was
no place like home. But the plain setting may have helped set a
tone of candor for the meeting that was about to unfold. "It
allowed the human element to become part of the drama. The
MEC saw the guy, flesh and blood, and he saw us."

Hoglander introduced Carl to the Master Council. "Carl
started by making a statement in his usual five different ways.
But one of the guys cut through the shit and said to him, 'What
have you got against pilots?' " Carl looked him in the eye and
said, "You guys do a marvelous job. I could never fly like that. I

have all the confidence in the world in you. The only problem is you get paid too much money."

It was time for the facts of life. "All right, you don't like Lorenzo. But Lorenzo is telling you something—that it's a free enterprise society. How can one airline pay one guy $120,000 a year when the guy at the other airline is flying the same plane for $30,000 or $40,000? It makes no sense. The company will go bankrupt. You'll get another two years out of it, and they'll go bust, and what good does that do you?" They were tough words for these guys to hear, mostly senior pilots with everything to lose. It was painful, but Icahn was looking them straight in the eye, and they were listening. "Like the steel industry," Carl went on. "The union did such a great job that they lost their jobs. They lost the industry! If the unions do too good a job, it's no good."

The hijacking in Lebanon was just over, and the pilots had come to the meeting basking in a brief return to the old stature and respect. The nation had been riveted by the drama of the terrorist hijacking that, on June 17, had diverted to Lebanon a TWA plane en route to Athens. The crew and planeload of hostages had been held, at gunpoint, for several weeks. With their own and the lives of passengers constantly at risk, TWA's pilots had performed as heroes. A captain who flies the Athens route said to himself, "Every time I see the picture of Captain Sestrake with the gun pressed to his temple, I say, '*Tell* me he makes too much money.'" It had been a terrible personal ordeal for these men. Icahn sympathized. He knew it seemed cold-blooded. But he and Kingsley had to look at hijackings also in economic terms; they meant lost business on the overseas routes and would contribute to severe losses in fourth-quarter revenues. They meant lost value.

The pilots defended their worth. As Icahn remembers it, the pilots argued, "Look, we're older pilots. We're capable. And look how we dealt with the Lebanon crisis. Look how cool and capable we were under fire." Icahn responded, "Let me ask you a question: what about a young captain who goes to war and wins a battle for us and gets the Congressional Medal of Honor when he's twenty-four years old? Doesn't he show a hell of a lot of capability? Isn't he cool? He does a hell of a job for the country, doesn't he? Look at the fighter pilot, or the captain who takes his whole company and leads it on to great victory and still can run the whole thing." No matter how Hoglander had described Icahn's style, nothing could have the impact of the man himself, telling them how it was. He was being a hard-driving businessman, demanding wage concessions the pilots didn't want to give. Finally he gave them the ultimatum: "If we're going to make the company successful, you are going to have to look reality in the eye, and reality is lower wages." He had used the word *we,* Hoglander thought. He was counting them in as the company never had. It was a tough argument, but Icahn believed they knew it was right. Then he softened a little: "Hey, I'm not fighting pilots. That's not my function. I'm saying, 'Look, Lorenzo's not all wrong on this subject.' What he did wrong, from what I hear, is that he didn't live up to his word. Made promises he didn't keep." After more than three hours of questions and answers, Hoglander guessed that there were few members of the MEC who doubted Carl Icahn would keep his promises. *Reneging,* the word that had become the metaphor for Lorenzo, would not be applied to Icahn.

Hoglander sensed that a critical turning point was being reached. Icahn had struck their fancy. "He came forward as an honest individual, despite his terrible accent." Hoglander was tense with hope.

Toward the end of the meeting, Carl was asked a straight question, and he reverted to the equivocating style that drove Harry crazy: "Well, I could, but at the same time maybe I will, on the other hand, I shouldn't do this, but I'd make a deal with you if . . ." One of the pilots cut in and said, with a wry smile, "Well, Carl, do I understand that to mean 'maybe'?" The dingy room filled with a roar of laughter.

"That meeting may have been the turning point," Hoglander says. "But Icahn came to the meeting with a different spirit. Somewhere over the summer, Carl fell in love with the idea of owning an airline. He changed from thinking he could make the most money *selling* it to thinking he could make the most money *running* it." Al Kingsley was amused by the theory. "I think it was the *unions* that had the metamorphosis. I think they felt all along that owning the airline was not Carl's game, and *they* began to believe we really wanted to own the airline. For us, the whole thing was always the union negotiation. Without the concessions—without the negotiating we had with the unions and the outcome—we were content to let someone else take the airline, because to us it wasn't worth what was being bid for it. When we made our earlier bid at $18, that's what it was worth to us. It would only become worth more to us if we had the concessions locked up in a contract." The hidden assets still lay in labor.

But as Icahn moved from his meeting with the MEC into the final negotiations, it did seem as if a new dimension was coloring and shaping his moves. The man who loved to say, "If you want a friend, get a dog," was using words like *loyalty* and *moral obligation*. Even in his first agreement on July 1, he had committed to keeping the airline intact, sacrificing the raider's prerogative to dispose of assets as he wishes. Was it possible that Icahn was doing the thing Freund was convinced he never did—getting emotionally involved with the property?

◆   ◆   ◆

As they all met next evening at 8:00 P.M. at Lazard Frères' offices to renegotiate the agreement, there was a new will to work it out. But it deteriorated rapidly into the old yelling match. The issue was percentages. The percentages the pilots would agree to cut from their salaries. Harry knew they had to move up from the 20 percent they'd ·agreed to before. He proposed to Icahn a cut of 22 percent from everybody, all three unions. "Carl said, 'Absolutely not,' and we went into one of our shouting matches again. I'd heard it all before. I was wasting Carl's fucking time. Lorenzo was waiting across the street. Carl was going to walk across the street, right? Hell, I didn't know where across the street *was!*"

They battled it down to 30 percent—almost a third of their pay! Hoglander was beside himself. "I'm a labor unionist. I can't give away guys' money like that." He asked Icahn to come out in the hall, sensing that this was the most important negotiating he would ever do. His intense eyes blazing down on Hoglander from a superior height of several inches, Icahn said, "Harry, you're a nice guy and we've tried to do business. But I'll tell you it's either that, or no deal." Hoglander was crushed, but snapped back, "Carl, it's got to be some middle ground. I'll try a number, and you tell me if it's acceptable." He tried a number near 23 percent. He knew it wasn't close to what Icahn was talking, but he had a wild card. Word had just come in that the United pilots had won their fight. It strengthened Hoglander's hand as he tried to force one of the nation's shrewdest entrepreneurs down to a percentage the pilots could live with. He doubted that you got to call Carl Icahn's bluff more than once.

Icahn just laughed at the number and said, "I'll see you around," and prepared to leave. Christ! That was it. They'd lost the deal. Just like that. Hoglander went back in the room and told his team what had happened, and Simon said, "Any hope?" Hoglander shook his head as Icahn knocked on the door and then stuck his head in to say, "See you around. It's been nice doing business with you," waved goodbye, and left. He was going across the street to Lorenzo, as he'd been threatening to do for six weeks, to take the $40 million they understood he'd be getting.

Simon and Hoglander went downstairs to a restaurant in Rockefeller Center. Keilin wouldn't be back from vacation until the next morning, and they missed him. They were too miserable to eat, so they went up to Hoglander's apartment. Hoglander was desolate. In a day, they had won the victory at United and lost TWA. "The deal is cooked. If he sells to Lorenzo, nobody can stop it." He'd fought all the way down to save it, but he'd crashed. And taken thirty-three hundred pilots with him. The MEC was meeting next morning at nine. He dreaded facing them. "I don't know how to tell them that I've lost the deal, that the deal is over," he agonized to Simon. Simon said to him, "You can't look back. We'll think of something by tomorrow. We'll try to think of another deal."

After a fitful sleep, Hoglander got to his office in the Pan Am Building at 8:00 A.M. He needed a few more minutes to think before facing the guys. As he walked out of his office to head for the meeting, his secretary, Diane, came running up to him. "Harry, Mr. Icahn's on the phone." He raced to an adjoining office as Keilin was asking Icahn if they could still get their deal back on track, and Icahn was saying, "Well, how do you mean?" Hoglander could hear it. Icahn was opening the door to a compromise.

Hoglander would never know for sure what had happened. He was told later that Carl had gone "across the street" and Lorenzo wouldn't make the deal with him. He had told Icahn that without the signed contracts with the unions, buying him out wasn't worth a $40 million fee to him—the fee Icahn had threatened them with like Chinese torture all these weeks. "He walked out saying, in effect, 'Go ahead, strike, I don't give a damn,' and now he was saying, 'I do give a damn.' " Hoglander was exhilarated. "In labor negotiations, it's a classic ploy. If you ever call a guy's bluff like that, and he comes back, you know you got him. I hadn't been trying to call his bluff. I was just trying to keep the deal alive. And I had him. *I had Carl!*"

Whatever had happened, the game wasn't over.

He ran out of the Pan Am Building and up Lexington five blocks to the MEC meeting, and blurted out the story. But there was no way he could really transmit the roller-coaster emotions of the last day. Next day, they got back in the ring with Icahn to hammer out the final agreement. Time had almost run out. Lorenzo had his financing from Drexel, and the proxy material would soon be going out to the TWA shareholders for approval of the merger. The three unions returned to rounds of visits to Icahn's office at Fifty-sixth Street, urgently lobbying each other, their teams colliding in halls and elevators. An explosion of anger trailed Vicki Frankovich, the flight attendants' representative, when she walked out of Icahn's office in the middle of negotiations. She was entertaining a hundred people at her elementary school reunion and had to fly home to Los Angeles. Hoglander arrived in Icahn's office just after she'd left. "Can you believe that woman? She's representing her people in something so important, and she goes home for an elementary school reunion!" Icahn couldn't believe it.

After another thirty-six hours of negotiations, Icahn and Hoglander finally arrived at numbers they could both accept: a package of 26 percent—22 percent hard money, 4 percent soft. Deregulation had extracted its price. But there would be profit sharing, stock ownership, and an ESOP for the employees. There would be an airline, and planes to fly. And even if TWA later merged with another airline, it would not be with Lorenzo. That was the deal. They signed.

Harry and his team had scarcely slept for sixty hours. Whenever Hoglander fell asleep, Icahn would phone and wake him up with a better idea. Hoglander wanted ratification immediately. It would keep Icahn from any more changes and give Hoglander the formal support of the pilots. They couldn't get ratification from the rank and file until August 20, but he determined to get it from the MEC the day they signed, August 5. Harry got on the phone to lobby the MEC members who were sitting on the fence, told them a vote would be taken within the hour, and ran downstairs to see the MEC. He said, "Here's the deal. I want you guys to ratify with the understanding that we get membership ratification also," and he called for a vote. He had just said, "All those in favor . . ." when the phone rang outside the meeting room. He knew it was Icahn. "If it's Icahn, tell him I'm not here." The man answering the phone nodded, and he went on with the vote. "All those in favor?" Right down the line and around the table. Aye. Aye. Aye. Aye. Aye. Seventeen ayes. "All those opposed?" One hand went up. They had approved the agreement seventeen to one, and Hoglander took the phone.

"Wait a minute, wait a minute," said Icahn. "You can have it but only if—"

"Carl, we already voted."

"You already voted?"

With indescribable satisfaction, Hoglander said, "Yeah."

Unshaven and exhausted after another night and morning of wind-up meetings with the machinists and Icahn, Hoglander and Simon ordered hamburgers and beer from the outdoor café in front of General Motors across from the Plaza Hotel and just sat there with the midday sun shining. Icahn walked in with his team and joined them. Nervous energy began to erupt and they started joking and acting a little giddy. Icahn was restless. "I can't sit here too long. I gotta go buy some stock," he kept saying. The agreement he had just signed not only obligated him not to sell to Lorenzo, but to make a higher bid, and to make positive efforts to acquire TWA. It had taken forever to get him to an agreement. But once there, Carl Icahn was proving to be a man of his word. He finally leaped up from lunch, saying, "I'm going to strap my guns on now!" and went upstairs to start buying. In the next two days, he bought nearly 3 million shares, and emerged on August 7 with a stake of 40.6 percent. "That blitz was the most decisive act of the whole thing," Icahn said later. With that bold step, he moved himself to the crest of the hill, able, with a phone call to his trading desk, to claim control. And everyone knew it. In the press, he changed overnight from the man who had lost to Texas Air to the man about to take over TWA.

As Icahn went back to sweep the Street, Hoglander went back to the office, dodging cars as he plunged into noon-hour gridlock at the base of the Pan Am Building, almost sleepwalking. At his desk, eyes half closed, the sleeves of his crumpled plaid sports shirt rolled up, he looked rather like a hung-over Harrison Ford with a four-day beard. With his elbows on the table, his head slowly sinking toward the desk, he rasped out his daily report to Duffy. "We got an agreement, Hank. Twenty-two hard, four soft. The guys gotta ratify by August 20." Then Diane pushed him out of the office, and he went home to sleep.

On August 5, Icahn sent another letter to the TWA board, raising his bid to $24. His was now the best bid on the table. He enclosed copies of the revised agreement with the pilots' and machinists' unions, a stunning improvement in the power of his position. And he alerted the board that he owned over 40 percent.

◆ ◆ ◆

As Hoglander and Icahn thrashed through the negotiations that kept a takeover alive, another was about to abort. Many of the takeover club had been on airplanes or Amtrak in transit to Washington when the FCC made its announcement on the eve of the August 1 hearings on Turner's bid for CBS. The hearings had promised to be a production number. Two former chairmen of the FCC would face each other as lawyers for Turner and CBS. Walter Cronkite was rumored to be a surprise witness. But responding to an emergency petition from CBS, the FCC had canceled the hearings. Next day, Washington law offices and hotels held dozens of lawyers, bankers, and arbs struggling to deal with an unexpected free day. The cancellation was triggered by news from the Atlanta courtroom where Turner had filed an injunction to block the CBS buyback that would devastate Turner's junk-bond bid. Federal Judge Robert L. Vining, Jr., had rejected the injunction, making an FCC ruling moot. There was now only the faintest chance that Turner could keep his bid alive.

"This show is not over as we sit here today—it's a viable deal! It would pay CBS shareholders $21 dividends a year, compared to the $3 CBS pays," said one of Turner's Washington lawyers, Bruce Sokler, the day of the cancellation. "But I think it was foreseeable from day one that this whole deal was going to live or die in New York. In the marketplace. On the financial resources that Turner Broadcasting would be able to bring to the deal and how the market would react to it. Why? Because CBS is basically institutionally held, about 70 percent, and an institutional shareholder isn't really going to care that much about the ratings "Dallas" or whether this was the network of Edward R. Murrow. It is just looking at the bottom line. Turner will have to come forward with a new proposal that doesn't violate the poison pills, or get them removed, or go for a proxy fight, or . . ."

Instead, Turner sold back to the CBS buyback and turned his restless eye westward, to MGM/United in Los Angeles.

CHAPTER 15

◆◆

THOSE same early August days had been as tense for the management team of TWA. Marty Lipton came back from London bruised by the news of Crown Zellerbach's capitulation to Goldsmith. He had promised months earlier to address the American Bar Association meetings in London, sharing a podium with several distinguished British merger specialists, and, ironically, had been lecturing as an expert on takeovers when Crown's fall occurred. He had been with the board and management through the protracted agony, and said of the news, "It was the worst disappointment of my professional life." "What does it mean, Mr. Lipton?" a journalist asked, hoping for some scholarly comment on the implications of the event on poison pills and on defensive devices in general. "It means," he said quietly, "we lost." He could argue in speeches, interviews, law journals, and memos to his clients that his poison pill had been meant to prevent takeover only in the case of a merger. But the most basic strategy had been to keep the company independent. The entire Wachtell Lipton office had been cast into gloom, as the poison pill became the day's joke on Wall

Street. "But you can't afford to spend many days moping around," he said.

Dick Katcher was on vacation, and Lipton plunged into helping Lorenzo push for the lockups he now desperately needed to keep his deal with TWA alive as rumors grew that Icahn was coming close to a contract with the unions.

"What do we have to do to get them?" Lipton asked Freund, as the two met with other advisers in Freund's office, negotiating deals as Lipton and Flom have done for twenty-five years.

"We need a substantial bump in price," Freund told him.

"What's substantial?" Lipton wanted to know.

Freund told him, "Nothing less than two bucks."

Freund checked with the TWA board, and called Lipton on August 3 to tell him that if Lorenzo would go up $2, the board would reconsider the lockups on that basis. They would be considered at a TWA board meeting on August 13.

"We had little contact with the pilots, and our information was imperfect," says Freund. "We knew they were negotiating, but I kept hearing from my people, 'Ah, forget it. He'll never make a deal with the unions.' My guys were convinced that the machinists would never reach agreement. The pilots perhaps, but not the machinists."

On August 5, Freund received word that Lipton had tried, but failed, to get Lorenzo to bump his bid by $2. Frank's betting that Carl won't come up with a deal, Freund thought. A little later in the day, as he took a call from Steve Jacobs it appeared that Frank's bet was not only wrong but quite possibly fatal to his deal with TWA. "I'm sending something over to you, Jim. It's a letter from Carl," Jacobs told him. "He's signed a deal with both the unions, and he's bumping his bid to $24."

Freund put down the phone and shook his head, amazed. I got to hand it to Carl, he mused. It's a hell of a feat. It took endurance, and skill. The man deserves credit. But in war there are limits to the time you can allow for admiration of the enemy. Icahn's stunning achievement had put the Lorenzo deal in terrible jeopardy. News of his $24 bid was followed rapidly by news of his blitz. On August 7, he went to 40.7 percent. Then, spending $38.2 million in one day, he leaped, the next day, to 45 percent. "Now Carl has real clout. He has the best bid on the table. Clearly, he's in the driver's seat," Freund said.

In the press and the market, Icahn was suddenly perceived as the heir-apparent to the chairmanship of TWA. But the Skadden Arps lawyers, forever searching for means to defer what seemed inevitable, discovered a technicality that temporarily halted Icahn from buying more stock and going over the top to absolute control. It was a small pocket of time. Only forty-eight hours. But for Freund, buying time had become a way of life. The entire battle had been marked off by these narrow, desperate envelopes of time. The incredible pressures of the deal had been contained and intensified within them. Freund's role had been to create or identify them, then work like hell to expand or exploit them to their fullest. Scrutinizing an agreement, he found that, as part of the "no spoiler" pact made with TWA back in June, Icahn had promised that, before he went over a stake that equated to roughly 45 percent of TWA's common stock, he would give TWA two business days' notice. Freund's nerves were now alert for a letter from Carl. Once he had given notice and let forty-eight hours elapse, it would take only a phone call to take him over 45 percent to controlling interest. Until Icahn gave notice, the clock that would mark off his final march to control would not start ticking.

The roles had reversed 180 degrees from that meeting in June where Icahn had been the seller. Now the Icahn, TWA, and Lorenzo teams entered secret and intense negotiations to try to get Lorenzo to give up his bid for a $45 to $50 million break-up fee plus profit on the stock option plan—a fee that would pay him several million dollars profit, even after he paid a multimillion-dollar fee due to Drexel Burnham for raising his financing. On August 8, with Icahn holding roughly 45 percent, they seemed to have struck a deal. Lorenzo agreed to accept a $50 million breakup fee and withdraw his bid. Now Lorenzo was the seller. But that possibility came and went in an evening.

In a subsequent letter to the TWA board, Icahn described his frustration with Lorenzo as, for the second time, he walked

away from a deal Icahn had thought was done. "At a meeting
on Thursday of last week at Mr. Freund's office, this agreement
was being formalized for presentation to the TWA board. At
approximately 10:00 P.M. that night, representatives of Mr.
Lorenzo informed us that Mr. Lorenzo had reneged on our
agreement and was now demanding approximately $20 million
in addition to the approximately $50 million already ear-
marked for 'breakup' fees." Lorenzo had violated the code of
the handshake; in spite of the widely held belief that a deal was
not a deal until it was locked up with a signed contract,
honoring a deal finalized with a handshake was still a tradition
on Wall Street and the way Icahn did business. "We work on a
handshake. A guy's word over the telephone is his bond," says
Icahn. Lorenzo had broken that, he claimed. From now on,
Icahn would resist paying any breakup fee to Lorenzo. The
second chance to end the struggle had come and gone.

Gathering up apparently bottomless reserves of *chutzpah*,
Lorenzo, the next day, August 9, finally bumped his bid to $26,
making Icahn's $24 the second-best bid on the table.

Freund met with Icahn to try to get him to raise his bid to top
Lorenzo's. It was their most intense and abrasive meeting.
Gentlemanly quests to maintain a level playing field had been
reduced to the exhausted bickering and dogged trench warfare
of the endgame. Stress and frustration were taking their toll on
them all. But Freund was feeling confident about taking a
decisive role. "I've never worked over anybody like that in my
life," says Freund of the meeting with Icahn. "It went on for
hours, trying to get more dollars out of him." Freund challenged Icahn: "You said you wouldn't stand in the way of the
best bid, and Texas Air has the best bid. You should either go
along with this $26 dollar bid or match it." Icahn burst in,
"Bullshit! It's a spurious bid because Texas Air can't possibly
win. I'm not going to raise my bid, I'm going to buy stock." Any
raised bid by Lorenzo became "spurious," in Icahn's view, the
moment Icahn had signed agreements with the unions. When
Lorenzo made his $26 bid, he knew full well, Icahn believed,
"that any Texas Air bid could not be accepted by TWA's
shareholders because I was compelled to stand by the unions

and vote my 45 percent of the TWA common stock . . . to defeat virtually any bid by Texas Air." Without Icahn's stock, no bid by Lorenzo could win shareholder approval. He could certainly be a spoiler of the deal with Texas Air.

Finally, Freund struck where he knew it would hit home. "You always like to say you're a man of your word, and if you do this—if you block the best bid for shareholders—in my book, Carl, you're only 50 percent a man of your word."

Icahn blazed back, indignant, "Wait a second, wait a second. Didn't I say that I wouldn't buy more stock if Lorenzo didn't buy more stock? Didn't I keep my word there?"

"Yes, Carl, you did," Freund admitted, as Icahn recited a litany of kept promises. "Okay, okay, Carl, let's say you're a 75 percent man of your word, okay?" Freund offered reluctantly.

Then Icahn paused and smiled the slightly sheepish smile of a man who knows he's been caught. "Hey, I'm at least 80 percent. Jim, give me 80," and the ten men in the room broke up laughing.

The deal's standing joke had been created, and Icahn flew to Sun Valley with his family for a few days of vacation.

But he had still not raised his bid. Icahn was going to win control in the marketplace. On Friday, August 9, at 1:00 P.M., he made the move Freund had expected, the move to go over 45 percent and take control. TWA received a letter from Icahn's lawyers giving them two business days notice. The weekend plus the forty-eight hours would bring them to Tuesday at 1:00 P.M., August 13. The board was meeting that day, at 11:00 A.M. After all the threats, he was finally pulling the trigger. But there was pressure on Icahn, too. He could be hurt if Lorenzo got his lockups. The board could grant them as they convened at 11:00 A.M., two hours before he was free to buy at 1:00 P.M. Lockups would be impossible once he reached 51 percent. TWA was a Delaware corporation, and there was a rule in the Delaware law that forbade issuing lockups or other dilutive measures once you had gained majority control.

Both sides needed time. Icahn led Freund to believe that, at $26—and within the bounds of his contract with the unions, which meant no Lorenzo—Icahn might still be a seller. But he needed time to find out if there were any takers at that price. Freund needed time, too, to fashion possible lockups with Texas Air to take to the TWA board. So, on Monday, Freund and Jacobs agreed to push everything back one week; Icahn wouldn't buy any more shares before 1:00 P.M. on August 20, and TWA wouldn't issue any lockups before 11:00 A.M. on that same day. The two-hour time differential that existed on August 13 had been preserved.

On August 13, Lorenzo wrote to the TWA board making a formal request for the lockups the board had promised to consider if he bumped his bid $2. He had done that, and now he wanted action. Here were the dilution devices Icahn had condemned at the Diebold seminar, devices that would create a level playing field at the cost, to Icahn, of millions of dollars of stock value and a reduction in his percentage share of TWA stock.

Lorenzo demanded the issuing of a special voting stock that would give Texas Air the same number of votes as Icahn, canceling Icahn's voting advantage, an act that would "assist in preventing the Icahn ownership of TWA from being used to block stockholders from the best available price." And Lorenzo wanted an "asset option" to buy the transatlantic routes and possibly the PARS reservation system—TWA's crown jewels. Lorenzo's comment "We believe TWA would be unattractive to Mr. Icahn without these assets" was a gross understatement. Even with his labor contracts, the loss of these premier assets would destroy the valuations on which he had based his bid. And it would bust up the airline, the very thing Icahn was contractually committed not to do.

From Sun Valley, Icahn volleyed back with a letter to the board condemning the lockups, lockups Icahn claimed would "enrich Mr. Lorenzo at the expense of your minority share-holders," a disastrous result for which, he believed, "every board member would be personally liable." He threatened also to lower his present bid if lockups or breakup fees were granted. And for the first time, he played another strong card—the speed with which his merger could be completed. The merger of two airlines would require at least six months of examination by the DOT and the president before approval, months of uncertainty and potential delay that could cost TWA dearly. Applying to himself some of the pressure he was so skillful at applying to others, he made an expensive promise: "We are so confident that our merger transaction could be consummated by November 30, 1985, . . . we would be willing to increase our $24-per-common-share proposal by 25 cents for each thirty-day period following November 30 during which our merger has not been consummated."

Icahn's bombardment of the board reinforced a letter Harry Hoglander had delivered to them on August 6, when he had bribed a night watchman with a case of beer to let him place it personally on Ed Meyer's desk, a letter in which he had pleaded with the board not to award the "unconscionable sweeteners . . . that would frustrate the will of the shareholders and employees of TWA . . . and bolster the position of the clear spoiler in this situation, one whose clear record establishes without a doubt that discord and disruption follow him as night follows day." Hoglander was fuming, too, about the golden passes and had convinced Icahn that he should resist giving them in any deal he struck with the company.

Opposition to the golden passes, like seniority, was religion to Hoglander. Lorenzo had agreed to honor the golden passes. When Icahn and Hoglander had discussed them, Icahn had said, "I don't want to give them the goddamn passes," and Hoglander had declared, "The captain has the authority to let only certain pass riders on, and I'll be damned if I'm letting any of those bastards on the airplane. . . . They've never cared for the employees, us in particular." During the past three months, Meyer had never called Hoglander. Never even tried to strike any of the concessions Icahn had won. The pilots did not dislike TWA president Richard D. Pearson. He had been a marine, a pilot, and had a background they could identify with. But it was too much when, at this final stage, Pearson called Hoglander to talk about the passes. As Hoglander blew off with his feelings about them, Pearson said, "I'm not interested in those guys on the board, but what about the widow, Mrs. Breech?" Mrs. Breech, widow of a former TWA chairman,

Harry had been told, was worth about $15 million. His heart did not bleed for her.

"Call them on the phone? Hell, we should have _sued_ them!" says Freund. "From TWA's point of view, its employees, led by Harry, were, in effect, mutinying—making a deal with the very raider the company had tried so hard to fend off; trying their best to break up a deal the company had worked like _hell_ to put together."

Freund had begun to understand the depth of Icahn's resistance to bidding over Lorenzo's $26. But it didn't change the fact that Icahn was sticking with his bid. "The fact was that he was so confident he was going to win at $24 that he was unwilling to raise the ante," Freund observed.

They had precisely a week to work out the best possible destiny for TWA. All the pressures and issues of the war would converge on the TWA boardroom next Tuesday, August 20. At 11:00 A.M., TWA would be free to issue lockups. At 1:00 P.M., Icahn would be free to start buying again. With his stock lined up, he could probably gain majority control within hours. As Freund, Easton, and Zimmerman went into last-ditch talks with the two combatants in the last few days before the meeting, it was clear that TWA was in a tough spot. Before Lorenzo raised his bid, they had cooperated in Icahn's effort to get Lorenzo to release TWA from its merger obligation. But Lorenzo was unwilling to budge; they had tried to get Icahn to raise his $24 and outbid Lorenzo, but he wouldn't budge. "_Everybody_—our lawyers, bankers—told us we should bid up," says Kingsley. "Carl and I were the only ones who felt that Lorenzo's bid was spurious, and that we didn't have to." Our negotiations with Lorenzo finally focused on two main lockups: a super-voting preferred stock that would be issued for real money and would give Texas Air as many votes as Icahn had, and, second, a license on the PARS system that kept the system within TWA, but required Texas Air's consent for some uses Carl may have had in mind—things that would make Carl unhappy without detracting from its value to TWA," says Freund. Letters from Icahn, Lorenzo, and the pilots peppered Freund's desk those last few days as the TWA deal built to its climax.

◆　◆　◆

It was August 17, a Saturday, and Carl Icahn stretched out by the pool of his estate in Westchester, relaxed and confident in that moment's quiet before the climactic battle began. He was just back from Sun Valley, where the TWA deal had been as constant a companion as his wife, Liba, a pretty, dark-haired Czechoslovakian ballerina. After all the drama and convolutions of the past three months, the board meeting August 20 would be the decisive event. The board would vote for or against lockups. It would choose between the two—him or Lorenzo. He mused on the easier routes he might have taken.

He was in it now to the finish. But there were no tight-muscled twitches visible on Icahn's body. Just eight years into his first marriage, he seemed to relish being a family man and country squire after the years of obsessive focus on his work as he built his fortune, and ten years of living in New York. Although he had seven full-time gardeners to care for the sweeping acres of lawn and trees, his hobby was landscaping and gardening around the house and pool. The orderly rows of shrubs and beds of marigolds were precise and methodical, like Icahn's mind. Icahn's chauffeur marveled at how the man could keep three telephone calls going at once, complicated calls, and keep track of each of them.

This was the first day in weeks that the phone wasn't ringing off the hook. Today, Icahn chatting with a neighbor who came by with his son to play tennis on Icahn's court, stretched his lanky frame out on a tan canvas chaise by the pool, golf-club sporty in tan slacks and bright green polo shirt. His dark hair, just beginning to thin and graying at the temples, was damp and wavy in the heat, and he kept pushing back his green visor, wiping perspiration from his forehead and rubbing on suntan lotion. In spite of the intense heat, he kept his face directed to the sun, maximizing the value of rare leisure moments as compulsively as he did corporate assets. Sipping pink lemonade and nibbling hot cheese puffs brought by a uniformed maid from the rambling brick mansion close by, he felt, as he has always felt, "intellectual security . . . the confidence that I can outthink and control a situation."

He reviewed the options as if he were studying a chess board. He didn't need any more money. He didn't need the aggravation. He was obsessed with the game. The board had two options, as he saw it, both "risk averse" for him, the way he liked it. "One: they give Lorenzo the lockups, I buy 51 percent and pay less because they gave him all those things that made the stock worth less. Two: we go to court, and the court awards the deal to Lorenzo at $26. I've bought stock cheap, I sell at $26, and I'm a hero for getting that price for all the shareholders. But in the thirty to sixty days it takes to complete the deal with Lorenzo, what does the airline have? Unrest into the endgame—a lousy company, stock falling back. They're trapped.

"I'm 98 percent sure I'm going to win. I'm not going to raise my price, and I'm going to win it." Smiling at the irony of how things change in three months, he said, "I think the board would rather have me. The unions won't be on strike. The shareholders are getting $24. And I think the board is getting tired of Lorenzo. I think they're relieved—I'm almost their white knight." There was still risk. "We're taking chances. But the risk/reward ratio is in our favor." He went thoughtful: "There's no question I *can* lose, but I don't think there's anybody as good at this game as I am."

The big difference, he believed, was in having the wherewithal to finish, as Pickens had not, in Unocal once the Delaware court went against him. "I sympathize with Pickens. I think he got a very bad deal. The SEC agrees it was a bad deal. Pickens was 100 percent in the right about the company belonging to the shareholders." But like a general fighting on many fronts, had Pickens's supply lines stretched too thin?

Here was the crux of it all for Icahn. "The cardinal rule is to have enough capital at the end of the day." Always replaying other deals, many in the takeover club had speculated that Pickens might have weathered Phillips. If he had not been so leveraged, would he have used the same strategy in Unocal? "If he'd been able to go to 51 percent he could have got the company any time he wanted," said Icahn. "In TWA it would take me ten minutes." Before Christmas, Icahn's cocksureness would have crumbled as he broke his own cardinal rule. And the hubris of August would come back to haunt him.

But as a chess player, he saw the endgame now nearing

checkmate. Whatever option carried the day, it was time to end the war. Ultimately, he believed that "the smart thing, instead of fighting, is to try to make peace." He was closer to Freund's philosophy than perhaps even Freund knew.

◆   ◆   ◆

ON the eve of TWA's showdown meeting, Marty Lipton and Felix Rohatyn were in Revlon's boardroom holding the hand of an alarmed board about to face a hostile bid for control. Pantry Pride, a Florida grocery store chain that hardly seemed a match for the institution that meant beauty for America's women, had just announced its $45 hostile tender offer. The friendly acquisition suggested to Revlon's CEO, Michel Bergerac, on June 17 by Pantry Pride's chairman, Ronald O. Perelman, had gradually deteriorated over the summer as Bergerac had been unable to shake Perelman, an unknown upstart to the Revlon board. Now Revlon was in crisis. Beginning to build its defenses, Revlon's board had adopted staggered terms and been lectured on poison pills in late July. At this meeting on August 19, the two highest-profile men for the defense had been called to help.

Rohatyn told the board that he foresaw the classic scenario: Pantry Pride would finance a tender offer with junk bonds, then sell Revlon's divisions separately to pay the financing and make a profit. Lazard Frères' analysis showed $45 to be a grossly inadequate price for Revlon's shares—shares that could be worth $60 or $70, he felt, if the divisions were sold off at the proper time.

Marty Lipton recommended a double defense: a buyback of 5 million shares—the device that had just undercut Ted Turner's bid for CBS. And he proposed adoption of a Note Purchase Rights Plan, another name for the same poison pill. Like Crown Zellerbach's pill, it would be triggered when anyone acquired 20 percent of Revlon's shares. Although Crown Zellerbach had fallen to Goldsmith just three weeks earlier, even with a pill in place, Lipton's stature was undiminished, and the pill was adopted unanimously. But only after Rohatyn's warning that if the pill was put in place, liquidation of the company was likely to follow.

Within blocks of TWA's war rooms, another major battle had

begun. Freund's colleagues at Skadden Arps would carry the legal banner for Pantry Pride. Within a month, the same battle over lockups that would be decided in TWA's board meeting the next day would carry Revlon and Pantry Pride to a decisive test in the Delaware courts.

♦ ♦ ♦

WHILE the Revlon board met with Lipton and Rohatyn, Rohatyn's colleague, Gene Keilin, was preparing to spend the evening before the decisive TWA board meeting with Harry Hoglander in a tense vote watch at the ALPA office. All evening, the ratification votes would be coming in by conference calls from Los Angeles, Kansas City, Chicago, St. Louis, and New York. Hoglander had flown to St. Louis and Kansas City to present the contract, but he was nervous. He was asking the pilots to swallow the agreement whole, with very little emotional preparation. They had shown enormous guts and faith standing behind him so far, but he was asking them to ratify the end of an age. Was the membership ready to deal with the issue? By the time Simon and Keilin arrived at about 10:00 P.M., Hoglander was getting very excited. The West Coast vote had come in first, and was 93 percent in favor. The machinists were calling in with their vote, and reporting three to one in favor. By midnight, all the votes were counted, and the pilots had approved the contract by a whopping 82 percent. Hoglander, Simon, and Keilin went on conference call to Icahn, who was at his offices, to give him the news. Icahn was elated. They would go into the crucial board meeting tomorrow with a much stronger hand.

But Icahn wasn't planning to go. Freund had invited him and offered him equal time with Lorenzo to speak to the board. Icahn was convinced the board would just try to pressure him to match what he considered a phony bid. "You've got to go, Carl," Keilin argued with all his persuasiveness. "If you don't, it'll be like the 'empty chair' syndrome in political debates." Hoglander agreed. The empty chair—Icahn's—would not be able to answer accusations from questioners. Doubt would hover over his seriousness. Icahn agreed to go and asked Hoglander to write the board another letter urging it to reject

Lorenzo and accept the ratified agreement, and to hand-deliver it to the board. This time, Hoglander would come in the front door of 605 Third Avenue and deliver it to Meyer and the entire board in person. As he finished the letter about 2:15 A.M., Harry called Icahn to propose another course of action. He had been thinking, This might well be my swan song. If Lorenzo wins the airline, I'll probably get fired. If you're going to go, Harry, it might as well be in style. "Hey, Carl," he said, "not only am I going to read this letter, but I'm going to read it with my uniform on."

As he dressed next morning, he bypassed his rumpled seersucker suit and the sports coats in his closet and pulled out the navy blue captain's jacket with the four stripes around the sleeves and the gold wings on the chest. He put on the hat with the TWA crest and the gold laurel wreaths on the visor—the "scrambled eggs" that only a captain wore. "I knew it might be one of the last times I would ever wear the uniform, and I decided that now is the time, and this is the place, for a TWA pilot to be seen and heard in uniform."

He got to his office early to get the letters individually typed up and signed for each director, and as he, Keilin, and Simon discussed the meeting, Simon said to him, "You know, you ought to go beyond that letter. You ought to make a few remarks. Tell them what's on your mind." There would be risk in that, because, if it was going to be honest, it couldn't be a diplomat's speech. It would have to hold his venom toward Lorenzo and bitter feelings of abandonment by management. He would have to say things about pride that could sound corny to that sophisticated board. With Simon prodding him to say the things he really wanted to say, he scrawled his thoughts on the back of an envelope. Then they walked south to the TWA offices to meet Icahn at 9:30.

People bustling to work south of Grand Central Station were unaware that converging on a boardroom at Fortieth and Third were several dozen men who would decide control of TWA. That the notorious Carl Icahn, an airline pilot, million-dollar teams of lawyers and investment bankers, and a "world-class" board—McNamara, Ueberroth, Valenti, Miller—were gathering for a meeting that would be, for Freund, the most dramatic event of twenty years of law—"the best show in town. We could have sold tickets."

As the board settled in, it struck Freund that the mood had changed from early summer. "There was not a clear-cut feeling for Lorenzo going into that meeting. And Carl had gone from a guy they were fighting to a guy who had acted 80 percent responsible and achieved something with the unions nobody else had ever been able to achieve." Lorenzo was brought into the boardroom first and seated at the large oval table with the directors. Chairman of the Board Ed Smart introduced him. "Frank took a high-road kind of approach," said Freund. "He was soft-spoken, didn't shout, and stressed the strength of the two airlines and how he would be able to work things out with the unions. But he didn't come up with any concrete proposals of how to deal with them. I felt that, inside, he felt furious at the pilots for opposing him and that he would have liked to get even. But he talked pretty well."

While Lorenzo was speaking, Icahn and Hoglander sat waiting in an adjoining room talking of Garibaldi, an epoch of nineteenth-century Italian history they had both studied. "Carl reminded me of an event in the war of 1870 when all the forces had been on one side; that evening they made a deal with the pope, the forces reversed and came down on the other side, and the war was over. 'That's just what the board is going to do now,' Carl said." The board obviously wanted to avoid a confrontation, and Lorenzo was ushered out so that the two groups would not see each other. Icahn and his team were ushered in.

Smart introduced Icahn to the board. Perhaps he felt too confident to put his best effort into it. He's not doing well, Freund thought, not as well as Lorenzo. He's being more of a blusterer, threatening "you do this and I'll do that." He was acting, it seemed to Freund, "like a guy who sees something behind every rock and who, for all his bravado, knew the lockups *could* happen. If it was going to be a personality contest, so far Lorenzo would win."

Hoglander, seated next to Icahn at the board table, was thinking, "He's not nearly as good as before the Master Council. Where is the man who devastated Meyer at the congressional hearings? For some reason he's just not clicking with the board." Carl told them about the labor concessions and said, "I've brought Harry Hoglander to tell you about that."

Hoglander was determined to read the letter aloud so that he could warm up before delivering the comments that held his personal feelings. "I wanted to get my juices up, because I knew these were the last things I would say to them if it didn't work out." But with the letters already distributed around the table, reading it seemed redundant. He noted that Brock Adams and two other directors were absent and joining in by conference call. He addressed the absent three: "Since you gentlemen do not have a copy of the letter, I shall read it to you."

He was sitting, flanked by Icahn and Pearson with Valenti across, and the principals' teams ranged on chairs behind the table. He determined he would try to make eye contact with each board member during his presentation. He hit them first with a powerful statistic. "We are very pleased to inform you that our members ratified the agreement with Mr. Carl Icahn by an 82 percent margin of approval." It is an agreement, he went on, that "obligates Mr. Icahn to preserve the integrity of TWA's assets and obligations, insures labor peace at TWA, and protects the communities where TWA plays an important role. No matter what nonbinding assurances you have been given, you will misread the record of recent years if you believe Texas Air will satisfy these same objectives." A good tack for him to take, thought Freund, since the board's goals were to keep the airline intact and running. Hoglander closed his letter with a call to the moral ethic he had been raised with: "Your lawyers will tell you what decisions are permitted, but they cannot tell you what decision is right."

Freund sensed that Hoglander was getting their attention. This board never talks to employees. They get letters, but here is a pilot. Here is the person who, more than anyone else, represented the strength of feeling that has led union employ-

ees to take massive pay cuts. It was a smart move on Carl's part
to bring Hoglander, Freund mused. Hoglander knew he had
no more than five more minutes in which to try to sway the
board. He caught the eye of Frank Salizzoni, the financial vice-
president of Trans World Corporation, and held it as he began
his comments. He hoped Salizzoni would be on the pilots' side;
they had always considered him a friend. He didn't know if
those things meant anything, but he was naive enough to hope
they did.

"I'm appearing before you in my uniform not as any sort of
publicity stunt, but as an example of my pride as a TWA pilot. I
share my pride with thirty-three hundred pilots . . . who
average about twenty-four years of hard work and service to
our company. We pilots are loyal employees, conservative politically, socially, and financially. We respect entrepreneurship
and despise the cheat and the fast-buck artist. We side with
those who side with dignity. . . . And that's the way we think
America also feels."

It was a little overstated, Freund thought, but apparently
from the heart.

"And when I don't wear this uniform, which I consider a
symbol of authority, I also wear the uniform of a lieutenant
colonel in the National Guard. . . . I have respect for authority."
He saw Valenti give him a nod of kinship; he'd been a marine
pilot. "But having seen combat," he went on, "I also know that
the exercise of leadership and authority can be destructive as
well as constructive. . . . I state to you that the TWA pilots do
not care to work for Lorenzo. We don't want to work for a man
whose airplanes hit seawall dikes at La Guardia."

That's a cheap shot, a very cheap shot, Freund thought. No
one has ever suggested before that Frank ran an unsafe airline.
But it was becoming an electrifying presentation. As Hoglander's emotion grew, forty people focused on the words of a
rough-cut, straight-shooting pilot.

Harry had seen the two women on the board—Jewel S.
LaFontaine, a Chicago lawyer who had been a United Nations
delegate and deputy solicitor general, and Patricia Stewart,
whom he knew nothing about—perk up when he'd mentioned

TWA's ten-year crash-free safety record in his letter, and he looked at them and pursued the theme. "We have flown you and your families to your destinations safely. Don't give Lorenzo an opportunity to degrade our company." As he closed, he evoked the worst fears of the board—employee disruptions that could halt the airline and damage property. "You have heard cries for wildcat strikes on TWA. I want to assure you that if the board of directors takes actions to lock us into Lorenzo, the Air Line Pilots Association will call an *authorized* strike, and I will lead it against you."

Brian Freeman, the lawyer who represented the machinists, compounded the threats of strikes, warning that being sold into bondage to Lorenzo would provoke nighttime trashing of airplanes and other sabotage. In a few short minutes, the board had heard threats of lawsuits, formal strikes, and sabotage. Nobody likes to be threatened, Freund knew, but the reality was there. He suspected the board would believe that people with such strong feelings would be capable of doing just about anything.

Then Icahn fielded some questions, and Hoglander smiled. It was the Icahn he'd seen in the Master Council meeting. He was terrific! He talked of the future of the industry as consolidation and said he could see that TWA, as part of that, could well be sold to another airline. And then, an effective stroke. When Icahn was asked how he was going to run the airline, he said, "I'm not going to run the airline. I'm going to hire the best talent I can find to run it—men like your own Dick Pearson."

Freund knew Icahn had not bought Pearson's vote with the promise. It had been on his mind. Earlier, Icahn had told Freund and Zimmerman, "I hear good things about him. I'd like to talk to him. But Pearson has said some terrible things about me—and I've never even *talked* to him." He paused, then added, "At least Ed Meyer *met* me!" as Freund and Zimmerman cracked up.

It was close to noon. Freund guided Icahn out of the room. He told Icahn, "Go back to your office and relax, Carl. Take it easy. I'll call you to let you know what happened. Don't go crazy, don't buy any stock." Icahn looked at Freund and said,

"Come on, Freund, you got your guy in Delaware, I got my guy on the floor of the exchange. At one o'clock, he buys everything in sight." TWA did, indeed, have a lawyer poised at the office of the secretary of state in Dover, Delaware, ready to file the charter amendment creating the preferred stock—the lockup. And Icahn had his stock all lined up.

The Icahn team emerged to a wall of reporters and TV cameras and worked their way to the sidewalk. Icahn loves to walk, and the group walked from Fortieth Street to his office at Fifty-sixth Street, a twenty-five-minute walk. While the board prepared to vote, Hoglander trudged like an automaton, thinking, In half an hour, it will all be over. These months of anguish and exhaustion. We'll know in half an hour.

Freund, in his old mode of presenting all sides, summarized what he thought the two men had said and what the implications were. He felt strongly that it was not his job to tell the board what to do; they must decide. But he knew that, if he could vote, it would be against issuing the lockups. It would be for Icahn. "Let's look at the upside of Lorenzo. He's offering $2 more per share than Icahn, and the airlines would be a good fit. But let's look at the downside: Carl's $24 seems much surer than Frank's $26. And it would happen much sooner. There's no way to predict whether the lockups—which Carl would surely challenge—would stand up in court. If they did *not*, Carl would get the company and feel free to force a much lesser deal on the TWA shareholders."

And waiting for completion of Lorenzo's deal, there could be labor unrest, Freund warned. Hoglander's intensity had cast the specter of strikes, slowdowns, trashing of airplanes, lawsuits—anything. And, Freund posed, would Drexel's financing hold together? There was a clause in Drexel's contract with the committing group that if TWA's financial condition was "severely adversely changed," investors could back away from their commitments. Over the next six months, "severe adverse changes" could well occur. An unknown, threatening prospect.

Freund believed he knew the way voting would go, but that, in a close vote, Pearson would be the linchpin. "Pearson had more to gain from Lorenzo. He'd keep his job and his golden pass." Pearson spoke very quietly. Very controlled. And he voted against the lockups. The board went with him, unanimously, and Icahn had won the day.

Freund picked up the phone and called Icahn's office. How cool could you be! He wasn't back yet. He left a message, then prepared to put out the press release. He had written two press releases the night before—one for each outcome. As he waited for Icahn to return his call, Freund felt the tension of the morning released. He believed the board had reached the right decision, and he was pleased with the role he had played. Yes, and pleased, too, to discover that working on hostile takeovers wasn't just lobbing mortar shells back and forth between an irreconcilable raider and target. More subtle skills—strategizing, negotiating, persuading—did come into play. In the ten years since he'd written *Anatomy of a Merger,* the two strands of hostile and friendly had fused. The dichotomy had evolved into a continuum. In any deal now, you had to be a fighter and a lover.

◆　◆　◆

WALKING back, Icahn's aides joked to keep up their spirits. But as they gathered in Icahn's office, tension built as the staff filed in—secretaries, lawyers, maybe twenty people, all waiting for the call. Harry was amazed as Carl opened the door off his office and revealed a whole room of traders, poised to buy stock if the vote went against them. Harry collapsed into a sofa that had a pillow embroidered with the words "Happiness is a positive cash flow." Carl's secretary told Icahn that Freund had left a message to call. He had her return the call, and the room went absolutely silent as she buzzed in, "Call for you, Carl." Freund came on the other end. They couldn't hear. Icahn had turned off the conference call button. Hoglander could hardly bear it, listening to Carl saying his usual, "Yeah, yeah, I understand. Yeah, no bullshit. Yeah, okay, yeah, right, Jim," but the thumb of his left hand was slowly turning *up.*

They couldn't hear Freund at the other end trying to implement a delicate piece of strategy. They had all—Freund, Zimmerman, the TWA board—felt uncomfortable about not paying Lorenzo the $45 million he was entitled to by his merger

agreement with TWA in the event the agreement terminated.
Icahn had warned the board not to pay, and Freund knew how
negatively Icahn reacted to overt pressure. He didn't want to
make Lorenzo's breakup fee a condition of not giving the
lockups. He took a different tack. "Carl, the board has gone
your way, no lockups"—the good news that sent Icahn's thumb
up. His team began to applaud and whistle. Then Freund went
on: "But we don't want to be in the position of not honoring
our obligation. So I'd like you to agree that we can pay Frank
what's coming to him if he terminates the agreement."

He was giving Carl the opportunity to be magnanimous in
victory. At the negative news, Icahn turned his thumb down
and flattened his hand, the order for the room to shut up. In
that tense silence, Icahn went on, "Okay, if he agrees to stand
aside this week. He has to do it *this week.*" That was it! Harry
tried to divine what was happening, as Carl went on with his
"Yeah, yeah, a week, I said a week." But his thumb was turning
up again. It was turning up. Carl put down the phone, leaned
forward on his elbows as a grin spread across his face, and said,
"We've got ourselves an airline." Icahn's arm shot up in the V-for-
Victory sign, and the room exploded. "Okay, Keemosabi, we do
good in this town. We go on to next town now," Kingsley said,
playing Tonto to Icahn's Lone Ranger as he did at the end of
every deal, and Al and Carl hugged each other. After a victory
lunch of deli sandwiches in the board room, Harry handed
Carl his captain's jacket. Icahn put it on and paraded. *"We've got
ourselves an airline!"*

AFTERMATH

EARLY September. The deals are done, the endgames over. The mop-up of Unocal, Crown Zellerbach, and TWA moves forward but commands a less obsessive commitment of energy and resources as new deals—Revlon, Beatrice, Kaiser Aluminum, Union Carbide—gain momentum and play through.

Jim Freund spotted Carl Icahn in his center court box at the U.S. Open in Queens in late September, watching a tennis match between McEnroe and the Swede, Nystrom, as intensely as Icahn had negotiated for the airline. It was the calm of armistice after the wars; they were settling with Lorenzo that weekend, and to all intents and purposes, the fight for TWA was over. As McEnroe overwhelmed the Swede and got into an angry fight with the umpire, images of Icahn flashed through Freund's mind. On the phone to Icahn a few days later, Freund tried out his analogy.

"Carl, I saw you at the tennis matches, and it struck me that there was a real parallel between you and McEnroe. I don't mean the screaming at the umpire part, but his *play*." He had Icahn's attention. "There are lots of good tennis players around, but some balls they hit are apparently without purpose. Any shot that McEnroe hits always has a plan, a design. That's the way you are in the game."

Icahn murmured a little approval, as Freund built his metaphor.

"McEnroe hits some shots with great power, and that's you

going out and buying 2 million shares. He hits others very deftly—little unreturnable drop shots—and you can play it deftly, too. You don't stay at the base line."

"Yeah," Carl agreed with a grin, "I like to go to the net. But not all the time, not all the time."

Freund didn't mention the final parallel between the two. But as Icahn got louder and more intense, recalling the fury he'd felt when Lorenzo had, by his judgment, reneged on agreements, he suddenly stopped and laughed. "And when that happened, I got *angry* . . . just like McEnroe!" To Freund's delight, Icahn himself had completed the metaphor.

The toughest sets were yet to come. Icahn must now run an airline, one that was not fully his until he had the financing to buy the 48 percent he did not own.

In the relative calm of late October, Captain Harry Hoglander flew with Judith to Anaheim for an AFL-CIO convention. The pilots union, ALPA, was an affiliate. With the peak of a plastic Everest in the background, the scene was as unreal as the takeover world had been. Several thousand hard-drinking, tough-talking delegates filled two gigantic conference hotels at the edge of Disneyland. Judith stood out in that crowd, with her classy white slacks and shirt and gold jewelry. He felt out of place here, too. Maybe it was elitism, but pilots were a different kind of union man. How many of the delegates here were continuing to stick their heads in the sand fighting for wage scales and benefits that could kill their industries? How many were willing to see their jobs in the context of change they couldn't stop? It was damn painful. Nobody here was going to bleed over Harry, or his personal cut of $26,000 a year. But that was the price of keeping the union and the airline intact. He could still put on the blue uniform with pride and dignity.

After the meetings, he and Judy were going to drive up the coast—the Hearst castle, Carmel, San Francisco. He needed a little time to talk and decompress. And figure out. How did you go back flying the line after this? Cincinnati. Cleveland. Six legs a day. He loved flying. And every time he flew, now, he was getting fantastic feedback from the pilots. During the fight, they'd swarmed around him every time he arrived at the ramp, anxious and full of questions. Now it was, "Great job, Harry," and thumbs raised at him in a sort of "Well done!" gesture. Every time he broke through the clouds, he still said to himself, "Hey, every day's a sunshine day up here." But it took adjustment, after Icahn.

By November, the TWA deal was in serious trouble and the war rooms were filling again.

On November 13, a reporter thrust a tape recorder toward Icahn and asked him, "Are you glad you bought an airline?"

"Oh, yeah, sure, we're having a lot of fun with it," said Icahn, sitting at his desk, distracted and growling, his fingers spread on his forehead and his head down as he studied the papers before him, as if fierce intensity could force "the way out" to reveal itself. In his shirt sleeves, his raincoat tossed over a chair, he took a string of phone calls and yelled orders to his aides and secretaries to find files and papers he needed. His closest aide, Al Kingsley, his airline analyst Sanford Rederer, and about six others were piling up at the back of his office, like planes backed up on a ramp, waiting to get his attention as the day ground into a dark, wet evening. As the reporter tried again with a question on air safety, Icahn's head jerked up, shocked and exasperated. "Don't ask me about air safety right *now!*" he snapped, then turned back to his work.

"We could have made $150 million profit by selling back to Lorenzo," Al Kingsley said with a shrug as he worked at his desk behind the mountain of paper that threatened to engulf his substantial bulk if it ever started sliding. They had fired most of the board and replaced it with six people—Icahn, Kingsley, and Icahn's uncle Elliot Schnall, plus three carry-overs from the old board, Dick Pearson, now president, and two outside directors. Those outside directors would be made a committee of two to represent shareholder interests; Freund would be named the committee's counsel. Icahn's team was trying to separate and spin off the reservations system, PARS, which had enchanted Icahn back in the summer with its hidden value. "There's nothing else to spin off. It's an airline. That's it." They were marketing PARS's charms. But so far, no one had been willing to pay Icahn's price of half a billion dollars.

And the financing wasn't going well. They needed "in the neighborhood of $800 million to a billion dollars" to buy out all the shares beyond the 52 percent Icahn owned. Until then, he would not, in fact, own an airline. Through October, Icahn and Hoglander had staged the "Carl and Harry Show," helicopter- ing to Boston and Hartford, calling meetings in New York and Los Angeles, trying to convince investors of TWA's strong future while its balance sheet showed a net loss of nearly $70 million for the first nine months of 1985, and its stock fell to $21. Potential investors flew in from London and Paris, as European money took an increasing interest in takeover op- portunities. With Drexel still obligated to Lorenzo until the moment Icahn signed with Lorenzo, Icahn had turned to Paine Webber to raise the money.

The road show put Hoglander back in action. Landing at a midtown heliport after one of the meetings, Hoglander had lured Icahn and Dick Pearson in for a drink at a little Italian restaurant where some of Hoglander's union guys were waiting for him to join them. Hoglander urged Icahn to come in. When Icahn resisted, Hoglander told him, "Carl, you've got to come in, or they'll never believe what I tell them about how we're working to put this thing together." Carl came in, had drinks and dinner, and when Harry finally dragged himself out and took the limousine home at eleven, Carl was still there, fresh as a daisy, talking about how to make the thing work. This guy is incredible, thought Hoglander. He'd gone down into the pits with the workers to forge his concessions; he was still willing to go there. "We fight every day. But what the hell."

Paine Webber's efforts failed, although the market would not know that until the end of November, the deadline Icahn had promised for achieving his financing. By then, Drexel Burnham was back on the job as his lead investment banker. "We haven't got a 'highly confident' letter yet, but we'll get one, I'm sure," said Kingsley on November 13. "They haven't failed us yet." Soon Icahn would have to start paying 25 cents per share for every month he didn't have his financing. It was a self-imposed penalty he had offered as a ploy to dramatize to the TWA board that he could complete his purchase of TWA faster, months faster, than Lorenzo. The payments had been scheduled to start on November 30, but he had a short reprieve. In the agreement's small print, it said the payments were not to begin until TWA had sent out shareholder materials concerning the transaction; the mailings were still hung up in the SEC approval process. But the envelope was closing.

By late November, the deal that should have been wrapped up was unraveling. It was highly unusual in Jim Freund's experience. "Normally, after a deal, all you read about is how it's going. This one is falling apart," said Freund. Icahn's obligation to do the merger had been conditional on getting the financing, but the financing wasn't there. Icahn was caught in a frustrating catch-22. He could not take control of the board until he had bought all outstanding TWA stock and completed his merger. He could not buy stock and complete his merger without financing from Drexel. Drexel, under increasing threat of restraints on junk bonds from the Federal Reserve Board and nervous about TWA's deteriorating operating results, would not write a "highly confident" letter and do the financing until Icahn had even more concessions from the unions. Icahn could not turn operating results around until those concessions were signed and in place. The pilots and machinists were resisting the new cuts that, for the pilots, would amount to a total package of 34 percent of their income; the flight attendants were intransigent and were threatening to strike. Drexel also wanted Icahn to put up a strike chest for an attendants' strike, cash that would probably have to come from Icahn's pocket. Drexel was also demanding less cash and more paper in the merger deal, trying to preserve TWA's cash at a time when the airline's cash flow was under pressure. There were clearly limits, even for the man who lectured that you should never launch a big takeover without your reserves stretched out before you.

Meetings as stormy and intense as any of July and August hammered round the clock in Freund's offices at TWA, Icahn's office, and at Skadden Arps. The culminating meeting trying to hold the merger together was in a conference room at Skadden Arps on Sunday night, December 8—the same room where they had tried to talk Icahn out of coming after the company. Drexel's Leon Black took the lead. After exhausting rounds of meetings, Icahn had converted his $24 offer to $13 cash, $11 securities. The TWA board had accepted it. But it wasn't good enough for Drexel. Dick Pearson had just flown to Los Angeles to see Mike Milken; it would have to be a package of even less cash and more paper for Milken to market it to his investors. To get his commitments. As the men ranted and argued, Steve Jacobs and Black heightened the drama by dashing in and out of the room. Upstairs, at another law firm they were working with GAF lawyers to prepare the launch, the next morning, of GAF chairman Sam Heyman's tender offer for Union Carbide. Controlling himself with "quiet outrage," Freund reminded Icahn that it was just this nickel-and-dime stubbornness that had made Lorenzo blow his chance to get TWA, to which Icahn raised his chin and, in words whose quaintness had surprised Freund in the past, "took umbrage" at Freund's comment. Icahn had reached the limits of the cash that would be in the deal, and the meeting ended in a frustrating impasse. Next morning, as Heyman began his formal assault on Union Carbide, the press reported that Icahn's TWA deal was collapsing.

The next day, Jim Freund called Icahn with the disastrous third-quarter operating results. On the basis of those, the year's loss would be close to $150 million. Ten days later, Icahn would get the news of the shootings at the Rome airport." PARS was hit with a flood of cancellations of bookings on the golden European routes. "Welcome to the airline business," a seasoned board member said to Icahn. "If you think this is bad, wait till you see the *first* quarter. That's always a real character builder."

He could still sell the airline. Freund and others had advised him, "See if anybody wants to do a deal." TWA's investment banker, Salomon's Mike Zimmerman, had reopened talks with Resorts International and was talking to Northwest and American. But it was Texas Air's Lorenzo who had put a firm deal on the table—$22 per share, all cash. It was an attractive option for Icahn. He couldn't dump his stock on the open market; his block was too big. And the stock price had dropped from the low 20s to the mid-teens. His average price had been $19. Lorenzo's bid now would offer him a handsome profit. Freund called the unions in for a meeting at Skadden, Arps and outlined the desperate choices. "We've had a bad fourth quarter. Icahn refuses to go through with the deal as it's structured, and the revised deals are unattractive. The only company prepared to bid is Texas Air. Lorenzo's $22 is better than any other deal; he wants to negotiate with the unions. Texas Air *wants* to meet with you. What's your reaction?"

The reaction of the machinists and pilots was instantaneous, completely negative, and loaded with not-so-veiled threats. Given the reaction, Icahn told Freund he would not sell to Lorenzo.

The unions were resisting concessions, as well as Lorenzo. Yet the only route to profitability, Icahn believed, lay in extracting even more from men who had already given up over 30 percent of their income. At one meeting, when he learned that the unions had not accepted new concessions, Freund saw Icahn tear into his own people with a violence that shocked him. "He's become a man possessed with demons. But the demons keep changing. One day it's the unions. Next day, it's Drexel. Next day it's the terrorists." Watching Icahn with a writer's eye for character, Freund was observing a transformation from the confidence of August, when Icahn had kept them all under pressure with his threats. "Then, no matter which way he turned, he couldn't lose. Now, every option he looked at, he *could* lose. It's the *zugzwang* in chess, where, wherever you move, you can be hurt."

TWA's open letter to Icahn months earlier taunted him now: "You see, Mr. Icahn, running a major airline . . . is not like speculating with paper on Wall Street." Was he losing heart? During one of the bleakest hours, late at night at Skadden Arps, Icahn was walking down the hall with Freund. They'd struck some friendly bonds. The "sweater joke" had become a trigger for laughs: at an endless night meeting, Icahn had been cold and Freund had lent him his cashmere sweater, and he'd worn it home. At a subsequent meeting, when Icahn had again borrowed the sweater and was taking a very tough negotiating stance, Freund broke the tension by quipping, "Hey, Carl, give me back my sweater." They were comfortable trading frank talk, and Icahn said to Freund now, "Jim, sometimes I think I was a *schmuck*. In a way, I'm in this mess because of my loyalty to the pilots, my *moral obligation!*" For Freund, it was a wonderful moment. The rock-hearted man of commerce who loved to say, "If you want a friend, get a dog," was admitting to being in a pickle. Because he'd been nice.

Icahn flew to Palm Beach, dragging the demons of uncertainty with him. He called Freund from Florida. "Jim, I don't want to do a merger." He would not do the full leveraged buyout of TWA. He would remain as controlling head of TWA. The shareholders wouldn't get their promised $24 a share package, although many had taken their profits when the stock was selling in the 20s. But there was a lot of humiliation in it for Icahn. After the *American Lawyer* story congratulating him on having done everything right, *Fortune* would put him on its February 17 cover with the headline, "THE COMEUPPANCE OF CARL ICAHN." Carl now proposed, instead of a merger, to have Drexel raise $750 million for the company to weather tough times. Freund had negotiated certain standstill provisions to protect the minority stockholders if Icahn were to change his mind and sell or merge the company in 1986 or 1987. "He had agonized, but once he had made up his mind," Freund said, "the old affirmative Icahn emerged."

By January 10, Icahn could finally write a letter headed "Dear fellow employees" and report that "the recent uncertainties concerning TWA's future have at last been resolved . . . and I can now address you as Chairman of TWA's Board of Directors." TWA, he hoped, "would emerge as one of the financially strongest airlines in the world. After the Drexel Burnham financing, TWA will have between $750 million and $1 billion in cash. My prediction is that in the next few years airlines with weak capital structures will have difficulty surviving." And then he spoke to them in a personal way that confirmed to Hoglander that Icahn had, indeed, struck some kind of personal bond with the pilots, the feelings that had made him a *schmuck* and almost lost him the airline. "Like most of you, I did not have

wealthy parents and have worked extremely hard for what I
have earned. I started on Wall Street in 1961, and I began
Icahn & Co. in 1968 with my own savings and some borrowed
capital. The original net worth has increased to over $150
million. I cannot promise I will do as well for all of you at TWA,
but I can assure you that if I do not, it will not be from lack of
trying." He ended with a call to arms. "Now that our uncertainties are over and we return to profitability, I have faith that all
of you will take a renewed pride in your work and this great
airline's tradition. I can assure you that in addition to profit
sharing, we will all share in the great sense of achievement
when TWA will once again be 'Leading the Way.'" Hoglander
read the letter several times. It was powerful. Moving even.
"We're losing our shirts, but he's still a good guy." Whatever
else, Icahn had kept faith with the unions. Hoglander gave
Icahn a captain's coat on his fiftieth birthday in February, and
even compromised on the golden passes. They would remain;
Icahn, the airline executive, had his picture taken for his own
golden pass.

Over New Year's, the unions had begun to fall into line. First
the mechanics, then the pilots. Saudi Arabia's acts sent oil
prices plunging, dramatically reducing the cost of fuel. And at
the end of February, Icahn merged with an agreement to
acquire Ozark Airlines, a $250 million acquisition that would
strengthen TWA's St. Louis hub and its competitive position as
the trend to consolidation grew. Hoglander said, "A very smart
move. Ozark has no debt. He'll hock it to the hubcaps to get his
money out!"

The same week, a deal was struck between Frank Lorenzo
and a deeply troubled Eastern Airlines. If it passed antitrust
challenges in Washington, Eastern would be acquired by Texas
Air. Frank Borman had, indeed, achieved the largest airline in
the nation, but lost his job and his airline. Hoglander watched
the takeover teams move into place and noted that Skadden
Arps was representing the Eastern pilots on this one. "I sat on
the fringes and shuddered," he says, as the Eastern pilots
capitulated to Lorenzo. As ALPA's Henry Duffy flew to Houston and stayed with the pilots during the death watch, Hoglan-

der claimed, "Hank's a hero. The pilots had no consensus. They couldn't even agree on the union contract with the airline. After an all-night session of parliamentary procedure they were counting angels on a head of a pin when someone came in and said, 'Borman's just sold to Lorenzo.' It was three in the morning. Duffy jumped in a car, got Borman up. Borman said he *had* to sign with Lorenzo." In the wake of that shock, the pilots had at least struck a deal that would protect them for a year and a half. "We gave up a lot of things to get away from Lorenzo; they gave up a lot of things and got him," said a glum Hoglander. It made the deal struck between Icahn and the TWA unions seem all the more remarkable.

Icahn had a final demon to exorcise. Victoria Frankovich, head of the flight attendants union. The attendants had struck in late February 1986 while TWA pilot Bill Tantau was flying his last Mideast flight as co-pilot, about to give up London, Cairo, and Athens to fly the "shitty" midwestern routes as captain of his own plane, as Harry Hoglander had. As attendants walked off in Cairo, they staffed the 747 with ground personnel, and as Tantau deadheaded home to Napa Valley, California, he had a chance to see Icahn's "new hires" in action—"smiling, fresh-faced, a little scared, but doing just fine." In preparation for the strike, Icahn had started a training program for fifteen hundred attendants to be paid $1,000 a month, the same rate Lorenzo's Continental Airlines paid.

Tough challenges ahead for the attendants had been inadvertently forecast by a flight attendant Jim Freund chatted with on a flight to California during the tense days before the final board meeting last August. When it came out that he was a lawyer for TWA, she'd said, "Oooh, I just got a call from my father, who went to Princeton with Carl Icahn, and he said, 'Why are you people being so hard on my ex-classmate?' " Freund had been at Princeton at the same time and had known her father. Crazy small world. Their last name started with a Z. As he left the plane the last thing she'd said to him was: "Please tell Mr. Icahn, if he gets the airline and starts firing people, to do it in alphabetical order!"

"TWA's attendants get, typically, $45,000," Icahn told a national television audience as he debated Frankovich on PBS's nightly MacNeil-Lehrer report on March 11. "I like the flight attendants. They do a good job. But Miss Frankovich is leading them over a cliff."

"That's why we agreed to $12,000 starting pay," Frankovich said, eyes steely, teeth clenched as she talked. Wearing her navy uniform and white blouse, her curly streaked-blond hair clipped short, she had the taut and tired look of an attendant at the end of a long overseas flight. Hoglander had grappled with the end of an age with hollering and profanity in the privacy of the war rooms. Frankovich played out the agony on prime-time TV. "We want fairness. Sexism is the only reason we can find to explain why we are being asked to take larger pay cuts and more work rules concessions than comparable jobs in TWA, and flight attendants in comparable airlines—United, American, Northwest. He has told us in negotiations, 'We're not breadwinners, we're second incomes.' "

"I won't dignify that with an answer," Icahn snapped back. The attendants would take a 15 percent cut; Icahn was demanding 17 percent. But the pay cuts are not the issue, he reiterated. It's the work rule concessions—more hours. "It's the *productivity* we have to have if we are going to survive." Attacking the two more hours of flying time a week he is trying to extract, Frankovich argued that overwork will lead to exhaustion and compromise the primary job of attendants—passenger safety. The pilots, he reminds her, took a 30 percent cut, with pay cuts and work rule concessions, and have just recently taken more work rule concessions that moved it up to 34 percent. "The pilots have been terrific. They've worked with us right along and they understand what has to be done."

He confronted her with the school reunion incident last August. Her face went hard, and the strain of a year of fighting showed in the dark arcs under her eyes and the knots of tight muscles in her cheeks. If only she had struck a deal on August 5 instead of flying home to a party in California, Icahn told her again, she could have got the same deal machinists and pilots got. "Those were different days," he said. "Conditions are different now. I wouldn't strike that deal today. We need more cuts to stay in business." He will be forced to break up the airline, he declares, if flying it is not economic. "I have to look out for the shareholder's interests, and I'm the largest share-holder."

Frankovich bitterly dismissed "that famous weekend you keep talking about" and volunteered that, in negotiations beginning the next day, "we'll look at every option." But like Icahn she was trapped by the economics of deregulation. Her striking union had already lost two thousand of its total six thousand jobs to the fresh-faced new hires eager to work for less than a third of TWA's wage scale. "And people *like* them," Icahn emphasizes. "Vicki might have worked it out with the old management," says pilot Tantau, feeling sympathy for TWA's super "stews," "but she doesn't seem to understand. This is *takeover!*"

The attendants were still striking on Wednesday morning, April 2, when the first fragmentary news came across the Reuters tape in Icahn's New York office. An explosion on a TWA flight to Athens. Suspected terrorist bomb. Four dead, nine wounded. Icahn set up a press conference for 12:45, as his staff and TWA officials tried frantically to get more details.

A shepherd near the Greek village of Statheika northwest of Argos had seen bodies and an airplane seat raining from the air. Aboard Flight 840, Captain Richard Petersen had poured on power to overcome the wind drag created by a hole blown in the side of his 727, and radioed Athens that he would be making an emergency landing. Four people had been sucked out in the explosive decompression that followed the explosion at window seat 10F as the plane was descending through fifteen thousand feet on its approach to Athens. The flight had originated Tuesday morning in Los Angeles, stopped in New York, then proceeded to Rome for the final legs to Athens and Cairo. It was the kind of linkage of domestic and international routes that was TWA's pride, strength, and major income source. But as banner headlines like the *San Francisco Chronicle*'s "BOMB RIPS TWA JETLINER OVER GREECE—4 KILLED" spread the horror, travel agents reported a flood of tourists canceling European trips and diverting to California and Mexico.

"You see, Mr. Icahn, running a major airline is a big job," TWA's open letter to Carl Icahn had cautioned him nearly a year earlier. As terrorism created international panic and TWA's bookings fell, Icahn said, "It could be argued that I paid a high price for nobility."

♦   ♦   ♦

JOHN Sorte's wife still hadn't worn the dress she'd bought for Drexel Burnham's black-tie partners' dinner last Easter. As they were dressing, Sorte had been called to Los Angeles to put together Boone Pickens's junk-bond financing for Unocal. The partners' Christmas party was coming up. But she wouldn't be able to wear it there, either. She was pregnant with twins, to be born in March.

The Christmas party was festive. But Drexel was not as "highly confident" as it had been about the future of junk-bond financing for hostile takeovers and leveraged buyouts. After months of lobbying against efforts to restrain the use of junk bonds—after defeating the bill that had sat on New York Governor Cuomo's desk—Drexel had received its first formal setback.

The seeds of fear of junk bonds planted back in March 1985 by Fred Hartley when he wrote to the Federal Reserve Board chairman, Paul Volcker, had sprouted and bloomed. In trying to stop Pickens and prevent his bank, Security Pacific, from lending to Pickens, Hartley had railed against excessive debt, junk bonds, and the overleveraging of America. He had demanded that the Federal Reserve Board take action. In early December, it did. Its rounds of hearings, letters of comment and review had finally culminated in a proposal to eliminate some uses of junk-bond financing of takeovers. It was only a limited attack—the margin requirements would be raised on shell companies created expressly for the purpose of financing hostile takeovers—but it was the first sign that the negative mood about takeovers was still growing and could lead to more restrictions. Governor Cuomo was about to sign a rewritten version of the bill he had vetoed in July, one that would also discourage the use of junk bonds. Drexel Burnham continued to lobby in Washington and searched for ways to broaden its base of financial services and involve its network of investors in more conventional investment banking.

Mike Milken's virtuoso creation—high-yield financing applied to mergers and acquisitions—had never gained respectability. With fears of excessive debt continuing to grow as 1985 ended, it seemed unlikely that they ever would. As the firm set out on an aggressive program of diversification, Wall Street watched to see where Drexel Burnham's ingenuity would lead it next. By April, falling interest rates were making junk bonds' high yields look appetizing as an investment, as Dan Dorfman was reporting in his nationally syndicated column.

◆   ◆   ◆

SIR James Goldsmith was in his town house on Eightieth Street on the eve of a special Crown Zellerbach board meeting in New York on November 13. His young French companion in New York rushed upstairs with her arms full of paper-wrapped bouquets of flowers for the evening's dinner party. Slim, wearing tight faded designer jeans, no makeup, and her brown hair pulled back into a braid, she vanished as Sir James took calls and received a stream of manila envelopes. The sounds of a child echoed off the walls of the three-story stairwell, and a white-coated butler and black-uniformed maid flitted in and out of the salon. His principal officer in America, Roland Franklin, called to invite himself to dinner, no doubt to chat about the meeting. Tomorrow, a special committee of the Crown board appointed last summer would report its recommendations for further restructuring. "We'll have announcements a week from now," said Sir James as he went to dress for dinner.

Since Sir James had assumed the chairmanship on July 25, silence and mystery had shrouded the disposition of Crown's assets. A large timber company, James River Corporation, had been reported negotiating to buy some paper divisions. Joe Perella's secret visit to the town house with a client in August to try to do some dealmaking in the wake of the Crown deal had not produced results. Crown was carrying forward a streamlining announced last April as a move to drive Goldsmith away—one thousand layoffs, selling off a few plants and divisions, some consolidation of engineering and research. That effort, and the costs of the fight, had led to a third-quarter loss of over $84 million—only the second time in sixty years it had posted a loss. But the stripping away of divisions that would give Goldsmith his treasures, the timber—the move everyone expected—had yet to be announced.

As intrigued as he was with strategy, Goldsmith made a point of not getting personally involved in management. He left that to Franklin. What engaged Goldsmith's passions on the eve of this meeting was not Crown Zellerbach but his final triumph in the French courts after a five-year battle against French oil giant Elf-Aquitaine, "France's largest corporation, the Exxon of France except for one big difference—it's controlled by the state. Nationalized!" A fight to recoup his damaged investment and prove Elf's wrongdoing in a Guatemalan oil venture in which the French bank he had sold on the eve of nationalization in 1981 had a relatively small investment, "it was an ideological battle in which I was 100 percent emotionally involved." The kind of exotic international deal Goldsmith is drawn to, it involved a holding company in Luxembourg, a subsidiary in the Bahamas, partial ownership by Elf-Aquitaine, and a flamboyant oil concessionaire, a "bigger-than-life Orson Welles playing the role of the Texas wildcatter." Above all, "it represented everything I most hate. The arrogance of the establishment backed by the arrogance of the civil servant in a socialist country. The arrogance and dishonesty of the nationalized company that feels it is above the law—that it can *write* the law." Goldsmith had risked $100 million to prove that Elf had been guilty of "systematic destruction of the wells, bribing a court official, a conspiracy to undermine production and bankrupt the company" for geopolitical or economic reasons he never fully fathomed.

"They collapsed last July. We won. We got a couple of hundred million dollars, the biggest settlement ever made, I believe, outside of the United States."

To the Crown board meetings he did attend, Goldsmith brought an air of drama, sweeping in, as his biographer sees him, like a nomadic Mongol chief miscast in the twentieth century. In fact, Crown board member Warren Hellman, sitting opposite and observing Goldsmith at one of the many meetings in San Francisco during the spring, speculated that this campaign for Crown and all the other campaigns were simply theater pieces staged to satisfy some inner agendas—perhaps huge egos. That day, Goldsmith had excoriated the Crown board for its inept management. His electric delivery and skewering wit had left the board limp. As he finished, he'd caught Hellman's eye, winked, and shrugged, as if to ask, "How did I do?" Hellman was developing a theory that takeovers weren't really necessary at all. If the timber divisions were the assets Goldsmith wanted, there were simpler and more peaceable means to acquire them.

By early December, there was still no word on the disposition of Crown's assets.

◆　◆　◆

ICAHN and Goldsmith were not the only entrepreneurs with their plates full.

"We'll show them a white blackbird yet," Boone Pickens had said, as the collapse of the Unocal deal sent the stock of his own Mesa Petroleum sliding from $20 to $13—and lower. He could win or lose almost anything else—a court decision, a proxy vote, even a *company*—as the vagaries of war. But for Pickens to fail to look after his own shareholders was to put his long crusade and his carefully crafted image at serious risk.

By late August, Pickens had found his white blackbird. Heeding his own call for restructuring of corporate America, he announced that he would do precisely that to Mesa Petroleum. In a "fundamental shift of direction . . . that will give shareholders a much better return on their investment," he would transform the entire Mesa Petroleum into a publicly traded limited partnership. Mesa Limited Partnership. It was projected that by the spring of 1987, Mesa, the vehicle for Pickens's stunning assault on the oil industry, would be liquidated. Gone as a corporation, not as Gulf, Getty, and Cities Service were gone, but transformed into a radically different organizational structure. An oil analyst calculated that Pickens's share of the partnership could be up to $20 million a year, a respectable war chest for financing new deals as the wave that had begun in oil washed over other industries to banking, retail, chemicals, cosmetics, food, media. But his staff reported that it would be more like half that.

The market responded to Pickens's white blackbird with a frenzy of trading on the New York Stock Exchange, and Mesa surged to $17.12. "This is the grand finale," said an oil analyst. "Mesa will ride into the sunset and Mr. Pickens will become a private merchant banker." As 1985 wound down, Boone Pickens was writing his autobiography, but it was still uncertain whether Pickens would direct his resources and energy to making acquisitions through the new partnership, or into a small, private deal team independent of Mesa. But no one doubted that he would be back.

In February 1986, he answered the question. Mesa Limited Partnership made an unsolicited offer for KN Energy, but was rebuffed. In March, the partnership made its first acquisition, an $800 million merger with Pioneer Corp. of Midland, Texas, the largest independent producer of natural gas in America—a deal in which Pickens came in as a white knight. Pickens was back, still buying reserves rather than drilling for them and apparently still ahead of the pack, taking advantage of the bargains created in the oil industry by declining oil prices. The Mesa offer won out over a higher offer by Minneapolis financier Irwin Jacobs, proof, according to the new president of Mesa Petroleum, Dave Batchelder, that the limited partnership, which gives more cash and less taxation than dividends to investors, was ideally suited for the energy industry's new era of low prices.

While Pickens regrouped in Amarillo, the Delaware decision that had knocked him out of Unocal swelled into a landmark case. It was being quoted in any lawsuit that tested the Business Judgment Rule and the limits of a board of directors' powers to protect itself from the threat of takeover. As precedent, *Unocal Corp.* v. *Mesa Petroleum Co.* would pepper the pages of two important Delaware decisions that came down that fall, Revlon and—at last, in late November—Household. The Unocal decision would shape Justice Andrew Moore's thinking as he struggled to complete the long-awaited Household decision. It had already changed the way takeover wars were waged. "The Unocal decision in Delaware effectively ended two-tier tender offers," said Drexel Burnham's John Sorte, who had raised junk bonds for Pickens's two-tier tender for Unocal.

While Unocal was a setback for the shareholder revolution Pickens had championed, Jesse Unruh was carrying its goals forward, formalizing them in a "Shareholder Bill of Rights," adopted at the annual meeting of the Council of Institutional Investors in Santa Monica on April 8, grown by then to 31 public pension funds with assets of $160 billion. Confirming the founding principles of shareholder democracy—such self-evident truths as one share–one vote and rejection of corporate entrenchment devices like greenmail, poison pills and exclusionary self-tenders as in Unocal—events at the Holiday Inn April 3, 1986, may not seem as significant as adoption of that earlier statement of liberties on December 15, 1791. But with its ink barely dry, the new Bill of Rights would go head-to-head against the New York Stock Exchange, as the exchange prepared to abandon its longheld one share–one vote rule to accommodate member companies who were trying to avoid takeover by creating special classes of stock with unequal voting rights. Faced with relaxing its rules or losing listings to the other two exchanges, the Big Board appealed to the SEC, whose ruling, when it came, would be a clear and resounding summation of the state of the takeover wars and of the shareholder revolution.

◆ ◆ ◆

"LIMITED Partnerships In, Oil Megacorporations Out," Kurt Wulff cheered in his October 1, 1985, newsletter, in response to Pickens's plans. It was all coming to pass! For the oil analyst who had been in the trenches with Pickens throughout the revolution, Mesa's partnership completed the dramatic circle of events he and Pickens had both helped trigger in the early sixties. Pickens was still, as he had always been, the boldest implementer of Wulff's heretical theories. His actions, more than anyone else's, had made Wulff's goals for a transformation of the structure of America's big oil companies a reality.

His pleasure poured forth in a special research bulletin on Mesa he had sent to his clients in late September: "Already a leader in the formation of royalty trusts and especially in the restructuring of integrated companies (Cities Service, Gulf, Phillips, and Unocal), Mesa is now the leading implementer of the limited partnership technique as well."

Limited partnerships separated out certain of a company's assets—the oil and gas reserves usually—distributed them as units that could be bought and sold just like stock, and sent the profits straight out to shareholders. They were taxed at only one level—the individual—and put control of the cash flow in the hands of stockholders, where it belonged. And by splitting up an integrated oil company's different functions—refining, production, gas stations—they achieved what Wulff had been arguing for for years. Smaller companies. *Deintegration!*

"Growing at 200 percent a year, publicly traded limited partnerships will own all U.S. oil and gas reserves by 1988 if the current trend continues. Nowhere is the rejection of the old oil megacorporation more obvious than in the case of Unocal," he said in his October newsletter. The market had spoken. Units of Unocal's partnership—the units whose release into the market had been awaited by oil analyst Lester Winterfeld at Manufacturers Hanover Trust last July—were trading in the market in November at more than twice the value of Unocal's common stock. With this example, Unocal might yet be inspired to transform itself into ten small companies, Wulff hoped. With continued restructuring, "oil will be with us at least another forty years," Wulff predicted with his usual boyish enthusiasm, "and with increased consumption, and oil shortages pushing prices up, I see some good plays coming in the 1990s." The oil industry would go raging into its dark night.

Within two months, oil prices had crashed. In January 1986, Saudi Arabia played chicken with the rest of the oil-producing nations and cut oil prices adrift. Fed up with countries that violated OPEC's production quotas, which had kept prices buoyed, the Saudis removed them, allowing prices to plunge, knowing that, at some level, countries that could not produce oil as cheaply as Saudi Arabia would be forced to reinstate production quotas. A boon to the consumer and a stimulant to the economy, the drop in oil prices devastated oil companies' income and the value of their reserves in the ground. From the benchmark price for Texas intermediate crude of $27, the price crashed to below $15 in February. Restructured companies with massive debts to pay down were watched nervously. ARCO was trimming five thousand jobs and would sell its headquarters building in downtown Los Angeles. Unocal's third-quarter earnings declined 12 percent, its profits from sale of the partnership units offset by the cost of fighting T. Boone Pickens. As Chevron continued to digest Gulf, it reduced its $10.9 billion debt from 51 to 42 percent of total capitalization, but earnings were down and Gulf's landmark art deco headquarters in Pittsburgh was being sold. Phillips, trying to reduce a debt that stood at a staggering 80 percent of capitalization after fending off Pickens and Icahn, was selling off $2 billion worth of assets, cutting wherever it could—offshore leases, geothermal production, pipelines and exploration in Canada, and giving three thousand employees early retirement.

In late March, even Exxon, the world's largest corporation, responded to the downturn with an announcement that it, too, would trim and slim for more efficiencies, restructuring divisions and cutting the work force.

No one had said it would be easy, but it was healthy, Wulff argued, as he continued to recommend takeover targets. In his November newsletter, he named names. Amoco and Mobil, Chevron and Texaco. Topping his list of candidates among the small integrated companies were three longtime recommendations—Amerada Hess, Sun, and, yes, Unocal. Still nervous, Unocal announced an antitakeover move in the early spring, the issuing of special stock to dilute a raider. Exxon, alone, still seemed invulnerable.

In October, Wulff broke his rule and called his wife, Louise, from the office with the good news. He'd been voted for the second consecutive year to the First Team of analysts in *Institutional Investor* magazine's rankings, the most prestigious of all measures of an analyst's performance. Looking back over the twenty years Louise had pushed and prodded him to develop and promote his ideas, he realized that she had the skill that made a good raider. As early as any of them, she had spotted his own undervalued assets and shrewdly set about to maximize their value.

◆　◆　◆

BY early spring, the spot price of oil had fallen below $10. And Kurt and Louise Wulff were planning to attend Unocal's annual meeting in Los Angeles April 28. Their presence promised to stir some trouble. Louise, owner of several thousand shares of Unocal, had made a shareholder proposal in the notice of the meeting mailed to all shareholders. Listed as Item 6, her proposal asked that Unocal "act to divide the properties of Unocal along functional . . . lines into about ten separate, independent, publicly traded business entities. . . ." Wulff knew he'd got Hartley's attention when he read, in *USA Today* on March 24, that the proposal made by the wife of "one of Wall Street's brightest and most controversial analysts" had been rejected by Unocal's management as "based on shortsighted and speculative reasoning," one that was probably impossible by the terms of its newly refinanced debt—"a costly and irreversible act . . . whose major beneficiaries would be lawyers and investment bankers." But *USA Today* also made sly note that Wulff's suggestions for restructuring Gulf had been followed, six months later, by Gulf's $13.3 billion sale to Chevron, the largest deal ever.

As oil prices crashed, the warring factions of the Getty family gathered to declare peace over dinner. Their timing in selling to Texaco was looking shrewder every day. They had sold in early 1984 for $128 a share; now, with oil prices having devastated the value of Getty Oil's reserves, they would have been lucky, they felt, to get $78. There were no tears spilled over the loss of the company. The family now controlled several of the world's largest trusts, their fortunes simply made liquid and converted from one form to another. If there were regrets it was that the billions paid to the trust and museum by Texaco were trapped in low-interest ninety-day treasury bills, contractually locked up for now. If he had had control, Gordon Getty wryly suggested, the family would have been fully in-

vested, profiting in a stock market that was going through the
sky. In the unbundling of the Getty fortune, Getty had slipped
from *Fortune* magazine's list as "richest man in America" to
rank as merely one of the richest, a welcome chance to return
to the relative privacy he had enjoyed before he had entered
the takeover arena. In April, there would be a concert of his
music at Carnegie Hall.

◆   ◆   ◆

For Robert Roudebush, flying home to Cincinnati on People
Express after a visit to National Can's plants in Fairfield, New
Jersey, in November, takeover had not meant the creation of
multibillion-dollar family trusts. It had been an experience of
helplessness. "Our CEO, Mr. Considine, sent us a letter telling
us that an attack was on. Then he sent a letter that, all of a
sudden, overnight, National Can Corporation had been sold to
Triangle Industries. We heard they made juke boxes and
vending machines. But who are they? How could it happen?
How could a company with $3.8 million profits take over a
company with $26 million?" For Bob Roudebush, the shock
had compounded the sense that stability was crumbling. The
collapse of the Homestate Savings & Loan in Ohio threatened
to spread to the bank that held his life savings, Charter Oak
S&L. "My wife went down at five in the morning and joined the
line of people who'd been there all night in sleeping bags,
waiting to take out their money. The police came with bull
horns and ordered them home, saying that the governor was
guaranteeing the bank's deposits with state funds."

Uncertainty now haunted the final months before his retirement. A project engineer, Roudebush had joined National Can
twelve years earlier at a time of fast growth and had helped
move the technology of safe food packaging forward. "I've seen
the change from the three-piece can to the two-piece can with
no more lead seams," he says with pride at having spared the
American consumer botulism. "The only letter I've had from
Considine since the takeover said I was getting 14 percent of
my gross salary for 1985. But what is it? Is it cash or profit
sharing? It can't be National Can stock—it doesn't exist anymore. Is it Triangle stock? What *is* it? My wife gets anxious and

says, 'Go find out,' but I can't just go up to the top floor and ask
Mr. Considine."

◆   ◆   ◆

BY fall 1985, there was a collective reach for respectability
among the first generation of raiders. The biggest hitters
seemed tired of being kicked around. "You get weary of your
efforts not being appreciated," Boone Pickens said dispiritedly
to *Barron's* as he restructured Mesa and turned, at least for the
time being, from the firing line. He had not announced his
candidacy for the Texas governorship, as there had long been
speculation he would. His deadline to announce had been
November.

Ivan Boesky was on the road with his book *Merger Mania,*
flashing its glossy red-and-gold cover like the Dead Sea Scrolls.
A competitor at a large investment banking house slammed the
book shut at the pages where Boesky described his strategy in
the Getty deal, which had earned him an estimated $50 million
gross profit, expressing the dislike many in the arbitrage community feel for Boesky.

But in dapper black suit, gold watch chain, and dazzling
smile, Boesky had become a celebrity. Lean-boned and bright-
eyed, he is the silver fox of risk arbitrage. Along with Pickens,
Icahn, and Goldsmith, he is metamorphizing into a senior
statesman. He has started his own merchant bank, a term with
a respectable British ring to it. His fight for respectability may
have been privately motivated in part. A tombstone ad in the
Wall Street Journal announcing that Ivan Boesky, merchant
banker, had negotiated financing for the Beverly Hills Hotel
Corporation revealed a bitter family fight. He had married the
daughter of the owner of the Beverly Hills Hotel over the
objections of her father, who never approved of him, it was
reported in a February 1986 article in *Vanity Fair*. His father-in-
law's death had triggered a family war for control of the hotel.
Deprived of respect for too long, Boesky had lured several
family members to his side and gained a controlling interest.
Taking over the presidency, he had stripped the sister-in-law
who had sided with her father of her poolside cabana at the
hotel. For those who paused to read his book's dedication,

Boesky revealed another side of family, and the classic self-made origins of the new financial warriors, in his tribute to a father "whose courage brought him to these shores from his native Ykaterinoslav, Russia in the year 1912."

In polished and witty speeches to universities and bond clubs breakfasts, Boesky was slickly cleaning up the raiders' image. "Icahn, Pickens, Steinberg. Some people call them raiders. I call them 'corporate entrepreneurs.' And if you read the *New York Times* now, you will see that they are called 'financiers.' All of a sudden, these men are getting some respect in our society, as they should." Boesky continues, "Because in all kinds of revolutions, it's always the first who get stomped on until they finally convince the world what they were trying to say is right, and become the nation's heroes. They may try to stomp out the Icahns of the world, but they are noble gentlemen! It took Icahn to find out that if you get a 20 percent wage concession from pilots, you increase your cash flow $320 million a year. It doesn't seem reasonable that he should have to go to war to demonstrate to the people who were sitting on these assets that they could have done it themselves."

Boesky waved a sheet of paper at a packed hall of Berkeley business students in mid-September. "On this list are more than fifty companies that in the last two months have announced voluntary restructuring. Finally corporate America is saying, 'I really have to get to work and improve myself.' So what you're seeing is the great restructuring of corporate America on a voluntary basis." His final comment drew appreciative roars of laughter: "Greed is all right by the way. I want you to know that. I think greed is healthy. You can be greedy and still feel good about yourself."

◆　◆　◆

SAUL Steinberg may never be forgiven for greenmailing Mickey Mouse. But with some persuasive public relations by Gershon Kekst, Steinberg's image, too, was being massaged into more respectable shape. Steinberg and his wife, Rodwyn, dominated the November issue of *Town & Country* magazine. A lavish story, "Barony on Park Avenue," celebrated the Steinberg collection of old masters that hangs in their thirty-four-room triplex, a palatial setting once owned by John D. Rockefeller. As the magazine broke on the stands, a spokesman for Steinberg's Reliance Financial Services denied as "unfounded" fears of a hostile takeover that had led Green Tree Acceptance, a finance company in St. Paul, Minnesota, to sue Drexel Burnham for selling a commanding chunk of its stock to Steinberg in an underwriting Drexel had done for Green Tree. By the end of October, Steinberg and his associates held 24.8 percent of Green Tree's stock.

Like the wave of radical chic two decades earlier, the flossy upscale magazines, it seemed, were making fall 1985 the season of the raider. Carl Icahn was the darling of the December *Vanity Fair*'s gossipy story on parties of the year, a guest along with Norman Mailer, Malcolm Forbes, Norman Lear, and Arianna Stassinopoulos at Alice Mason's September 17 "black-tie dinner for fifty in her art-stuffed rooms," a party at which Icahn, "not content with grabbing TWA . . . accused all CEOs of being 'waspy guys who sit on blue-ribbon boards and cheat the shareholders out of their rightful dues.' " When another guest defended the Revlon board, then under terminal takeover attack, as "a fine board, an honorable board, Mr. Icahn," Icahn had roared, "Don't patronize me!" *Vanity Fair* reported: "In fact, the tycoon preying on Revlon, Ron Perelman, was craning his ears at the next table . . . while Forbes walked away with a half million bucks from Icahn for Princeton."

Underlying that juicy glimpse of Alice Mason's party was a subtle transformation of the takeover wars. It was the season of new raiders. And Perelman led the pack.

◆ ◆ ◆

ON October 28, Stuart and Noreen Shapiro stood in the middle of a moss garden surrounding a Zen Buddhist temple in Kyoto. A hundred different species of moss rolled like jade velvet to an exquisite lake that centered the garden. It was as serene a place as Stuart had ever seen.

Three days later, he was in court in Wilmington arguing the appeal that could give a brash entrepreneur, Ron Perelman— owner of Pantry Pride, a chain of food and retail stores in Fort Lauderdale, Florida—control of one of the nation's best-loved companies: Revlon. American women had grown up with Revlon; their cosmetic bags held its Love Pat and Moon Drops lipsticks, its blushes, mascara, and moisturizers. In fact, such Revlon health-care products as Tums antacids and its acne creams were more alluring to the stock market. But it was the Beauty Group that had helped shape the image and self-confidence of millions of teenagers. Revlon was an intimate friend. Now it was Pantry Pride against Fire and Ice, and the fight was shaping into a classic struggle that attracted the club. Perelman had hired Skadden Arps and Drexel Burnham. Revlon had hired Lazard Frères and Wachtell Lipton. Revlon's white knight was the prestigious LBO specialist, Forstmann Little, who brought its investment bankers, Goldman Sachs, to the war. The importance of the struggle could be measured by the fact that Flom, Lipton, Rohatyn, and Milken were personally involved.

It was a dramatic clash of style: Perelman, forty-two, controlled through his holding company, MacAndrews & Forbes, the Florida food chain and a prospering miniconglomerate of cigar, chocolate, and film processing companies. He was an entrepreneur so heavily leveraged and hurting for cash that he was forced to make an acquisition to get cash flow to pay down his debt and dividends. He moved in the glitzy fast lane in New York, loved show biz and movie stars, and was married to ABC newscaster Claudia Cohen. At his wedding reception at the Palladium, his lawyer, Roy Cohn, reported that "an investment banker at our table started to add up the net worth of those at the party and stopped at $10 billion."

Revlon's chairman and CEO, Michel Bergerac, was an elegant Frenchman, with balding head and thick moustache. Brother of actor Jacques Bergerac, he sat in the office that had been Charles Revson's. Recruited from ITT by Revson as his successor in 1974, Bergerac had inherited a tarnished glamor queen losing market share in its mainstays—lipstick, nail polish, and mascara. He planned a bold diversification into the burgeoning health-care field, which now accounted for nearly 70 percent of Revlon's $2.4 billion sales.

"Although those who knew him gave him higher odds, the

smart money on the Street gave Perelman a million-in-one
chance to win," said Stuart Shapiro. As he swiftly prepared his
argument before the Delaware Supreme Court in Wilmington
on October 31, Stuart Shapiro had the sense of déjà vu endemic to the incestuous world of takeover law. Only the names
on the briefs seemed changed. This one read *MacAndrews &
Forbes* v. *Revlon*. His colleagues had already argued before the
same chancery court judge he had lost to on the first Household trial, Vice-chancellor Walsh. Arguing against him, for
Revlon, would be Gil Sparks and Herb Wachtell, familiar
Skadden Arps opponents. And as with Household, he would be
fighting one of Marty Lipton's poison pills, one very similar to
Crown Zellerbach's. Its adoption by the Revlon board on
August 19 had triggered Perelman's lawsuit. Unlike his father's
position when arguing the appeal on Household, Stuart would
be arguing from strength. His colleagues had already won the
first hearing before Vice-chancellor Walsh.

Conquering jet lag to prepare his argument, Stuart had
smiled as he read the minutes of two of Revlon's board meetings. "Those minutes are going to make our case!" he said, as
he read detailed notes from the meetings of October 3 and 12.
They were a priceless insight into the thought processes and
responses of the board of a great corporation under siege. But
it was like a psychiatrist letting you see his notes. Why had
Marty Lipton had his lawyers take full notes at the meetings?
"He apparently believes in the blanket right of boards to make
judgments. These notes reveal his philosophical position. But
they can only be useful to the opposition." They were laced with
juicy discussion on the poison pills and lockups the board had
adopted, about Forstmann Little's proposed leveraged buyout,
and the strong urgings by both Marty Lipton and Felix Rohatyn to accept that proposal, although lower than Perelman's.
The notes revealed a frank and admitted effort to eliminate
Pantry Pride's, or any other company's, bid for Revlon.

The battle had begun on June 17, 1985, when Perelman had
gone to visit Bergerac to inform him of his interest in the
company. It had been as friendly as such a meeting can be. It
wasn't until August 19, the day before the TWA board meeting

that gave Icahn his airline, that the Revlon board focused on
the threat. On that day, it had adopted Marty Lipton's Share
Purchase Rights Plan—the poison pill. Liquidation was not
discussed. The game plan was to keep Revlon independent.

As early as the August 19 board meeting, when Lipton
introduced his Rights Plan, Rohatyn had cautioned, "If the
Rights are put in place, liquidation of the company is likely to
follow." The Rights Plan was adopted at that meeting, another
weapon in what Revlon still viewed as a fight for independence.
But by the October 3 board meeting, a change had taken place,
an attitudinal change in the board vividly described by Judge
Walsh in his final decision in October: "When in late September, Pantry Pride increased its offer to $53 a share, it became
clear to Revlon that Pantry Pride would not fade away, and its
substantial increase in the ante required the Revlon board to
consider what previously was unthinkable—the breakup of
Revlon. . . . The directors' role changed from that of a board
fending off a hostile acquirer bent on a breakup of the corporation to that of an auctioneer attempting to secure the highest
price for the pieces of the Revlon enterprise." And he added a
telling caveat to Revlon's subsequent actions: "From this point
on the Revlon board permitted considerations other than price
to dictate its approach."

Now that the liquidation Rohatyn had warned would come
with the poison pill seemed inevitable, the Revlon board
seemed bent on at least choosing a respectable liquidator.
Invited to both the October 3 and 12 meetings was Ted Forstmann, whose young firm was still second to Kohlberg, Kravis
Roberts & Co. in leveraged buyouts, but had managed to gain
enormous success as specialists in that hot and highly competitive field and yet operate in the banking and corporate circles
enjoyed by only the most powerful old-line investment banking
houses. Bergerac introduced Forstmann Little as a group that,
in a few short weeks, had become more than a white knight,
"they have become good friends." They had put a cash offer of
$56 per share on the table. The board had no illusions that Ted
Forstmann was coming in to keep Revlon intact. "In embracing
Forstmann Little as its merger partner," Judge Walsh said,

"Revlon knew that it was not merging with an operating company but with a firm which specialized in leveraged buyouts. They knew that their white knight did not have a long-term 'home and family' relationship in mind."

The romance between Revlon and Forstmann would later provoke Vice-chancellor Walsh to ask, "What motivated the Revlon directors to end the auction with so little objective improvement? Revlon's repeated claim that it favored Forstmann Little at every stage because Forstmann Little seemed better able to finance its acquisition does not withstand hard analysis." And yet Revlon believed it needed them. Marty Lipton and Felix Rohatyn kept telling them so. Perelman already owned thirty thousand shares. And he was coming for more. At the October 3 board meeting, Lipton had reported that he and Flom had had one of their legendary power meetings two days earlier. Over lunch, Flom had planted the veiled threat that Perelman would buy some stock under his tender offer that Friday. It had not been lost on the board that if Perelman went back into the open market, he could buy voting control and oust the board. That had been the meeting where Forstmann Little's bid had been introduced and accepted.

By the October 12 meeting, Perelman had raised his bid several times, topping Forstmann Little's bid by 25 cents. His was the higher bid, and he looked determined enough to keep bidding up until he won. How could a board, by the Business Judgment Rule, not accept a bid that would be more profitable for the shareholders? More than ever, Rohatyn and Lipton argued, Revlon must hold on to Forstmann Little. If they let Forstmann's bid go, the only obstacle to Perelman would be gone. He could then lower his bid and snatch the company for far less than it was worth.

In Ted Forstmann's presentation to the board on October 12, the stylistic clash erupted. He had come to the meeting for lockups—a commitment of the company's Vision Care and National Health Laboratories to him, which would lessen the allure of Revlon to anyone else. And he wanted a $25 million breakup fee, whether or not the deal went through with Forstmann. Even from the impersonal printed page of the

minutes, Forstmann's distaste stood out. Forstmann's financing
sources for the LBO would be "conservative, well-established
organizations with fiduciary duties" such as the GE, Boeing,
and Standard Oil of Indiana pension funds, Manufacturers
Hanover, and Bankers Trust Company; Perelman's would
come from junk bonds. Forstmann was not a common raider,
but had been invited in, he reminded the board, by Lazard
Frères. "Before this transaction, I had never heard of Ronald
Perelman. It took some persuasion for me to agree to meet with
him." He had not entered into the transaction to make a deal
with Mr. Perelman, he said. And he would not now enter into a
nickel-and-dime bidding war with him. "I hope the board will
not think me rude or pushy. It is not the nature of my company
to give ultimatums, but this deal demands it. The offer is open
only for this evening, and if it is not accepted, it will be
withdrawn and the company will be left to deal with Pantry
Pride on its own." The board voted Forstmann both his lockups
and his $25 million fee.

As Stuart Shapiro read the minutes, his delight grew. This
was the best gift the shareholder revolution had received in
months.

The Supreme Court agreed with Shapiro's argument. On
November 1, the decision came down for Perelman and Pantry
Pride, clearing the way for Perelman's $1.83 billion takeover of
Revlon. With Michael Milken personally directing, Drexel
Burnham had its commitments for $1.1 billion in what it
considered its most important junk-bond deal to date. And in
loaning $450 million to Perelman's financing, the nation's sixth-
largest bank, New York's dignified Chemical Bank, had overcome intense internal opposition at the highest levels. It had
pushed its lending limits to the edge to do its first hostile deal,
and given Perelman priceless credibility in a game in which
perception is everything. That successful entry into the takeover wars would speed Chemical Bank's parent, Chemical
New York, to the decision in early 1986 to create an arbitrage
desk to speculate in takeovers—unprecedented for a bank—
and it was reported in the *Wall Street Journal* to be trying to hire
one of the Street's top arbitragers. It was a daring step into the

investment bankers' territory. Could the invisible "Chinese Wall" that insulated a bank's several functions from each other, preventing insider trading, withstand the arbitrager's cosmic power to know all, see all, on the Street?

Stuart left the courtroom to get to a telephone and call Perelman in New York within minutes of the decision. But the arbs had beaten him to it. Perelman, his wife and aides, the senior Skadden Arps lawyer, Don Drapkin, and his wife, and a small crowd of colleagues were gathered, waiting, in the office of Perelman's town house on East Sixty-third Street. They were surrounded by an art collection that dispelled the barbarian image painted by Ted Forstmann—Giacometti, Degas, Miró, Dubuffet, and rare Karsh photos. The call came in, and in a replay of the scene in a Los Angeles courtroom a year earlier when Hawley had hugged Joe Flom, Perelman threw his arms around Don Drapkin and kissed him. When Stuart's call came in moments later, the champagne had already been popped.

On November 5, Ronald O. Perelman moved into the office of Charles Revson and Michel Bergerac as chairman of the board. Bergerac left with a $35 million severance package, the largest golden parachute ever paid. On November 30, Pantry Pride announced the sale of Revlon's prescription drug unit, the third division to be sold in the swift dismemberment of Revlon.

Stuart Shapiro tried to read the decision for clues on how Delaware might rule on Household. Arbs had called him with the rumor that the Household decision would be coming down within a week. He felt cautiously buoyant. In Revlon, the courts had said, in effect, that the adoption of a poison pill was okay *if* the Revlon board felt a genuine threat, but it must not stand in the way of legitimate takeover bids. Perelman had already made his first bid—a hostile tender offer for $47.50 per share—when the board adopted the pill. No such threat had existed in the case of Household. In chancery, Walsh had congratulated the Revlon board on using the pill's deterrent effect to buy itself some time to get competing bids that ultimately moved Revlon's stock price up 16 points—a boon to shareholders. But he had lectured the board that the pill, "having served to permit the Revlon board full negotiating power, cannot now stand in the way of the bidding process."

As Shapiro interpreted it, the judge accepted the notion that a pill would kill other tender offers and made it the obligation of any pill-armed board that makes itself, instead of the competitive marketplace, the arbiter of who should buy or sell the company to create its own market for bids. It must negotiate with any serious suitor! Vice-chancellor Walsh was calling the Revlon board to a higher level of responsibility to shareholders than boards without a pill. It was a pro-takeover decision from the very heart of corporate defense, the Delaware courts. If the same kind of thinking was in Justice John McNeilly's mind as he wrote his Household decision, it would mean that, even if Irving Shapiro lost his argument for Moran to have adoption of the pill outlawed, a pill would be allowed to do no more than give a board breathing time. Marty Lipton's great weapon might be permitted, but it would be drained of its poison. In Walsh's court, it had been enjoined! The signs, Stuart Shapiro felt, were very, very good.

◆ ◆ ◆

SIR James Goldsmith was finding, like Icahn, that winning the war was only the beginning. The poison pill was the problem. Since Goldsmith had taken over the chairmanship of Crown Zellerbach in July, they had all crept around the poison pill on tiptoe, trying to avoid it. James River had emerged as the principal customer for the Crown assets Goldsmith wanted to sell. Goldsmith had done business with the paper and forest products company before; he had sold them some of Diamond International's assets. It was Roland Franklin, who had picked up the phone and called Brenton S. Halsey, James River's CEO, shortly after Goldsmith took over, recognizing that their products and markets meshed beautifully. James River was a strong young company, well managed and forward looking. It would have been a natural merger, with Goldsmith keeping only the forest lands for himself. But the pill was there, triggered, and lying in wait to destroy Goldsmith's investment if he did a formal merger with James River. "If you did a merger of Crown with anybody, the pill's flipover would take effect, and Rights holders could buy Crown's stock two for the price of one. So you couldn't do a merger. It had to be an exchange offer," explained Goldsmith's lawyer, Fin Fogg.

But how? "The challenge was to design a solution that would convince the courts it was not just a clever disguise for a merger, but something distinctly different," said Fogg. "The pill would not expire for ten years. James River was very concerned about not being able to merge for ten years, until the pill expired. Until then, the two must run as separate companies. We discussed it at the first meeting with James River; we discussed it at the last. We all wanted a transaction that would not be declared illegal. Roland and I had discussed an exchange offer in our earliest talks with them. And that is what was finally achieved."

In mid-December, after a weekend of continuous meetings, the transaction had finally been beaten into a shape acceptable to everyone. Goldsmith would keep the 1.2 million acres of forest lands. "James River will end up owning 90 percent of Crown Zellerbach stock after the spin-off of forest lands," said Fogg, who felt they had achieved a rather elegant solution. "The market has responded well. Crown stock closed up yesterday, December 17, at $41 5/8. But even now, it's possible it won't work. I hope it does." It was the end of more than one marathon for Fogg. He would no longer be doing midnight runs down Fifth Avenue to the printers in the south Village in the heat of a tender offer. He had run a marathon in Rome in the summer, in the over-forty "veterans" category. He had found himself in a world-class field. Olympians. He had collapsed in the race with a knee injury and had had cartilage surgically removed. He would leave the field to Warren Hellman, the San Francisco deal maker Goldsmith had kept on as a Crown board member, a man who continued to impress Fogg as "very active, very bright. Wants to do what's right for the shareholders." An ultradistance runner, Hellman was so committed to his training that one of his neighbors in the fashionable Presidio Heights district of San Francisco said with amusement after meeting Hellman at a dinner party, "At ten o'clock, he just got up and went home to bed. He leaves wherever he is at ten."

In January, Crown reported its fourth-quarter results.

There was a net loss for the year of $26.8 million, caused mostly by the costs of the ongoing restructuring. But there were results that delighted Goldsmith. Net income had jumped 66 percent in the fourth quarter. And though earnings on its paper and container businesses were down, earnings in two divisions were up. In timber and wood products.

How could the time, money, talent, energy, and resources consumed by Lipton's clever creation during the course of the Crown Zellerbach deal ever be measured? There was still a shareholder suit against the pill in Chicago—a wild card with a class of pill holders countersuing non-pill-holding shareholders who had attacked the legality of the pill in court. An epidemic of poison pill cases was expected, challenge and counterchallenge. For on November 19, the Household decision came down.

◆ ◆ ◆

NOVEMBER 19 was a day of two massive shocks for the takeover community. For Skadden Arps, it was Black Tuesday. Their lawyers had lost in both.

On that day, the award against Texaco came down. The *Wall Street Journal* headline on November 20 would read: "PENNZOIL WINS $10.53 BILLION IN TEXACO SUIT." It was the largest civil judgment in history. The numbers were staggering even for the megadealers. With the court thrust being to demonstrate Getty's duplicity, no one from Skadden Arps or First Boston had been called as a witness. But the award put their triumph and takeover ethics in general under a cloud. In shock and disarray, the U.S.'s third-largest oil company staggered into the appeals process, struggling, first, to avoid having to post a $10.6 billion bond to the Texas court. Watched by the nation, a morality play that began in a Houston courtroom would continue to unfold as tarnished old notions of honor and the worth of a handshake were tested against the code of contracts and agreements that governed not only Wall Street but the buying and selling of assets in America—a test that could well be carried to the U.S. Supreme Court before it was resolved.

Skadden's Morris Kramer had been hired by First Boston to represent Texaco. "Morris is keeping a low profile," said one of his colleagues sympathetically. It could have been any of them. Anyone in the deal flow. Kramer, Perella, and Wasserstein had been indemnified from guilt by Texaco, such standard operating procedure that, said Perella, "We've never worked on a deal without indemnification." While Lipton and Goldman's Boisi had been called to testify, the three had been blessedly free of involvement. For anyone ensnared in the aftermath, a manic phase of court hearings, subpoenas, depositions, and appeals at all levels had begun, a process that threatened to become a permanent lifestyle. "But this is not Watergate. They ran into a lynch mob," Perella said, expressing the widely held view on Wall Street that the Houston award was not so much a moral judgment as an expression of the parochial biases of a Texas state court. "It's well documented," Perella reminded, "that Jamail, Pennzoil's lawyer, made a $10,000 political contribution to the presiding judge in the case."

When the award against Texaco came down, Kurt Wulff swiftly rewrote his December newsletter, and titled it "Bhopal!" Says Wulff, "I didn't mean there was any loss of life in Texaco, but the corporate implications were the same. They are both burdened with this huge liability." But he felt talks of Texaco's bankruptcy were exaggerated. "Texaco gets sympathy from the press and government with talks of bankruptcy. But as long as oil stays above $18 a barrel, they could pay Pennzoil the $10.5 billion award, liquidate the company, pay off all their debts, and still pay every shareholder $60 a share." But would they be able to keep underwriting the Metropolitan Opera radio broadcasts, a worried fan asked.

◆　◆　◆

ON the same day, November 19, the Household decision came down. The supreme court in Wilmington had called Irving Shapiro's office at two in the afternoon to report that the decision would be released at 4:00 P.M. At the Skadden Arps office in New York, Stuart Shapiro and the half dozen people who had worked most closely on the case gathered in Mike Mitchell's office to wait. A light flashed on the speaker phone at 4:10, and the call was broadcast to the group: "We lost." There was a moment of numbed silence. They had lost Household.

Justice McNeilly had not believed, as Vice-chancellor Walsh had not, that poison pills precluded tender offers. He had not believed they limited the options of a board to get the best deal for its shareholders. He had declared the pill a proper corporate defense.

At Skadden Arps, they peppered Ward with questions. "What did they say?" "Read us the words." Within two minutes the decision had been telecopied to New York, and Stuart had the text in his hand. Then the press calls began.

The elder Shapiro masked his disappointment with humor. "You're a hell of a son, Stu," he said a few hours later. "You give *me* the case to argue that you lost in front of Judge Walsh, and *you* argue the appeal on the case where Judge Walsh ruled in your favor!"

"Dad, yours was a great oral argument," Stu tried to convince his father. "The decision is not related to the quality of the argument."

Household's primary lawyer, Michael Schwartz, had called to say, "Of course we're thrilled to win. But the professional experience of being in the courtroom with your father is the one I'll cherish all my life." And Moran had called and said, "I've had the best representation I could have had. I'm thrilled your father argued it." They were gallant calls. "If you can't stand the pain, you shouldn't be in law," said the senior Shapiro. Stuart Shapiro predicted that a flood of lawsuits would follow Household, "but they won't be about the legality of the pill; they'll be about its implementation."

Household had been a case about power, its use and abuse. "That decision was just wrong," Irving Shapiro believed, "and I predict that time will show the decision was in error." The court had said that a corporate board had the right to assume extraordinary powers, seizing them from the shareholders without approval. "But the court never explained what the source of that power could be."

Walking across the treed square flanked by the elegant old Du Pont Hotel and the chancery court after lunch at the Rodney Square Club several weeks later, Shapiro reflected on power. "Power is not the exercise of some great force to force action by someone else. It is not hitting people over the head. It's rather a series of relationships where people accommodate people, when they can, in practical and proper terms. The ability to call any number of different people and say, 'I have a problem. Can you help me in such and such a way?' is one of the great luxuries of power. In doing that, you expect that you may very well get your own phone call. If I invite a key executive to make a speech for some favorite cause, there is an implicit commitment that when he calls I will say yes. That's what power is all about. And it's an unspoken association. Lee Iacocca and I had worked together in Washington on public policy matters, so we were friends. When I was involved in the sale of the Hughes Aircraft Company and he was considering being a bidder, he came to see me. He simply wanted to register his presence, and hoped that, all things being equal, I would remember that Lee Iacocca had a serious interest."

The most satisfying exercise of power for Irving Shapiro in recent months had been negotiating the sale of minority interest in a family-owned newspaper in Minneapolis. He had had a long relationship with the stockholding family. After agonizing over whether to sell, the family had made the decision and come to Shapiro. He had called Bob Greenhill at Morgan Stanley, head of their corporate finance. It had taken two years of work. But Greenhill had found a buyer, the deal was done, and the family had their capital liberated at last to do the things they wanted to do. The most satisfying moment had come at a celebration dinner in New York. A son-in-law had thanked Shapiro for giving him the financial freedom to stay in the cancer research he had almost given up for a job that would put his kids through college. In that deal, there had been no hostile posturing. No arrogant abuses. It had been, for Shapiro, the use of power at its best.

◆ ◆ ◆

By the end of 1985, it was clear to *Time* magazine that mergers and takeovers, successful and failed, and the increasingly popular leveraged buyouts were "the most important and far-reaching business story of the year," as it made "Merger Tango" its December 23 cover story. When finally tallied by the authoritative merger consultants W. T. Grimm & Co., total purchase price in 1985 of acquired companies was $179.6 billion, 47 percent higher than 1984's record of $122.2 billion. There had been 3,000 deals announced, highest since the 4,040 in 1973's tidal wave of mergers—an average of nearly ten a day. They had spread from oil to broadcasting, foods, drugs and medical services, to chemicals, electronics, the aerospace industry, and airlines.

Crown Zellerbach had had a domino effect in the forest products industry, with San Francisco's Potlatch greenmailed, as many believe, by Canada's Belzbergs and Pacific Lumber falling to the MAXXAM group. As the airlines continued their consolidation, People Express was acquiring a commuter airline, Britt Airways, Texas Air proposed to take over Eastern, and Icahn's TWA gobbled up Ozark Air.

Sam Heyman still stalked Union Carbide as he had since the summer; by late November, he controlled 10 percent of the stock and had requested Justice Department clearance to buy more. Union Carbide, woefully unprepared after the Bhopal disaster to wage a takeover battle, was vigorously restructuring but claimed to feel no threat from Heyman. "Bhopal is the ultimate poison pill," said CEO Warren Anderson, who believed the tens of billions of dollars of contingent liability that hung over the company would make it impossible for any suitor to get financing for a takeover.

Yet Samuel J. Heyman had. With a creative package of junk notes, stock, and warrants that offered instant profit to investors, Drexel Burnham had, in fact, got commitments of $3.75 billion of the $4.8 billion bid. But on January 8, 1986—the day the Federal Reserve announced restrictions on junk bonds—Sam Heyman withdrew his bid for Union Carbide, saying that he might try again later. Carbide's defensive acts, a massive stock repurchase and sale of the prized product division that made Glad plastic bags and Eveready batteries—plus the lingering liability of Bhopal—had made Carbide too risky and too big a bite. Heyman returned to running GAF, but like Pickens in his first assault on one of the Big Oil "elephants," he had had a taste of the big time. He had earned his way into the Club that had tried to defeat him in his bid for GAF Corp, a Wayne, New Jersey–based chemical and building material company, a fight in which his wife, Ronnie, had filibustered at a shareholder's meeting and faced-down Joe Flom. He had launched the GAF takeover with a mere 5 percent of GAF stock. On Carbide, Heyman would make an estimated $200 million profit, and GAF would continue to hold 10 percent of Union Carbide's stock.

While Union Carbide "crawls away from the fight deep in debt and stripped of its prized consumer product lines," as the *Los Angeles Times* described it, Heyman saw his new clout reflected in the Dow Jones averages on February 26. Because of his assault on Carbide, two stocks, Kodak and Union Carbide, moved the Dow Jones 8 points closer to the 1,700 level, the most active stocks of the day; it was Carbide's sell-off of its consumer lines, and rumors that Kodak was Heyman's next target, that had sparked the action. In late March, he watched his Carbide and GAF stock climb as Carbide achieved a remarkably low settlement for the Bhopal disaster. While Texaco limped with the burden of the $10.5 billion award against it, Carbide settled for a mere $350 million. It was an odd measure of a corporation's ethics and social responsibilities; the violation of a handshake agreement had, it seemed, been deemed a far greater moral lapse than the death of two thousand Indians by toxic leaks.

By year end, General Foods had gone to Philip Morris, and Nabisco to R. J. Reynolds. RCA's $6 billion-plus acquisition of GE was the largest nonoil deal in history. Kaiser Aluminum had won a proxy fight with Tulsa entrepreneur Joseph Frates but was still in play. Genentech, and the nation's largest department store chain, Federated Department Stores, were rumored targets, as were Anheuser-Busch and Western Union. Carter Hawley Hale's stock jumped 2 points on takeover rumors that still circulated two years after The Limited's attack. Macy's and Levi Strauss had gone, or were going, private in leveraged buyouts. As Drexel Burnham delivered its "highly confident" letter for the financing of the $6.1 billion leveraged buyout of the nation's largest food and consumer products company,

Beatrice, by Kohlberg Kravis Roberts, a happy private investor said, "Drexel's treasure chest has no bottom," as he made 20 points per share in the largest leveraged buyout so far.

Boesky whispered to an audience that there were still good takeover prospects in communications, chemicals, health care, and retail. Banks and the computer industry braced for attack. In England and Australia, the largest hostile takeovers yet were in progress, and, in Japan, the first.

And yet, as 1986 dawned, the pace slackened from its 1985 peaks. The stock market's explosive rise in the first few months of the year had closed the gap between low stock price and high appraised value in which takeover profits lay. On March 20, the Dow Jones averages broke the 1,800 barrier, having gained 16.6 percent since the first of the year. The warriors collectively caught their breath, and raised their heads to watch the action abroad. Australia's wealthiest man, Robert Holmes a Court, was making a $1.3 billion bid for his nation's leading oil and steel producer, his third tilt at the company. Signs that the stock market would not be going up forever appeared two days later, when the market plummeted 35 points.

The raiders were already on the move. Asher Edelman was stalking Fruehauf Corp. Saul Steinberg was moving on Silicon Valley. As famous authors attending the international PEN Congress strolled by the Rodins, Rubens, and Cranachs in his Park Avenue triplex for PEN's opening-night bash, Steinberg revealed that he had large holdings "for investment purposes only" of Quadrex Corp. and Spectra-Physics. "Steinberg's intention is as stated," said Gershon Kekst on his behalf, but, evoking Pickens's march on Unocal, admitted that there had been times when investments turned into acquisitions.

As Canada's Prime Minister Mulroney traveled to Washington in March to talk about acid rain, his countrymen were raiding across the border: emboldened by the Belzberg's and Reichmanns' successes, Canada's leading tobacco company, Imasco Ltd., had launched a $1.74 billion takeover bid for Vancouver-based Genstar, the building materials and financial services conglomerate with its U.S. base in San Francisco, and Toronto-based People's Jewellers made its second takeover offer for the Dallas jewelry retailer Zale Corp. The Belzbergs prepared to make a hostile bid for Kentucky-based Ashland Oil.

An epidemic of defensive acts was proof that, in corporate boardrooms, a threat was still perceived. Safeway, Borden's, and McDonald's led the rush for poison pills. Kaiser Aluminum adopted rich golden parachutes for its executives. Unocal issued special antitakeover stock. Dozens of restructurings continued to reshape corporate America.

On the heels of the Household decision, Skadden Arps did its own flipover, becoming a veritable poison pill factory. "We lawyers can turn on a dime," laughed Jim Freund. "Many of our clients have wanted them, but we couldn't recommend them until their legal status was clarified," explained Irving Shapiro, as winter turned to spring. "Now, it's hard to fit all the companies who want pills into our schedules." And Fin Fogg told Corporate Control Alert, "The consensus in our firm is that we owe an obligation to our clients." Joe Flom had even prepared a thick three-ring brochure very much like the one Marty Lipton had delivered to the Household board and had designed a new, improved pill that it was hoped would prevent repeats of the Crown Zellerbach disaster. Its poison would be released when a bidder acquired 50 percent of a company's stock, not 100 percent as in Lipton's, so that a Goldsmith could no longer march to control in the open market. "We're popping a pill a day into corporate bylaws," Freund said, chuckling. "We're becoming a regular apothecary."

And proxy season was approaching. How many challenges to board seats lurked? CBS rejected a bid by oilman Marvin Davis, only to be forced to a proxy fight with Jesse Helms's right-wing Fairness in Media at its annual meeting April 16, where Helms would try to prohibit CBS from taking antitakeover measures by shareholder vote.

Proxy season was Artie Long's season. On February 11, he received a call from San Francisco. From the nation's second-largest bank. The call came from the bank's executive vice-president and general counsel, George Coombes. Long had worked for him in 1969 and 1970 when Coombes was assistant general counsel for General Motors. And now the bank was in that state of amorphous fears and feelings of vulnerability when Long usually got his first call.

"What are they worried about?" John Cornwell asked his long-time partner. "If you had a loss of $2.6 billion on bad loans, a net loss of $337 million, dividends cut to zero, and stock down from the 30s to $12 in three years, what the hell would you be worried about!" said Long. A threat of real substance had emerged. Sanford Weill, former head of Shearson Lehman Brothers, had appeared from nowhere, proposing to bring in a billion in capital and install himself as new chairman. His bid had been rejected by a shaken board. Like IBM and Exxon, the bank still wore an aura of impregnability. But, with oil prices on a slide that would see them below $10 a barrel by late March, could oil-producing countries like Mexico and Venezuela keep up payments on over $4 billion in loans? What if they defaulted? In that vulnerable open wound, predators could strike. "I don't know of anybody in our business who isn't constantly looking with some envy at that remarkable base of customers," Chairman Richard Flamson of the flourishing Security Pacific Bank told the *Wall Street Journal* mid-March, as he admitted his interest in acquiring the troubled bank.

So big that it was virtually a utility, the bank would be difficult to win with a tender offer; it would be ensnared in a web of regulatory obstacles. But with an army of individual shareholders, a proxy fight could be swift and effective. The annual meeting was coming up April 29. There was nothing tangible out there now. But the Weill threat could return as a proxy fight. There could be a run at board seats. Artie Long was put on retainer, and he hollered at his secretary to book a flight to San Francisco.

Artie Long entered the dark carnelian granite megalith that dominates the San Francisco skyline for his first meeting with the bank. These would be *some* war rooms, if it came to a proxy fight. His client was Bank of America.

INDEX